Advances in Longitudinal Methods in the Social and Behavioral Sciences

A volume in
CILVR Series on Latent Variable Methodology
Gregory R. Hancock, *Series Editor*

Advances in Longitudinal Methods in the Social and Behavioral Sciences

edited by

Jeffrey R. Harring
University of Maryland

Gregory R. Hancock
University of Maryland

INFORMATION AGE PUBLISHING, INC.
Charlotte, NC • www.infoagepub.com

Library of Congress Cataloging-in-Publication Data

Advances in longitudinal methods in the social and behavioral sciences / edited by Jeffrey R. Harring, Gregory R. Hancock.
     p. cm. – (CILVR series on latent variable methodology)
  ISBN 978-1-61735-889-0 (pbk.) – ISBN 978-1-61735-890-6 (hbk.) – ISBN 978-1-61735-891-3 (e-book) 1. Social sciences–Methodology. 2. Social sciences–Longitudinal studies. 3. Longitudinal method. I. Harring, Jeffrey, 1964- II. Hancock, Gregory R.
  H61.A3937 2012
  300.72'1–dc23
                                                                    2012020193

Copyright © 2012 Information Age Publishing Inc.

All rights reserved. No part of this publication may be reproduced, stored in a retrieval system, or transmitted, in any form or by any means, electronic, mechanical, photocopying, microfilming, recording or otherwise, without written permission from the publisher.

Printed in the United States of America

CONTENTS

Foreword vii
Preface ix
Acknowledgments xiii

PART I

MODELING LONGITUDINAL DATA: EXAMINING FACETS OF CHANGE OR VARIABILITY

1 A Template for Describing Individual Differences in Longitudinal Data, with Application to the Connection Between Learning and Ability 3
Robert Cudeck and Casey L. Codd

2 On Interpretable Reparameterizations of Linear and Nonlinear Latent Growth Curve Models 25
Kristopher J. Preacher and Gregory R. Hancock

3 Mood Changes Associated with Smoking in Adolescents: An Application of a Mixed-Effects Location Scale Model for Longitudinal Ecological Momentary Assessment Data 59
Donald Hedeker and Robin J. Mermelstein

4 Tethering Theory to Method: Using Measures of Intraindividual Variability to Operationalize Individuals' Dynamic Characteristics 81
Nilam Ram, David Conroy, Aaron Pincus, Amanda Hyde, and Lauren Molloy

5 Dynamic Systems Analysis of Affective Processes in Dyadic
   Interactions Using Differential Equations 111
   Emilio Ferrer and Joel Steele

PART II

DRAWING VALID INFERENCES: LONGITUDINAL DESIGN CONSIDERATIONS AND MODEL ASSUMPTIONS

6 Sensitivity Analysis of Mixed-Effects Models When
   Longitudinal Data Are Incomplete 137
   Shelley A. Blozis

7 Finite Mixtures of Nonlinear Mixed-Effects Models 159
   Jeffrey R. Harring

8 Growth Mixture Modeling and Causal Inference 193
   Booil Jo

PART III

THE ROLE OF MEASUREMENT IN MODELING WITHIN-SUBJECT AND BETWEEN-SUBJECT EFFECTS

9 Disaggregating Within-Person and Between-Person Effects in
   Multilevel and Structural Equation Growth Models 217
   *Patrick J. Curran, Taehun Lee, Andrea L. Howard, Stephanie Lane,
   and Robert MacCallum*

10 Considering Alternative Metrics of Time: Does Anybody Really
   Know What "Time" Is? 255
   Lesa Hoffman

11 Valid Measurement Without Factorial Invariance:
   A Longitudinal Example 289
   Michael C. Edwards and Robert J. Wirth

12 The Discrimination-Censoring Paradox in Item Response
   Growth Models 313
   Jennifer Koran

About the Contributors 333

FOREWORD

Being born in the mid-1960s, I never got to tell the story of where I was when Chuck Yeager broke the sound barrier, or when Martin Luther King, Jr. gave his speech at the Lincoln Memorial, or when John F. Kennedy was shot, or any of a variety of other remarkable events that my parents remembered firsthand. Although admittedly not in the same league as Mach 1, MLK, or JFK, I do distinctly recall when I saw my first growth model; it's not necessarily a story I'll tell my grandchildren, but it turned out to be quite meaningful to me. It was 1992 and my graduate advisor, Laurie Chassin, gave me a handout that Jack McArdle had distributed during a conference symposium held a few days earlier. She told me that I had the weekend to figure out what he was doing and to see if we could apply these methods to her longitudinal dataset. Two things immediately struck me when reading Jack's handout: (1) growth modeling was totally cool; and (2) I had absolutely no idea how it worked or how to do it. Interestingly, I think that both of my initial reactions still ring true 20 years later.

The first point is self-evident: growth modeling remains totally cool. The second point is a bit more intriguing. It's not that I haven't tried to learn these methods and to apply them in potentially meaningful ways; I have (or at least have tried, that is). The second point remains relevant for me today because, quite honestly, they keep moving the goal posts on me. Just when I start to feel like I'm beginning to understand the core of these models, some exciting new development is proposed that shoves me backward in my understanding. But this is exactly why I so love working in this field. It's a pipe dream to think that I'll ever *master* growth modeling; instead, I simply strive to stay in the game despite the constantly changing rules. And you are witnessing these changing rules yourself in the book you hold in front of you right now.

When I say "they keep moving the goal posts," the *they* are authors like those contained in this volume. This book contains an even dozen chapters authored by some of the leading authorities and rising stars currently working in longitudinal data analysis. Although varied in topic, the common denominator is a coordinated attempt to narrow the gap between the substantive models that give rise to our research hypotheses and the statistical models we use to empirically test these hypotheses. The skills of editors Jeff Harring and Greg Hancock have resulted in a cohesive collection of chapters that push us forward as a field as we continue to strive to do the best empirical research possible. The chapters are organized into three clusters: *Modeling Longitudinal Data, Drawing Valid Inferences,* and *The Role of Measurement.* Each entry helps us think more carefully about how we can build better models for our data and how we can draw stronger inferences back to our theories.

I may not have had the chance to witness Chuck Yeager's historic flight, but in my own little world this is just as exciting.

—**Patrick J. Curran, PhD**
Professor of Psychology
University of North Carolina at Chapel Hill

PREFACE

Recent years have seen an explosion of empirical longitudinal research. If you pick up any flagship journal in education or psychology, for example, you are likely to see multiple articles employing modern longitudinal methods, in particular latent growth curve modeling and its many variants. These studies often share common research objectives, namely to gain an understanding of typical behavior of the phenomena under study as represented by the parameters of a model, of the extent to which parameters and hence phenomena vary across subjects, and of whether some of this variation is systematically associated with individual attributes. The importance that practitioners are placing on longitudinal designs and analyses signals a critical shift toward methods that enable a better understanding of developmental processes thought to underlie many human attributes and behaviors.

The ability to recognize growth, however, is made more complicated by the practical realities of the environments in which we gather data, of the instability in the attributes being measured, and of the vagaries of the individuals believed to be changing over time. Thus, a common and ongoing challenge across research domains is to make meaningful inferences regarding the traits underlying observed but fallible response profiles of longitudinal data both at the group and individual levels. While the basic statistical methods used for addressing these types of questions have been extended in numerous ways in recent years, methodological progress must be sustained in order to be able to react to, and indeed plan for, the myriad complex data analytic conditions often found in practice.

To that end, the Center for Integrated Latent Variable Research (CILVR) at the University of Maryland hosted a conference on June 17–18, 2010,

---

Advances in Longitudinal Methods in the Social and Behavioral Sciences, pages ix–xi
Copyright © 2012 by Information Age Publishing
All rights of reproduction in any form reserved.

bringing together a diverse panel of quantitative researchers to present innovative, state-of-the-art longitudinal methodology within a latent variable framework. With a longitudinal methods training workshop the day before, the three-day event was designed to expose its regional, national, and international participants to new ways of examining facets of change that could be addressed using these methods; to raise awareness of some of the methodological hazards, challenges, and nuances therein; and to stimulate discussions among and between applied researchers and methodologists. Given CILVR's goal of scholarly dissemination of research spanning the continuum of latent variable methods, the current volume, *Advances in Longitudinal Methods in the Social and Behavioral Sciences*, is comprised of chapters written by presenters who participated in the 2010 CILVR conference. Not only does this volume represent a glimpse of what is occurring currently in the field, but it chronicles innovative refinements, extensions, and new developments in latent variable methods for analyzing longitudinal data, providing the methodological contexts for modeling complex multifaceted theories, and foreshadowing exciting emerging research in this broad domain.

The volume is divided into three complementary sections. Part I, *Modeling Longitudinal Data: Examining Aspects of Change or Variability*, focuses on the development and refinement of longitudinal methods, specifically the construction of models whose parameters reflect particular facets of change or variability—with some developments occurring at the population level whereas others are directed at the level of the individual. Part II, *Drawing Valid Inferences: Longitudinal Design Considerations and Model Assumptions*, describes current analytic methods of handling missing data, which are frequently seen as the rule and not the exception when collecting longitudinal data. Sampling units are often thought to be homogeneous in relation to the repeated measures. In two chapters, latent classes are incorporated in nuanced ways to account for unobserved population heterogeneity. In both cases, the appropriate handling of missing data and modeling of population heterogeneity are needed to draw valid inferences of the characteristics underlying the change process. Part III, *The Role of Measurement in Modeling Within-Subject and Between-Subject Effects*, focuses on some methodological issues associated with the challenges inherent in accurately gathering and modeling measurements that may change over time or in measurement procedures that are time-sensitive.

We are excited about the information on longitudinal methods conveyed in this volume because it represents current methodological advancements that will certainly have important implications for future applied research. Note, however, that this volume is not intended to be a first exposure to latent variable methods nor modern methods of longitudinal data analysis. Interested readers lacking in essential knowledge of these methods are encouraged to consult primary and/or secondary didactic resources in order to get the most from the chapters. Once equipped with an understanding of the core modeling methods, we are sure that readers will be equally enthusiastic about this volume's enlightening content and perspectives. We anticipate that the infusion of these methods throughout the applied literature and these methods' continued progression and development will aid in our collective understanding of the processes underlying human behavior broadly defined.

—**Jeffrey R. Harring and Gregory R. Hancock**
University of Maryland

ACKNOWLEDGMENTS

Editing a book is a cooperative effort that incorporates the input, support, and assistance of many people. We are grateful for the opportunity to publically acknowledge their contributions here.

We greatly appreciate the editorial assistance of Min Liu, Nidhi Kohli, Junhui Liu, Jui-Chen Hsu, and Ying Li (the EDMS graduate student lunch bunch). They provided insightful and thoughtful comments on each chapter and we appreciated their willingness to engage in this type of professional activity and collegial fellowship. We are also very grateful for the assistance of Xiaodong Hou for her diligent coordination of book-related materials as well as her role as liaison between us, the authors, and the publisher.

Very special thanks go to our CILVR conference coordinator, Elizabeth Lintz. In addition to her incomparable organizational skills, Elizabeth intelligently handled a multitude of administrative challenges and logistical issues behind the scenes so that the conference itself ran very smoothly. We would also like to thank the Society of Multivariate Experimental Psychology for its financial support, which paid for some conference expenses and which helped sponsor minority fellowships for three graduate students to attend the conference.

Lastly, we would like to thank George Johnson and his team at Information Age Publishing for their professionalism and support in making this edited volume possible.

PART I

MODELING LONGITUDINAL DATA:
EXAMINING FACETS OF CHANGE OR VARIABILITY

CHAPTER 1

A TEMPLATE FOR DESCRIBING INDIVIDUAL DIFFERENCES IN LONGITUDINAL DATA, WITH APPLICATION TO THE CONNECTION BETWEEN LEARNING AND ABILITY

Robert Cudeck and Casey L. Codd
Ohio State University

INTRODUCTION

In an influential series of experiments published a century ago, Ballard (1913) reported that under some conditions children could recall a passage of poetry better after a short period of time and without additional rehearsal than they did immediately after learning the piece. For example, the mean percent of lines of a poem correctly recalled by one group of Ballard's 12-year-old children over 7 days after the initial learning was 111, 117, 113, 112, 111, 99, and 94, where the percentages were scaled to be 100 on the last day of practice (p. 6). The demonstration of improved memory without rehearsal or review runs counter to the almost universal finding that retention of recently learned material declines quickly over time. Ballard coined the term *reminiscence* to describe unrehearsed improvement in memory for text typically after a delay. McGeoch (1935) traced the phenomenon back as far as 1903 to Alfred Binet, among others. The experiments provoked wide interest. Researchers later showed that reminiscence effects can be obtained using nonsense syllables, three-letter digits, consonants, abstract words, standard prose, and pictures of objects or of people. It was shown to occur in younger and older learners, and in depressed and nondepressed samples, in those with both high and low IQ. Eysenck and Frith (1977) studied reminiscence as a correlate of personality characteristics.

In addition to the effect based on some components of verbal learning, reminiscence also has been demonstrated using the completely different domain of psychomotor tasks. A case in point is performance on the pursuit rotor task. The data in Figure 1.1 show the effect for participants who worked on the task over 3 consecutive days. On each day there were 25 trials of 20 seconds each with a 10-second intertrial interval. The 75 time-on-target responses were averaged into blocks of five trials, for a total of 15 trial blocks over the 3 days. The striking reminiscence effect is apparent after days 1 and 2, where, at least for this group, performance improves even in the absence of active practice.

Although reminiscence has been widely documented, the exact conditions under which it is known to occur are not completely understood. Consequently, work is ongoing to investigate characteristics of the experiment or features of the learners in which reminiscence occurs (e.g., Groninger & Murray, 2004; Wheeler & Roediger, 1992).

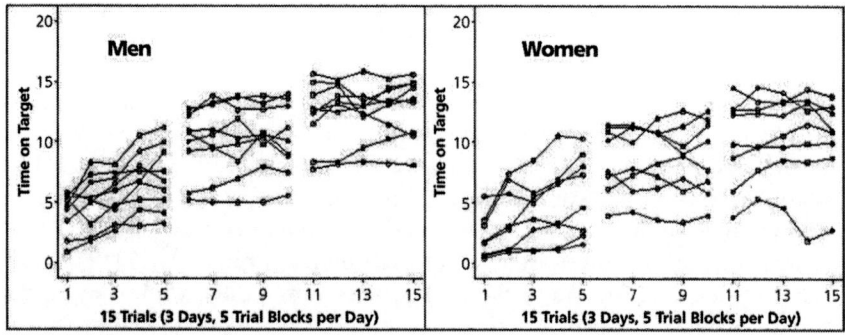

Figure 1.1 Performance on the pursuit rotor task for a selected group of individuals over 15 trials across 3 days. The reminiscence effect is the improvement between days which occurs without direct practice.

UNDERSTANDING REMINISCENCE WITH A SUBJECT-SPECIFIC MODEL

Mastering a task in the laboratory is a skill, and some individuals acquire it faster and perform it better than others. There is a very large literature on the correspondence between skill acquisition and traditional measures of human ability such as intelligence tests. Reminiscence is one of those aspects of learning and memory in which individual differences are evident but for which reliable covariates have not been identified. One goal of this chapter is to investigate the connection between learning a task and background covariates that effectively predict performance. Quantifying the reminiscence effect is essential in the overall statistical model.

The majority of experiments investigating the effect are based on the study of mean profiles over acquisition trials. For an effect that is essentially defined for individuals, the focus on group means is not the ideal level of analysis. Very early on in this literature, McGeoch (1935) argued that the study of average profiles "is not valid in the study of reminiscence, for reminiscence is an affair of the memory of an individual subject, who either improves or does not. Averages can conceal the fact that many subjects have improved slightly while one happens to lose greatly in retention score." And again later she noted, "There are individual differences in the display of this phenomena—some subjects are reminiscers, some are not" (cited in Buxton, 1943, p. 323).

The random coefficient model (RCM) is especially well suited for studying individual differences in learning. What gives the method its appeal is the great flexibility in adapting to measurement designs, functional forms, and especially the distinction of between- and within-subject variability. Certainly the most important feature of the RCM is that it is a subject-specific model, focused on individual patterns of change. This approach is in marked contrast to other statistical models that apply to the mean performance and in which individual differences are averaged over. The emphasis on individual change patterns is natural and appealing, as much in education and the social sciences as it is in public health research. Most of the numerous text-length summaries and substantive applications in which the RCM is featured address this central capability of the method.

At the same time, it is an odd fact that the existing literature has given the practical implications of a subject-specific model very short shrift. The current curious state of practice is to sing the praises of the model as an ideal method for the study of individual change, but then ignore the individuals and resort to an analysis of the mean change profile. The reason for the inconsistent practice is easy to understand: the analysis of mean change is not a trivial exercise, but it is more straightforward than is an appropriate analysis with a subject-specific model. A completely idiographic approach applied to a large sample is a sobering undertaking. It also requires subjective decisions above what are needed for an analysis of the mean change. Tailoring the analysis to individuals, then selecting the most important parts of the statistical summary to present again at an individual level, are steps that involve choices. With these problems in mind, a second goal of this research is to suggest a template for how individual differences in a longitudinal study can be effectively investigated with the RCM without finessing the problem presented by individuals and retreating to an analysis of the average performance.

A classic example of how to do this was presented in a venerable article by Thurstone in 1919, based on his doctoral dissertation investigating algebraic functions for learning data. From our perspective Thurstone was concerned with the problem of justifying a subject-specific approach to repeated-measures data for skill acquisition. The immediate problem was investigating how students learned to use a manual typewriter. As a way of dealing with the overall statistical issues, the procedure he followed is quite interesting. It constitutes a template for how this approach can be carried out.

To summarize, the goal of this chapter is to describe the pursuit rotor data with a version of the RCM. The particular function selected gives information about the dynamics of skill acquisition on this task and is constructed to highlight the reminiscence effects that exist. To understand individual differences in learning, the model is extended to include latent variable covariates that are based on a battery of ability tests. This addresses the question of which aspects of learning are associated with traditional ability factors. In all this we want the final model to have a consistent subject-specific orientation. The example provided by Thurstone's study of learning is a guidebook for the way this kind of research can be conducted.

THURSTONE'S LEARNING STUDY

Thurstone's (1919) work on skill acquisition in using a typewriter was a quantitative description of individual learning. His article does contain averages; however, it is a case study in research with repeated measures from a subject-specific point of view. The approach is conceptually simple: accumulate results from multiple individuals and aggregate them into general themes that pertain to all learners. Even the language used in the process is informative: "The majority of learning curves... have this initial performance" (p. 13). He was distilling from many particular curves to understand common features. The analysis of the average learning profile would not have accomplished the same objective as the synthesis of many individual learner profiles did. The implications of the individual-oriented viewpoint are not yet widely appreciated, even though statistical methods are available that make such an analysis feasible, and even though an individual focus is natural in the behavioral sciences.

Another aspect of Thurstone's (1919) study that makes it a useful example is the way that the main algebraic function was chosen. He did not report all of the alternative functions that were considered, except to observe that there were more than 40. The list is impressive in an era of hand calculations. The reason for examining such a large number of functions was because he required a model that worked well with the characteristic form of the learning data that he studied. One function in particular provided an especially good match to the data and had parameters that were effective summaries of the learning profiles. The function was the simple two-parameter hyperbola, recognizable as the Michaelis-Menten model (Bates & Watts, 1992, Chap. 2):

$$f = \frac{\beta_f x}{\beta_h + x}.$$

The parameters are β_f, the level of learning at an advanced level of practice, and β_h, the number of trials when half of the total gain has been achieved. Thurstone viewed it as essential that the function fit the context, work well with data, and have interpretable parameters. And this required that he shop around.

The third issue to note in Thurstone's (1919) article is the strict criteria for inclusion and exclusion of participants and what he was trying to accomplish by such careful selection. The training program in his study was demanding. It ran 2 hours per day, 5 days per week for 7 months. He recruited a total of 83 vocational school students who almost all finished the program. Yet before carrying out the full statistical analysis he excluded a sizeable number, 32 cases or 39%. Of the 32, 20 were dropped because of irregular attendance, three were excluded because of variability in response, and nine because the form of their learning curve did not correspond to the function he believed to be appropriate. Excluding subjects who do not meet study criteria is routine in some research domains but almost unheard of in others. The goal of Thurstone's study was to describe how a typical subject acquired the skill. It was essential to identify blue-blooded, highly pedigreed members of the class of genuine typing learners. He wrote, "We have eliminated 12 out of 63 complete records. Generalizing from this fact we may conclude that the speed-amount form of learning for typewriting takes the hyperbolic form in about four cases out of five. This justifies our reference to it as the typical but not as the universal form of learning curve" (p. 28).

The point of this example is the individual-focused procedure itself. It had a clear-cut emphasis on individual learning. The function he chose was selected from among many because it was especially appropriate for the behavior and because it adequately described most individuals in his sample. To be sure that the model worked well, he deliberately selected subjects so the match of function to data was close among those whom he judged to be most representative of the class. It goes without saying that some of these procedures are open to debate, especially with regard to the selection of participants who are ultimately retained in the final sample. It is nonetheless instructive that the focus on individual learning was the motivation for the whole approach and dictated the strategy he followed subsequently. The emphasis on individual learning affects research practice, especially in the initial phases of work with the RCM. The approach comes into play when the function is developed, when participants are included for further study, and when the appropriateness of the function for the data is evaluated.

MORE ON THE DATA AND ORIGINAL SAMPLE

Work for this chapter was motivated by data collected in the Minnesota Study of Twins Reared Apart (Bouchard, Lykken, McGue, Segal, & Tellegen, 1990). The research participants are members of an invaluable sample of adult twins that also includes some adoptive and biological family members, and other close associates of the twins. In most cases, the twins were separated early in life, reared in adoptive families, and not reunited until adulthood. The subset used for this project was 176 adults (63 men and 113 women) who ranged in age from 18 to 77 years old. As part of a detailed assessment, participants were tested individually on a standard pursuit rotor apparatus in three successive morning sessions that lasted approximately 30 minutes each (Fox, Hershberger, & Bouchard, 1996). The data collection protocol also included three batteries of cognitive ability tests that we will use as latent variable covariates to explain individual differences in learning on the pursuit rotor task. Although the parent project is primarily devoted to the study of behavior genetic studies, the sample has also been used to investigate a number of substantive questions concerned with measurement and statistics (Johnson, Bouchard, Krueger, McGue, Gottesman, 2004). In this work we did not take advantage of the special characteristics inherent in twin designs.

SOME CANDIDATE RESPONSE FUNCTIONS

To represent the individual pursuit rotor records of Figure 1.1, the first step is to choose an appropriate function. The goal is to use a subject-specific model, so the function should provide a good fit for the majority of individuals. A reasonable exploratory procedure is to examine each function by plotting individual data and fitted functions in a trellis display. It is convenient initially to use nonlinear least squares for what is called "individual-specific regression" by Davidian and Giltinan (1995, Chap. 5). One benefit of this approach is that it keeps the analysis focused on individuals. It is always the case that data for some individuals are fit better by one function than others. It is also true that even a generally effective function does not work well for everyone. Consequently, the goal is to decide on a function that seems most appropriate for the largest number of individuals. In some situations, the response patterns in the sample seem almost qualitatively different, and a simple function may not describe the different kinds adequately. For some of these, it may be possible to find a more complex function that works well with the different kinds of response. In other examples, the existence of different response styles can be evidence of different classes of learners. In this situation, a mixture model that allows different subpopulations to follow fundamentally different trajectories may be appropriate.

The repeated measures, $y_i = (y_{i1}, \ldots, y_{in_i})'$, are assumed to follow the model

$$y_i = f_i(x_i, \theta_i) + e_i$$

where $f_{ij}(x_i, \theta_i)$ is the function for the ith individual at the jth measurement, $f_i(x_i, \theta_i) = (f_{i1}(x_i, \theta_i), \ldots, f_{in_i}(x_i, \theta_i))$ are predicted values, and $e_i = \{e_{ij}\}$ are residuals. The number of repeated measures, n_i, varies according to the measurement protocol and the presence of missing data. The vector x_i contains covariates such as background measurements or demographic variables, and almost always includes the occasion or elapsed time since the beginning of the study to the jth assessment; the vector θ_i contains the function coefficients for the ith person. The idea is that a common function applies to all, but with varying coefficients and differing covariate scores that tailor the function to the repeated measurements of the ith case. This is level 1 of the hierarchical RCM.

We review five functions for the pursuit rotor data. They are representative of a large number of alternatives. Functions 1–4 ignore the fact that trials are spread over 3 days. Including information about days complicates the function, so if the data can be represented effectively without incorporating the days into the function, the models are simpler. The particular versions shown in Figure 1.2 are the least squares fit to four or five participants to give a sampling of the range of individual responses. In this section the vector x_i is specialized to be the trial blocks of the experiment, $x_{ij} = j$ where $j = 1, \ldots, 15$, where trial blocks are a proxy for continuous time.

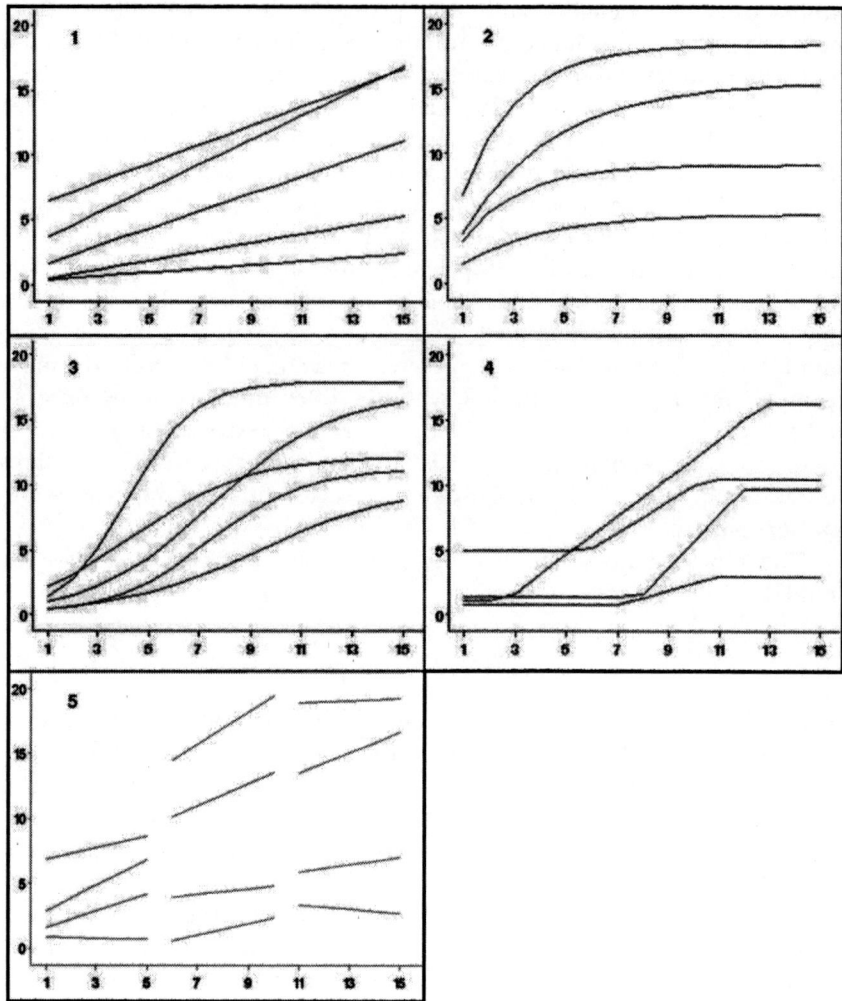

Figure 1.2 Five candidate functions for the pursuit rotor data, fit to selected individuals. The functions are (1) linear; (2) exponential; (3) logistic; (4) three piece linear spline with unknown knots; and (5) three discontinuous segments including two coefficients for reminiscence effects.

1. *Linear*: Parameters $\theta_i = (\beta_{i0}, \beta_{i1})$ are intercept and slope

$$f_{ij} = \beta_{i0} + \beta_{i1}x_{ij}$$

Function (1) thus assumes a constant rate of improvement over trials with no periods where learning is any more rapid than others.

2. *Exponential:* $\theta_i = (\eta_i, \beta_{if})$ are rate of increase and final performance at an advanced level of learning.

$$f_{ij} = \beta_{if}\left(1-\exp(-\eta_i x_{ij})\right) \qquad \eta_i > 0$$

Function (2) applies to individuals who learn rapidly during early trials and then gradually improve to a personal asymptote.

3. *Logistic:* $\theta_i = (\eta_i, \beta_{i0}, \beta_{if})$ are rate of increase, initial performance, and final performance.

$$f_{ij} = \frac{\beta_{i0}\beta_{if}}{\beta_{i0}+(\beta_{if}-\beta_{i0})\exp(-\eta_i x_{ij})} \qquad \eta_i > 0$$

The logistic function also describes participants who learn rapidly initially and then improve to a personal maximum level. An important feature of this function is that it includes an inflection that marks the point in trials where the function changes from positive to negative acceleration.

4. *Three restricted linear segments:* $\theta_i = (\beta_{i0}, \beta_{if}, \tau_{i1}, \tau_{i2})$ are initial performance, final performance, and two changepoints or knots.

$$f_{ij} = \begin{cases} \beta_{i0} & x_{ij} \leq \tau_{i1} \\ \beta_{i0} + \dfrac{\beta_{if}-\beta_{i0}}{\tau_{i2}-\tau_{i1}}(x_{ij}-\tau_{i1}) & \tau_{i1} < x_{ij} \leq \tau_{i2} \\ \beta_{if} & \tau_{i2} < x_{ij} \end{cases}$$

The function has initial intercept β_{i0} until the first knot is reached at $x = \tau_{i1}$. At that point the function increases to a second intercept β_{if}, which occurs at the second knot $x = \tau_{i2}$ (Pauler & Laird, 2000). This is a restricted three-piece linear spline with two unknown knots, continuous between segments over trials. During early trials the time on target score is constant and equal to β_{i0}. During later trials, the response is constant at a different level and equal to β_{if}. The unknown knots, τ_{i1} and τ_{i2}, determine when the transitions between early and late levels occur. Between knots, the function increases from β_{i0} to β_{if} with slope $(\beta_{if}-\beta_{i0}),(\tau_{i2}-\tau_{i1})$. This function applies to learning data that exhibits an early period with no improvement, followed by a period of steady linear increase, reaching a plateau with no further change. The knots are especially informative because they mark the points in time when the function changes fundamentally.

5. *Three discontinuous linear segments,* one for each day. Each of the segments is linear; however, the overall function is nonlinear.

$$f_{ij} = \begin{cases} \alpha_{i0} + \alpha_{i1}x_{ij} & 1 \leq x_{ij} \leq 5 \\ \beta_{i0} + \beta_{i1}x_{ij} & 6 \leq x_{ij} \leq 10 \\ \gamma_{i0} + \gamma_{i1}x_{ij} & 11 \leq x_{ij} \leq 15 \end{cases}$$

To measure change between days, define ρ_{i1} and ρ_{i2} to be the difference in performance between trials 5 and 6 and between 10 and 11, using $x_1^* = 5.5$ and $x_2^* = 10.5$ as the points of discontinuity. These parameters are essentially reminiscence effects under the model.

$$\rho_{i1} = \beta_{i0} + \beta_{i1}x_1^* - (\alpha_{i0} + \alpha_{i1}x_1^*)$$
$$\rho_{i2} = \gamma_{i0} + \gamma_{i1}x_2^* - (\beta_{i0} + \beta_{i1}x_2^*)$$

If performance at the end of Day k is the same as at the beginning of Day $k+1$, then $\rho_{ik} = 0$ and the two segments are continuous at x_k^*. Rewrite the function in a more usable form by solving for β_{i0} and γ_{i0} in terms of the other six coefficients.

$$f_{ij} = \begin{cases} \alpha_{i0} + \alpha_{i1}x_{ij} & 1 \leq x_{ij} \leq 5 \\ \alpha_{i0} + \alpha_{i1}x_1^* + \rho_{i1} + \beta_{i1}(x_{ij} - x_1^*) & 6 \leq x_{ij} \leq 10 \\ \alpha_{i0} + \alpha_{i1}x_1^* + \rho_{i1} + 5\beta_{i1} + \rho_{i2} + \gamma_{i1}(x_{ij} - x_2^*) & 11 \leq x_{ij} \leq 15 \end{cases}$$

Parameters are thus $\theta_i = (\alpha_{i0}, \alpha_{i1}, \beta_{i1}, \gamma_{i1}, \rho_{i1}, \rho_{i2})$.

Apart from the fact that all five functions are increasing, they are very different in terms of the learning styles they describe and the information produced by the parameters. They also vary in terms of the number of parameters and in how well they fit individual data. Every one of the five is best for a subset of participants, and each also is poorer than at least one other function for some individuals.

FITTING FUNCTIONS TO INDIVIDUALS

To summarize performance of the candidates, we fit the functions to every individual by least squares and recorded whether the procedure converged.

If a solution could be obtained, the individual mean square residual was calculated,

$$MSR_i = \left(\sum_j (y_{ij} - f_{ij})^2\right) / n_i.$$

Results are shown in Table 1.1. The linear function (1) converged for all $N = 176$ with median MSR_i of 35.0. The exponential function (2) had a better median MSR_i but only converged for 162 cases. The logistic function (3) was able to fit 170 individual datasets and had a median MSR_i of 17.1. Both (3) and (4) were much better than (1) or (2); however, (4) did not converge for 48 participants.

Function (5), the three-piece spline, could be fit to all subjects. It also had the best median MSR_i. Function (5) is also valuable because it produces an estimate of the reminiscence effects between days. All of these characteristics made it the best candidate from among the alternatives. It is worth emphasizing that the other functions worked well for some. Function (5) is best for the majority of participants, but was not best for all.

The main impression with all the functions is the tremendous range of individual differences in the learning pattern. Figure 1.3 displays data and fitted equations for nine individuals with (5). The values at the top of each panel are the least squares fit and subject ID number. The panels are ordered in terms of increasing MSR_i. The reminiscence effects are quite variable across individuals and are different from day 1 to day 2 for a given person. For example, individual #73 in the lower right panel showed strong improvement between days 1 and 2; however, during active practice on days 2 and 3 he or she did steadily worse and the reminiscence effect between days 2 and 3 was negligible. Individual #43 in the third row showed a strong increase between days 1 and 2, but a decrease between days 2 and 3.

Figure 1.4 shows those who had the worst individual fit to function (5). With poor-fitting models it can be difficult to judge whether the problem

TABLE 1.1 Performance of Five Functions with the Pursuit Rotor Data

Function	Parameters	N*	Median MSR
(1) Linear	2	176	35.0
(2) Exponential	2	162	26.9
(3) Logistic	3	170	17.1
(4) Three restricted linear segments	4	128	15.4
(5) Three discontinuous linear segments	6	176	7.3

Note: N* is the number of individual datasets out of 176 for which the least square algorithm converged. Column 4 is the median individual mean square residual out of N* converged cases.

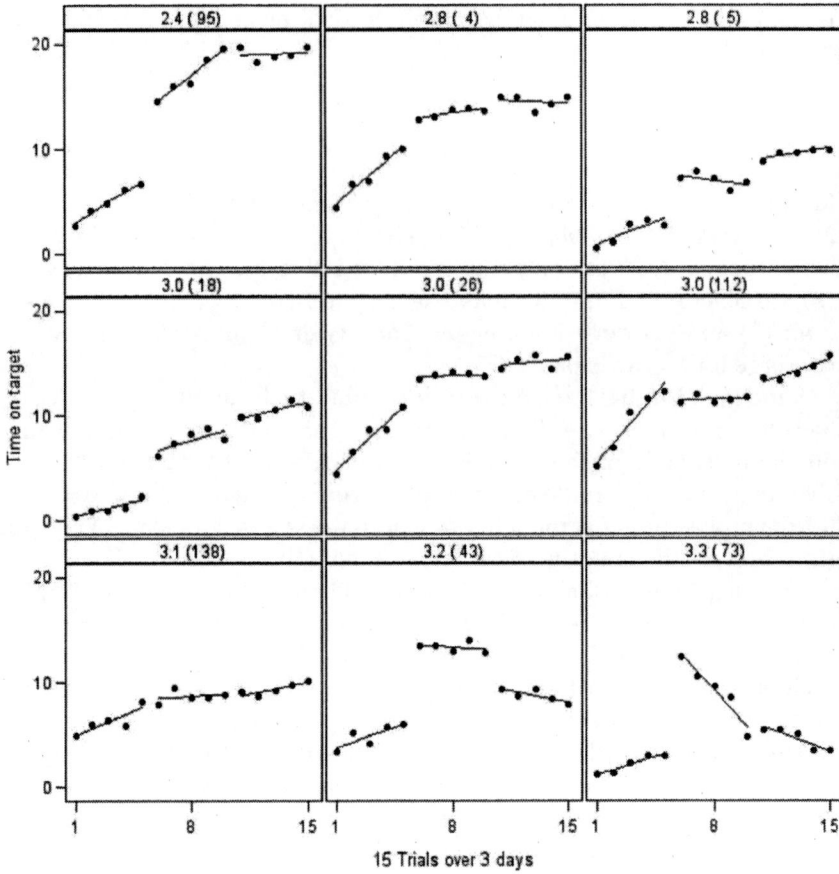

Figure 1.3 Nine individuals with functions that fit function (5) well.

is due to high within-subject variability with an otherwise adequate function, or if instead the function is simply inappropriate. Examining graphs of those with the poorest fit is also valuable as a check for outliers and other anomalies. Even among this group, the learning styles are varied. For example, individual #164 in the top-right panel showed very strong reminiscence between both of the days; however, under direct practice on day 2, performance was consistently worse over trials. Person #53 in the upper left corner had a whopping 10-second improvement from trial 3 to trial 4 then maintained consistently high scores for the duration of the experiment. Individual #170 in the center panel showed beautiful linear increases over the first 10 trial blocks, and then become somewhat inconsistent on trials 11–15.

Results in Figure 1.3 and especially Figure 1.4 demonstrate that function (5) worked satisfactorily for almost all individuals in the sample. Judging

A Template for Describing Individual Differences in Longitudinal Data ▪ 15

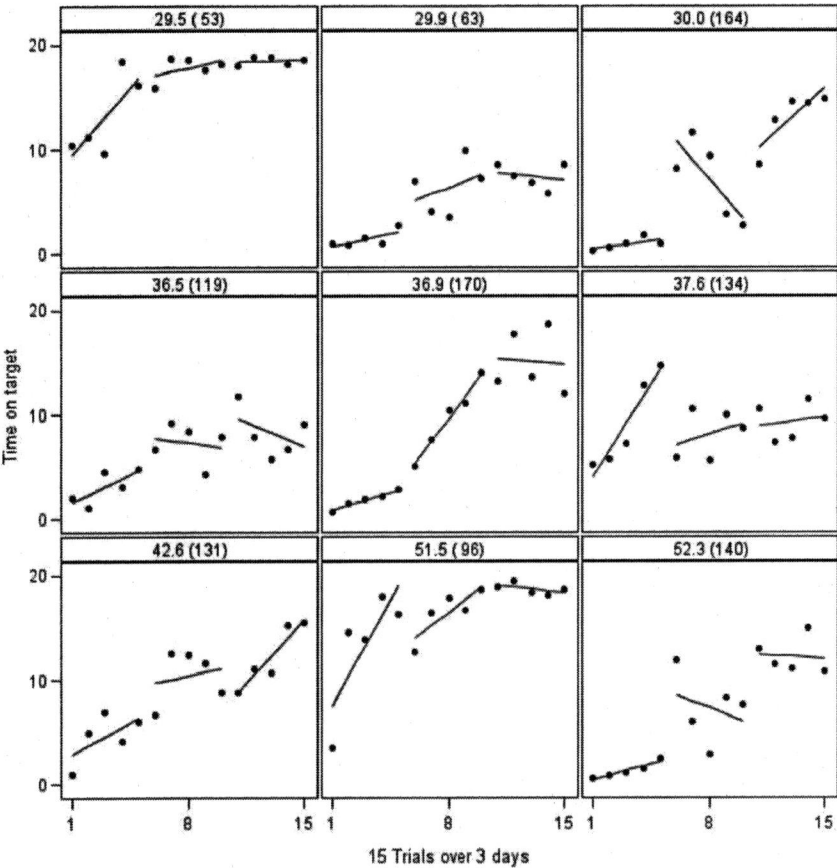

Figure 1.4 Participants who had the worst-fitting individual models.

the success of a function in terms of number of individuals who are reasonably well fit is in many ways preferable to relying exclusively on an overall goodness-of-fit statistical test. As valuable as the latter result is, it does not take into consideration the many and varied issues regarding how, to what degree, and with which complications the model works at the subject level.

A RCM FOR THE PURSUIT ROTOR DATA

After deciding on the function and verifying that it is generally appropriate for the sample, the next step is to fit a full RCM. Instead of treating each person independently, one assumes that the individual coefficients are part of a distribution, the most common of which is $\theta_i \sim N(\theta, \Phi_{\theta\theta})$. A population structure is also assumed for individual residuals. The typical approach uses $e_i \sim N(0, \Psi_e)$, where the covariance matrix has a simple form such as that Ψ_e is a diagonal matrix. The marginal distribution of the response depends on the function selected for the repeated measures as well as the distribution selected for θ_i and e_i. The theory is fully reviewed by several authors (Davidian & Giltinan, 1995; Fitzmaurice, Laird, & Ware, 2004; Hand & Crowder, 1996), who also present information on computing strategies and software options. Although we are taking a subject-specific perspective in this analysis, fitting the full model allows one to investigate characteristics of the population that are unavailable when data are examined on a person-by-person basis.

The function for the repeated measures is nonlinear in form but is linear in the random effects, and so the setup is straightforward. Repeating from above, the coefficients of the model are $\theta_i = (\alpha_{i0}, \alpha_{i1}, \beta_{i1}, \gamma_{i1}, \rho_{i1}, \rho_{i2})$. Let $\mathbf{X}$ (15 × 6) be the design matrix for the ith case over trials. The three-phase model is specified by writing rows as

$$\{X\}_j = \begin{cases} (1, x_{ij}, 0, 0, 0, 0) & 1 \leq x_{ij} \leq 5 \\ (1, x_1^*, 1, (x_{ij} - x_1^*), 0, 0) & 6 \leq x_{ij} \leq 10 \\ (1, x_1^*, 1, 5, 1, (x_{ij} - x_2^*)) & 11 \leq x_{ij} \leq 15 \end{cases}$$

Then the model for an individual is

$$\mathbf{y}_i = \mathbf{X}\theta_i + \mathbf{e}_i.$$

Maximum likelihood estimates of the fixed effects and of the variances of the individual coefficients over the population are listed in Table 1.2. Standard errors are in parentheses. Figure 1.5 displays a graph of the function evaluated at the estimates $\hat{\theta}$, together with a 20% random sample of

TABLE 1.2 Maximum Likelihood Estimates of the Parameters of Function (5) and of the Variance of the Individual Coefficients

Parameters of function (5)

$\hat{\alpha}_0$	$\hat{\alpha}_1$	$\hat{\beta}_1$	$\hat{\gamma}_1$	$\hat{\rho}_1$	$\hat{\rho}_2$
2.79(.15)	0.86(.04)	0.15(.04)	0.01(.04)	2.32(.19)	1.61(.19)

Variance of individual coefficients

$\hat{\alpha}_{i0}$	$\hat{\alpha}_{i1}$	$\hat{\beta}_{i1}$	$\hat{\gamma}_{i1}$	$\hat{\rho}_{i1}$	$\hat{\rho}_{i2}$
4.640(.47)	0.351(.04)	0.167(.02)	0.176(.03)	6.380(.76)	6.150(.78)

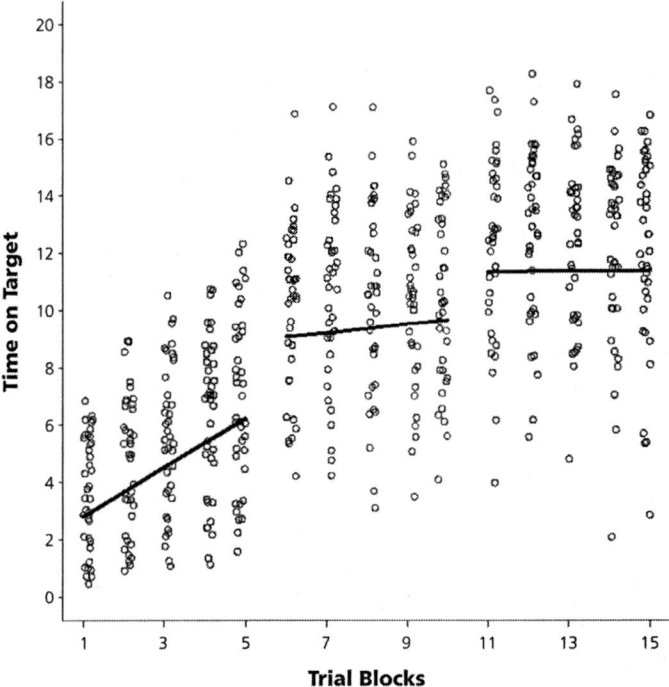

Figure 1.5 Plot of function (5) evaluated at the parameter estimates, with a 20% random sample of individuals. Data points are jittered.

the data. The points have been jittered to better show density. Because the parameters are the means of the individual coefficients, the estimated curve that corresponds to these values should run through the middle of the point cloud. The curve for the typical subject starts with the intercept at $\hat{\alpha}_0 = 2.79$. It improves on day 1 and 2 with positive slopes of $\hat{\alpha}_1 = 0.86$ seconds and $\hat{\beta}_1 = 0.15$ seconds per trial. The mean slope on day 3 could be zero in the population: $\hat{\gamma}_1 = 0.01, se(\hat{\gamma}_1) = 0.04$. The function also has improvement due to reminiscence effects of $\hat{\rho}_1 = 2.32$ and $\hat{\rho}_2 = 1.61$ seconds. It can be seen in the second line of Table 1.2 that all of the individual coefficients have appreciable variability. Thus, one of the interesting possibilities when using an RCM has occurred here, namely that γ_{i1} varies significantly across persons, although γ_1 is small and may be zero.

The variability across individuals on the pursuit rotor task is striking. For example, the predicted response under the model at the last trial, $\hat{y}_i \mid x = 15$, had range 0.92 to 19.7. Similarly, the predicted total gain between the first and 15th trials under the model, $(\hat{y}_i \mid x = 15) - (\hat{y}_i \mid x = 1)$, varied from 0.4 to 17.6 seconds. Overall, however, the RCM based on function

(5) performed well with these data. The model adequately describes the heterogeneous patterns of learning, including the major differences in initial performance, learning rates, and reminiscence effects over the 3 days, even though the latter are quite complicated.

A procedural issue is worth noting here. Examining many subjects and fitting candidate functions using the "individual-specific regression" approach reviewed above is not the same as fitting a RCM by maximum likelihood and evaluating results from that method. The former approach is intentionally exploratory and somewhat ad hoc statistically, although invaluable for judging the appropriateness of the response function for the repeated measures that are observed in the sample. On the other hand, estimating a full RCM by maximum likelihood gives estimates and predicted values both of parameters and individual coefficients that are more efficient than are obtained from an individual approach. An important part of a complete analysis of the RCM is to obtain predictions of θ_i and use them to again check that the individual-level functions fit particular subjects. Generally the correspondence between the two methods is good. This also keeps the emphasis on the subject-specific nature of the approach.

LATENT VARIABLE COVARIATES

In order to better understand the variability between subjects that is evident in learning the pursuit rotor task, we extend the model to include correlates of the individual coefficients. Johnson and colleagues (2007) reviewed work based on a large battery of ability tests that was administered to the sample in this study. They suggested a factor analysis model with eight factors for the complete set of ability variables. For the current analysis, we used 17 variables and five factors from Johnson et al.'s investigation. The goal of extending the RCM to incorporate covariates is to obtain information about which abilities are associated with which coefficients of the three-phase model. We use latent variables rather than manifest variables in order to summarize the relatively large number of ability tests into a smaller set of latent factors, and also to minimize the effects of measurement error on the correlations and regression coefficients for these components.

The ability tests and factors are, respectively, $\mathbf{z}_i = (z_{i1}, \ldots, z_{i17})'$ and $\mathbf{f}_i = (f_{i1}, \ldots, f_{i5})'$, so the model for the tests is

$$\mathbf{z}_i = \Lambda \mathbf{f}_i + \mathbf{d}_i$$

where Λ (17 × 5) is the matrix of factor loadings, the distribution of factors is $\mathbf{f}_i \sim N(\mu, \Phi_{ff})$, and $cov(\mathbf{d}_i) = \Psi_d$, with $cov(\mathbf{e}_i, \mathbf{d}_i') = \mathbf{0}$. In typical applications of the RCM, covariates are included in a level-2 regression as explanatory variables for the individual coefficients

$$\theta_i = \theta + \Gamma f_i + u_i$$

where Γ are coefficients in the regression of θ_i on f_i, and u_i are residuals. Alternatively, and especially in an exploratory study, it can be more informative to simply examine elements of the covariance matrix between θ_i and f_i. To do this, write the combined model for the repeated measures on the pursuit rotor task and for the ability tests, (y_i, z_i), as

$$\begin{pmatrix} y_i \\ z_i \end{pmatrix} = \begin{pmatrix} X & 0 \\ 0 & \Lambda \end{pmatrix} \begin{pmatrix} \theta_i \\ f_i \end{pmatrix} + \begin{pmatrix} e_i \\ d_i \end{pmatrix}$$

Then, a parameter matrix of special interest is the joint covariance matrix between the random effects and the ability latent variables,

$$\mathrm{cov}\begin{pmatrix} \theta_i \\ f_i \end{pmatrix} = \begin{pmatrix} \Phi_{\theta\theta} & \\ \Phi_{f\theta} & \Phi_{ff} \end{pmatrix}$$

where in particular

$$\Phi_{f\theta} = cov(f_i, \theta_i').$$

The five latent variables used here are Memory, Spatial, Verbal, Quantitative, and Object Rotation. Three of these, Memory, Spatial, and Object Rotation, were chosen because of their relevance to skill acquisition on the pursuit rotor task. Verbal and Quantitative were included because of their general importance in ability research. The tests that made up the factors were selected by Johnson et al. (2007) from three test batteries: the Hawaii Battery, the Comprehensive Ability Battery, and the Weschler Adult Intelligence Scale. Because the learning task involves physical dexterity, we also included the participant's age as a single manifest variable.

The factor pattern for Λ is in Table 1.3 along with maximum likelihood parameter estimates of the loadings. In Table 1.4 are estimated correlations between and within θ_i and f_i. Among the regression coefficients, $corr(\alpha_{i0}, \alpha_{i1}) = 0.38$ and $corr(\beta_{i1}, \gamma_{i1}) = 0.36$. We interpret these correlations to be weak evidence of an initial learning component on day 1 and a later learning component on days 2 and 3. Also among the regression coefficients, it was found that $corr(\beta_{i1}, \rho_{i2}) = -0.61$ and $corr(\gamma_{i1}, \rho_{i2}) = -0.53$. These estimates imply that those learners who had high slopes during the last 2

TABLE 1.3 Estimated Factor Loadings on the Five-Factor Solution for 17 Ability Tests Taken from Three Batteries

	M	S	V	Q	R	Age
M_1: Immediate visual memory (H)	66					
M_2: Delayed visual memory (H)	55					
M_3: Associative memory (C)	41					
M_4: Meaningful memory (C)	59					
S_1: Flexibility of closure (C)		69				
S_2: Identical patterns (H)		85				
S_3: Hidden pattern (H)		72				
V_1: Vocabulary			78			
V_2: Word fluency (H) (C)			74			
V_3: Vocabulary (W)			86			
Q_1: Numerical ability (C)				75		
Q_2: Subtraction/multiplication (H)				70		
Q_3: Arithmetic (W)				88		
R_1: Mental rotation (H)					42	
R_2: Card rotations (H)					79	
R_3: Cubes (H)					40	
R_4: Spatial ability (C)					92	
Age						1*

Note: Test batteries are H, Hawaii; CAB, Comprehensive Ability Battery; W, WAIS. Factors are M, memory; S, spatial; V, verbal; Q, quantitative; R, rotation. Age is included as a single manifest variable, with loading fixed to 1 (as indicated by the asterisk). Nonzero loadings shown, all others are fixed zero.

days tended to have low reminiscence coefficients between days 2 and 3. In other words, those with high rates of learning during practice tended to have lower levels of improvement between days.

It has been suggested in the literature on reminiscence effects that, as McGeoch (1935) put it, "Some subjects are reminiscers, some are not." This is an interesting conjecture, but it is not supported with these data. In moving from one day to the next, the $corr(\rho_{i1}, \rho_{i2}) = 0.18$. At both periods there is quite a lot of variability in ρ_{i1} and ρ_{i2}; however, it is not the same people who are reminiscing at each occasion.

Information on correlations between θ_i and f_i is in the lower left section of Table 1.4. Correlations above $|0.30|$ are underlined. It can be seen that moderate correlations only exist between the coefficients of the first day, α_{i0} and α_{i1}, and the latent variables Spatial and Rotation. This implies that these two abilities are somewhat associated with better initial performance and rate of learning during day 1, but not with learning rate during day 2 or 3, or with the reminiscence coefficients. There are also moderately negative correlations between age and α_{i0} and α_{i1}, such that younger participants

TABLE 1.4   Estimated Correlations between Regression Coefficients of the RCM and Latent Variables of the Ability Test

α_{i0}	1.00										
α_{i1}	.38	1.00									
β_{i1}	.12	.13	1.00								
γ_{i1}	.00	.23	.36	1.00							
ρ_{i1}	−.09	−.33	−.34	−.22	1.00						
ρ_{i2}	−.17	−.24	−.61	−.53	.18	1.00					
Memory	.26	.01	.13	−.22	.15	.14	1.00				
Spatial	**.30**	**.30**	.06	−.03	.23	.05	.64	1.00			
Verbal	−.01	.04	−.07	−.03	.06	.07	.58	.57	1.00		
Quant	.01	.13	.06	.06	.13	−.02	.57	.66	.81	1.00	
Rotation	**.40**	.25	.11	.05	.16	.00	.56	.82	.30	.42	1.00
Age	**−.36**	**−.34**	−.11	−.02	−.23	.05	−.39	−.60	.05	−.16	−.58	1.00

Note: Age is a single manifest variable. Correlations above |0.30| between regression coefficients and factors are in bold.

tend to have higher values on both coefficients. All other correlations between ability factors and coefficients of the learning function are negligible.

DISCUSSION

The goal of this research was first to describe learning on the pursuit rotor task, and then to relate acquisition of this skill to latent variable covariates of ability. In the learning literature, reminiscence is universally defined as the simple difference in performance on a task immediately at the end of practice and again at a second time somewhat later. In contrast, we have defined reminiscence to be part of a model-based, explicit function that covered the whole range of the experiment. The three-component spline function presented here included two parameters for reminiscence between adjacent days and were not simple difference scores. Defined in this manner, the estimated reminiscence effects borrow strength from both the full profile of repeated measures and covariates for an individual, as well as from the data of all others in the sample. These estimates are therefore expected to be more reliable and more accurate than a simple difference would be. As always occurs with learning tasks of this kind, performance on the pursuit rotor varied enormously between subjects. Our version of reminiscence estimated from the model also showed considerable individual differences. This flexibility in adapting the function to the available data is an attractive feature of the overall approach.

We argued that this kind of learning can be fruitfully investigated as a subject-specific model in which the focus of attention is the way that individuals change. In this approach, average change is of secondary importance. Many applications of the RCM begin with the statement that the model is effective for describing individual change, but then abandon the emphasis on individuals and go on to present a model for the mean learning curve. We believe that in many cases it would be much more informative to maintain the emphasis on individuals.

A subject-specific model is a single general function that is assumed to apply to all. It accommodates differences between persons by varying the coefficients. The RCM is ideal for this type of statistical analysis because it is focused on persons but at the same time synthesizes a possibly large number of individual functions into an integrated whole. This is a more complicated way of investigating repeated-measures data than is the analysis of mean change. But it has the potential to produce a richer picture of the way that individuals learn. This sentiment has often been voiced in the past and from many different quarters (e.g., Barlow & Nock, 2009; Kent & Hayward, 2007; Rogosa, Brandt, & Zimowski, 1982; Rogosa & Willett, 1985). One problem with investigating repeated-measures data from a truly individual perspective is that there are few examples of how to conduct a project of this kind. Thurstone's (1919) classic study of learning curves is a jewel and can be read as a kind of template for how a subject-specific study can be carried out.

A few substantive points can be made based on these analyses. One theme in this literature is that reminiscence is a trait, a stable feature of a person's learning style. In this model the two reminiscence coefficients had correlation of only 0.18. This implies that different persons exhibited the effect on different days and that there was not a consistent ordering of the sample on these measures.

The subject-specific functions for time on target scores fit the great majority of individual datasets well. This implies that the six coefficients of the function summarize performance on the pursuit rotor effectively. From the battery of 17 ability tests, we defined a five-factor latent variable structure and estimated correlations between the ability factors and the regression coefficients. There were only modest correlations between these two sets of variables. This suggests that the individual differences observed on learning the pursuit rotor task are a rather different kind of ability than the abilities that are measured by traditional paper-and-pencil tests. If traditional measures of ability cannot explain performance on a laboratory task, what other variables might account for this skill? One obvious untapped domain is personality. Such traits as motivation, conscientiousness, and persistence may be explanatory variables that could be explored in future research. The models and emphasis on individual change presented here can be adapted easily to include other types of covariates and their own latent variable structures.

ACKNOWLEDGMENT

We are grateful to Professor Thomas J. Bouchard for permission to use data from the incomparable Minnesota Study of Twins Reared Apart for work in this chapter.

REFERENCES

Ballard, P. B. (1913). Oblivescence and reminiscence. *British Journal of Psychology Monograph Supplements, 1,* 1–82.

Barlow, D. H., & Nock, N. K. (2009). Why can't we be more idiographic in our research? *Perspectives on Psychological Science, 4,* 19–21.

Bates D. M., & Watts D. G. (1988). *Nonlinear regression analysis and its applications.* New York: Wiley.

Bouchard, T. J., Lykken, D. T., McGue, M., Segal, N. L., & Tellegen, A. (1990). Sources of human psychological differences: The Minnesota Study of Twins Reared Apart. *Science, 250,* 223–228.

Buxton, C. E. (1943). The status of research in reminiscence. *Psychological Bulletin, 40,* 313–340.

Davidian, M., & Giltinan, D. M. (1995). *Nonlinear models for repeated measurement data.* London: Chapman & Hall.

Eysenck, H. J., & Frith, C. D. (1977). *Reminiscence, motivation, and personality: A case study in experimental psychology.* New York: Plenum Press.

Fitzmaurice, G., Laird, N., & Ware, J. (2004). *Applied longitudinal analysis.* New York: Wiley.

Fox, P. W., Hershberger, S. L., & Bouchard, T. J. (1996). Genetic and environmental contributions to the acquisition of a motor skill. *Nature, 384,* 356–358.

Hand, D. J., & Crowder, M. J. (1996). *Practical longitudinal data analysis.* London: Chapman & Hall.

Groninger, L. D., & Murray, K. N. (2004). Reminiscence, forgetting, and hypermnesia using face-name learning: Isolating the effects using recall and recognition memory measures. *Memory, 12,* 351–365.

Johnson, W., Bouchard, T. J., Krueger, R. F., McGue, M., & Gottesman, I. I. (2004). Just one g: Consistent results from three test batteries. *Intelligence, 32,* 95–107.

Johnson, W., Bouchard, T. J., McGue, M., Segal, N. L., Tellegen, A., Keyes, M., et al. (2007). Genetic and environmental influences on the verbal-perceptual image rotation (VPR) model of the structure of mental abilities in the Minnesota study of twins reared apart. *Intelligence, 35,* 542–562.

Kent, D., & Hayward, R. (2007). When averages hide individual differences in clinical trials. *American Scientist, 95,* 60–68.

McGeoch, G. O. (1935). The conditions of reminiscence. *American Journal of Psychology, 47,* 65–89.

Pauler, D. K., & Laird, N. M. (2000). A mixture model for longitudinal data with application to assessment of noncompliance. *Biometrics, 56,* 464–472.

Rogosa, D. R., Brandt, D., & Zimowski, M. (1982). A growth approach to the measurement of change. *Psychological Bulletin, 92,* 726–748.

Rogosa, D. R., & Willett, J. B. (1985). Understanding correlates of change by modeling individual differences in growth. *Psychometrika, 50,* 203–228.

Thurstone, L. L. (1919). The learning curve equation. *Psychological Monographs, 26*(No. 114).

Wheeler, M. A., & Roediger, H. L. (1992). Disparate effects of repeated testing: Reconciling Ballard's (1913) and Bartlett's (1932) results. *Psychological Science, 3,* 240–245.

CHAPTER 2

ON INTERPRETABLE REPARAMETERIZATIONS OF LINEAR AND NONLINEAR LATENT GROWTH CURVE MODELS

Kristopher J. Preacher
Vanderbilt University

Gregory R. Hancock
University of Maryland

One of the primary goals of longitudinal modeling is to estimate and interpret free model parameters that reflect meaningful aspects of change over time in a parsimonious manner. Perhaps the simplest example is to estimate a linear slope in regression analysis when the predictor is time (t) and the criterion (y) is measured repeatedly at several occasions; this slope may be interpreted straightforwardly as the expected change in y given a unit change in t in the population, holding constant all other predictors. Of course, the nature of longitudinal change may be far from this simplest

Advances in Longitudinal Methods in the Social and Behavioral Sciences, pages 25–58
Copyright © 2012 by Information Age Publishing
All rights of reproduction in any form reserved.

scenario, and as such researchers are increasingly seeking theoretically appropriate ways to model more complex nonlinear systems as well (see, e.g., Grimm & Ram, 2009; Ram & Grimm, 2007).

In many circumstances, a given linear or nonlinear model may be sensible from a theoretical perspective and may fit the data well, yet may have parameters that are difficult to interpret in a meaningful way. Such models often may be reparameterized. *Reparameterization* is the reexpression of a target model so that parameters of the reexpressed model more closely align with questions of substantive interest to the researcher. In this chapter we discuss various ways in which reparameterization may be used in the context of latent growth curve modeling (LGM), a powerful and flexible application of structural equation modeling (SEM) often used to model trends in longitudinal data and individual differences in those trends.

As is seen in this chapter, reparameterization can be extremely useful to researchers for several reasons. First and foremost, it is often more convenient to directly estimate some quantity of interest as a model parameter than it is to compute it post hoc as a function of other estimated parameters. Direct estimation of these parameters permits researchers to obtain both point and interval estimates of the quantity of interest, allowing the researcher to test hypotheses and determine precision of estimation. Reparameterization also allows researchers to determine whether an aspect of change or some other important quantity is predicted or moderated by other variables, and generally allows the flexibility of treating a parameter as a fixed known value, as an unknown value to be estimated, or even (in some cases) as a random coefficient reflecting individual differences in some aspect of the function.

To provide a framework for our discussion, we describe three illustrative (but by no means exhaustive) classes of reparameterization, and present exemplars from each class: (1) quantifying homogeneity or heterogeneity of individuals, (2) estimating and predicting aspects of change, and (3) estimating and predicting time-specific individual differences. To illustrate the quantification of homogeneity or heterogeneity, we use the context of adolescents' delinquent peer associations to discuss how a linear growth curve model may be reparameterized so that the aperture (the point in time associated with the least variable individual differences) is directly estimated as a model parameter. As an example of estimation and prediction of aspects of change, we demonstrate the estimation of individually varying surge points and surge slopes (Choi, Harring, & Hancock, 2009) in elementary school children's mathematics scores, and show how gender can be used as a person-level predictor of these random effects. To illustrate the estimation and prediction of time-specific individual differences, we show how to reparameterize a nonlinear function of infant growth so that individual differences can be operationalized as a random effect and predicted by maternal breastfeeding behavior. Clearly, individual differences are central to each of these exemplars, as they often are in models of change over time. In each case, the target of reparameterization will become an estimated parameter or a random effect reflecting individual differences in the target aspect.

This chapter thus serves as an introduction to the general concept of reparameterization. It is our intention and hope that readers will gain an understanding of reparameterization that will allow them to generalize the procedure to new contexts. In the next section, we discuss the concept of reparameterization as a general tool that can be used in the context of modeling longitudinal data. Then we elaborate on our empirical examples as exemplars reflecting the three broad classes of reparameterization. At the end, we suggest other potential reparameterization classes as well.

REPARAMETERIZATION

As indicated earlier, reparameterization is the reexpression of a target model so that parameters of the reexpressed model more closely align with questions of substantive interest to the researcher. The use of reparameterization assumes that the researcher has first identified an appropriate target function to represent growth or change over time, and that the researcher wishes to quantify some aspect of the function (e.g., a point in time, an aspect of change, or a prediction coefficient) not already represented in the standard parameterization of the function. A reparameterized model should have the same number of estimated (free) parameters, and ideally will be statistically equivalent to the original model (although sometimes reparameterization will involve approximation).

In the methodological literature there is a history of reparameterizing conventional models to aid in addressing specific substantive questions. For example, using SEM, Choi et al. (2009) reparameterized a logistic model of change to estimate lower and upper asymptotes, surge points, and jerk points. The latter two parameters represent points in time corresponding to key points of change in the logistic trend. Cudeck and du Toit (2002) reparameterized the common and familiar quadratic curve to estimate the intercept, the time at which the curve attains its maximum/minimum, and the predicted value at that point in time, using single- and multilevel regression modeling. Using multilevel modeling, Rausch (2004, 2008) reparameterized the negative exponential curve to estimate a "half-life" parameter, which represents the amount of time that must elapse for the mean trend to reach a point halfway between the current point and the upper asymptote. Finally, Harring, Cudeck, and du Toit (2006) reparameterized two-segment linear spline models so that the knot (or transition point) is estimated directly as a parameter. In each of these examples, the objective of reparameterization is to recast some aspect of change as either a model parameter or as a random effect that varies and covaries across sampled cases.

Despite the evident potential and usefulness of reparameterization, it is rarely applied outside the methodological literature. We can speculate about why this strategy has failed to catch on among social scientists. First, reparameterization typically has been demonstrated in the context of a single functional form in isolation. It may not be clear to potential users how essentially the same procedure could be adapted to a variety of functional forms. Second, when reparameterization has appeared in prior literature, it typically has not been the primary focus of the study, but rather a tool used to achieve a specific end (e.g., enhancing the probability of successful convergence or isolating a scientifically interesting aspect of the functional form). Third, there have been too few linkages with applied topics to motivate substantive researchers to make the extra effort to use unconventional model specifications.

Clearly, there is a need for a general explanatory framework for reparameterizing models, the goals and outcome of which are closely tied to substantive questions. Below we describe a general approach for obtaining interpretable reparameterizations using LGM. In broad strokes, this general approach involves the following four steps:

1. Reparameterizing the target function to contain substantively important parameters or random coefficients.
2. Linearizing the target function to render it specifiable in SEM software.
3. Specifying the model using the structured latent curve approach.
4. Estimating model parameters (point and interval estimates).

We begin by describing this framework conceptually, and then in the next section illustrate the details in the context of the exemplars of our three classes of reparameterization. Throughout, we highlight the generality of the approach and the new substantively relevant information that can be obtained by using it.

1. Reparameterizing the Target Function

Reparameterization begins with a model expression. The researcher needs to decide what aspect of that model could benefit from explicit quantification. If the aspect of interest is already represented in the model (e.g., slope mean, intercept variance), then there is no need to reparameterize the model. Assuming the desired aspect is not already in the model as a parameter or random effect, the researcher must determine how it could be expressed in terms of existing model parameters. An expression is derived, often using simple calculus, for that aspect of change in terms of existing parameters; the result is then solved back in terms of an existing parameter and substituted into the original model expression. The result is the reparameterized model.

2. Linearizing the Target Function

In many cases, reparameterization will result in an intrinsically nonlinear function, in the sense that no transformation will render a linear function. For example, some parameters may enter the model embedded within reciprocals, radicals, trigonometric terms, exponents, or logarithms. This intrinsic nonlinearity poses a practical problem in latent growth curve modeling because SEM is a fundamentally linear framework. Hence, the researcher may need to "linearize" the function to enable fitting the model in SEM software.

To linearize the target function, we approximate it with a first-order Taylor series expansion, which can be described simply as consisting of the target function itself (evaluated at the parameter estimates) plus the linear sum of coefficients (e.g., intercepts, slopes, asymptotes) in the target function times partial first derivatives of the target function taken with respect to each coefficient. Taylor series linearization has long been used in fitting nonlinear regression and nonlinear mixed models (e.g., Beal & Sheiner, 1982; Davidian & Giltinan, 1995; Hand & Crowder, 1996).

3. Specifying the Model

As a third step, we employ the principles of *structured latent curve modeling* (SLCM) (Browne, 1993; Browne & du Toit, 1991) to rearrange the linearized function in a way that makes it possible to specify the model using SEM. SLCM involves treating the partial derivatives obtained in Step 2 as factor loadings. New parameters that conceptually reflect person-level (level-2) characteristics can be treated as fixed values or estimated parameters. New within-person (level-1) aspects of a reparameterized model may be treated as fixed values, estimated parameters, or random coefficients that vary from person to person. In fact, nearly any aspect of growth can be treated as a random coefficient in this framework.

4. Estimating Model Parameters

Once the model is specified, it can be fit using SEM software capable of imposing nonlinear constraints.[1] It is important to note that the framework described here accommodates missing data that are missing at random, and can be modified to accommodate individually varying occasions of measurement. Both capabilities are made possible by the use of full-information maximum likelihood (FIML) estimation.

EXEMPLARY APPLICATIONS

Thus far, we have covered in conceptual terms four steps that can be taken to proceed from a conventionally parameterized latent growth model to a reparameterized model with parameters serving specific interpretive purposes. Now that the groundwork has been laid, we present concrete details in the context of the exemplars in our three illustrative classes of reparameterization.

Quantifying Homogeneity or Heterogeneity of Individuals

Our first exemplar is of the broader class of reparameterizations of longitudinal models that quantify homogeneity or heterogeneity of individuals. Clinicians and education researchers are often interested in tracking the degree of children's affiliation with delinquent peers. In particular, researchers may wish to locate the point in time when children are the most similar to each other in their degree of affiliation with delinquent peers, before their trajectories begin to diverge from one another. Locating this point may help clinicians properly time interventions to delay or prevent negative behaviors that tend to spread through peer associations, such as drug use, truancy, and juvenile crime.

More generally, the point in time at which individuals demonstrate the greatest similarity is termed the *aperture* (Hancock & Choi, 2006). The aperture has previously been discussed by Rogosa and Willett (1985) (who called it the *centering point*) and by Mehta and West (2000). The aperture may be directly estimated in a number of ways. We use a method based on the four steps described in the preceding section. To illustrate the method, we make use of peer affiliation data reported by Stoolmiller (1994) and subsequently analyzed by Hancock and Choi (2006).

First, we parameterize the linear latent growth model (with random intercepts and slopes) such that the point in time corresponding to the minimum model-implied variance is represented as a parameter in the model. Note that there is only one such point in time in a linear trajectory model, and it characterizes the entire sample, so it cannot be treated as a random effect that varies across people. We begin with a model expression for an unconditional latent growth model, which may be expressed in an equation for the outcome y at time i for individual j:

$$y_{ij} = \eta_{1j} + \eta_{2j}(t_{ij} - t^*) + \varepsilon_{ij}. \tag{2.1}$$

In equation 2.1, y_{ij} is delinquent peer association (a measure of aggregated child, parent, and teacher responses); t_{ij} is the value of time (in this example, grade in school); t^* is the time chosen as the origin (zero point) of the time variable for all subjects, η_{1j} and η_{2j} are the latent intercept and slope, respectively, for subject j; and ε_{ij} is an occasion-specific disturbance term, here assumed to have homoscedastic[2] variance over time and to be uncorrelated across occasions, with $\varepsilon_{ij} \sim N(0, \sigma_\varepsilon^2)$. The latent growth factors are assumed to be jointly normally distributed:

$$\begin{bmatrix} \eta_{1j} \\ \eta_{2j} \end{bmatrix} \sim \text{MVN}\left(\begin{bmatrix} \mu_1 \\ \mu_2 \end{bmatrix}, \begin{bmatrix} \psi_{11} & \\ \psi_{21} & \psi_{22} \end{bmatrix} \right). \tag{2.2}$$

Thus, there are six parameters (two factor means, three level-2 (co)variances, and a level-1 disturbance variance). The model is depicted graphically in Figure 2.1.

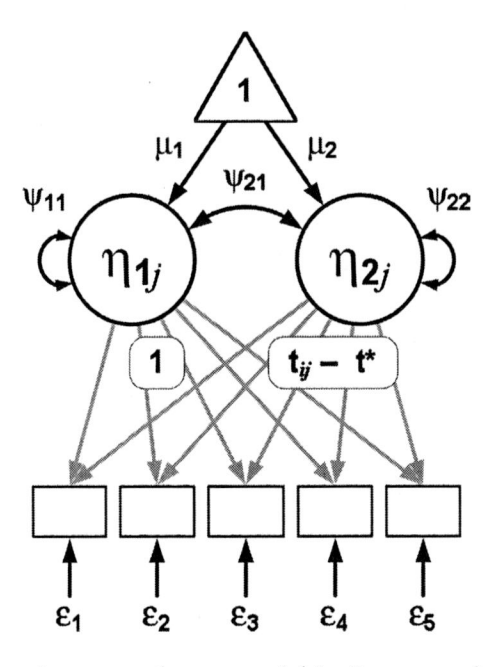

Figure 2.1 A linear latent growth curve model for five repeated measures.

In this example we would like to estimate the aperture—the value of t_{ij} at which children are the most similar to one another in terms of affiliation with delinquent peers—as a model parameter. The aperture occurs where the model-implied variance of y_{ij} is the smallest, a characteristic upon which we can capitalize. The first step, then, is to express the model-implied variance of y_{ij} in terms of existing model parameters. That variance is:

$$\sigma_y^2 = \text{var}\left[\eta_{1j} + \eta_{2j}(t_{ij} - t^*) + \varepsilon_{ij}\right] \tag{2.3}$$

$$= \text{var}(\eta_{1j}) + 2(t_{ij} - t^*)\text{cov}(\eta_{1j}, \eta_{2j}) + (t_{ij} - t^*)^2 \text{var}(\eta_{2j}) + \text{var}(\varepsilon_{ij})$$

$$= \psi_{11} + 2(t_{ij} - t^*)\psi_{21} + (t_{ij} - t^*)^2 \psi_{22} + \sigma_\varepsilon^2.$$

To find the temporal reference point of t_{ij} at which the time variable would have to be centered in order to achieve minimum variance (i.e., t^*), we apply elementary calculus, setting the first partial derivative of equation 2.3 with respect to centered time ($t_{ij} - t^*$) equal to zero:

$$\frac{\partial \sigma_y^2}{\partial (t_{ij} - t^*)} = 2\psi_{21} + 2(t_{ij} - t^*)\psi_{22} \tag{2.4}$$

$$0 = \psi_{21} + (t_{ij} - t^*)\psi_{22}$$

$$(t_{ij} - \eta_a) = -\frac{\psi_{21}}{\psi_{22}}.$$

The quantity η_a is the aperture. Notice also that if we center at η_a, $\psi_{21} = 0$. This permits us to reexpress the model equivalently as:

$$y_{ij} = \eta_{1j} + \eta_{2j}(t_{ij} - \eta_a) + \varepsilon_{ij}, \quad \varepsilon_{ij} \sim N(0, \sigma_\varepsilon^2) \tag{2.5}$$

where

$$\begin{bmatrix} \eta_{1j} \\ \eta_{2j} \\ \eta_a \end{bmatrix} \sim \text{MVN}\left(\begin{bmatrix} \mu_1 \\ \mu_2 \\ \mu_a \end{bmatrix}, \begin{bmatrix} \psi_{11} & & \\ 0 & \psi_{22} & \\ 0 & 0 & 0 \end{bmatrix}\right). \tag{2.6}$$

The reparameterized model in equations 2.5 and 2.6 still has six parameters; we have simply sacrificed the estimation of ψ_{21} (which we know to be zero at the aperture; see equation 2.4) for the ability to estimate the aperture, parameterized as the mean of a latent variable with zero variance.

The second step is to linearize the model in equations 2.5 and 2.6 in order to make it possible to specify the model in SEM software. The model is already in linear form, so no linearization is technically necessary here, but we apply linearization anyway to illustrate the method in a simple context. A first-order Taylor series approximation is given by the function:

$$\tilde{y} \approx y|_\mu + \sum_p \frac{\partial y}{\partial \eta_{pj}}\bigg|_{\mu_p} (\eta_{pj} - \mu_p) \tag{2.7}$$

where $y|_\mu$ is the target function evaluated at the parameters,

$$\frac{\partial y}{\partial \eta_{pj}}\bigg|_{\mu_p}$$

is the first partial derivative of the reparameterized model with respect to the pth coefficient evaluated at the coefficient means, and $(\eta_{pj} - \mu_p)$ is the pth mean-centered growth coefficient. In the reparameterized model there are three coefficients (η_{1j}, η_{2j}, and η_{aj}), and the required partial derivatives evaluated at the coefficient means are, respectively, 1, $(t_{ij} - \mu_a)$, and $-\mu_2$. Although it may not be immediately obvious, this linearized form adheres to the standard expression of the confirmatory factor model, where $y|_\mu = \Lambda\mu$,

$$\sum_p \frac{\partial y}{\partial \eta_{pj}}\bigg|_{\mu_p} (\eta_{pj} - \mu_p) = \Lambda \eta_j^*,$$

and η_j^* is a vector of *mean-centered* latent variables. The loadings in Λ are the derivatives evaluated at each occasion of measurement:

$$\Lambda = \begin{bmatrix} 1 & (0-\mu_a) & -\mu_2 \\ 1 & (1-\mu_a) & -\mu_2 \\ \dots & \dots & \dots \\ 1 & (T-\mu_a) & -\mu_2 \end{bmatrix}. \tag{2.8}$$

The reparameterized model is depicted in Figure 2.2 in a somewhat simplified form.[3]

Three aspects of change (intercept, linear slope, and aperture) are represented as factors in the reparameterized model. The intercept and slope are represented as random coefficients that do not covary, whereas the ap-

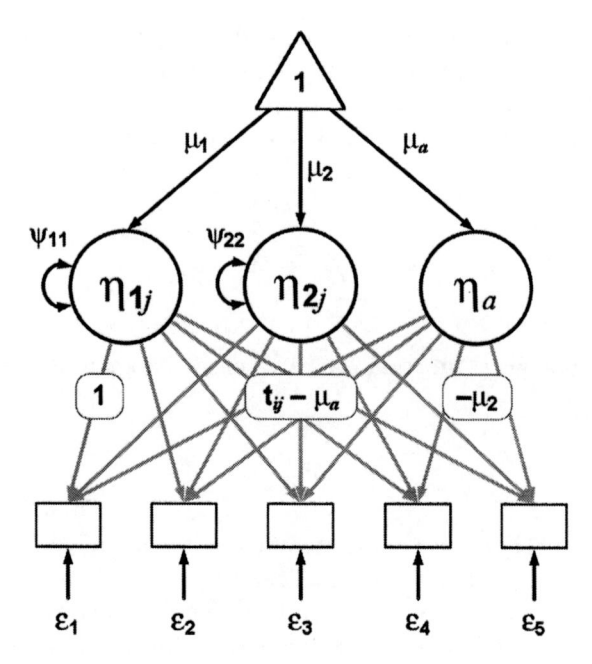

Figure 2.2 A reparameterized linear latent growth curve model for five repeated measures, with the aperture parameterized as μ_a.

erture is represented as a fixed coefficient (a latent variable with zero variance) because it cannot vary across individuals.

Applying this reparameterized model to Stoolmiller's (1994) data, we find that the model fits well ($\chi^2_8 = 1.725$, $p = .988$; RMSEA = .000, 90% CI = [.000,.000], NNFI = 1.277)[4] and yields the following parameter estimates (and standard errors):

$$\begin{bmatrix} \eta_{1j} \\ \eta_{2j} \\ \eta_a \end{bmatrix} \sim \text{MVN} \left(\begin{bmatrix} 4.048 & (.489) \\ 0.229 & (.067) \\ 3.668 & (.926) \end{bmatrix}, \begin{bmatrix} 5.819\,(1.168) & & \\ 0 & .290\,(.098) & \\ 0 & 0 & 0 \end{bmatrix} \right) \quad (2.9)$$

and $\hat{\sigma}_e^2 = 5.117(.365)$. The aperture is estimated to occur at $t_{ij} = 3.668$; that is, according to the model, children are most similar in their affiliation with delinquent peers approximately ⅔ of the way through the third grade. Therefore, third grade might be a good opportunity to implement interventions designed to inoculate children against peer influence and prevent them from engaging in negative behaviors that are spread through peer associations. LISREL syntax is provided at http://quantpsy.org/pubs/preacher_hancock_2012_code.pdf.

This may seem like a rather involved procedure for estimating just one additional parameter. We agree, and certainly there are easier ways to estimate the aperture parameter. We merely used the aperture to illustrate a general procedure that can be used in much more complex settings, as we illustrate next. One advantage of using the specific approach to reparameterization we described in steps 1–4 above in the case of apertures is that the procedure not only yields a point estimate and an interval estimate, but also treats the aperture as a variable in the model (η_a). Representing the aperture as a variable allows the researcher to test moderation hypotheses; for example, we can test whether the timing of greatest similarity differs between boys and girls, or as a function of social network size or socioeconomic status.

Estimation and Prediction of Aspects of Change

Our second example is also drawn from the field of education. We make use of the Early Childhood Longitudinal Study, Kindergarten Class of 1998–1999 (ECLS-K) data (Tourangeau, Nord, Lê, Sorongon, & Najarian, 2009). The ECLS-K data span kindergarten through the eighth grade. The limited dataset we use includes data on math, reading, and gender. Here we focus on modeling the nonlinear trend in math skills assessed in the fall and spring of kindergarten, fall and spring of first grade, and spring of third, fifth, and eighth grades. A random subset of 250 children's scores are depicted in Figure 2.3.

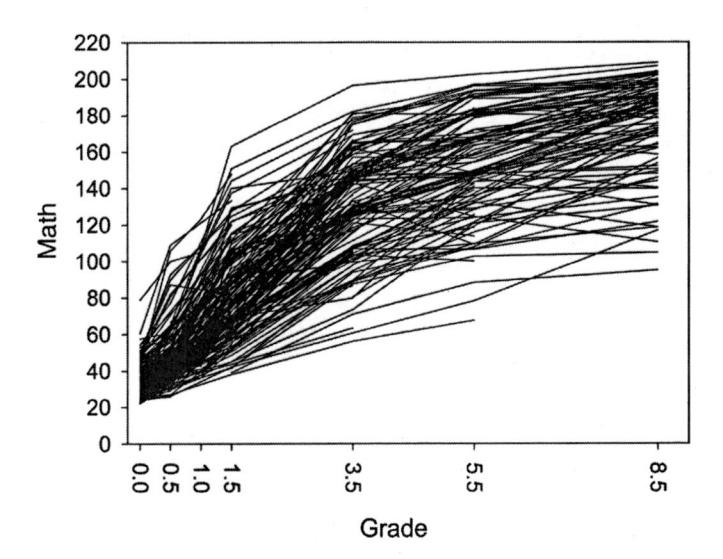

Figure 2.3 A random sample of 250 children's observed mathematics score trajectories from the ECLS-K data.

An appropriate model for learning data such as those in ECLS-K might be the sigmoidal Gompertz curve, which increases slowly from a lower asymptote to a region of relatively faster change, followed by a gradual approach to an upper asymptote. Unlike logistic functions, Gompertz curves need not be symmetric about their points of inflection—a potentially realistic reflection of actual learning rates. There are several versions of the Gompertz curve, some with three parameters (e.g., Browne, 1993; Gompertz, 1825; Sit & Poulin-Costello, 1994; Winsor, 1932) and some with four (e.g., Grimm, Ram, & Estabrook, 2010). We begin with a parameterization of the Gompertz curve presented by Sit and Poulin-Costello (1994), with all coefficients random:

$$y_{ij} = \eta_{1j} \exp\left(-\exp\left(\eta_{2j} - \eta_{3j} t_{ij}\right)\right) + \varepsilon_{ij}, \qquad (2.10)$$

where η_{1j} is the upper asymptote, η_{2j} controls the shape of the curve, and η_{3j} shifts the curve horizontally.

Of the three parameters in the expression in equation 2.10, only η_{1j} may be of interest to education researchers. However, the curve is governed by two other parameters that are rather more difficult to treat substantively. Thus, we wish to reparameterize the function to replace η_{2j} and η_{3j} with more interesting parameters: the *surge point* (the point in time at which the maximum rate of change occurs; Choi et al., 2009) and the *surge slope* (the slope, or instantaneous rate of change, at that point). These parameters may be of greater interest to researchers; treating the surge point as a random coefficient would enable educators to determine what environmental factors moderate the surge point, and what individual differences predict children's different rates of learning at that point.

We begin with the target function in equation 2.10. In this example, we allow heteroscedastic error variances over time. The first step is to reparameterize the target function to contain the three desired aspects of change (upper asymptote, surge point, and surge slope) as either estimated parameters or random coefficients. For full generality, we choose to treat all three as random coefficients. The target function and its first and second derivatives are:

$$y_{ij} = \eta_{1j} \exp\left(-\exp\left(\eta_{2j} - \eta_{3j} t_{ij}\right)\right) \qquad (2.11)$$

$$\frac{\partial y_{ij}}{\partial t_{ij}} = \eta_{1j}\eta_{3j} \exp\left(\eta_{2j} - \eta_{3j} t_{ij}\right) \exp\left(-\exp\left(\eta_{2j} - \eta_{3j} t_{ij}\right)\right)$$

$$\frac{\partial^2 y_{ij}}{\partial t_{ij}^2} = -\eta_{1j}\eta_{3j}^2 \exp\left(\eta_{2j} - \eta_{3j} t_{ij}\right) \exp\left(-\exp\left(\eta_{2j} - \eta_{3j} t_{ij}\right)\right)$$

$$+ \eta_{1j}\eta_{3j}^2 \left(\exp\left(\eta_{2j} - \eta_{3j} t_{ij}\right)\right)^2 \exp\left(-\exp\left(\eta_{2j} - \eta_{3j} t_{ij}\right)\right)$$

The surge point is defined to occur where

$$\frac{\partial^2 y_{ij}}{\partial t_{ij}^2} = 0.$$

Setting the second derivative to zero and solving for t_{ij} yields the new surge point random coefficient t_{0j}:

$$t_{0j} = \frac{\eta_{2j}}{\eta_{3j}}. \tag{2.12}$$

At this point it is possible to express either η_{2j} or η_{3j} in terms of t_{0j}, yielding:

$$\begin{aligned}\eta_{2j} &= t_{0j}\eta_{3j} \\ \eta_{3j} &= \eta_{2j}/t_{0j}.\end{aligned} \tag{2.13}$$

We could replace either η_{2j} or η_{3j}, leading to

$$\begin{aligned}y_{ij} &= \eta_{1j}\exp\bigl(-\exp(t_{0j}\eta_{3j} - \eta_{3j}t_{ij})\bigr) \\ &= \eta_{1j}\exp\bigl(-\exp(\eta_{3j}(t_{0j} - t_{ij}))\bigr)\end{aligned} \tag{2.14}$$

or

$$\begin{aligned}y_{ij} &= \eta_{1j}\exp\left(-\exp\left(\eta_{2j} - \frac{\eta_{2j}}{t_{0j}}t_{ij}\right)\right) \\ &= \eta_{1j}\exp\left(-\exp\left(\eta_{2j}\left(1 - \frac{t_{ij}}{t_{0j}}\right)\right)\right).\end{aligned} \tag{2.15}$$

We chose equation 2.14 because its parameters are potentially of greater interest and are more easily interpretable; it has the additional benefit that it does not involve division by t_{0j}, thus avoiding potential problems of dividing by zero or by very small numbers. The reparameterized function is:

$$y_{ij} = \eta_{1j}\exp\bigl(-\exp(\eta_{3j}(t_{0j} - t_{ij}))\bigr), \tag{2.16}$$

where η_{1j} and η_{3j} are defined as before, and t_{0j} is the surge point.

We also want the surge slope as a coefficient in the model. This slope is the first derivative (local linear slope) at the surge point (Choi et al., 2009). We obtain the first derivative using the new parameterization to avoid reintroducing η_{2j} into the model. The target function and its first derivative are:

$$y_{ij} = \eta_{1j} \exp\left(-\exp\left(\eta_{3j}\left(t_{0j} - t_{ij}\right)\right)\right) \quad (2.17)$$

$$\frac{\partial y_{ij}}{\partial t_{ij}} = \eta_{1j}\eta_{3j} \exp\left(\eta_{3j}\left(t_{0j} - t_{ij}\right)\right) \exp\left(-\exp\left(\eta_{3j}\left(t_{0j} - t_{ij}\right)\right)\right)$$

At the surge point t_{0j}, $(t_{0j} - t_{ij}) = 0$, yielding the new surge slope random coefficient s_{0j}:

$$s_{0j} = \eta_{1j}\eta_{3j} \exp(-1). \quad (2.18)$$

Reexpressing η_{3j} in terms of the surge slope, we obtain:

$$s_{0j} = \eta_{1j}\eta_{3j} \exp(-1) \quad (2.19)$$

$$\eta_{3j} = \frac{s_{0j}e}{\eta_{1j}}$$

where $e = \exp(1)$, or Euler's number. Replacing η_{3j} in equation 2.17 yields:

$$y_{ij} = \eta_{1j} \exp\left(-\exp\left(\frac{s_{0j}e}{\eta_{1j}}\left(t_{0j} - t_{ij}\right)\right)\right) \quad (2.20)$$

where η_{1j} and t_{0j} are defined as before, and s_{0j} is the surge slope.

The second step is to linearize the reparameterized model to express it in a form more palatable to SEM software. The first partial derivatives of equation 2.20 with respect to $\eta = [\eta_{1j}\ t_{0j}\ s_{0j}]'$ and evaluated at the coefficient means $\mu = [\eta_1\ t_0\ s_0]'$ are:

$$\frac{\partial y}{\partial \eta} = \begin{bmatrix} \exp\left(-\exp\left(\frac{s_0 e(t_0 - t_{ij})}{\eta_1}\right)\right) \\[2ex] +\dfrac{s_0 e(t_0 - t_{ij})\exp\left(\dfrac{s_0 e(t_0 - t_{ij})}{\eta_1}\right)\exp\left(-\exp\left(\dfrac{s_0 e(t_0 - t_{ij})}{\eta_1}\right)\right)}{\eta_1} \\[3ex] -s_0 e \exp\left(\dfrac{s_0 e(t_0 - t_{ij})}{\eta_1}\right)\exp\left(-\exp\left(\dfrac{s_0 e(t_0 - t_{ij})}{\eta_1}\right)\right) \\[2ex] -e(t_0 - t_{ij})\exp\left(s_0 e(t_0 - t_{ij})\eta_1^{-1}\right)\exp\left(-\exp\left(s_0 e(t_0 - t_{ij})\eta_1^{-1}\right)\right) \end{bmatrix} \quad .(2.21)$$

We use these derivatives as factor loadings, substituting values of t_{ij} where appropriate. The linearized model can then be expressed in matrix form as:

$$y_j = \Lambda\mu + \Lambda\eta_j^* + \varepsilon_j, \tag{2.22}$$

where $\Lambda\mu$, the loading matrix multiplied by the factor means, represents the target model evaluated at the parameter estimates, and $\Lambda\eta_j^*$ represents the deviation of individual j's trajectory from the mean implied by $\Lambda\mu$. The vector ε_j contains occasion-specific residuals for individual j.

In the third step, we make use of SLCM to specify the model in equation 2.22. This involves treating the derivatives in equation 2.21 as factor loadings using software capable of imposing nonlinear constraints. In SLCM, parameters that enter the reparameterized target function linearly have corresponding factor means estimated in μ, whereas those that enter the function nonlinearly have corresponding factor means constrained to zero. As the ambitious reader may derive, η_{1j} and s_{0j} enter the reparameterized target function linearly, whereas t_{0j} enters nonlinearly because the first partial derivative of the function with respect to t_{0j} contains t_{0j}; thus, $\mu = [\eta_1 \ 0 \ s_0]'$. This step is taken so that $\Lambda\mu$ will equal the desired mean trajectory at the parameter estimates.[5] The model is depicted graphically in Figure 2.4, Panel A. Symbols for elements of the random coefficient covariance matrix are omitted from the figure for simplicity, but can be represented as:

$$\Psi = \begin{bmatrix} \psi_{\eta_1} & & \\ \psi_{t_0,\eta_1} & \psi_{t_0} & \\ \psi_{s_0,\eta_1} & \psi_{s_0,t_0} & \psi_{s_0} \end{bmatrix}. \tag{2.23}$$

This *unconditional* model does not consider gender as a covariate (we include gender next). Fitting the model to data yields:

$$\begin{bmatrix} \eta_{1j} \\ t_{0j} \\ s_{0j} \end{bmatrix} \sim MVN \left(\begin{bmatrix} 145.775(.232) \\ .000(\text{N/A}) \\ 22.601(.056) \end{bmatrix}, \begin{bmatrix} 407.249 \ (9.018) & & \\ -3.069 \ (.147) & .250 \ (.006) & \\ 93.129 \ (1.772) & -2.007 \ (.047) & 37.868 \ (.563) \end{bmatrix} \right) \tag{2.24}$$

with the variance of ε_{ij} increasing from 12.165 to a maximum of 87.257 in the spring of first grade, and decreasing to 61.129 by the spring of eighth grade. The estimated mean surge point was $\hat{t}_0 = 1.303$ (.005), with corresponding surge slope $\hat{s}_0 = 22.601$ (.056).

The goal of this example was not only to show how parameters such as the surge point and surge slope may be treated as random coefficients within

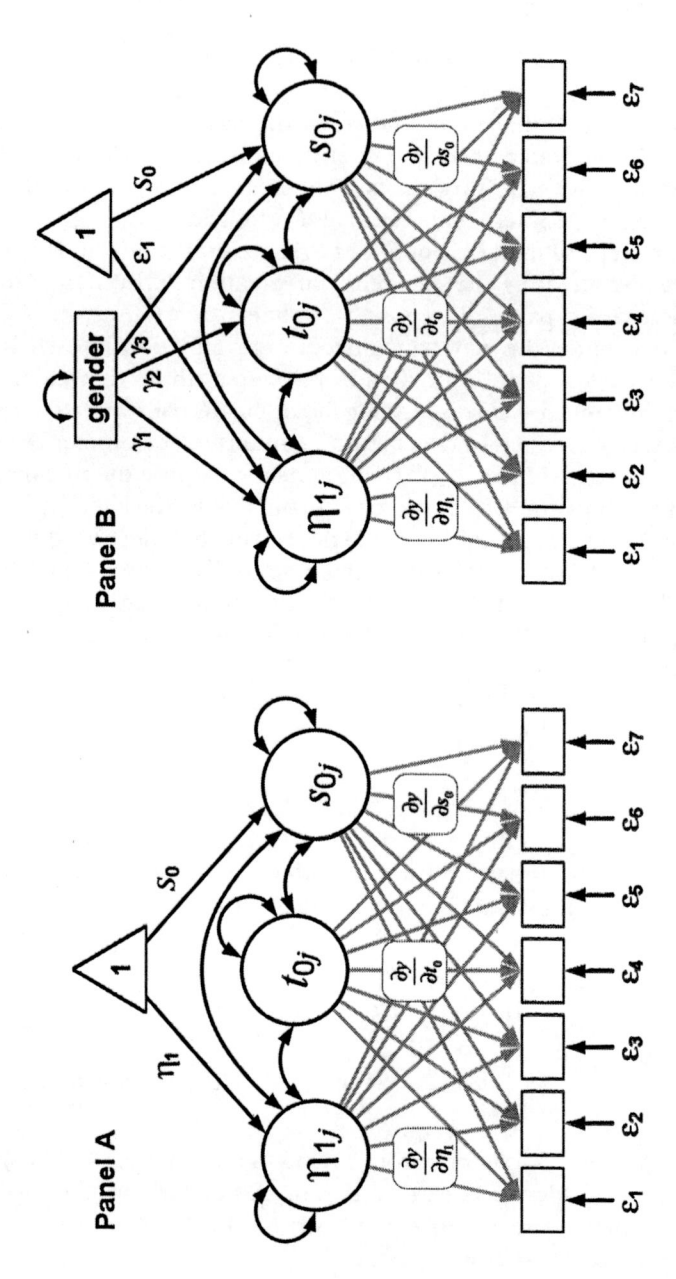

Figure 2.4 Panel A: An unconditional Gompertz growth curve model for mathematics learning among grade school children. For full loading expressions, see equation 2.21. Panel B: The same model is represented with gender as a level-2 predictor of growth coefficients. Because gender is coded (boys = 0, girls = 1), the γ coefficients represent the expected difference for girls with respect to boys.

the SEM/LGM framework, but also to predict individual differences in these coefficients using gender as a level-2 predictor. The structural equation for the random coefficients η_j in the *conditional* model may be written as:

$$\eta_j = \mu + \Gamma x_j + \zeta_j, \qquad (2.25)$$

where Γ contains structural coefficients linking growth factors to exogenous measured variables in x_j. Regressing the growth factors on gender (boy = 0, girl = 1) yields the following results:

$$\begin{bmatrix} \eta_{1j} \\ t_{0j} \\ s_{0j} \end{bmatrix} \sim \text{MVN}\left(\begin{bmatrix} 146.447(.308) \\ .000(\text{N/A}) \\ 23.238(.079) \end{bmatrix}, \begin{bmatrix} 413.179\ (8.886) & & \\ -3.052\ (.137) & .228\ (.006) & \\ 96.052\ (1.806) & -1.884\ (.047) & 37.838\ (.575) \end{bmatrix}\right) \qquad (2.26)$$

$$\hat{\Gamma} = \begin{bmatrix} -1.454\ (.408) \\ .043\ (.008) \\ -1.339\ (.106) \end{bmatrix}. \qquad (2.27)$$

Because boys were coded 0 and girls were coded 1, the means in equation 2.26 reflect model-implied values of the growth coefficients for boys. Thus, the mean surge point for boys was $\hat{t}_0 = 1.282(.007)$, with corresponding surge slope $\hat{s}_0 = 23.238(.079)$. Based on equation 2.27, being a girl is associated with a slightly lower value of the upper asymptote (i.e., 146.447 − 1.454 = 144.993), a significantly later surge point (i.e., 1.282 + .043 = 1.325), and a significantly lower surge slope (i.e., 23.238 − 1.339 = 21.899) than for boys. Mplus syntax for both the unconditional and conditional models is provided at http://quantpsy.org/pubs/preacher_hancock_2012_code.pdf.

Using these reparameterized models, we were able to predict individual differences in the timing of key growth events: the point in time at which children are learning math the fastest. The advantages of specifying the moderated Gompertz curve with random coefficients in SEM are clear. Unlike in multilevel modeling, we could additionally consider latent covariates if the situation demanded it.

Estimation and Prediction of Time-Specific Individual Differences

Our third example is drawn from the field of public health. Public health researchers often are concerned with tracking infant development in countries that are susceptible to child malnutrition. Recent studies sponsored by UNICEF (2003, 2008a, 2008b) found that African and South Asian children are particularly likely to suffer from stunted growth due to malnutrition, and stunting can begin *in utero*. The aim of these studies is to identify determinants of optimal and suboptimal infant growth so that interventions can be implemented. In order to identify these determinants, it is necessary to have a model that accurately reflects growth in infant weight. However, we may also want not only to describe individual differences in growth trends, but also to predict these individual differences—at any desired age—with environmental variables such as breastfeeding versus bottle-feeding, rural versus urban status, and others. In this section, we show how to reparameterize a nonlinear function of infant growth so that individual differences can be operationalized as a random effect that is potentially predicted by breastfeeding behavior.

The Cebu Longitudinal Health and Nutrition Survey (Adair & Popkin, 1996; Adair et al., 2011) includes weight data for Filipino infants every 2 months from ages 0 to 24 months ($n = 2632$).[6] The aims of the survey study included tracking individual differences in weight gain at various ages, as well as discovering the extent to which environmental factors (including maternal breastfeeding behavior) impact weight gain. The first step in our approach to modeling these data was to choose a plausible functional form to describe individual and mean trajectories of change. We selected the Jenss-Bayley model (Jenss & Bayley, 1937) because it was designed specifically to model human growth in the first 6 years of life. The Jenss-Bayley function is well suited for infant growth data because early biological growth often follows an exponential process where growth acts to limit further growth, but the asymptote is not horizontal during the early years as in an ordinary exponential function. One common expression of the Jenss-Bayley model (with random coefficients) is:

$$\begin{aligned} y_{ij} &= \eta_{1j} + \eta_{2j}t_{ij} - \exp(\eta_{3j}^* + \eta_{4j}t_{ij}) + \varepsilon_{ij} \\ &= \eta_{1j} + \eta_{2j}t_{ij} - \eta_{3j}\exp(\eta_{4j}t_{ij}) + \varepsilon_{ij} \end{aligned} \quad (2.28)$$

where η_{1j} and η_{2j} are the intercept and slope coefficients for the line defining the asymptote of the function, $\eta_{3j} = \exp(\eta_{3j}^*)$ is the vertical distance between the intercept of the Jenss-Bayley function and the linear asymptote's intercept, and $\exp(\eta_{4j})$ is the ratio of the acceleration of growth at age t to

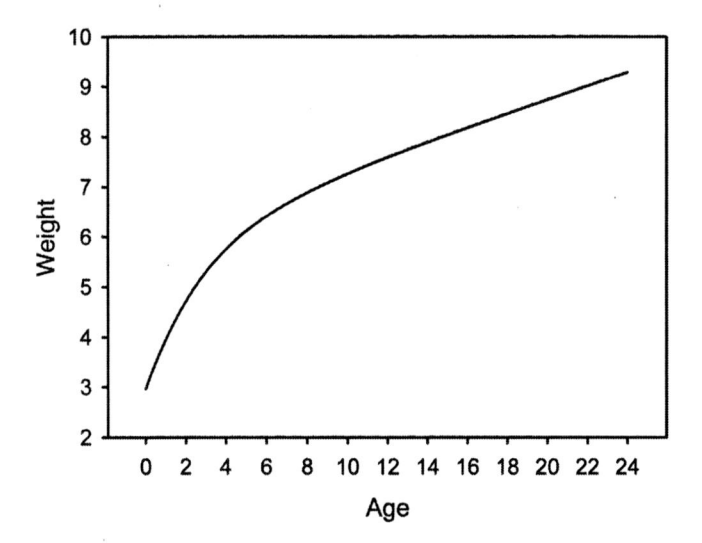

Figure 2.5 The Jenss-Bayley function defined by $\eta_1 = 6$, $\eta_2 = .137$, $\eta_3 = 1.11$, and $\eta_4 = -.334$.

that at age $t-1$. Thus, the Jenss-Bayley function combines exponential and linear growth. A generic Jenss-Bayley function is depicted in Figure 2.5.

For this example we are interested in reparameterizing the Jenss-Bayley function to permit the prediction of individual differences in model-implied weight at any given point in time between 0 and 24 months of age. In addition, the reparameterization needs to be such that this model-implied weight is treated as a random effect in the model. In a linear growth curve model this would be a straightforward task—simply centering age at any desired value would render the intercept factor interpretable as model-implied weight at that age, and the intercept factor then could serve as the dependent variable in a latent structural regression. However, because the Jenss-Bayley model is intrinsically nonlinear we do not have this luxury. Centering age elsewhere would result in a different functional form. With intrinsically nonlinear functional forms like the Jenss-Bayley function, the task is not so simple.

To reparameterize the Jenss-Bayley function, we express model-implied weight at an arbitrary age t^* of the investigator's choosing. The model-implied weight for the jth infant, η_j^*, can then be expressed as:

$$\eta_j^* = \eta_{1j} + \eta_{2j}t^* - \eta_{3j}\exp(\eta_{4j}t^*). \tag{2.29}$$

This expression, in turn, can be solved for an existing coefficient (we chose η_{1j}) and the result substituted back into equation 2.28, yielding:

$$y_{ij} = \eta_j^* + \eta_{2j}(t_{ij} - t^*) + \eta_{3j}\exp(\eta_{4j}t^*) - \eta_{3j}\exp(\eta_{4j}t_{ij}) + \varepsilon_{ij}. \quad (2.30)$$

In equation 2.30, we have given up the option of estimating parameters associated with the linear intercept η_{1j}, a random coefficient that may not be particularly interesting, for the ability instead to estimate parameters associated with η_j^*, the random coefficient of central interest.

The model in equation 2.30 is still intrinsically nonlinear, so in order to specify it using SEM we must first obtain a linear approximation. The partial derivatives of equation 2.30 with respect to each coefficient (i.e., η_j^*, η_{2j}, η_{3j}, and η_{4j}), evaluated at the growth factor means, are:

$$\frac{\partial y}{\partial \eta} = \begin{bmatrix} 1 & (t_{ij} - t^*) & e^{\mu_3}(e^{\mu_4 t^*} - e^{\mu_4 t_{ij}}) & e^{\mu_3}\left[(t^*)e^{\mu_4 t^*} - t_{ij} e^{\mu_4 t_{ij}}\right] \end{bmatrix}'. \quad (2.31)$$

We use these derivatives as factor loadings:

$$\Lambda = \begin{bmatrix} 1 & (0-t^*) & e^{\mu_3}(e^{\mu_4 t^*} - 1) & e^{\mu_3}(t^*)e^{\mu_4 t^*} \\ 1 & (2-t^*) & e^{\mu_3}(e^{\mu_4 t^*} - e^{\mu_4(2)}) & e^{\mu_3}\left[(t^*)e^{\mu_4 t^*} - (2)e^{\mu_4(2)}\right] \\ \cdots & \cdots & \cdots & \cdots \\ 1 & (T-t^*) & e^{\mu_3}(e^{\mu_4 t^*} - e^{\mu_4(T)}) & e^{\mu_3}\left[(t^*)e^{\mu_4 t^*} - (T)e^{\mu_4(T)}\right] \end{bmatrix} \quad (2.32)$$

where t^* is a constant time point chosen by the researcher, corresponding to the age at which individual differences in weight are desired.

Specifying the linearized model in SEM proceeds as before. That is, we use the general confirmatory factor analysis model in equation 2.22 with the loading matrix in equation 2.32 and the latent mean vector $\mu = [\mu_1\ \mu_2\ \mu_3\ 0]'$. The mean of the latent variable corresponding to the exponential rate coefficient is set equal to zero so that $\Lambda\mu$ will equal the desired mean trajectory at the parameter estimates (η_{4j} enters the model nonlinearly). The model is depicted graphically in Figure 2.6, Panel A. As with the previous example, elements of the random coefficient covariance matrix are omitted from the figure, but can be represented as:

$$\Psi = \begin{bmatrix} \psi_{\eta^*} & & & \\ \psi_{\eta_2,\eta^*} & \psi_{\eta_2} & & \\ \psi_{\eta_3,\eta^*} & \psi_{\eta_3,\eta_2} & \psi_{\eta_3} & \\ \psi_{\eta_4,\eta^*} & \psi_{\eta_4,\eta_2} & \psi_{\eta_4,\eta_3} & \psi_{\eta_4} \end{bmatrix}. \quad (2.33)$$

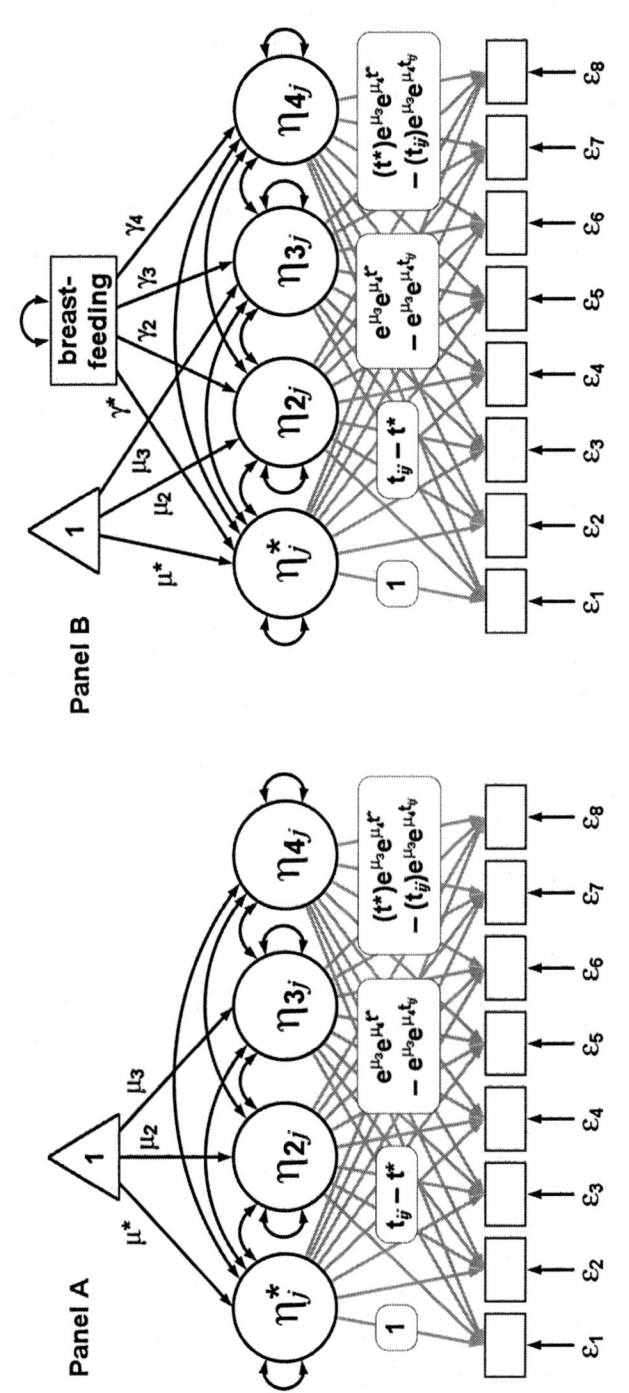

Reparameterization in Latent Growth Curve Models ▪ 45

Figure 2.6 Panel A: The reparameterized and linearized Jenss-Bayley model specified as a structured latent curve model. The Cebu data had 13 repeated measurements; only 8 are depicted here for simplicity. The mean of model-implied infant weight is represented by μ^*, whereas the variance of the η_j^* factor represents interindividual variability in this model-implied weight. Panel B: The same model is represented with cumulative breastfeeding as a level-2 predictor of growth coefficients. Because cumulative breastfeeding is the average of a bimonthly binary breastfeeding indicator coded (0 = did not breastfeed the previous day, 1 = breastfed the previous day), γ^* represents the weight difference between hypothetical infants who never received breastfeeding versus those who always received breastfeeding (on days prior to measurement).

The unconditional model does not include breastfeeding as a predictor. As one example of the kind of output generated by this model, consider what happens when we set $t^* = 6$, that is, we wish to estimate the mean and variance of model-implied individual differences in infant weight at age = 6 months. We also permit residuals at adjacent occasions to covary with a constant covariance. Fitting the unconditional model yields adequate fit ($\chi^2_{88} = 1274.024$, $p < .0001$; RMSEA = .072, 90% CI = [.068, .075], NNFI = .982) and parameter estimates (and standard errors) as follows:

$$\begin{bmatrix} \eta^*_j \\ \eta_{2j} \\ \eta_{3j} \\ \eta_{4j} \end{bmatrix} \sim \text{MVN} \left(\begin{bmatrix} 6.778\,(.017) \\ .136\,(.001) \\ 1.841\,(.008) \\ .000\,(\text{N/A}) \end{bmatrix}, \begin{bmatrix} .899\,(.035) & & & \\ -.008\,(.002) & .002\,(<.001) & & \\ .515\,(.026) & -.014\,(.001) & .380\,(.021) & \\ .019\,(.002) & -.001\,(<.001) & .016\,(.001) & .002\,(<.001) \end{bmatrix} \right) \quad (2.34)$$

with

$$\begin{bmatrix} \varepsilon_{ij[t]} \\ \varepsilon_{ij[t-1]} \end{bmatrix} \sim \text{MVN} \left(\begin{bmatrix} 0 \\ 0 \end{bmatrix}, \begin{bmatrix} .102\,(.003) & \\ .028\,(.001) & .102\,(.003) \end{bmatrix} \right), \quad (2.35)$$

and $\hat{\mu}_4 = -.334(.004)$. The model-implied mean weight at age 6 months is 6.778 kg, with a standard deviation of $(.899)^{1/2} = .948$ kg. This procedure can be repeated any number of times, substituting a new t^* each time, yielding a series of models that are equivalent in terms of fit. The model-implied mean weight is plotted at 13 different ages in Figure 2.7, along with a 95% interval based on the estimated time-specific variance and the observed means (i.e., $\hat{\mu}^* \pm 1.96\sqrt{\hat{\psi}_{\eta^*}}$).

The preceding represents an informative, convenient way to model and illustrate the model-implied mean and variance of infant weight at any desired age, even if the desired age falls somewhere between two observations. However, our primary interest—and the reason we reparameterized the model in the first place—lies in predicting individual differences in weight at any given age by cumulative breastfeeding *up to that point*. At every occasion of measurement, mothers were asked whether they had breastfed the previous day (0,1). We defined *cumulative breastfeeding* as the average of all breastfeeding responses up to a given point in time. It serves as an indicator of how much a given infant has been breastfed since birth, relative to other infants of the same age. We introduced cumulative breastfeeding as an

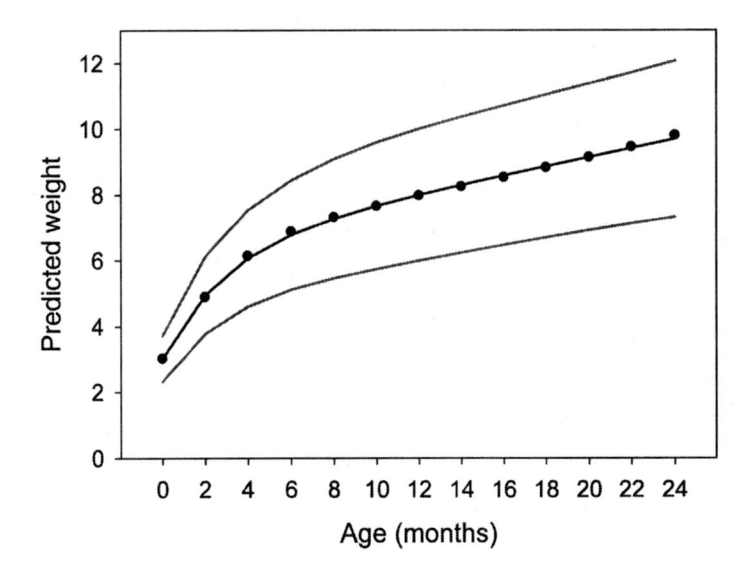

Reparameterization in Latent Growth Curve Models ■ 47

Figure 2.7 Observed and model-implied infant weight at 13 different ages, plotted with 95% interval based on the estimated time-specific variance (i.e., $\hat{\mu}^* \pm 1.96\sqrt{\hat{\psi}_{\eta^*}}$). Solid dots represent observed means.

infant-level predictor of all four random coefficients. Our main interest was in the effect of cumulative breastfeeding on infant weight at particular ages.

As with the second example, the structural equation for the random coefficients η_j in the conditional model may be written as equation 2.25. Regressing the model-implied weight factor (along with the other growth factors) on cumulative breastfeeding at each point in time yields different parameter estimates and model fit at each age because cumulative breastfeeding is a different variable at each occasion of measurement. All of the models fit well by standard criteria (minimum RMSEA = .051 at ages 4–8 months; maximum RMSEA = .062 at birth). The pattern of effects in Figure 2.8 tells us something useful: The effect of cumulative breastfeeding on infant weight is positive in the early months, but negative at 10 months and beyond. A steep drop occurs in the effect of breastfeeding on weight by about the 6-month mark. This corresponds to the age at which the American Academy of Pediatrics, the World Health Organization, and UNICEF recommend supplementing breast milk with solid food. Investigating the reasons for the change from a positive effect to a negative effect by 10 months is beyond the scope of this example, but we may conjecture that infants who still rely heavily on breastfeeding at or beyond 10 months of age are probably experiencing other dietary deficiencies that explain their relatively lower weight. Perhaps mothers need to continue breastfeeding because of other comorbid factors, like poverty, which are linked to these other deficiencies. Mplus syntax for both the

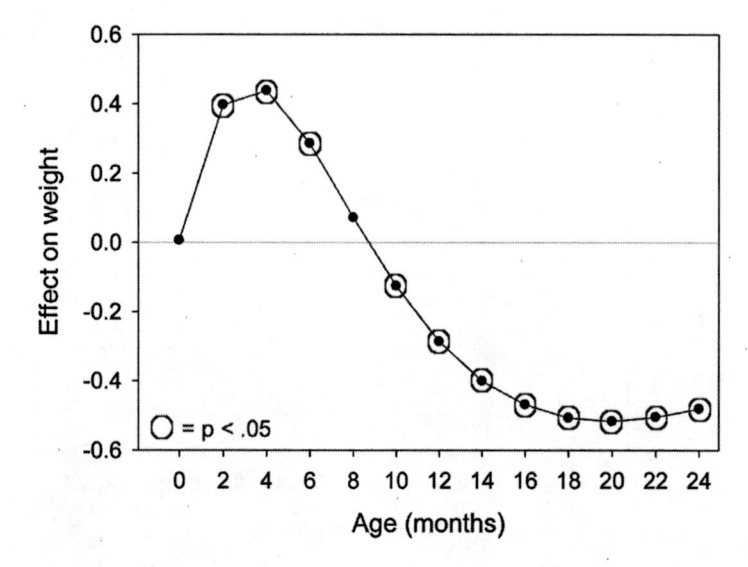

Figure 2.8 The effect of cumulative breastfeeding on model-implied infant weight at 13 ages. Circled slope estimates are statistically significant at $\alpha = .05$.

unconditional and conditional models is provided at http://quantpsy.org/pubs/preacher_hancock_2012_code.pdf.

SUMMARY AND EXTENSIONS

In this chapter we have provided a framework for reparameterizing linear and nonlinear LGMs to yield new parameters and latent variables to answer important substantive questions. Often a model can be reparameterized to yield a point estimate and interval estimate for a new parameter that is of central interest to the researcher because it represents some salient aspect of change that was initially inaccessible. In other models, reparameterization permits treating the new parameter as a random coefficient that varies across individuals.

We presented four steps for using SEM (specifically, the SLCM approach) to model trends using reparameterized models. Again, they are:

1. Reparameterizing the target function to contain substantively important parameters or random coefficients.
2. Linearizing the target function to render it specifiable in SEM software.
3. Specifying the model using the structured latent curve approach.
4. Estimating model parameters (point and interval estimates).

We described this approach conceptually, then gave more detailed explanations in the context of exemplars representing different classes of the kinds of reparameterizations in which researchers might reasonably be interested. Specifically, we illustrated the steps using a clinical/educational psychology example on affiliation with delinquent peers, a mathematics learning example in which aspects of learning could be predicted by gender, and a public health example involving prediction of infant growth.

Reparameterization has the potential to make the already versatile SEM framework even more flexible. Particularly in longitudinal settings, reparameterization permits the researcher to treat virtually any aspect of change as a fixed and known value, an estimated parameter, or in many cases a random coefficient that varies across individuals. The latter two options provide a way to investigate whether these aspects of change are predicted or moderated by level-2 predictors (e.g., mathematics learning or cumulative breastfeeding). These examples illustrated three kinds of reparameterization researchers might be interested in using. The first example focused on estimating parameters associated with homogeneity or heterogeneity; the second example treated three aspects of change as random coefficients; and the third example focused on the estimation and prediction of time-specific individual differences in an outcome. We feel that reparameterization has great potential for helping researchers create models that more closely align with theoretical predictions, and should be emphasized to a greater extent in graduate training.

We now close this chapter by emphasizing that the general approach to reparameterization described in our steps is by no means limited to the classes of reparameterization illustrated in this chapter. Other examples of potential use are readily devised, as follows:

1. Hipp, Bauer, Curran, and Bollen (2004) fit a partially nonlinear growth curve model to seasonal crime trend data in which intrinsically nonlinear parameters were treated as fixed coefficients. Using the reparameterization approach described in this chapter, similar models could be fit to cyclic data treating, for example, instantaneous rate of change as an individual-differences variable, amenable to prediction by person-level characteristics. The variance of this random coefficient could serve as a proxy for cycle synchrony versus asynchrony.
2. The field of metabolism biochemistry is full of examples in which it is of interest to assess the rate at which a drug is absorbed and metabolized. Often the functions used to model these dynamics are complex nonlinear trajectories (see Davidian & Giltinan, 1995). Reparameterization could be used in tandem with SLCM to treat

salient characteristics of growth as random effects, and to embed the trajectory function into a larger causal network.
3. In education research it is often of interest to gauge the rate of learning from year to year when academic years are separated by summer breaks (Entwistle & Alexander, 1992; Hancock & Koran, 2005). When multiphase segmented spline models are used, it is possible through reparameterization to treat the angle separating the slopes of adjacent linear segments (in radians or degrees) as a random coefficient.

We are confident that many more uses for reparameterization will become apparent to researchers, and we look forward to the expanded scope of research questions that these methods will help to answer.

APPENDIX
LISREL and Mplus Code to Accompany Examples

Three Ways to Estimate an Aperture Parameter

Method 1: Lambda shift method

```
LATENT GROWTH CURVE OF HANCOCK & CHOI DATA, EX. 2
DA NI=4 NO=198 MA=CM
CM
11.000
5.860 13.000
6.205 8.094 14.000
6.103 8.798 10.177 16.000
ME
3.3 3.7 4.0 4.2
MO NY=4 NE=2 LY=FU,FI BE=FU,FI TY=FI AL=FR PS=SY,FI TE=DI,FR AP=1
LE
INT SLP
FR PS 1 1 PS 2 2 !PS 2 1
VA 1 LY 1 1 LY 2 1 LY 3 1 LY 4 1
CO LY 1 2 = 4-PA 1
CO LY 2 2 = 6-PA 1
CO LY 3 2 = 7-PA 1
CO LY 4 2 = 8-PA 1
PD
OU IT=5000 AD=OFF ND=4
```

Method 2: Phantom variable approach

```
LATENT GROWTH CURVE OF HANCOCK & CHOI DATA, EX. 2
DA NI=4 NO=198 MA=CM
CM
```

```
11.000
5.860 13.000
6.205 8.094 14.000
6.103 8.798 10.177 16.000
ME
3.3 3.7 4.0 4.2
MO NY=4 NE=3 LY=FU,FI BE=FU,FI TY=FI AL=FI PS=SY,FI TE=DI,FR
LE
INT SLP PHANTOM
FR AL 1 AL 2
PA PS
 1
 0 1
 0 0 0
MA PS
 .5
  0 .5
  0 0 0
PA LY
0 0 0
0 0 0
0 0 0
0 0 0
MA LY
1 4 -1
1 6 -1
1 7 -1
1 8 -1
PA BE
 0 0 0
 0 0 0
 0 1 0
MA BE
 0 0 0
 0 0 0
 0 -4.3 0
PD
OU IT=5000 AD=OFF ND=4
```

Method 3: Structured latent curve approach

```
LATENT GROWTH CURVE OF HANCOCK & CHOI DATA, EX. 2
DA NI=4 NO=198 MA=CM
CM
11.000
5.860 13.000
6.205 8.094 14.000
6.103 8.798 10.177 16.000
ME
3.3 3.7 4.0 4.2
MO NY=4 NE=3 LY=FU,FI TY=FI AL=FR PS=SY,FI TE=DI,FR AP=1
LE
```

```
INT SLP APERTURE
PA PS
 1
 0 1
 0 0 0
MA PS
 .5
  0 .5
  0  0  0
PA LY
 0 0 0
 0 0 0
 0 0 0
 0 0 0
MA LY
 1 0 0
 1 0 0
 1 0 0
 1 0 0
CO LY 1 2 = 4-PA 1
CO LY 2 2 = 6-PA 1
CO LY 3 2 = 7-PA 1
CO LY 4 2 = 8-PA 1
CO LY 1 3 = -1*AL(2)
CO LY 2 3 = -1*AL(2)
CO LY 3 3 = -1*AL(2)
CO LY 4 3 = -1*AL(2)
CO AL 3 = PA 1
PD
OU IT=5000 AD=OFF ND=4
```

A Reparameterized Gompertz Structured Latent Growth Curve Model with Random Coefficients

Example application to ECLS-K mathematics data (kindergarten through eighth grade). Random coefficients represent the upper asymptote, surge point, and surge slope (see Choi et al., 2009) for definitions of these terms.

```
TITLE: ECLS-K math, reparameterized Gompertz curve;
DATA: FILE = eclsk.dat;
VARIABLE: NAMES = id
!gender !0=M/1=F; uncomment gender for conditional model
m_fk m_sk m_f1 m_s1 m_s3 m_s5 m_s8;
USEVARIABLES ARE gender m_fk-m_s8;
MISSING = .;
ANALYSIS:
ALGORITHM = INTEGRATION;
INTEGRATION = MONTECARLO;
```

Reparameterization in Latent Growth Curve Models ▪ 53

```
MODEL:

!Factor Loadings
g0 BY m_fk*(Lg01)
m_sk-m_s8(Lg02-Lg07);
t0 BY m_fk*(Lt01)
m_sk-m_s8(Lt02-Lt07);
g3 BY m_fk*(Lg31)
m_sk-m_s8(Lg32-Lg37);

!Means
[m_fk-m_s8@0]; [g0*147](mu_g0); [t0@0]; [g3*22](mu_g3);

!Variances and covariances
m_fk-m_s8; g0*495 t0*.24 g3; g0 WITH t0 g3; t0 WITH g3;

!Regressions
!g0 t0 g3 ON gender; !uncomment line for conditional model

MODEL CONSTRAINT:
NEW(mu_t0*.7); !Introduce mean of surge point

!Asymptote loadings
Lg01 = exp(-1*exp(((mu_g3*exp(1)*(mu_t0-0.0))/mu_g0)))
+((mu_g3*exp(1)*(mu_t0-0.0)*exp(mu_g3*exp(1)*(mu_t0-0.0)/mu_g0)
*exp(-1*exp(mu_g3*exp(1)*(mu_t0-0.0)/mu_g0)))/mu_g0);
Lg02 = exp(-1*exp(((mu_g3*exp(1)*(mu_t0-0.5))/mu_g0)))
+((mu_g3*exp(1)*(mu_t0-0.5)*exp(mu_g3*exp(1)*(mu_t0-0.5)/mu_g0)
*exp(-1*exp(mu_g3*exp(1)*(mu_t0-0.5)/mu_g0)))/mu_g0);
Lg03 = exp(-1*exp(((mu_g3*exp(1)*(mu_t0-1.0))/mu_g0)))
+((mu_g3*exp(1)*(mu_t0-1.0)*exp(mu_g3*exp(1)*(mu_t0-1.0)/mu_g0)
*exp(-1*exp(mu_g3*exp(1)*(mu_t0-1.0)/mu_g0)))/mu_g0);
Lg04 = exp(-1*exp(((mu_g3*exp(1)*(mu_t0-1.5))/mu_g0)))
+((mu_g3*exp(1)*(mu_t0-1.5)*exp(mu_g3*exp(1)*(mu_t0-1.5)/mu_g0)
*exp(-1*exp(mu_g3*exp(1)*(mu_t0-1.5)/mu_g0)))/mu_g0);
Lg05 = exp(-1*exp(((mu_g3*exp(1)*(mu_t0-3.5))/mu_g0)))
+((mu_g3*exp(1)*(mu_t0-3.5)*exp(mu_g3*exp(1)*(mu_t0-3.5)/mu_g0)
*exp(-1*exp(mu_g3*exp(1)*(mu_t0-3.5)/mu_g0)))/mu_g0);
Lg06 = exp(-1*exp(((mu_g3*exp(1)*(mu_t0-5.5))/mu_g0)))
+((mu_g3*exp(1)*(mu_t0-5.5)*exp(mu_g3*exp(1)*(mu_t0-5.5)/mu_g0)
*exp(-1*exp(mu_g3*exp(1)*(mu_t0-5.5)/mu_g0)))/mu_g0);
Lg07 = exp(-1*exp(((mu_g3*exp(1)*(mu_t0-8.5))/mu_g0)))
+((mu_g3*exp(1)*(mu_t0-8.5)*exp(mu_g3*exp(1)*(mu_t0-8.5)/mu_g0)
*exp(-1*exp(mu_g3*exp(1)*(mu_t0-8.5)/mu_g0)))/mu_g0);

!Surge point loadings
Lt01 = -1*mu_g3*exp(1)*exp(mu_g3*exp(1)*(mu_t0-0.0)/mu_g0)
*exp(-1*exp(mu_g3*exp(1)*(mu_t0-0.0)/mu_g0));
Lt02 = -1*mu_g3*exp(1)*exp(mu_g3*exp(1)*(mu_t0-0.5)/mu_g0)
*exp(-1*exp(mu_g3*exp(1)*(mu_t0-0.5)/mu_g0));
Lt03 = -1*mu_g3*exp(1)*exp(mu_g3*exp(1)*(mu_t0-1.0)/mu_g0)
*exp(-1*exp(mu_g3*exp(1)*(mu_t0-1.0)/mu_g0));
```

```
Lt04 = -1*mu_g3*exp(1)*exp(mu_g3*exp(1)*(mu_t0-1.5)/mu_g0)
*exp(-1*exp(mu_g3*exp(1)*(mu_t0-1.5)/mu_g0));
Lt05 = -1*mu_g3*exp(1)*exp(mu_g3*exp(1)*(mu_t0-3.5)/mu_g0)
*exp(-1*exp(mu_g3*exp(1)*(mu_t0-3.5)/mu_g0));
Lt06 = -1*mu_g3*exp(1)*exp(mu_g3*exp(1)*(mu_t0-5.5)/mu_g0)
*exp(-1*exp(mu_g3*exp(1)*(mu_t0-5.5)/mu_g0));
Lt07 = -1*mu_g3*exp(1)*exp(mu_g3*exp(1)*(mu_t0-8.5)/mu_g0)
*exp(-1*exp(mu_g3*exp(1)*(mu_t0-8.5)/mu_g0));

!Surge slope loadings
Lg31 = -1*exp(1)*(mu_t0-0.0)*exp(mu_g3*exp(1)*(mu_t0-0.0)/mu_g0)
*exp(-1*exp(mu_g3*exp(1)*(mu_t0-0.0)/mu_g0));
Lg32 = -1*exp(1)*(mu_t0-0.5)*exp(mu_g3*exp(1)*(mu_t0-0.5)/mu_g0)
*exp(-1*exp(mu_g3*exp(1)*(mu_t0-0.5)/mu_g0));
Lg33 = -1*exp(1)*(mu_t0-1.0)*exp(mu_g3*exp(1)*(mu_t0-1.0)/mu_g0)
*exp(-1*exp(mu_g3*exp(1)*(mu_t0-1.0)/mu_g0));
Lg34 = -1*exp(1)*(mu_t0-1.5)*exp(mu_g3*exp(1)*(mu_t0-1.5)/mu_g0)
*exp(-1*exp(mu_g3*exp(1)*(mu_t0-1.5)/mu_g0));
Lg35 = -1*exp(1)*(mu_t0-3.5)*exp(mu_g3*exp(1)*(mu_t0-3.5)/mu_g0)
*exp(-1*exp(mu_g3*exp(1)*(mu_t0-3.5)/mu_g0));
Lg36 = -1*exp(1)*(mu_t0-5.5)*exp(mu_g3*exp(1)*(mu_t0-5.5)/mu_g0)
*exp(-1*exp(mu_g3*exp(1)*(mu_t0-5.5)/mu_g0));
Lg37 = -1*exp(1)*(mu_t0-8.5)*exp(mu_g3*exp(1)*(mu_t0-8.5)/mu_g0)
*exp(-1*exp(mu_g3*exp(1)*(mu_t0-8.5)/mu_g0));
```

The Jenss-Bayley Model Reparameterized to Estimate the Effect of Cumulative Breastfeeding on Infant Weight at Any Desired Age

We did not have permission to post the Cebu infant data, but we provide Mplus code below to show how to estimate the model.

```
TITLE: cebu growth data (jenss-bayley) with mobile intercept;
DATA: FILE IS cebu_wide_more.dat;
VARIABLE: NAMES ARE id momht rural male age0-age12 br0-br12 h0-h12
w0-w12 b0 b2 b4 b6 b8 b10 b12 b14 b16 b18 b20 b22 b24 xb6 xb8 xb10
xb12 xb14 xb16 xb18 xb20 xb22 xb24;
USEVARIABLES ARE cbf !comment out 'cbf' for unconditional model
x0-x12; !b0-b24 cumul BF means from age 0m; xb6-xb24 from age 6m
MISSING ARE ALL (-999);
USEOBSERVATIONS ARE id NE 1600044; !omit outlier
DEFINE: !below, choose to model height or weight
!x0=h0;x1=h1;x2=h2;x3=h3;x4=h4;x5=h5;x6=h6;
!x7=h7;x8=h8;x9=h9;x10=h10;x11=h11;x12=h12;
x0=w0;x1=w1;x2=w2;x3=w3;x4=w4;x5=w5;x6=w6;
x7=w7;x8=w8;x9=w9;x10=w10;x11=w11;x12=w12;
!comment out next line for unconditional model
cbf=b12; ! <- SET AGE FOR CUMULATIVE BREASTFEEDING (mos.);
ANALYSIS: ESTIMATOR IS ML; ITERATIONS ARE 10000; !BOOTSTRAP IS 300;
MODEL: [x0-x12@0]; x0-x12*.1(v1); x0-x11 PWITH x1-x12*.027(v2);
```

```
fa*1.2; fb*.005; fc*.288; fd*.02; fa WITH fb fc fd;
fb WITH fc fd; fc WITH fd;
[fa*9](mfa); [fb*.13](mfb); [fc*1.2](mfc); [fd@0];
! fa, fb, & fc are linear
fa BY x0-x12@1;
fb BY x0*(b0); fb BY x1-x12(b1-b12);
fc BY x0*(c0); fc BY x1-x12(c1-c12);
fd BY x0*(d0); fd BY x1-x12(d1-d12);
!comment out next line for unconditional model
fa ON cbf*-.53; fb ON cbf*.05; fc ON cbf*-.55; fd ON cbf*-.23;

!jenss-bayley with a mobile intercept
MODEL CONSTRAINT: NEW(mfd*-.334 t0);
t0=12; ! <- SET INTERCEPT LOC. (mos.)

b0=0-t0;  c0=exp(mfc+mfd*t0)-exp(mfc+mfd*0);
b1=2-t0;  c1=exp(mfc+mfd*t0)-exp(mfc+mfd*2);
b2=4-t0;  c2=exp(mfc+mfd*t0)-exp(mfc+mfd*4);
b3=6-t0;  c3=exp(mfc+mfd*t0)-exp(mfc+mfd*6);
b4=8-t0;  c4=exp(mfc+mfd*t0)-exp(mfc+mfd*8);
b5=10-t0; c5=exp(mfc+mfd*t0)-exp(mfc+mfd*10);
b6=12-t0; c6=exp(mfc+mfd*t0)-exp(mfc+mfd*12);
b7=14-t0; c7=exp(mfc+mfd*t0)-exp(mfc+mfd*14);
b8=16-t0; c8=exp(mfc+mfd*t0)-exp(mfc+mfd*16);
b9=18-t0; c9=exp(mfc+mfd*t0)-exp(mfc+mfd*18);
b10=20-t0; c10=exp(mfc+mfd*t0)-exp(mfc+mfd*20);
b11=22-t0; c11=exp(mfc+mfd*t0)-exp(mfc+mfd*22);
b12=24-t0; c12=exp(mfc+mfd*t0)-exp(mfc+mfd*24);

d0=t0*exp(mfc+mfd*t0)-0*exp(mfc+mfd*0);
d1=t0*exp(mfc+mfd*t0)-2*exp(mfc+mfd*2);
d2=t0*exp(mfc+mfd*t0)-4*exp(mfc+mfd*4);
d3=t0*exp(mfc+mfd*t0)-6*exp(mfc+mfd*6);
d4=t0*exp(mfc+mfd*t0)-8*exp(mfc+mfd*8);
d5=t0*exp(mfc+mfd*t0)-10*exp(mfc+mfd*10);
d6=t0*exp(mfc+mfd*t0)-12*exp(mfc+mfd*12);
d7=t0*exp(mfc+mfd*t0)-14*exp(mfc+mfd*14);
d8=t0*exp(mfc+mfd*t0)-16*exp(mfc+mfd*16);
d9=t0*exp(mfc+mfd*t0)-18*exp(mfc+mfd*18);
d10=t0*exp(mfc+mfd*t0)-20*exp(mfc+mfd*20);
d11=t0*exp(mfc+mfd*t0)-22*exp(mfc+mfd*22);
d12=t0*exp(mfc+mfd*t0)-24*exp(mfc+mfd*24);

OUTPUT: TECH1 TECH3 STDYX; !CINTERVAL(BCBOOTSTRAP);
```

ACKNOWLEDGMENT

We thank Kevin Grimm and Jeff Harring for valuable help with the Gompertz curve example.

NOTES

1. SEM software packages capable of imposing nonlinear constraints currently include LISREL, Mplus, SAS PROC CALIS and PROC TCALIS, Mx, and OpenMx.
2. We assume homoscedasticity for parsimony, not because the model requires it.
3. The Taylor series approximation uses mean-centered latent variables, but the diagrams and model specifications used in this chapter simplify matters by giving some of the latent variables mean parameters.
4. Computation of NNFI required a nonstandard null model; see Widaman and Thompson (2003).
5. If the parameters entering the function nonlinearly are fixed coefficients rather than random coefficients, the model is termed *conditionally linear* (Blozis & Cudeck, 1999).
6. We omitted from our analyses one infant who grew to be nearly twice the weight of his peers, yielding $n = 2{,}631$.

REFERENCES

Adair, L. S., & Popkin, B. M. (1996). Low birth weight reduces the likelihood of breast-feeding among Filipino infants. *Journal of Nutrition, 126,* 103–112.

Adair, L. S., Popkin, B. M., Akin, J. S., Guilkey, D. K., Gultiano, S., Borja, J., et al. (2011). Cohort profile: The Cebu longitudinal health and nutrition survey. *International Journal of Epidemiology, 40,* 619–625.

Beal, S. L., & Sheiner, L. B. (1982), Estimating population kinetics. *Critical Reviews in Biomedical Engineering, 8,* 195–222.

Blozis, S. A., & Cudeck, R. (1999). Conditionally linear mixed-effects models with latent variable covariates. *Journal of Educational and Behavioral Statistics, 24,* 245–270.

Browne, M. W. (1993). Structured latent curve models. In C. M. Cuadras & C. R. Rao (Eds.), *Multivariate analysis: Future directions 2* (pp. 171–197). Amsterdam, The Netherlands: Elsevier-North Holland.

Browne, M. W., & du Toit, S. H. C. (1991). Models for learning data. In L. M. Collins & J. L. Horn (Eds.) *Best methods for the analysis of change.* Washington, DC: American Psychological Association.

Choi, J., Harring, J. R., & Hancock, G. R. (2009). Latent growth modeling for logistic response functions. *Multivariate Behavioral Research, 44,* 620–645.

Cudeck, R., & du Toit, S. H. C. (2002). A version of quadratic regression with interpretable parameters. *Multivariate Behavioral Research, 37,* 501–519.

Davidian, M., & Giltinan, D.M. (1995). *Nonlinear models for repeated measurement data.* London: CRC Press.

Entwistle, D. R., & Alexander, K. L. (1992). Summer setback: Race, poverty, school composition, and mathematics achievement in the first two years of school. *American Sociological Review, 57,* 72–84.

Gompertz, B. (1825). On the nature of the function expressive of the law of human mortality, and on a new mode of determining the value of life contingencies. *Philosophical Transactions of the Royal Society of London, 115*, 513–585.

Grimm, K. J., & Ram, N. (2009). Nonlinear growth models in M*plus* and SAS. *Structural Equation Modeling: A Multidisciplinary Journal, 16*, 676–701.

Grimm, K. J., Ram, N., & Estabrook, R. (2010). Nonlinear structured growth mixture models in Mplus and OpenMx. *Multivariate Behavioral Research, 45*, 887–909.

Hancock, G. R., & Choi, J. (2006). A vernacular for linear latent growth models. *Structural Equation Modeling: A Multidisciplinary Journal, 13*, 352–377.

Hancock, G. R., & Koran, J. M. (2005, April). *A latent growth modeling strategy for interrupted longitudinal processes.* Paper presented at the annual meeting of the American Educational Research Association, Montreal, Quebec, Canada.

Hand, D., & Crowder, M. (1996). *Practical longitudinal data analysis.* Boca Raton, FL: Chapman & Hall/CRC.

Harring, J. R., Cudeck, R., & du Toit, S. H. C. (2006). Fitting partially nonlinear random coefficient models as SEMs. *Multivariate Behavioral Research, 41*, 579–596.

Hipp, J., Bauer, D. J., Curran, P. J., & Bollen, K. A. (2004). Crimes of opportunity or crimes of emotion: Testing two explanations of seasonal change in crime. *Social Forces, 82*, 1333–1372.

Jenss, R. M., & Bayley, N. (1937). A mathematical method for studying the growth of a child. *Human Biology, 9*, 556–563.

Mehta, P. D., & West, S. G. (2000). Putting the individual back in individual growth curves. *Psychological Methods, 5*, 23–43.

Ram, N., & Grimm, K. (2007). Using simple and complex growth models to articulate developmental change: Matching theory to method. *International Journal of Behavioral Development, 31*, 303–316.

Rausch, J. R. (2004). *Designing longitudinal studies of negative exponential growth according to the reliabilities of growth parameter estimators.* Unpublished thesis, University of Notre Dame, Notre Dame, IN.

Rausch, J. R. (2008). *Parametrizations for the negative exponential growth model.* Paper presented at the international meeting of the Psychometric Society, Durham, NH.

Rogosa, D. R., & Willett, J. B. (1985). Understanding correlates of change by modeling individual differences in growth. *Psychometrika, 50*, 203–228.

Sit, V., & Poulin-Costello, M. (1994). *Catalog of curves for curve fitting.* Biometrics Information, Handbook no. 4, B.C. Ministry of Forests, Victoria, BC, Canada.

Stoolmiller, M. (1994). Antisocial behavior, delinquent peer association and unsupervised wandering for boys: Growth and change from childhood to early adolescence. *Multivariate Behavioral Research, 29*, 263–288.

Tourangeau, K., Nord, C., Lê, T., Sorongon, A. G., & Najarian, M. (2009). *Early Childhood Longitudinal Study, Kindergarten Class of 1998–99 (ECLS-K), Combined User's Manual for the ECLS-K Eighth-Grade and K–8 Full Sample Data Files and Electronic Codebooks (NCES 2009–004).* Washington, DC: National Center for Education Statistics, Institute of Education Sciences, U.S. Department of Education.

UNICEF. (2003). *Drought, HIV/AIDS and child malnutrition in southern Africa: Part 1, Preliminary analysis of nutritional data on the humanitarian crisis.* Retrieved from www.tulane.edu/~internut/NIPSA%20I.pdf.

UNICEF. (2008a). *The state of Africa's children 2008: Child survival.* Retrieved from www.unicef.org/sowc08/docs/SOAC_2008_EN_A4.pdf.

UNICEF. (2008b). *The state of Asia-Pacific's children 2008: Child survival.* Retrieved from www.unicef.org/publications/files/SOAPC_2008_080408.pdf.

Widaman, K. F., & Thompson, J. S. (2003). On specifying the null model for incremental fit indices in structural equation modeling. *Psychological Methods, 8,* 16–37.

Winsor, C. P. (1932). The Gompertz curve as a growth curve. *Proceedings of the National Academy of Sciences, 18,* 1–8.

CHAPTER 3

MOOD CHANGES ASSOCIATED WITH SMOKING IN ADOLESCENTS

An Application of a Mixed-Effects Location Scale Model for Longitudinal Ecological Momentary Assessment Data

Donald Hedeker
Robin J. Mermelstein
University of Illinois at Chicago

INTRODUCTION

Modern data collection procedures, such as ecological momentary assessments (EMA; Smyth & Stone, 2003; Stone & Shiffman, 1994), experience sampling (Feldman Barrett & Barrett, 2001; Scollon, Kim-Prieto, & Diener, 2003), and diary methods (Bolger, Davis, & Rafaeli, 2001) yield relatively large numbers of subjects and observations per subject, and data from such designs are sometimes referred to as intensive longitudinal data (Walls & Schafer, 2006). Analysis of EMA data using mixed models (also known as multilevel or hierarchical linear models) is well described by Schwartz and Stone (2007). Additionally, Moghaddam and Ferguson (2007) analyzed EMA data using mixed models to examine smoking-related changes in mood. These articles focus on the effects of covariates, either subject-varying or time-varying, on the EMA mean responses. Here we extend this approach by examining the degree to which covariates influence the within-subjects variation inherent in the EMA data.

A few articles have described approaches for examining determinants of between- and within-subjects variance from EMA studies. Penner, Shiffman, Paty, and Fritzsche (1994) used basic descriptive statistical methods to examine relations among within-subject variation in several mood variables. Jahng, Wood, and Trull (2008) described generalized mixed models to analyze within-subject differences in sequential EMA mood responses, specifically characterizing these as mean square successive differences. Hedeker, Mermelstein, Berbaum, and Campbell (2009) described a mixed model that included determinants of the between-subjects variance, while Hedeker, Mermelstein, and Demirtas (2008) developed a model that additionally allowed determinants of the within-subjects variance plus a random subject scale effect. This model is referred to as a *mixed-effects location scale model* because subjects have both random location and scale effects. Models with random scale effects have been described in several articles where interest centers on variance modeling and/or accounting for heterogeneous variation across individuals or clusters (Chinchilli, Esinhart, & Miller, 1995; Cleveland, Denby, & Liu, 2002; James, Venables, Dry, & Wiskich, 1994; Leckie, 2010; Lin, Raz, & Harlow, 1997; Myles, Price, Hunter, Day, & Duffy, 2003).

In this chapter, we extend the mixed-effects location scale model to focus on the variation of mood change that is associated with smoking across measurement waves, and the degree to which subject and wave characteristics influence the variation in mood changes. Also, while Hedeker et al. (2008) only considered random subject intercepts for the one wave of EMA data, here we allow random subject time trends for the multiple waves of EMA data. We further consider a three-level model that treats observations nested within waves within subjects. To aid in making this class of models accessible, sample computer syntax is provided in the Appendix.

ADOLESCENT SMOKING, MOOD, AND VARIABILITY

Many prominent models of cigarette smoking maintain that smoking is reinforcing, and that smoking can relieve negative affect (Kassel, Stround, & Paronis, 2003; Khantzian, 1997). Indeed, both adults and adolescents often claim that smoking is relaxing and reduces emotional distress (Chassin, Presson, Rose, & Sherman, 2007; Kassel & Hankin, 2006). However, although the relation between mood and smoking has received substantial empirical attention for adult smokers, much less is known about the acute changes in mood with smoking among adolescents. The present study, with its focus on real-time assessments of mood and smoking among adolescents, helps to shed light on this important topic.

Although there is substantial consensus among both smokers and researchers that smoking helps to regulate affect, most of the empirical work investigating the smoking-mood relation has focused on the examination of changes in mean levels of mood with smoking. Surprisingly, although affect regulation inherently implies the modulation of variability in mood as well, the examination of variability in mood and smoking has largely been neglected. As Hertzog and Nesselroade (2003) noted, describing mean levels of variables is not always adequate for examining key features of developmental change. Variation also conveys important information about the phenomenon of interest. In the case of adolescent smoking and the development of dependence, variation in mood and mood changes may help to explain more of the development of tolerance. Examining individual variability may enhance our ability to predict changes in smoking behavior above and beyond what can be achieved by examining mean information alone.

Important, too, in the examination of mood and smoking is the distinction between within-person and between-person variability. Kassel and colleagues (Kassel & Hankin, 2006; Kassel et al., 2003) have argued persuasively for the need to differentiate causal within-person mechanisms from between-person data. Whether smoking relieves negative affect is essentially a within-person question, and thus analytic models need to similarly differentiate between within-subject and between-subject effects.

Much of the research on mood and smoking has also been limited to assessments of negative affect, while ignoring positive affect. This neglect is particularly problematic given the theoretical importance of differentiating between negative reinforcement models of smoking and positive reinforcement models, especially in the development of dependence among adolescents (Tiffany, Conklin, Shiffman, & Clayton, 2004). There is also considerable evidence to support the notion that positive and negative affect are distinct constructs, and not just opposite ends of a continuum (Watson & Tellegen, 1985; Watson, Wiese, Vaidya, & Tellegen, 1999). Thus, in the current study, we assessed both positive and negative affect.

Finally, there may well be individual differences in the extent to which adolescents' moods vary and whether these moods vary with smoking. Identifying potential moderator variables may also help in the prediction of smoking escalation among relatively novice smokers. Indeed, in a previous paper (Hedeker et al., 2009) it was observed that adolescent smoking level was associated with variation in mood changes associated with smoking, diminishing this variance for both positive and negative affect. While this finding was noteworthy, it represents a between-subjects effect of smoking level, rather than addressing the point of whether variation in mood changes associated with smoking diminishes *as a person increases their smoking level* (a within-subjects effect). Here, we aim to assess this within-subjects effect by modeling the EMA data across several measurement waves as a subject changes his or her smoking level. We hypothesized that the between-subjects effect of smoking level that we previously reported would also be observed as a within-subjects effect. Namely, as adolescents increase their level of smoking across time, their variation in mood changes associated with smoking would diminish. Thus, following along the lines of the development of tolerance with dependence, we hypothesized that as smoking level or experience increased, mood responses to smoking would decrease, as would variability in overall mood.

METHODS

Subjects

The data are drawn from a natural history study of adolescent smoking. Participants included in this study were in 9th or 10th grade at baseline, 55.1% female, and reported on a screening questionnaire 6–8 weeks prior to baseline that they had smoked at least one cigarette in their lifetimes. The majority (57.6%) had smoked at least one cigarette in the past month at baseline. Written parental consent and student assent were required for participation. A total of 461 students completed the baseline measurement wave. Of these, 57% were white, 20% Hispanic, 16% black, and 7% of other race.

The study utilized a multimethod approach to assess adolescents including self-report questionnaires, a week-long time/event sampling method via hand-held computers (EMA), and detailed surveys. Adolescents carried the hand-held computers with them at all times during a data collection period of 7 consecutive days and were trained both to respond to random prompts from the computers and to event-record (initiate a data collection interview) in conjunction with smoking episodes. Random prompts and the self-initiated smoking records were mutually exclusive; no smoking occurred during random prompts. Questions concerned place, activity, companionship, mood, and other subjective variables. The hand-held computers dated and time-stamped each entry. Following the baseline assessment, subjects completed additional EMA sessions at 6-, 15-, and 24-month follow-ups, for a total of four EMA measurement waves. Subject retention was good, with 405, 360, and 385 subjects completing the EMA sessions at these three follow-ups, respectively. Since estimation of model parameters is based on a full-likelihood approach, the missing data are assumed to be "ignorable" conditional on both the model covariates and the observed responses of the dependent variable (Laird, 1988). In longitudinal studies, ignorable nonresponse falls under the "missing at random" (MAR) mechanism of Rubin (1976), in which the missingness depends only on observed data. As Molenberghs et al. (2004) indicate, MAR is a relatively weak assumption, especially as compared to the more stringent missing completely at random (MCAR) assumption, and one that we will make here. For the interested reader, extended not missing at random (NMAR) approaches are described in Chapter 14 of Hedeker and Gibbons (2006).

Because of our interest in comparing mood *within subjects* from smoking events across measurement waves, we restricted our analysis to subjects who provided two or more waves of data, where at each wave the subject provided at least two smoking events. In all, there were 130 such subjects with data from a total of 3,388 smoking events. Of these, 47, 39, and 44 subjects provided data at two, three, and four waves, respectively. The number of subjects at each measurement wave equaled 116 (baseline), 91 (6 months), 92 (15 months), and 88 (24 months), and the average number of smoking events equaled 7.14 (range = 2–42), 7.65 (range = 2–32), 9.97 (range = 2–43), and 10.76 (range = 2–49) at these same four waves, respectively.

Measures

Negative and Positive Affect

Two mood outcomes were considered: measures of the subject's negative and positive affect (denoted NA and PA, respectively) at a smoking episode. Both of these measures consisted of the average of several individual mood items, each rated from 1 to 10, with "10" representing very high levels of the attribute that were identified via factor analysis. Specifically, PA consisted of the following items that reflected subjects' assessments of their positive mood: I felt happy, I felt relaxed, I felt cheerful, I felt confident, and I felt accepted by others. Similarly, NA consisted of the following items: I felt sad, I felt stressed, I felt angry, I felt frustrated, and I felt irritable. For the smoking events, participants rated their mood "before" and "now after smoking." Considering the five items of the "before" (and "now after smoking") PA mood assessments, Cronbach's alpha was equal to .84 (.77), .81 (.78), .85 (.83), and .83 (.82) at baseline, 6, 9, and 24 months, respectively. Similarly, in terms of the NA mood assessments, Cronbach's alpha equaled .90 (.90), .92 (.91), .88 (.91), and .93 (.90) at baseline, 6, 9, and 24 months, respectively. Because of our interest in smoking-related mood change, we used the difference (now − before) as our measure of reported mood change associated with smoking.

Gender and Wave

As covariates, we considered gender and measurement wave with the variables Male (coded 0 = female or 1 = male) and Wave (coded 0 = baseline, 1 = 6 months, 2.5 = 15 months, and 4 = 24 months). In our selected sample of 130 subjects, 46% were males.

Smoking Level

As a time-varying (within-subjects) measure of a subject's smoking level, we used the number of smoking events that a subject reported at a given measurement wave (denoted as NumSmk). To separate the between- and within-subjects effects of this time-varying variable on mood change, as described in Begg and Parides (2003), we also included the subject's mean of NumSmk as a covariate (denoted as AvgSmk). By including both the wave-varying NumSmk and the subject-varying AvgSmk, we can estimate, respectively, both the within-subjects and between-subjects effects of smoking level on mood change. The between-subject effect represents the association of a person's average smoking level with their average change in mood (both averages being taken over time). Conversely, the within-subjects effect indicates how a person's mood change differs as their level of smoking varies over waves. The latter is of primary interest here as it represents the degree to which a person's mood response to smoking (now − before) changes as their smoking level varies across time. Finally, because of the relatively large numerical range of these variables, to ease computation and interpretation, we divided both by a factor of 10 so that the coefficients of these variables represent changes attributable to 10 smoking events (rather than a single smoking event). Also, to increase the interpretation of the intercept-related parameters we centered these two smoking-level variables at the value of 10 smoking reports.

DATA ANALYSIS

Consider the following mixed-effects regression model for the measurement y, either smoking-related change in NA or PA, of subject i ($i = 1, 2, \ldots, N$ subjects) on occasion j ($j = 1, 2, \ldots, n_i$ occasions):

$$y_{ij} = (\beta_0 + \upsilon_{0i}) = (\beta_1 + \upsilon_{1i})\text{Wave}_{ij} + \beta_2\text{Male}_i + \beta_3\text{AvgSmk}_i + \beta_4\text{NumSmk}_{ij} + \varepsilon_{ij} \quad (3.1)$$

Here, the occasions refer to the multiple smoking events that a subject provides, which, based on our inclusion criteria, are obtained at two or more measurement waves for each subject. The random subject effect υ_{0i} indicates the influence of individual i on his or her mood change at baseline, while υ_{1i} represents how a subject's mood change varies over time. Both of these reflect individual deviations relative to the population intercept and slope, β_0 and β_1. The inclusion of the random slope υ_{1i} is important here because the data are collected across multiple waves. With two random subject-specific effects, the population distribution of intercept and slope deviations is assumed to be a bivariate normal $N(0, \Sigma_\upsilon)$, where Σ_υ is the 2 × 2 variance–covariance matrix given as:

$$\Sigma_\upsilon = \begin{bmatrix} \sigma^2_{\upsilon_0} & \sigma_{\upsilon_0 \upsilon_1} \\ \sigma_{\upsilon_0 \upsilon_1} & \sigma^2_{\upsilon_1} \end{bmatrix}.$$

The model includes the intercept and Wave effect at both the individual (υ_{0i} and υ_{1i}) and population (β_0 and β_1) levels. Thus, we are controlling for baseline mood change and mood change across time at both of these levels. The model additionally includes the subject-varying covariates Male and AvgSmk to allow for the effects of gender and overall smoking level on mood change. The final regressor, NumSmk, which varies within subjects and across waves, represents the within-subjects effect of smoking level; the effect of this variable indicates the degree to which smoking-related mood change (now − before) varies as a subject changes his or her smoking level across time.

The errors ε_{ij} are assumed to be normally distributed in the population with zero mean and variance σ^2_ε, and independent of the random effects. Here, σ^2_ε is the within-subjects (WS) variance, which indicates the degree of variation in mood change within a subject. Because our interest is in allowing covariates to influence mood change variation, in addition to the effects on the mean level of mood change, we posit the following log-linear model of the WS variance:

$$\sigma^2_{\varepsilon_{ij}} = \exp(\mathbf{w}'_{ij} \tau). \quad (3.2)$$

This type of log-linear representation is common in the context of heteroscedastic (fixed-effects) regression models (Aitkin, 1987; Davidian & Carroll, 1987; Harvey, 1976). The WS variance is subscripted by i and j to indicate that it varies depending on the values of the covariates in vector $\mathbf{w}_{ij}$ (and their coefficients). The number of parameters associated with these variances does not vary with i or j. The covariate vector $\mathbf{w}_{ij}$ includes a (first) column of ones for the reference WS variance (τ_0); the WS variance equals $\exp(\tau_0)$ when the covariates $\mathbf{w}_{ij}$ equal 0, and is increased or decreased as a function of these covariates and their coefficients τ. For a particular covariate w^*, if $\tau^* > 0$, then the WS variance increases as w^* increases (and vice versa if $\tau^* < 0$). Note that the exponential function ensures a positive multiplicative factor for any finite value of τ, and so the resulting variance is guaranteed to be positive.

As in Hedeker et al. (2008), the WS variance can vary across subjects, above and beyond the contribution of covariates, namely,

$$\sigma^2_{\varepsilon_{ij}} = \exp(\mathbf{w}'_{ij}\tau + \omega_i), \qquad (3.3)$$

where the random subject (scale) effects ω_i are distributed in the population of subjects with mean 0 and variance σ^2_{ω}. The idea for this is akin to the inclusion of the random (location) effects in equation 3.1, namely, covariates do not account for all of the reasons that subjects differ from each other. The parameters υ_{0i} and υ_{1i} in equation 3.1 indicate how subjects differ in terms of their means and the ω_i parameters in equation 3.3 indicate how subjects differ in variation, beyond the effect of covariates. Notice that taking logs in equation 3.3 yields $\log(\sigma^2_{\varepsilon_{ij}}) = \mathbf{w}_{ij}\tau + \omega_i$, which indicates that if the distribution of ω_i is specified as normal, the random scale effects serve as log-normal subject-specific perturbations of the WS variance. The skewed, nonnegative nature of the log-normal distribution makes it a useful choice for representing variances and it has been used in many diverse research areas for this purpose (Fowler & Whitlock, 1999; Leonard, 1975; Reno & Rizza, 2003; Shenk, White, & Burnhamb, 1998; Vasseur, 1999).

In this model, υ_{0i} and υ_{1i} are random effects that influence an individual's mean, or location, and ω_i is a random effect that influences an individual's variance, or (square of the) scale. Thus, the model with both types of random effects is called a *mixed-effects location scale model*. These three random effects are all allowed to be correlated with covariance parameters $\sigma_{\upsilon_0\upsilon_1}$ (intercept and slope), $\sigma_{\upsilon_0\omega}$ (intercept and scale), and $\sigma_{\upsilon_1\omega}$ (slope and scale). Details on model estimation can be found in Hedeker et al. (2008). A nice feature of the model is that standard software (i.e., SAS PROC NLMIXED) can be used for estimation, and we provide sample computer syntax in the Appendix.

Visually, Figure 3.1 presents the model for EMA data without the error variance model (i.e., only equation 3.1), while Figure 3.2 illustrates the addition of the error variance model and random scale effects (i.e., equations 3.1 and 3.3). These figures present artificial data in order to better highlight and describe the model features. In both figures, the average across all subjects is depicted with solid horizontal lines, and the lines of two subjects are presented as dotted horizontal lines. In a given dataset, there will be dotted lines for each subject, but for simplicity here we only plot two representative subjects. Also, for simplicity, only two waves of data are plotted. The slanted solid lines represent the population time-trends (averaged over

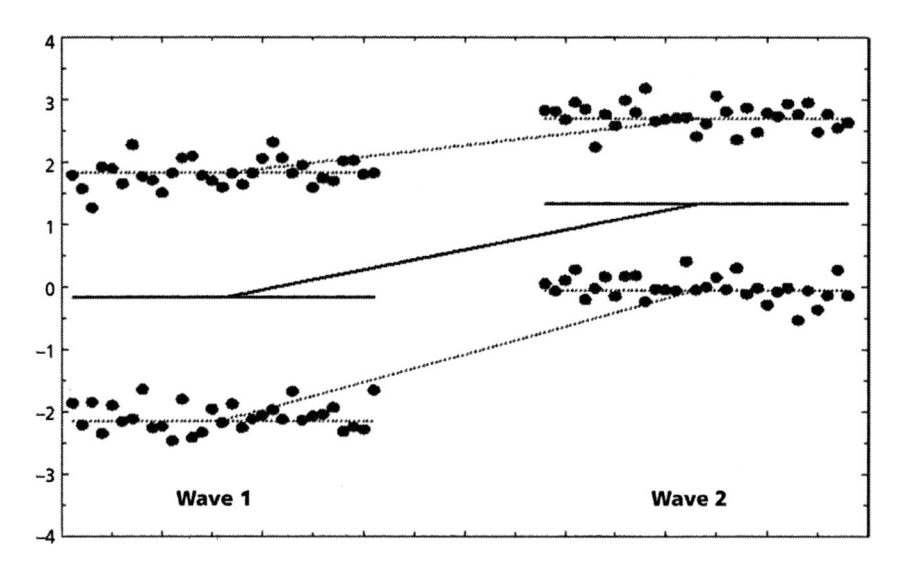

Mood Changes Associated with Smoking in Adolescents ■ 67

Figure 3.1 Mixed-effects model for longitudinal EMA data across two waves. Mean trend (solid lines), subject trends (dotted lines), and EMA observations (dots) for two representative subjects.

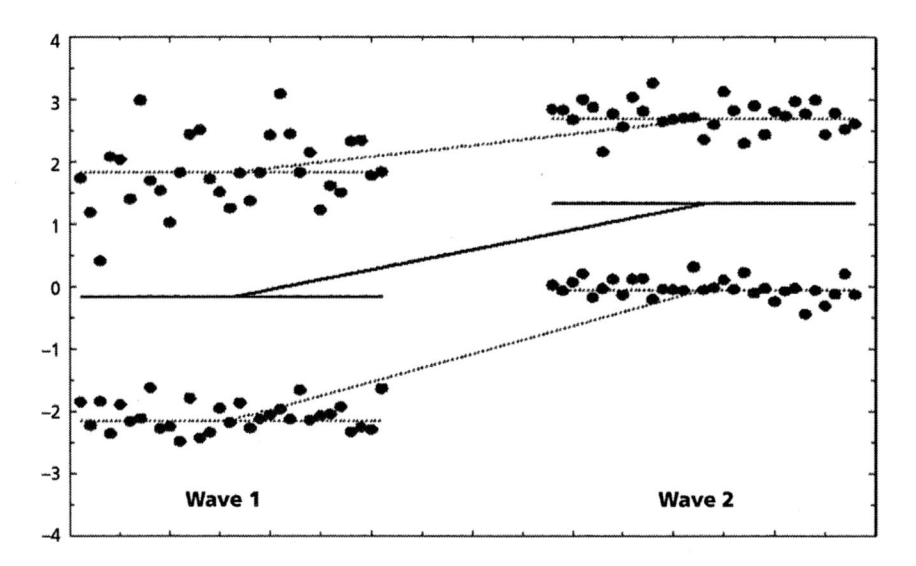

Figure 3.2 Mixed-effects location scale model for longitudinal EMA data across two waves. Mean trend (solid lines), subject trends (dotted lines), and EMA observations (dots) for two representative subjects.

subjects), while the slanted dotted lines represent the time-trends for the two subjects. Data points for these two subjects are also included in the plot; these represent the outcomes for a subject at a wave.

Considering Figure 3.1 first, the solid horizontal line at Wave 1 (i.e., baseline) corresponds to the population intercept and the slanted solid line is the population slope (β_0 and β_1, respectively). Covariates (besides Wave) can affect this mean response by either raising or lowering the slanted solid line (main effect) or change its slope (time interaction) in the usual way. The dotted lines of the two subjects at Wave 1 are indicative of a person's random intercept υ_{0i}, which indicates how a subject deviates from the mean response at Wave 1. In the figure, one subject is above and another subject is below the mean line. The heterogeneity in these dotted lines at Wave 1 is indicative of BS intercept variance ($\sigma_{\upsilon_0}^2$): if the dotted lines are close together then there is not much subject heterogeneity; conversely, if the dotted lines are spread out, then more heterogeneity is indicated. Similarly, the heterogeneity of the dotted trend lines is reflected by the BS slope variance ($\sigma_{\upsilon_1}^2$); in the plot these slopes vary between the two subjects, which corresponds to the notion that subjects vary in their time trajectories. Finally, the degree of variation of a person's data points around each of their horizontal dotted lines is the WS variance (σ_ε^2). In Figure 3.1, as in a standard mixed model, this is the same for all subjects at all waves.

Figure 3.2 illustrates the concept of the random scale effect and error variance modeling inherent in equation 3.3. Notice that the dispersion of the observations around each of the horizontal dotted lines varies. At both Waves 1 and 2, there is a great deal more WS variance for the subject above the mean line, relative to the subject below it. This disparate WS variation across subjects is precisely what the random scale effect ω_i captures, and the variance associated with this random effect (σ_ω^2) indicates the degree of subject heterogeneity in the WS variance. Notice also that the WS variance for both subjects is lessened at Wave 2 relative to Wave 1. This illustrates the effect that covariates **w** (and their coefficients τ) can have on the WS variance expressed in equation 3.3. As illustrated, the coefficient for Wave would be negative (i.e., as Wave increases, WS variance diminishes). Covariates of the WS variance could be occasion-varying like Wave, or subject-varying like Male, in which case the WS variation (across all occasions) of males would be more/less relative to females.

Second and/or Third Thoughts

The two-level model in equation 3.1 treats all observations at level 1 as nested within subjects at level 2. However, the observations are obtained across several measurement waves, and so a three-level structure of observations (level 1) within waves (level 2) within subjects (level 3) would seem more appropriate. For this, consider the multilevel decomposition of the model, where, for simplicity, we only include the covariate Wave (here, $i = 1, 2, \ldots, N$ subjects; $j = 1, 2, \ldots, n_i$ waves; and $k = 1, 2, \ldots, n_{ij}$ observations within a wave j for subject i):

Level 1 (within subjects, within waves)

$$y_{ijk} = b_{0ij} + \varepsilon_{ijk} \tag{3.4}$$

Level 2 (within subjects, between waves)

$$b_{0ij} = b_{0i} + b_{1i}\text{Wave}_{ij} + [\upsilon_{0ij}] \tag{3.5}$$

Level 3 (between subjects)

$$b_{0i} = \beta_0 + \upsilon_{0i} \tag{3.6}$$
$$b_{1i} = \beta_1 + \upsilon_{1i}$$

Here, b_{0ij} represents the subject means across time (i.e., the averages for a subject of the observations at a particular wave), and b_{0i} and b_{1i} are the subject intercepts and time trends of these means, respectively. The parameters in equation 3.6 of the level-3 model are as described above. In the proposed two-level model in equation 3.1, we have not included a wave-specific random effect, which is specified in equation 3.5 in brackets as $[\upsilon_{0ij}]$ for emphasis. Notice that without this term in the model, one is assuming that the subject means across time follow a line perfectly. This would seem to be a rather stringent assumption for subjects with more than two waves of data.

To test this assumption, therefore, we also estimated three-level models that include a random wave effect, in addition to the random subject effects. The three-level models also incorporate the modeling of the error variance given in equation 3.3. Namely, our full three-level mean model is specified as:

$$y_{ijk} = (\beta_0 + \upsilon_{0i} + \upsilon_{0ij}) + (\beta_1 + \upsilon_{1i})\text{Wave}_{ij} + \beta_2\text{Male}_i + \beta_3\text{AvgSmk}_i \tag{3.7}$$
$$+ \beta_4\text{NumSmk}_{ij} + \varepsilon_{ijk}$$

with the corresponding error variance model as:

$$\sigma^2_{ijk} = \exp(\tau_0 + \tau_1\text{Wave}_{ij} + \tau_2\text{Male}_i + \tau_3\text{AvgSmk}_i + \tau_4\text{NumSmk}_{ij} + \omega_i). \tag{3.8}$$

The random effects at the same level are allowed to be correlated; however, random effects at different levels are independent. Thus, the subject-level random scale effect and subject-level random location effects are correlated, but the random wave effect is independent.

RESULTS

First, to get a sense of the data, Table 3.1 lists the results of wave-stratified random intercept models of PA and NA, treating observations nested within subjects, namely, $y_{ij} = \beta_0 + \upsilon_{0i} + \varepsilon_{ij}$. The intercept of this model reflects the dependent variable mean, adjusting for the different numbers of observations per subject. Similarly, the variances are separated in terms of the between- and within-subjects components. As can be seen, the positive affect means are all positive, while the negative affect means are all negative, indicating the mood benefit attributed to smoking (both of these variables are mood assessments of now – before smoking). The benefit to positive affect does seem to diminish somewhat over time. What is also apparent is the general decline across time in both the between- and within-subjects variances.

Next, Table 3.2 lists the results of several two- and three-level models of smoking-related changes in positive and negative affect. For each of the models, the number of variance-covariance parameters, deviance (–2 log likelihood value), and Akaike information criterion (AIC) are provided. All models included the variables Wave, Male, AvgSmk, and NumSmk as regressors in both the mean and error variance structure.

The first two rows in this table are for the two-level models (labeled 2a–2b), while the remaining four rows are for three-level models (labeled 3a–3d). Computational issues arose for two of the three-level models, in that either a random effect correlation equaled unity in absolute value (model 3b), or

TABLE 3.1 Smoking-Related Positive and Negative Affect Change: Wave-Stratified Model-Based Descriptive Results

			Positive affect			Negative affect		
			Mean	BS var	WS var	Mean	BS var	WS var
Wave	N	$\sum_i n_i$	$\hat{\beta}_0$	$\hat{\sigma}_\upsilon^2$	$\hat{\sigma}_\varepsilon^2$	$\hat{\beta}_0$	$\hat{\sigma}_\upsilon^2$	$\hat{\sigma}_\varepsilon^2$
Baseline	116	828	0.730	0.792	2.240	–0.439	0.902	2.495
6 months	91	696	0.538	0.371	2.020	–0.445	0.350	2.399
15 months	92	917	0.353	0.457	1.574	–0.318	0.380	1.771
24 months	88	947	0.404	0.243	1.460	–0.391	0.267	1.507

Note: N equals the total number of subjects, $\sum_i n_i$ equals the total number of observations.

TABLE 3.2 Smoking-Related Positive and Negative Affect Change: Two- and Three-Level Model Results (Deviance and AIC Values)

Model	Subject-level random	Wave-level random	Variance-covariance parameters	Positive affect Deviance	AIC	Negative affect Deviance	AIC
2a	I, W		3	11763	11789	11999	12025
2b	I, W, S		6	11246	11278	11154	11186
3a	I	I	2	11756	11780	11997	12021
3b	I, W	I	4	\multicolumn{4}{l}{I,W correlation = –1}
3c	I, S	I	4	11228	11256	11150	11178
3d	I, W, S	I	7	\multicolumn{4}{l}{W variance = 0}

Note: I, intercept, W, wave, S, scale; Deviance = –2 log likelihood; AIC: Akaike information criterion. Regressors = Wave, Male, AvgSmk, NumSmk in both mean and error variance models.

a random effect variance equaled zero (model 3d). These computational issues occurred for both positive and negative affect. Of the remaining models, there is clear evidence for the three-level models, and also for the models including random scale effects. Thus, the model of choice is the three-level random scale model (model 3c). Estimates from this model are provided in Table 3.3.

In terms of the mean model, the intercept is highly significant for both mood change outcomes: positive for PA ($\hat{\beta}_0 = .547, p < .0001$) and negative for NA ($\hat{\beta}_0 = -.339, p < .0001$). This indicates that smoking had a beneficial effect by increasing positive affect change and decreasing negative affect change (when the covariates all equal 0, or for an average female at baseline with 10 smoking events). Wave had a diminishing effect on smoking-related PA mood change ($\hat{\beta}_1 = -.059, p < .005$), but no significant effect on NA. Namely, as time increased the smoking-related benefit to positive affect change decreased, while the negative affect change remained. Neither gender nor smoking level significantly influenced smoking-related mood change.

In terms of the error variance, Wave has a consistent significant effect in reducing variation for both PA change ($\hat{\tau}_1 = -.124, p < .0001$) and NA change ($\hat{\tau}_1 = -.095, p < .0001$); the variation in smoking-related mood change diminished across time. The BS effect of smoking level (AvgSmk) also significantly reduced variation in smoking-related PA mood change ($\hat{\tau}_3 = -.259, p < .018$). Thus, subjects who, on average, smoke more across time also exhibit less variation in smoking-related positive affect change, averaged across time. Controlling for these effects, the WS effect of smoking (NumSmk) significantly reduced variation in smoking-related mood change of both PA ($\hat{\tau}_4 = -.080, p < .046$) and especially NA ($\hat{\tau}_4 = -.220, p < .0001$). Thus, controlling for the effect of time and the between-subjects effect of

TABLE 3.3 Smoking-Related Positive and Negative Affect Change Estimates, Standard Errors (SE), and p-Values[a]

	Positive affect			Negative affect		
	Estimate	SE	p <	Estimate	SE	p <
Mean model						
Intercept β_0	0.547	0.078	0.0001	−0.339	0.064	0.0001
Wave β_1	−0.059	0.020	0.005	0.025	0.017	0.14
Male β_2	0.112	0.099	0.27	−0.114	0.079	0.15
AvgSmk β_3	−0.111	0.077	0.16	0.016	0.063	0.81
NumSmk β_4	−0.042	0.045	0.36	0.034	0.039	0.38
Error variance model						
Intercept τ_0	0.654	0.111	0.0001	0.650	0.152	0.0001
Wave τ_1	−0.124	0.020	0.0001	−0.095	0.021	0.0001
Male τ_2	0.217	0.151	0.16	0.166	0.214	0.44
AvgSmk τ_3	−0.259	0.107	0.018	−0.198	0.145	0.19
NumSmk τ_4	−0.080	0.040	0.046	−0.220	0.042	0.0001
Random effect (co)variances						
Subject intercept $\sigma^2_{\upsilon(3)}$	0.162	0.041	0.001	0.082	0.027	0.004
Subject scale $\sigma^2_{\omega(3)}$	0.560	0.091	0.0001	1.28	0.188	0.0001
Subject int,scale $\sigma_{\upsilon\omega(3)}$	0.139	0.041	0.001	−0.204	0.048	0.0001
Wave intercept $\sigma^2_{\upsilon(2)}$	0.071	0.024	0.004	0.033	0.017	0.06

[a] p-values are based on Wald statistics (Estimate/SE ~ standard normal distribution).

smoking level, as a person increases his or her level of smoking across time the variation in his or her smoking-related mood change is reduced.

Turning to the variance estimates, the subject-level intercept variance is seen to be significant for both outcomes ($\hat{\sigma}^2_{\upsilon(3)} = .162, p < .001$ for PA, $\hat{\sigma}^2_{\upsilon(3)} = .082, p < .004$ for NA); subjects do vary in their levels of smoking-related mood changes. The wave-level variance is observed to be significant for PA ($\hat{\sigma}^2_{\upsilon(2)} = .071, p < .004$), and near-significant for NA ($\hat{\sigma}^2_{\upsilon(2)} = .033, p < .06$), indicating that the data from subjects within a wave are also correlated, over and above the overall subject effect. The subject-level scale variance is observed to be highly significant for both outcomes ($\hat{\sigma}^2_{\omega(3)} = .560, p < .0001$ for PA, $\hat{\sigma}^2_{\omega(3)} = 1.28, p < .0001$ for NA), which indicates the importance of including the random subject scale effect. Subjects clearly vary in terms of the within-subject within-wave variance (over and above the influence of the covariates in the error variance model). In terms of the covariance, for both outcomes, the association of the random subject intercept and scale terms is seen to be significant. For PA it is positive ($\hat{\sigma}_{\upsilon\omega(3)} = .139, p < .001$), which indicates that subjects with higher positive affect levels (in terms of smoking-related mood change) have greater mood (change) variation. Conversely, for NA this covariance is negative ($\hat{\sigma}_{\upsilon\omega(3)} = -.204, p < .0001$), which suggests that subjects with higher negative affect levels (smoking-related mood change) exhibit less mood (change) variation. Expressed as correlations, these are .47 for PA and −.63 for NA. As the outcomes are change scores, these suggest that as the change score levels go toward zero (lower PA change and higher NA change), the scale variance is reduced. It is worth noting that zero is not a boundary value for these change scores, which varied from −9 to 9, and so these correlations do not necessarily reflect a floor effect of measurement.

DISCUSSION

This chapter has illustrated how mixed models for EMA data can be used to model differences in WS variances, and not just means. As such, these models can help to identify predictors of within-subjects variation, and to test psychological hypotheses about these variances. While estimation of the model goes beyond standard mixed model software (e.g., SAS PROC MIXED, SPSS MIXED, HLM, MLwiN, SuperMix), SAS PROC NLMIXED can be used for this purpose. In the Appendix, we provide sample syntax for maximum likelihood estimation of our mixed location scale models, making this class of models accessible to researchers.

Here, we focused on the degree of change in mood variation associated with smoking events (now − before), and whether covariates influenced this variation among adolescent smokers. One of the key concepts in dependence is the development of tolerance, or the diminishing of effects of a substance with continued use. A common experience reported by both adults and adolescents is mood change after smoking a cigarette, and the equally common notion is that these subjective feelings diminish over time as one's experience with smoking increases and tolerance may develop. However, heretofore, researchers have examined changes in these subjective experiences primarily through paper-and-pencil, retrospective questionnaire reports. Thus, it has been difficult to document adequately whether adolescents experience mood changes with smoking and also how symptoms of dependence develop or with what level of smoking experience. Overall, following smoking, adolescents reported higher positive affect and lower negative affect than before their smoking report. Additionally, our analyses indicated an increased consistency of subjective mood responses as a person's smoking experience increased over time and a diminishing of the mood change associated with smoking. Our data thus provide one of the few ecologically valid examinations of the development of tolerance.

Our study is one of the first to examine real-time subjective mood responses to smoking among adolescents who are still relatively early in their smoking careers and light or infrequent smokers (less than 9% of the sample smoked more than five cigarettes a day). As such, this study helps to add important information about the relatively early development of symptoms of dependence, a potential development of tolerance to the mood-regulating effects of smoking.

More potential applications of this class of models clearly exist in substance abuse and psychological research. For example, many questions of both normal development and the development of psychopathology address the issue of variability or stability in emotional responses to various situations and contexts. Often, an interest is with the variability of responses an individual gives to a variety of stimuli or situations, and not just with the overall mean level of responsivity. The models presented here also allow us to examine hypotheses about consistency of responses as well.

In order to reliably estimate variances, and the effects of covariates on these variances, a fair amount of both within-subjects and between-subjects data is required. Modern data collection procedures, such as EMA and real-time data captures, provide this opportunity. These procedures follow the "bursts of measurement" approach described by Nesselroade (1991). As noted by Nesselroade, such bursts of measurement increase the research burden in several ways; yet they are necessary for studying individual variation and allow researchers to examine important questions that were previously unanswerable. Along with these modern data collection procedures, it is useful to have statistical models that can effectively analyze the unique features of these datasets. Hopefully, this chapter has provided models for this purpose.

APPENDIX

Below are syntax samples for the two- and three-level mixed-effects location scale models. Expressions with all uppercase letters denote SAS-specific syntax, while expressions including lowercase letters are for user-defined entities. The dependent variable NAchange is the change in negative affect associated with a smoking event (now − before) and, for simplicity, we only consider the covariate Wave. The variable id is a subject-level identifier. For the random subject effects, u0 is the intercept and u1 is the trend across waves ("u" is used for the Greek upsilon of our equations), while omega is for the random scale effect.

The mean response model is given by mean, with regression coefficients named b0 and bWave. The model for the within-subjects (error) variance is denoted vare, with t0 for the reference variance (i.e., the variance when

Wave equals 0), in natural log units, and tWave as the coefficient for Wave. Finally, v0, v1, and vs represent the variances of the two random location and one random scale effects, with covariances c01, c0s, and c1s.

```
PROC NLMIXED GCONV=1e-12;
PARMS b0=-.3 bWave=.01 t0=.6 tWave=-.1
      v0=.2 v1=.1 vs=.005 c01=0 c0s=0 c1s=0;
mean = (b0 + u0) + (bWave + u1)*Wave;
vare = EXP(t0 + tWave*Wave + omega);
MODEL NAchange ~ NORMAL(mean,vare);
RANDOM u0 u1 omega ~ NORMAL([0,0,0], [v0,c01,v1,c0s,c1s,vs])
      SUBJECT=id;
```

Users must provide starting values for all parameters on the PARMS statement. To do so, it is beneficial to run the model in stages using estimates from a prior stage as starting values and setting the additional parameters to zero or some small value. For example, one can start by estimating a random-trend model using standard mixed model software to yield starting values for the fixed effects (β), random intercept variance (v0), random trend variance (v1), intercept-trend covariance (c01), and error variance (t0). Then, one can add covariates to the error variance model, perhaps one at a time, with starting values of zero. Finally, the full model with the parameters associated with the random scale effect (vs, c0s, c1s) can be estimated. In practice, this approach works well with PROC NLMIXED, which sometimes has difficulties in converging to a solution for complex models. Also, in our experience, it seems that specifying a small starting value for the random scale effect variance (vs) helps model convergence. Furthermore, for complex models, it is sometimes the case that the default convergence criterion is not strict enough. In the above syntax, the convergence criterion is specified as GCONV=1e-12 on the PROC NLMIXED statement. The results in this chapter did change a bit as this stricter criterion was applied, relative to the default specification; however, the results did not change beyond this level. It would seem that this level is reasonable; however, it probably should be examined on a case-by-case basis.

Three-Level Extension

PROC NLMIXED is set up for two-level models; however, it can be used for three-level analysis in some situations. Li (2010) developed a recursive conditional likelihood approach that can be used for this purpose. An alternative approach was described by Dale McLerran in a Web post at http://listserv.uga.edu/cgi-bin/wa?A2=ind0506b&L=sas-l&F=&S=&P=55. For the current example, we created four indicator variables for the four measurement waves, w1, w2, w3, and w4. These are then included in the mean model and specified as random effects (named below as d1, d2, d3, d4) with mean zero. Furthermore, they are constrained to have the same variance (vwave), and to be independent of each other and the subject random effects.

```
PROC NLMIXED GCONV=1e-12;
PARMS b0=-.3 bWave=.01 t0=.6 tWave=-.1
      v0=.2 v1=.1 vs=.005 vwave=.1 c01=0 c0s=0 c1s=0;
mean = (b0 + u0) + (bWave + u1)*Wave
       + d1*w1 + d2*w2 + d3*w3 + d4*w4;
vare = EXP(t0 + tWave*Wave + omega);
MODEL NAchange ~ NORMAL(mean,vare);
RANDOM u0 u1 omega d1 d2 d3 d4 ~ NORMAL([0,0,0,0,0,0,0],
       [v0,c01,v1,c0s,c1s,vs,
        0, 0, 0, vwave,
        0, 0, 0, 0, vwave,
        0, 0, 0, 0, 0, vwave,
        0, 0, 0, 0, 0, 0, vwave]) SUBJECT=id;
```

As noted by McLerran, the feasibility of this approach depends on the size of the problem because the number of random effects in the model can greatly increase the computational demands. In our case, with only four waves, including the random wave effect was not problematic, in and of itself. However, as noted in the chapter, once the random wave effect was included (vwave), the random subject wave variance (v1) went to zero, and so was removed from the final model.

ACKNOWLEDGMENTS

Thanks are due to Siu Chi Wong for assisting with data analysis.

This work was supported by National Cancer Institute Grant Nos. 5PO1 CA98262 and R21 CA140696.

REFERENCES

Aitkin, M. (1987). Modeling variance heterogeneity in normal regression using GLIM. *Applied Statistics, 36,* 332–339.

Begg, M. B., & Parides, M. K. (2003). Separation of individual-level and cluster-level covariate effects in regression analysis of correlated data. *Statistics in Medicine, 22,* 2591–2602.

Bolger, N., Davis, A., & Rafaeli, E. (2003). Diary methods: capturing life as it is lived. *Annual Review of Psychology, 54,* 579–616.

Chassin, L., Presson, C. C., Rose, J., & Sherman, S. J. (2007). What is addiction?: Age-related differences in the meaning of addiction. *Drug and Alcohol Dependence, 87,* 30–38.

Chinchilli, V. M., Esinhart, J. D., & Miller, W. G. (1995). Partial likelihood analysis of within-unit variances in repeated measurement experiments. *Biometrics, 51,* 205–216.

Cleveland, W., Denby, L., & Liu, C. (2002). Random scale effects (Bell Labs technical report). Retrieved from *http://cm.bell-labs.com/cm/ms/departments/sia/doc/randomscale.pdf.*

Davidian, M., & Carroll, R. (1987). Variance function estimation. *Journal of the American Statistical Association, 82,* 1079–1091.

Feldman Barrett, L., & Barrett, D. (2001). An introduction to computerized experience sampling in psychology. *Social Science Computer Review, 19,* 175–185.

Fowler, K., & Whitlock, M. C. (1999). The distribution of phenotypic variance with inbreeding. *Evolution, 53,* 1143–1156.

Harvey, A. C. (1976). Estimating regression models with multiplicative heteroscedasticity. *Econometrica, 44,* 461–465.

Hedeker. D. & Gibbons, R.D. (2006). *Longitudinal data analysis.* New York: Wiley.

Hedeker, D., Mermelstein, R. J., Berbaum, M. L., & Campbell, R. T. (2009). Modeling mood variation associated with smoking: An application of a heterogeneous mixed-effects model for analysis of ecological momentary assessment (EMA) data. *Addiction, 104,* 297–307.

Hedeker, D., Mermelstein, R. J., Demirtas, H. (2008). An application of a mixed-effects location scale model for analysis of Ecological Momentary Assessment (EMA) data. *Biometrics, 64,* 627–634.

Hertzog, C., & Nesselroade, J. R. (2003). Assessing psychological change in adulthood: an overview of methodological issues. *Psychology and Aging, 18,* 639–657.

Jahng, S., Wood, P. K., & Trull, T. J. (2008). Analysis of affective instability in ecological momentary assessment: Indices using successive difference and group comparison via multilevel modeling. *Psychological Methods, 13,* 354–375.

James, A. T., Venables, W. N., Dry, I. B., & Wiskich, J. T. (1994). Random effects and variances as a synthesis of nonlinear regression analysis of mitochondrial electron transport. *Biometrika, 81,* 219–235.

Kassel, J. D., & Hankin, B. L. (2006). Smoking and depression. In A. Steptoe (Ed.), *Depression and physical illness* (pp. 321–347). Cambridge, UK: Cambridge University Press.

Kassel, J. D., Stroud, L. R., & Paronis, C. A. (2003). Smoking, stress, and negative affect: Correlation, causation, and context across stages of smoking. *Psychological Bulletin, 129,* 270–304.

Khantzian, E. J. (1997). The self-medication hypothesis of substance use disorders: A reconsideration and recent applications. *Harvard Review of Psychiatry, 4,* 231–244.

Laird, N. M. (1988). Missing data in longitudinal studies. *Statistics in Medicine, 7,* 305–315.

Leckie, G. (2010). *Modelling the variance in multilevel models.* Colloquium presentation, Institute for Health Research and Policy, University of Illinois at Chicago.

Leonard, T. (1975). A Bayesian approach to the linear model with unequal variances. *Technometrics, 17,* 95–102.

Li, X. (2010). *A three-level mixed-effects location scale model with an application in ecological momentary assessment data.* Unpublished doctoral thesis, University of Illinois at Chicago, School of Public Health.

Lin, X., Raz, J., & Harlow, S. (1997). Linear mixed models with heterogeneous within-cluster variances, *Biometrics, 53,* 910–923.

Moghaddam, N. G., & Ferguson, E. (2007). Smoking, mood regulation, and personality: An event-sampling exploration of potential models and moderation. *Journal of Personality, 75,* 451–478.

Molenberghs, G. M., Thijs, H., Jansen, I., Beunckens, C., Kenward, M. G., Mallinckrodt, C., et al. (2004). Analyzing incomplete longitudinal clinical trial data. *Biostatistics, 5,* 445–464.

Myles, J. P., Price, G. M., Hunter, N., Day, M., & Duffy, S. W. (2003). A potentially useful distribution model for dietary intake data. *Public Health Nutrition, 6,* 513–519.

Nesselroade, J. R. (1991). The warp and woof of the developmental fabric. In R. Downs, L. Liben, & D. Palarmo (Eds.), *Visions of development, the environment, and aesthetics: The legacy of Joachim F. Wohlwill* (pp. 213–240). Hillside, NJ: Erlbaum.

Penner, L. A., Shiffman, S., Paty, J. A., & Fritzsche, B. A. (1994). Individual differences in intraperson variability in mood. *Journal of Personality and Social Psychology, 66,* 712–721.

Reno, R., & Rizza, R. (2003). Is volatility lognormal?: Evidence from Italian futures. *Physica A: Statistical Mechanics and its Applications, 322,* 620–628.

Rubin, D. B. (1976). Inference and missing data. *Biometrika, 63,* 581–592.

Schwartz, J. E., & Stone, A. (2007). The analysis of real-time momentary data: A practical guide. In: A. A. Stone, S. S. Shiffman, A, Atienza, & L. Nebeling (Eds.), *The science of real-time data capture: Self-report in health research* (pp. 76–113). Oxford, UK: Oxford University Press.

Scollon, C. N., Kim-Prieto, C., & Diener, E. (2003). Experience sampling: promises and pitfalls, strengths and weeknesses. *Journal of Happiness Studies, 4,* 5–34.

Shenk, T. M., White, G. C., & Burnhamb, K. P. (1998). Sampling-variance effects on detecting density dependence from temporal trends in natural populations. *Ecological Monographs, 68,* 445–463.

Smyth, J. M., & Stone, A. A. (2003). Ecological momentary assessment research in behavioral medicine. *Journal of Happiness Studies, 4,* 35–52.

Stone, A., & Shiffman, S. (1994). Ecological momentary assessment (EMA) in behavioral medicine. *Annals of Behavioral Medicine, 16,* 199–202.

Tiffany, S. T., Conklin, C. A., Shiffman, S., & Clayton, R. R. (2004). What can dependence theories tell us about assessing the emergence of tobacco dependence? *Addiction, 99,* 78–86.

Vasseur, H. (1999). Prediction of tropospheric scintillation on satellite links from radiosound data. *IEEE Transactions on Antennas and Propagation, 47,* 293–301.

Walls, T. A., & Schafer, J. L. (2006). *Models for intensive longitudinal data.* New York: Oxford University Press.

Watson, D., & Tellegen, A. (1985). Toward a consensual structure of mood. *Psychological Bulletin, 98,* 219–235.

Watson, D., Wiese, D., Vaidya, J., & Tellegen, A. (1999). The two general activation systems of affect: Structural findings, evolutional considerations, and psychobiological evidence. *Journal of Personality and Social Psychology, 76,* 820–838.

CHAPTER 4

TETHERING THEORY TO METHOD

Using Measures of Intraindividual Variability to Operationalize Individuals' Dynamic Characteristics

Nilam Ram
The Pennsylvania State University
Max Planck Institute for Human Development

David Conroy, Aaron Pincus, Amanda Hyde, and Lauren Molloy
The Pennsylvania State University

Within-person changes in behavior that manifest on relatively short timescales are indicative of, and can be used to, measure and model a variety of dynamic constructs. In particular, observations obtained from the same individuals at closely spaced intervals (e.g., seconds, minutes, hours, days, weeks) can be used as indicators of individuals' inherent capacity for change, or *dynamic characteristics*, and systematic patterns of change that describe behavioral transformations, or *dynamic processes* (Ram & Gerstorf, 2009). Intensive repeated-measures data are a central feature of diary, ecological momentary assessment (EMA), ambulatory, and other intensive longitudinal study designs wherein multiple reports or assessments are obtained over a relatively short span of time (e.g., Bolger, Davis, & Rafaeli, 2003; Csikszentmihalyi & Larson, 1987; Shiffman, Stone, & Hufford, 2008; Walls & Schafer, 2006). In this chapter, we illustrate how quantifications of intraindividual variability, as summaries of intensive repeated-measures data, can be used to examine dynamic characteristics. First, we introduce a set of *theories*/constructs (i.e., lability, diversity, polarity, complexity) that can be used to articulate individuals' capacity for change in many domains of inquiry (e.g., emotional experience, interpersonal behavior). Second, we review a set of *methods*/mathematical descriptions that, when applied to intensive repeated-measures data, can be used to quantify intraindividual variability. Third, we introduce a set of empirical *data* and illustrate how the set of theoretical constructs can be explicitly tethered to the mathematical descriptions of those data to examine individuals' dynamic characteristics. Finally, we highlight aspects of theory and study design that hold particular import for the tethering of dynamic constructs to intensive repeated-measures data.

THEORY: DYNAMIC CHARACTERISTICS

Across the domains of science, many theoretical frameworks have been developed to explain if, how, and when entities change. In statistical thermodynamics, for example, researchers search for the laws governing how particles (e.g., atoms, molecules) move in space and time, and how those movements differ in relation to control variables like temperature, volume, and pressure. Similarly, in the social and behavioral sciences, we search for general principles about how individuals' behaviors (used here as a general term encompassing thoughts, feelings, actions, perceptions, etc.) can change or be changed, and how the extent of those changes differ in relation to individuals' dispositions (e.g., personality) and features of the environment (e.g., social context).

Among the main building blocks of theory are the constructs that are used to describe specific behavioral phenomena. In our attempt to make meaning of the many theoretical constructs being used in our fields (the social and behavioral sciences) we have identified a subset of constructs that researchers use to describe individuals' inherent capacity or potential for behavioral change or stability–dynamic characteristics (Ram & Gerstorf, 2009). Connecting selected areas of the psychological literature to concepts used in the physical and biological sciences, we have homed in on a set of descriptors that provide a lexicon for defining and discussing individuals' capacities for change. Specifically, we forward a collection of terms (i.e., lability, diversity, polarity, complexity) that can, when applied to a particular behavior of interest, be used to communicate the essence of theoretically derived dynamic characteristics. For example, considered with respect to an individual's emotional states, *affective diversity* can be defined as the tendency of an individual to experience a variety of emotions (Ram, Gerstorf, Lindenberger, & Smith, 2011; Weiner, 2007; see correspondent definition of biodiversity; Morin, 1999). Conceptualized as "trait-like" descriptions, dynamic characteristics like affective diversity are generally considered fixed, inherent attributes of the individual. As with personality traits, cognitive abilities, or other dispositions, individuals can be described as having more or less of a given dynamic characteristic (e.g., more or less affective diversity). Hypotheses can be generated as to how these change-based characteristics are related to other between-person differences in characteristics and outcomes.

In sum, considered within a particular domain of behavior, many terms ending in *-ity* such as lability, diversity, and so on, can be used to label a set of theoretically defined constructs. In our substantive work, for instance, we are considering these descriptors in the context of individuals' emotional and interpersonal experiences and using them to define and examine a set of theoretically derived dynamic characteristics. Specifically, *emotional lability* describes individuals' proneness for fluctuation in intensity of an emotional state over time (Cattell, 1966; Eid & Deiner, 1999). For instance, an individual may be described as high in emotional lability if his or her sadness bounces around frequently from low to high during the course of a week. This could be thought of in contrast to emotional stability; for instance, somebody who consistently reports a similar level of sadness day after day. *Social diversity*, at the level of the individual, describes the tendency to engage with a variety of qualitatively different types of persons (e.g., friend, parent, roommate, supervisor). Similarly, *interpersonal behavior diversity* describes an individual's tendency to engage in a variety of different types of behaviors when interacting with others (e.g., dominant, submissive, agreeable, quarrelsome; see Moskowitz & Zuroff, 2004). *Affective polarity* is defined as the extent of mutual opposition between two opposite attributes: pleasant and unpleasant affect (see also Zautra, Affleck, Tennen, Reich, & Davis, 2005). *Socioemotional complexity* describes the extent to which interpersonal (evaluations of others) and intrapersonal (evaluations of self) aspects of individuals' social experiences cohere.

Of note, in much of the literature examining intraindividual variability, there has been a tendency to name the constructs being examined "intraindividual variability." In some cases it is not clear if the theoretical construct holds any more value than the observed variability. Ideally, theoretical constructs stand independent of specific indicators and models used to measure them. To highlight this concern we have purposively attempted to separate the definitions of the dynamic constructs listed above from the specific data and mathematical models that are used to render them operational. This is our attempt to encourage both the precise articulation of theoretical constructs, and the *explicit* use of "measurement models" (the quantifications of intraindividual variability) to render those theoretical constructs operational.

METHOD: MEASURES OF INTRAINDIVIDUAL VARIABILITY

Variation and covariation are among the main building blocks of statistical inquiry. Ensembles of scores are collected and their distributions described using measures of central tendency (e.g., mean), dispersion (e.g., variance), and association (e.g., covariance). These summaries of the data then serve as the basis for subsequent analysis and inferences. In intensive repeated-measures studies, repeated measurements are obtained from multiple individuals. The scores from each individual can be collected into its own ensemble—and the *intraindividual mean* of, *intraindividual variation* in, and *intraindividual covariation* among those scores described and examined. In this chapter we highlight that the person-level measures of dispersion and association provide the possibility to "measure" individuals' dynamic characteristics (Nesselroade, 1991).

For example, an *intraindividual standard deviation* (iSD), calculated on the ensemble of scores obtained from repeated measurements of a single individual, describes the extent to which the scores tend to differ from his or her mean score. A large iSD would indicate that the individual had a wide range of behaviors (e.g., high lability), whereas a small iSD would indicate a narrow range of behaviors (e.g., low lability). In essence the iSD quantifies the extent to which a person moves though a defined behavioral "space" (e.g., back and forth along a continuum of behavior). Calculated separately for each individual in the sample, the iSD (or other measures of dispersion) can be treated as a measure of interindividual differences in a capacity for change (e.g., lability) and can be examined in relation to other interindividual differences, including gender, personality, and other abilities or capacities using standard correlation, ANOVA, regression, and other between-person methods (see e.g., Jahng, Wood, & Trull, 2008; MacDonald, Hultsch, & Dixon, 2008; Ram & Gerstorf, 2009; Ram, Rabbitt, Stollery, & Nesselroade, 2005).

In addition to the iSD, many other measures of intraindividual variation and covariation can be used to describe how behaviors are dispersed in space—whether across a set of categories, along a line, in a plane, or within a multidimensional space. Measures of intraindividual variability for continuous variables (dispersion along a line) include the variance (iSD^2), root mean square, absolute range (max–min), interquartile range, median absolute deviation, mean difference, average deviation, coefficient of variation (variance/mean), signal-to-noise ratio (mean/variance), quartile coefficient of dispersion, and relative mean difference. Correspondent indices for count data (dispersion along a segmented line that begins at zero) include the index of dispersion (IDV; also called coefficient of dispersion or variance-to-mean ratio), and for categorical data (dispersion across categories) indices of qualitative variation (see Wilcox, 1973) and entropy statistics (Shannon, 1950; described later in this chapter). In some domains (e.g., human movement), skewness and kurtosis also provide useful indices for quantifying particular aspects of dispersion that can be tethered to specific dynamic characteristics (see Newell & Hancock, 1984).

Dynamic characteristics may also manifest as the amount or extent of association among multiple variables assessed in tandem—in intraindividual covariation (Fiske & Rice, 1955). The same operational principles used to quantify the dispersion along a single measure of behavior can be extended to quantifications of associations among multiple behavioral outcomes. Bivariate analogs to the univariate measures listed above would include the various within-person correlation coefficients (e.g., polychoric, Pearson) and, for categorical data, within-person odds ratios. Additionally, multilevel modeling has provided a useful framework for quantifying between-person differences in bivariate within-person associations using intraindividual regressions (see Bolger et al., 2003). Moving beyond two variables, multivariate intraindividual variation and covariation can be examined and quantified using P-technique analysis, wherein multivariate time-series obtained from single individuals are quantified during the application of data reduction methods (e.g., common factor models; Cattell, Cattell, & Rhymer, 1947) or other quantifications (e.g., network graphs; Fair et al., 2008). The obtained summary measures (e.g., number of principal components with large eigenvalues) provide an indication of the structure underlying individuals' behavior in multidimensional space. In sum, many of the methods and summary descriptors typically used to describe ensembles of data (e.g., variance, covariance) can be applied to repeated-measures data obtained from the same individual.

TETHERING DYNAMIC CHARACTERISTICS TO MEASURES OF INTRAINDIVIDUAL VARIABILITY

With dynamic characteristics, as with other constructs, a specific measurement model is used to render the construct operational. That is, there is an explicit tethering of the theoretical definition to the methodological procedures used to quantify the construct. Following our previous example, *affective diversity*—at the level of the individual—is defined as the tendency to experience a variety of qualitatively different feeling states (e.g., sadness, happiness, and anger). Some theories of emotion propose a core affect space defined by two dimensions, valence and activation (Posner, Russell, & Peterson, 2005). As an individual's feeling state changes over time, affective diversity manifests as the extent to which he or she "visits" different locations in the core affect space (locations on a geometric plane identified by their x = valence and y = activation coordinates). Thus, to render the construct operational we need to measure the extent to which those locations are dispersed around the space, or concentrated within a small zone of the space. Given the 2D space, we selected a measure of angular dispersion (spin) based on the circular standard deviation (equation given below) of the repeated measures of individuals' core affect (Kuppens, Van Mechelen, Nezlek, Dossche, & Timmermans, 2007). Using this measurement model we were able to quantify individual differences in affective diversity, and examine how it was related to other constructs (e.g., social diversity, personality).

In this chapter we illustrate how dynamic characteristics such as affective diversity can be operationalized using measures of intraindividual variability and examined in relation to a variety of interindividual differences (e.g., sex, personality, or other dispositions). Specifically, we measure *affective lability, social diversity, interpersonal behavior diversity, affective polarity,* and *socioemotional complexity* using quantifications of intraindividual variation and covariation (univariate, bivariate, and multivariate) as measurement models to summarize intensive repeated-measures data.

DATA-INTENSIVE REPEATED MEASURES

To illustrate a few of the possible intraindividual variability quantifications that can be tethered to dynamic characteristics, we introduce and make use of data from the Pennsylvania State University Affect Motivation and Interpersonal Behavior (PSU AMIB) study.

Participants

Participants were 190 undergraduate psychology students (66% female) from the Pennsylvania State University. They were between 18 and 54 years of age (Med_{Age} = 19, M_{Age} = 19.3, SD_{Age} = 2.8) and primarily in their first (61%) or second (25%) year of college. The majority indicated they were white (83%) with some representation of American Indian or Alaska Native (6%), Hispanic or Latino (5%), African American (3%), and Mixed or Other (3%) ethnicities. The sample might be considered representative of the student populations used in many laboratory-based psychological studies.

Procedure

Participants were recruited from the University's Psychology Department Participant Pool to take part in a 1-week experience sampling study for course credit during the Spring 2009 semester. Five cohorts of between 29 and 46 students began their participation by attending a 1½-hour introductory session in the evening at which they provided informed consent, were trained in the study procedures, and completed a Web-based questionnaire. Participants were given eight small booklets: one with an end-of-day questionnaire that would be completed during this introductory session, and seven with a series of eight interaction questionnaires to be completed immediately after interpersonal interactions they had throughout the day and an end-of day questionnaire to be completed shortly before going to bed. Care was taken that the definitions of terms, tasks, and our working model of an interpersonal interaction ("face-to-face interaction lasting 5 or more minutes") were clear and understood. At the conclusion of the session, participants completed a sample interaction report and the first end-of-day questionnaire. Over the course of the next week, participants completed the reports about their interpersonal interactions and end-of day questionnaires as they went about their daily lives. Each day, participants mailed completed booklets back to the research lab via campus mail. The speed and regularity at which the large quantity of booklets arrived back at the research office indicated that study procedures were followed well. In only a very few cases were problems encountered.

At Study Day 5, a subset ($n = 30$) of highly compliant participants (average of six or more interaction reports completed per day with no or very little missing data) were invited to continue participation for an additional 2 weeks for monetary compensation (up to $71.00 paid on an incremental scale based on number of days completed, $4.00 per booklet plus a $15.00 bonus for completing all booklets). The relatively large number of interpersonal interactions these "intensive" participants provided ($M = 140$, $SD = 31.3$, Min = 64, Max = 168) gave an opportunity to obtain estimates of reliability of our intraindividual variability measures and ask additional research questions that make use of analytic techniques requiring longer time series (e.g., P-technique factor analysis).

Occasions

The study was designed to obtain multi-timescale longitudinal data along a three-level hierarchy, interpersonal interactions nested within days nested within the 190 persons described above.

Persons. At the more macro level, individuals were described by a set of demographic (e.g., sex, age) and dispositional (e.g., motivation, personality) measures.

Days. From these 190 persons (main study), data were collected for a total of 1,498 person-days ($Med_{\text{\# of days}} = 8$, $M_{\text{\# of days}} = 7.67$, $SD_{\text{\# of days}} = 1.14$). Overall, data from 96% of the 1,520 possible persons-days were obtained (a 96% response rate), with 86.8% of participants ($n = 165$) completing all 8 days' worth of reports.

Social interactions. At the most micro level, participants provided data for a total of 7,591 social interactions. Data from the four individuals who did not provide data on at least 3 days, as well as that of two individuals who provided data on less than 10 total interactions, were removed. The remaining sample constituted 7,568 social interaction reports obtained from 184 participants who each provided data for between 10 and 56 interactions ($Med_{\text{\# of interactions}} = 43$, $M_{\text{\# of interactions}} = 43.1$, $SD_{\text{\# of interactions}} = 13.6$), with 75% reporting on more than 30 interactions across the 7-day protocol (the single social interaction reports obtained at the training session, called Day 0, were not used).

Measures

The multi-timescale design provided the opportunity to measure constructs at three levels of specificity: person level, day level, and interpersonal-interaction level.

Person level. Trait-like demographics and dispositions were measured once using a Web-based questionnaire. Demographic measures included age, sex, year in school, and race/ethnicity. Disposition measures included achievement motives (fear of failure, need for achievement), social desirability, trait self-conscious emotions (authentic pride, hubristic pride, shame, guilt), pathological narcissism (grandiosity, vulnerability), aggression (anger, hostility), emotion regulation styles (reappraisal, suppression), attachment (avoidance, anxiety), big five personality traits, interpersonal problem dispositions, self-theories of interpersonal flexibility (fixed, incremental), interpersonal dependency (exploitable, submissive, love), and interpersonal values (agentic, communal).

Day level. Day-level descriptions were obtained at the end of each day using the diary booklets. These reports included measures of participants' hours and quality of sleep, levels of physical activity, perceived stress, self-esteem, life satisfaction, state shame, guilt, and authentic and hubristic pride, a list of adjectives describing a variety of emotional and other states (i.e., *enthusiastic, calm, nervous, sluggish, happy, peaceful, embarrassed, sad, alert, satisfied, upset, bored, proud, relaxed, stress, depressed, excited, content, tense, disappointed, ashamed, relieved,* and *angry*), and whether the day had included an evaluative event (e.g., completion, submission, or delivery of an exam, assignment, presentation, or group project).

Social interaction level. Descriptions of participants' social interactions were provided in an event-contingent manner (i.e., self-initiated reporting after an interaction). These reports included descriptions of when the interaction occurred, the location and social setting, characteristics of the social partner (sex, status), how long and well they knew the partner, perceptions of the partner's behavior (agency, communion), and how participants themselves behaved (dominant, submissive, agreeable, quarrelsome) and felt (core affect, stress, physical health).

OPERATIONALIZING DYNAMIC CHARACTERISTICS

The nested design in the PSU AMIB study provided for the application of intraindividual variability-based "measurement-models," wherein the repeated measures were summarized into person-level or day-level scores. Specific to the examples included here, measures of central tendency, dispersion, and association were calculated and used as *person-level* operationalizations of individuals' dynamic characteristics.

Affective Lability (across Days)

In each end-of-day report participants indicated the degree to which they, "considering the day as a whole," had felt a number of feelings using a scale from 1 (did not feel this way at all) to 7 (felt this way strongly). The list of adjectives participants used to describe their daily experiences included 10 pleasant feelings (enthusiastic, happy, alert, proud, excited, calm, peaceful, satisfied, relaxed, content), and 10 unpleasant feelings (nervous, embarrassed, upset, stress, tense, sluggish, sad, bored, depressed, disappointed). For each participant on each day, responses were averaged separately across the positive and negative items, and an overall index of *affective experience* on that day was computed by subtracting the average of unpleasant feelings from the average of pleasant feelings (Carstensen et al., 2011). Person-level across-day affective *lability* was measured as the variability in their affective experiences across days 0 to 7. Specifically, we calculated *intraindividual standard deviation* (*iSD*) scores for each person as

$$iSD_i = \sqrt{\sigma_i^2} = \sqrt{\frac{1}{T-1}\sum_{t=1}^{T}(y_{ti} - \bar{y}_i)^2}.$$

Affective lability scores ($M = 1.34$, $SD = 0.66$) ranged from 0.23 (relatively "stable") to 4.59 (relatively "labile"). A selection of individual trajectories of affective experience is shown in Figure 4.1. Individuals in the left panel were characterized by low day-to-day affective lability, and individuals in the right panel by high affective lability.

Using the data from our 30 extended-study participants, we used bootstrapping principles to obtain an estimate of the reliability of the dispersion scores. Specifically, reliability was obtained by correlating the affective lability scores calculated on a randomly selected subset of 8 days of data for each person with scores calculated on all 22 days of data. Confidence intervals for reliability estimates were obtained using 1,000 resamples of the observed data, each obtained by random sampling with replacement (Yung & Chan, 1999; see also Ram et al., 2011). Reliability of the affective lability scores was $r = .80$ (95% confidence interval [CI] = .60, .90). For comparison, reliability of the corresponding intraindividual means was $r = .89$ (95% CI = .81, .94).

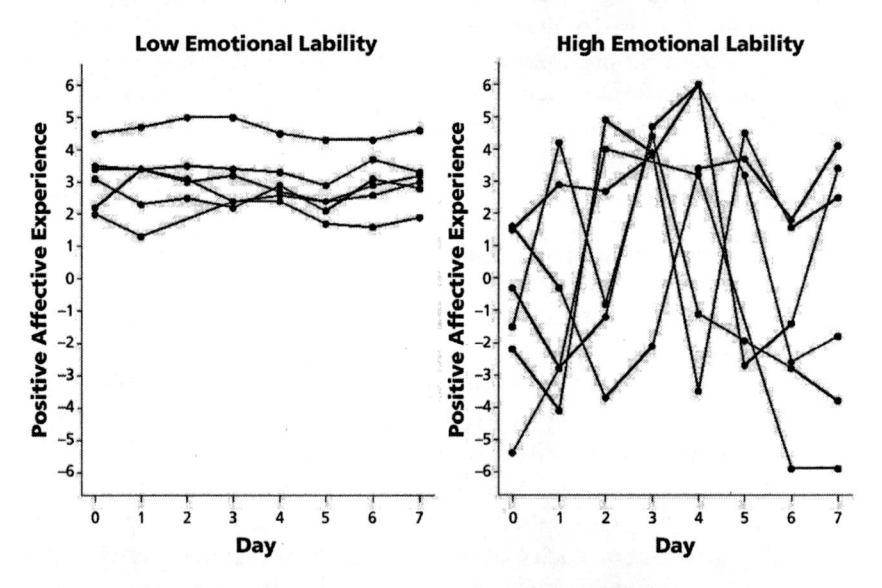

Figure 4.1 A selection of individual trajectories of *affective experience* across 8 days. Measured using an intraindividual standard deviation, the six individuals in the left panel were characterized by *low affective lability*, and the six individuals in the right panel by *high affective lability*.

Of note, compared to the rest of the sample ($n = 160$) the extended-study subsample ($n = 30$) was, on average, a bit less far along in years of school, $F(1,188) = 3.94$, $p = .049$, and higher on the hiding-of-self subscale of the PNI (Pincus et al., 2009), $F(1,188) = 4.60$, $p = .033$, the HI subscale, $F(1,186) = 7.63$, $p = .006$, and the JK subscale, $F(1,184) = 7.11$, $p = .008$, of the IIPSC (Hopwood, Pincus, DeMoor, & Koonce, 2008), and the submissive dependency subscale of the VDI (Pincus & Wilson, 2001), $F(1,183) = 7.8$, $p = .006$. They did not differ with respect to any other of the measured demographics or dispositional inventories, $Fs < 3.55$, $ps > .05$. Given the small number and unpatterned nature of differences, we treated the intensive participants as representative of the larger sample.

Interpersonal Behavior Diversity (across Social Interactions)

After each interaction, individuals indicated whether or not they had engaged in any of 12 agentic (dominant vs. submissive) and communal (agreeable vs. quarrelsome) behaviors during the interaction using the Social Behavior Inventory (SBI; Moskowitz, 1994). As per usual SBI scoring procedures, responses were tallied, normalized at the individual level (i.e., ipsatized; see Moskowitz & Zuroff, 2004) and placed in the two-dimensional (2D) interpersonal behavior space defined by orthogonal *Agency* and *Communion* dimensions. A selection of individual trajectories in this 2D space is shown in Figure 4.2. As seen in the plots, the behaviors of the two individuals in the left panel of the figure were concentrated in the upper right portion of the space, while the behaviors of the two individuals in the right panel were more dispersed around the entire space. Following the underlying circumplex-based theory of interpersonal behavior (Pincus & Gurtman, 2003), the location of each observation in the 2D space was then converted from Cartesian coordinates, X and Y, to polar coordinates, vector lengths, r, and vector angles, θ. The extent of an individual's *interpersonal behavior diversity* was then quantified as the dispersion of the vector angles (circular intraindividual standard deviation or *spin*; definitions and rationale of measure given in Moskowitz & Zuroff, 2004, 2005; specifics of the calculations follow Mardia, 1972). Specifically,

$$Spin_i = \sqrt{-2\ln\frac{\mathbf{R}_i}{T}}$$

where $\mathbf{R}_i$ is the resultant vector of all observations for one individual (see also Kuppens et al., 2007). Spin scores, our measure of interpersonal be-

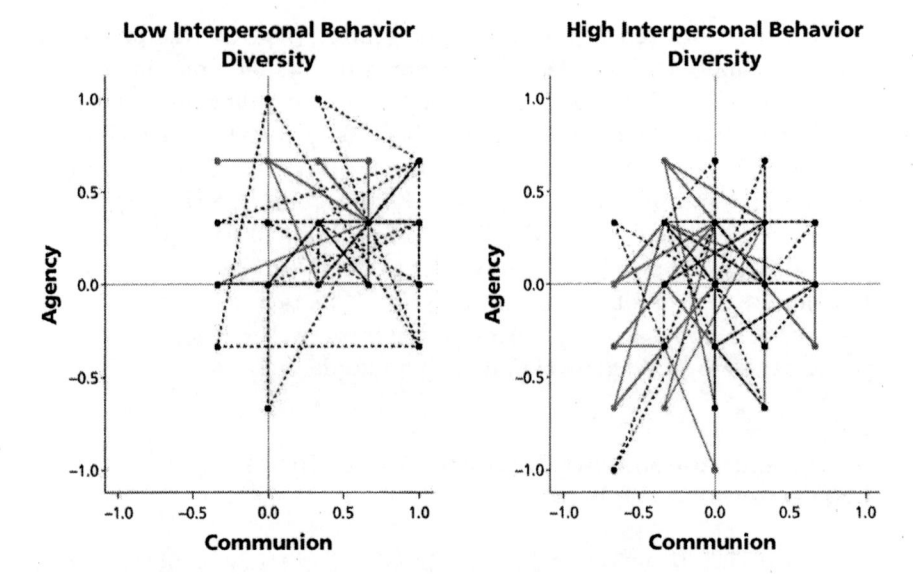

Figure 4.2 A selection of individual trajectories of *interpersonal behavior* in the two-dimensional plane defined by agency and communion. Measured using an angular dispersion (i.e., spin) score, the two individuals (solid gray line and dashed black line) were characterized by low *diversity* (behaviors located primarily in the upper right area of the space), while the two individuals in the right panel were characterized by high *diversity* (behaviors located in all areas of the space).

havior diversity, ranged from 0.69 to 2.65 on a scale that goes from 0 to $+\infty$ ($M = 1.60$, $SD = .32$).

Reliability was obtained using the same bootstrapping procedure outlined above, but with diversity scores calculated on a randomly selected subset of 43 observations per person (mean number of observations for the 8-day participants = 43.1) correlated with scores calculated on all available data, again using 1,000 resamples obtained by random sampling with replacement. Reliability of the interpersonal behavior diversity scores was estimated as $r = .87$ (95% CI = .77, .93).

Social Diversity (across Social Interactions)

Participants also indicated who they interacted with by classifying each interaction partner into one of 10 categories (supervisor/instructor, coworker, supervisee, friend, casual acquaintance, romantic partner, parent, sibling, roommate, other). Histograms for four individuals' reports of the types of social partners they interacted with during the study are shown in Figure 4.3. As can be seen, the two individuals in the left panels interacted primarily with one type of person (friend), while the two individuals in the right panels interacted with a wide variety of types of persons. The diversity of an individual's social partners was summarized within-person using *Shannon's* (1950) *entropy*, a measure of dispersion across categories, and often used in quantifications of biodiversity (Morin, 1999). Specifically, dispersion across categories was calculated as

$$Entropy_i = -\frac{1}{\ln m} \sum_{j=1}^{m} p_{ij} \ln p_{ij}$$

where the *entropy* score for person i is a function of the proportions, p_j, of the repeated observations that were in category j (where $j = 1$ to m catego-

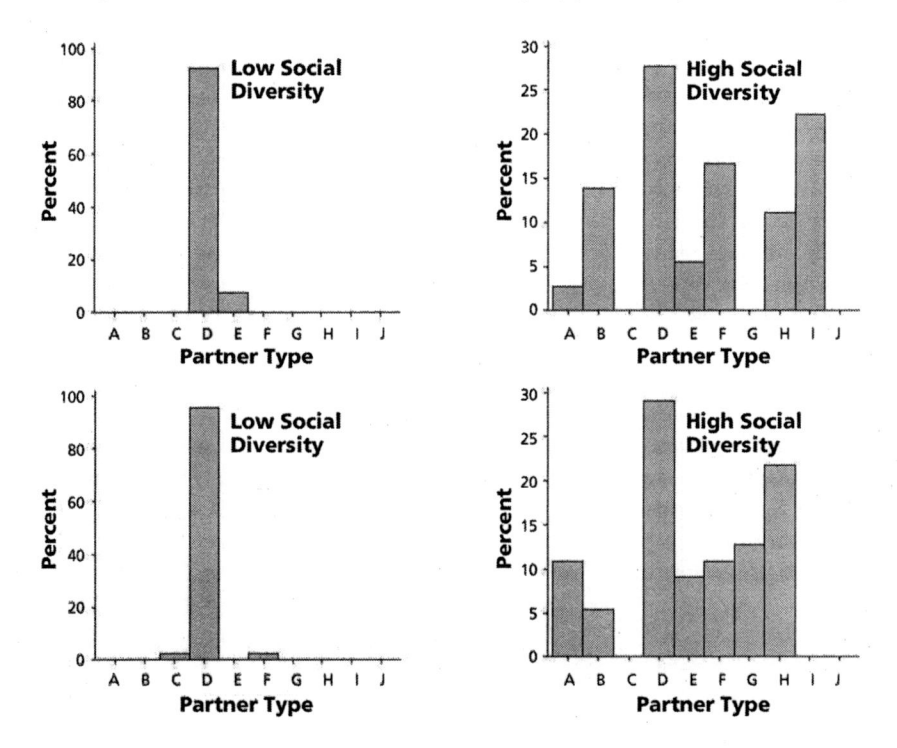

Figure 4.3 Histograms for the four individuals' reports of the *types of social partners* they interacted with during the study (A, supervisor/instructor; B, coworker; C, supervisee; D, friend; E, casual acquaintance; F, romantic partner; G, parent; H, sibling; I, roommate; J, other). As measured using an entropy statistic, the two individuals depicted in the left panels were characterized by low *social diversity* (primarily interacted with only one type of person), whereas the two individuals in the right panel were characterized by high *social diversity* (interactions dispersed across many types of persons).

ries), scaled so that scores range from 0.00 (all observations in a single category = no diversity) to 1.00 (equal number of observations in each of the j categories = complete diversity). Entropy scores, as a measure of individuals' diversity of social partners, ranged from 0.09 to 0.79 ($M = 0.43$, $SD = .14$). Using the bootstrapping procedure on the data from our 30 extended-study participants, reliability was estimated as $r = .86$ (95% CI = .75, .93).

Affective Polarity (across Days)

As noted above, participants provided daily reports about both pleasant and unpleasant feelings. In physics, *polarity* is defined as the extent of mutual opposition between two opposite attributes; in other words, the extent of negative association (e.g., correlation) between the two attributes. As such, affective polarity was quantified as the extent of negative association between an individual's pleasant and unpleasant affect across days (see also Zautra et al., 2005). Placed within a multilevel modeling framework for efficiency and precision, the measure of association between pleasant and unpleasant states took the form of a person-specific regression coefficient. Specifically, interindividual differences in affective polarity were extracted from the data using a typical two-level model with occasions nested within persons. The repeated observations were modeled at the individual level as

$$Y_{ti} = \beta_{0i} + \beta_{1i} X_{ti} + e_{ti}$$

where Y_{ti} is individual i's unpleasant affect score on day t; β_{0i} represents the individual's estimated base level of unpleasant affect; β_{1i}, the parameter of greatest interest, represents the within-person, across-day association between X_{ti}, the repeated observations of pleasant affect; and Y_{ti}, the repeated observations of unpleasant affect, and e_{ti} are residual errors. Collecting the individual-level estimates at the between-person level,

$$\beta_{0i} = \gamma_{00} + u_{0i}$$
$$\beta_{1i} = \gamma_{10} + u_{1i}$$

provides a simple framework for "calculating" and examining interindividual differences, u_{1i}s, in the within-person associations, β_{1i}s, that represent the construct of interest. Measured in this way, *affective polarity* scores ranged from –1.26 to –0.10 ($M = -0.45$, $SD = 0.20$). Individual-level plots of the bivariate relation between daily reports of positive and negative affect are shown in Figure 4.4. Individuals in the left panel had relatively low affective polarity, while individuals in the right panel had relatively high affective polarity. Using the bootstrapping procedure on the data from our

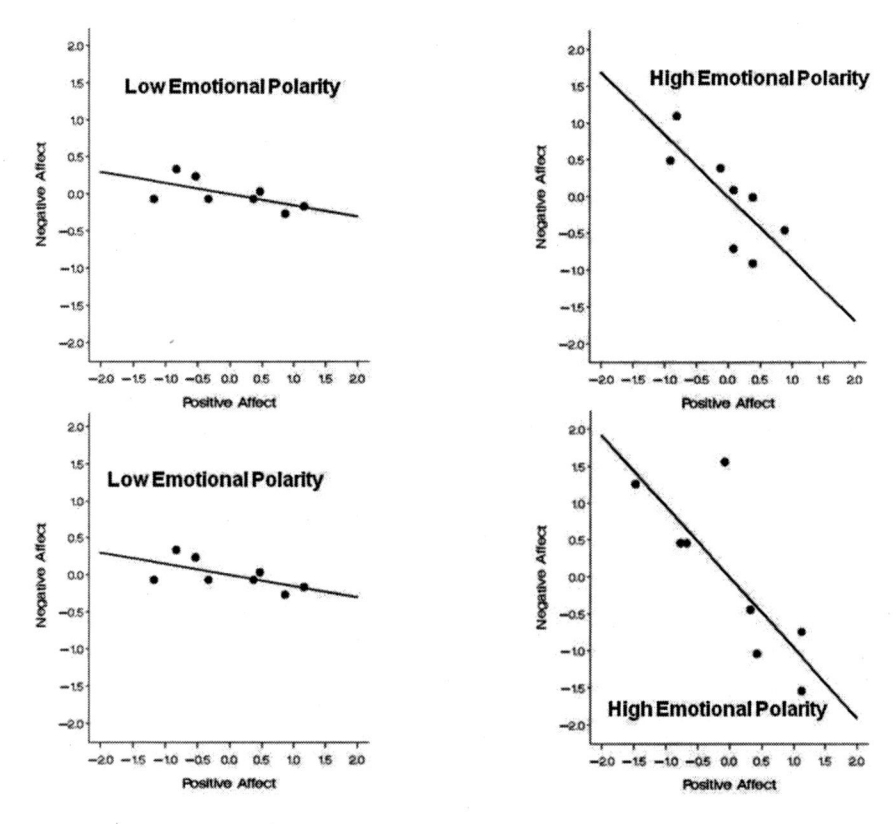

Figure 4.4 Individual-level regression plots showing the extent of within-person association between daily reports of *pleasant* and *unpleasant* affect. The within-person association, as a measure of *affective polarity*, was relatively low for the two individuals shown in the left panels, and relatively high for the two individuals shown in the right panels.

30 extended-study participants, reliability was estimated as $r = .68$ (95% CI = .42, .82). Due to the difficulty of estimating variance components in the multilevel model with such a small ($n = 30$) sample, this estimate is based on the intraindividual correlations (rather than the regressions) of negative and positive affect.

Socioemotional Complexity (across Social Interactions)

Immediately after each social interaction, participants provided ratings on eight items that assessed their core affect (valence and arousal) (Affect Grid; Russell, Weiss, & Mendelsohn, 1989), interpersonal behavior (agency and communion) (SBI; Moskowitz, 1994), perceptions of their social partner (agency and communion) (Interpersonal Grid; Moskowitz & Zuroff, 2005), and levels of stress and physical health (e.g., "How stressed out were you?"). Building from definitions of emotional complexity (e.g., Wessman & Ricks, 1966), the *socioemotional complexity* of an individual's social experiences was conceptualized as the extent to which all indices of experience and behavior covaried across his or her interpersonal interactions. To obtain a person-level summary measure of complexity among multiple (i.e., eight) variables, we fitted a P-technique factor analysis model separately to each person's data (see Brose & Ram, 2012, for a step-by-step primer). Specifically, the common factor model was applied to each multivariate single-participant time series (an occasions × variables matrix of scores),

$$y(t) = \lambda \eta(t) + \varepsilon(t)$$

where $y(t)$ is a p-variate time-series of observations (vectors) indexed by time ($t = 1, 2, \ldots, T$), λ is a $p \times q$ factor loading matrix, $\eta(t)$ is a q-variate time series of latent factor scores, and $\varepsilon(t)$ is a p-variate residual (specific error + measurement error) time series. The number of factors (q) determined as the number of eigenvalues ≥ 1 (Guttman, 1954) was used as a measure of an individual's complexity (see, e.g., Carstensen, Pasupathi, Mayr, & Nesselroade, 2000). Following this procedure, socioemotional complexity scores ranged from 2 to 4. However, when examining reliability of scores in our 30 extended-study sample, there was effectively no correspondence between the number of factors needed to represent the shorter (43 observation) time series and the longer ($M_{observations} = 140$, $SD = 31.3$) time series, $\kappa = 0.12$ (95% CI = –.21, .41). Thus, we only examined socioemotional complexity for the extended-study participants, using their relatively longer time series ($M_{observations} = 140$, $SD = 31.3$), which were at least closer to the recommended 100-observation minimum for factor analysis (Gorsuch, 1983). Of these 30 participants, 4 (13.33%), 19 (63.33%), and 7 (23.33%) were assigned complexity scores of 2, 3, and 4, respectively. Trajectories for socioemotional aspects of two individuals' social interactions are shown in Figure 4.5. The individual shown in the upper panel was characterized by two factors (i.e., low socioemotional complexity), and the individual shown in the upper panel was characterized by four factors (i.e., high socioemotional complexity).

INTERINDIVIDUAL DIFFERENCES IN DYNAMIC CHARACTERISTICS

Once the dynamic characteristics of interest have been operationalized and measured, the analysis shifts to a familiar examination of how the interin-

[Figure: two panels showing intensity trajectories over Social Interaction # from 0 to 170. Upper panel labeled "Low Socio-Emotional Complexity"; lower panel labeled "High Socio-Emotional Complexity".]

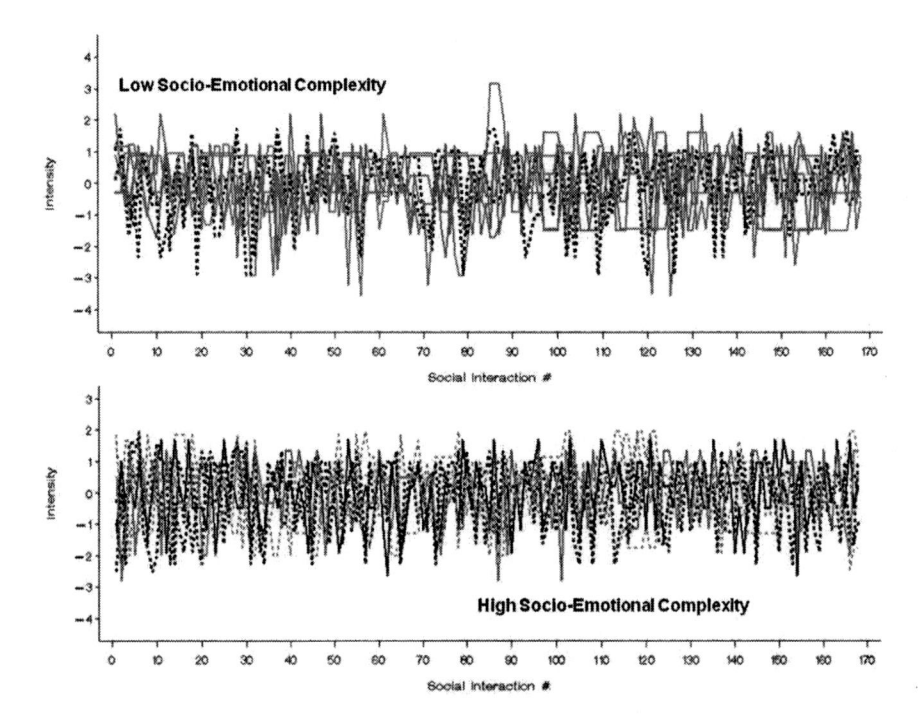

Figure 4.5 Trajectories for socioemotional aspects of two individuals' social interactions. Complexity, operationalized as the number of P-technique factors used to capture the structure of the data, is depicted by the number of different types of lines used to represent the occasion-to-occasion changes in eight variables (agentic and communal aspects of interpersonal behavior, agentic and communal aspects of interpersonal behavior, valence and activation dimensions of core affect, and stress and health). The individual shown in the upper panel was characterized by two factors (gray solid line and dashed black line), low socioemotional complexity, and the individual shown in the upper panel was characterized by four factors (gray dashed, gray solid, black dashed, and black solid), high socioemotional complexity.

dividual differences in those characteristics are related to one another and other dispositional tendencies (e.g., personality traits) using standard between-person methods (e.g., correlations, analysis of variance, regression). Below, we provide several examples of how one might explore interindividual differences in dynamic characteristics. Note that our interest with the following examples is not to reach formative substantive conclusions, but to demonstrate and illustrate how the intraindividual variability measures, which are in principle highly similar to the composite scores calculated for multi-item assessment batteries, may be used to operationalize and examine interindividual differences in individuals' dynamic characteristics—another layer of hypothesis testing. Illustrative purposes notwithstanding, we provide a brief theoretical introduction to each hypothesis test to reinforce our assertion that applications of these methods should be guided by clear and coherent substantive theory.

Application 1: Gender Differences in Affective Lability

Individual differences in affective lability are prominent features in many psychiatric disorders as well as being risk factors for cigarette smoking escalation and alcohol- and marijuana-related problems (American Psychiatric Association, 2000; Simons & Carey, 2006; Weinstein, Mermelstein, Shiffman, & Flay, 2008). Although sex differences in these disorders and problem behaviors have been documented, evidence for sex differences in affective lability is limited and largely equivocal. For example, depressed women report greater affective lability in general than depressed men, but college-aged men and women do not differ in affective lability (Dvorak & Simons, 2008; Winkler et al., 2004). Unfortunately, these limited findings are often based on retrospective self-reports of lability, which are known to be less valid than lability measures abstracted from intensive data collection (Anestis et al., 2010). Using data from the PSU AMIB study, we illustrate how sex differences in affective lability can be evaluated more validly using intensive, repeated-measures data. We hypothesized that women would exhibit greater affective lability than men.

As described above, affective lability was operationalized using the intraindividual standard deviation (iSD) of daily levels of affective experience. Men and women differed statistically significantly in their average affective lability $F(1,184) = 6.75$, $p = .01$. On average, men's daily reports of affective experience were characterized by less lability than were women's (men: $M = 1.17$, $SD = 0.58$; women: $M = 1.43$, $SD = 0.68$), $d = 0.41$.

Application 2: Linking Social Diversity and Diversity of Interpersonal Behavior

Individuals exhibiting high social diversity interact with a mix of others, ranging from intimate partners to complete strangers across a variety of settings. Some settings and interactions are more formal than others (a doctor's visit vs. morning coffee with one's spouse), more unfamiliar than others (interacting with a complete stranger vs. interacting with a longtime friend), and so forth. Buss (1989) proposed that situations vary in ways that impact the role of personality (vs. situational factors) in driving our behaviors. He proposed that situations have a strong impact on behavior (i.e., reduce variability) when they are formal, public, novel, have explicit culturally defined rules or norms, and provide few options for how one behaves. In contrast, characteristics of the person have a strong impact on behavior (i.e., allowing for greater variability) when situations are informal, private, familiar, have few explicit rules or norms, and provide many choices for how one behaves. By definition, individuals with low social diversity tended to interact with the same type of person over and over (in the AMIB sample, most often a friend). Such a pattern likely translates to consistently familiar, informal settings that allow for greater influence of the person on behavior. In contrast, individuals with high social diversity report engaging in a wider variety of behaviors. This pattern of reporting likely reflects a tendency for greater situational influences and more formalized and normative patterns of social behavior. We hypothesized that social diversity would be inversely related to interpersonal behavior diversity in a sample that was saturated with friend-to-friend interactions.

Among the variables characterizing individuals' social experiences was a categorical variable describing types of partners and a circumplex-based measure of interpersonal behavior. Dispersion for the former was quantified using an entropy statistic and the latter using a circular standard deviation (i.e., spin). These two person-level operationalizations of social diversity and interpersonal behavior diversity were negatively correlated, $r = -.19$, $p = .01$, suggesting that individuals who tended to interact with a less diverse set of social partners tended to engage in a more diverse set of interpersonal behaviors with those partners. It is not clear that this trend would hold in a sample where there was low social diversity based exclusively within, for instance, an employment setting (e.g., supervisor-supervisee) as might be of interest to industrial/organizational psychologists. Our results highlight the need to carefully consider the sampling frame when interpreting measures of dispersion.

Application 3: Extraversion as a Moderator of Affective Polarity

The latent structure of people's feeling states, or core affect, has long been controversial (Feldman Barrett & Russell, 1999b). Some evidence suggests that pleasant and unpleasant feelings are opposite affective states, and other evidence suggests that these feelings are independent dimensions of affect (for a review, see Feldman Barrett & Russell, 1999a). Several studies have examined this issue from an intraindividual perspective by testing within-person associations between pleasant and unpleasant feelings, and it is apparent that substantial variation exists in the magnitude of these associations (for a review, see Russell & Carroll, 1999). This finding raises the possibility that the bipolarity of affect ratings reflect an individual difference. From a personality perspective, individual differences in the bipolarity of pleasant and unpleasant feelings may reflect dispositional characteristics (e.g., extraversion, neuroticism; Warr, Barter, & Brownbridge, 1983) that influence people's sensitivity to pleasant and unpleasant daily events. For this illustration, we hypothesized that extraversion would influence people's sensitivity to positive daily events and therefore be associated with greater bipolarity of their feelings. To test for moderation, we expanded out the multilevel model to include extraversion as a between-person predictor (at level 2).

Affective polarity was operationalized as the extent of a negative within-person association between pleasant and unpleasant affect through a standard multilevel model. Controlling for individuals' mean levels of pleasant affect, affective polarity was moderated by trait extraversion (as measured using the Big Five Inventory–Short Version; Rammstedt & John, 2007) such that greater extraversion was associated with more extreme polarity, $\gamma_{11} = -0.06$, $p = .03$ (see, e.g., Schwartz & Stone, 2007, for model setup).

Application 4: Differences in Socioemotional Complexity and Attachment

Theories of personality development converge in the emphasis on the primacy of early attachment and its subsequent impact of social, cognitive, and relational functioning through the development of adult attachment styles (Cassidy, 1999; Horowitz, 2004; Luyten & Blatt, 2011). Attachment is undergirded by social-cognitive schemas that guide the organization of new relational experiences (Bretherton & Munholland, 2008). The capacity to differentiate aspects of experience and integrate them in a higher-order way is a hallmark of maturing personality functioning that is facilitated by secure attachment (e.g., Blatt, Auerbach, & Levy, 1997; Kernberg, 1984; Lukowitsky & Pincus, in press; Mahler, Pine, & Bergman, 1975). This led us to hypothesize that individual differences in socioemotional complexity calculated here would be inversely related to insecure attachment, such that low complexity reflects reliance on immature social-cognitive schemas and lower capacity for differentiation and higher-order integration of experience.

Individuals from our extended-study sample ($n = 30$) were categorized into socioemotional complexity groups based on the number of eigenvalues ≥ 1 that emerged during the fitting of P-technique factor analysis models to the eight-variable multivariate social interaction-level data noted above (i.e., core affect, interpersonal behavior, perceptions of the social partner, and stress and physical health). There were statistically significant differences between groups on average levels of attachment anxiety, $F(2,27) = 3.50$,

$p = .04$, but not on attachment avoidance, $F(2,27) = 0.74$, $p = .48$ (as measured using the Experience in Close Relationships Scale–Short Form; Wei, Russel, Mallinckrodt, & Vogel, 2007). Individuals with two-factor socioemotional complexity had the highest attachment anxiety ($M = 4.75$, $SD = 1.23$), followed by those with three-factor complexity ($M = 3.80$, $SD = 1.12$) and those with four-factor complexity ($M = 2.90$, $SD = 1.03$).

DISCUSSION

These examinations of interindividual differences in dynamic characteristics are intentionally simple and straightforward. Together they illustrate how capacities for change—theoretical constructs rendered operational using quantifications of intraindividual variation and covariation in intensive repeated-measures data—can be usefully placed and examined within usual interindividual differences frameworks. In our exploration of how construct definitions, measures of dispersion and association, and study design contribute to empirical investigation, we have noted that when working with intraindividual variability concepts, there is much to be gained from explicitly tethering the underlying theory, methods, and data in ways that promote further precision in our articulation of *timescale, model assumptions,* and *study design.*

Theory: Defining the Timescale

We have homed in on a lexicon of terms ending in *-ity* that are often used to identify constructs that describe individuals' inherent capacity or potential for behavioral change or stability–dynamic characteristics (Ram & Gerstorf, 2009). Descriptors (e.g., lability, diversity, polarity, complexity) are attached to content areas (e.g., affect, interpersonal behavior) to communicate the essence of theoretically derived dynamic characteristics. However, these descriptions, including our own, are limited in that they do not additionally identify the timescale on which the constructs manifest. For example, it is ambiguous if the construct *affective lability* pertains to changes in affective states that occur at the minute-to-minute, hour-to-hour, or day-to-day timescale. Operationalized at the day-to-day timescale, the intraindividual standard deviation does not inform us about affective lability that manifests at the hour-to-hour timescale.

Theory abounds with descriptions of dynamic characteristics. However, rarely are these descriptions or definitions precise with regard to the timescale on which individuals' capacity or tendency to change will manifest. Consider the concept of psychic splitting (vs. integration) in borderline personality disorder (BPD), which is considered an indication of the persistence of an immature cognitive coping or defense mechanism (Kernberg, 1984). Over the course of normal social-cognitive development, children shift from an inability to hold mixed feelings about the same object or person (e.g., self, other) to increased capacity to integrate their feelings and attributions (Harter, 2006). Prior to this cognitive development, young children tend to separate disparate attributions (e.g., Joe cannot be my best friend if I am angry at him). Once integrative capacity emerges, the child can hold two attributions simultaneously (e.g., Joe is my best friend, but I am mad he broke my toy). When normal integrative capacity fails to develop in adulthood, this is referred to as "splitting" and is associated with BPD (Clarkin, Yeomans, & Kernberg, 2006). Because of splitting, BPD patients are described as having chaotic emotions and interpersonal relationships characterized by variation among good (pleasant affects linked with positive attributions about the self and other) and bad (unpleasant affects linked with negative attributions about the self and other) states that impair their functioning and give rise to a variety of impulsive behaviors. Although the theory is rather refined, difficulties arise in tethering the theoretical concept of splitting to measures of intraindividual variability because the timescale is not explicitly defined. Variations at the minute-to-minute, day-to-day, and week-to-week timescales are all referred to as splitting in the clinical literature. As this and other work move forward it will become necessary to explicitly tie the resulting examinations of intraindividual variability (e.g., affect in BPD) to specific timescales, and thereby address the potential confounds and limitations in the theoretical definitions of dynamic constructs (see, e.g., Trull et al., 2008).

Method: Attention to Model Assumptions

In our examples, the dynamic characteristics were operationalized using straightforward calculations of dispersion or association that described particular aspects of individuals' data streams. In much the same manner that responses to multiple items are summarized as a composite, factor, or theta (in IRT) score, the repeated measurements (analogous to multiple items) are summarized as an intraindividual variability or covariation score.

As with other forms of measurement, among the key issues that must be considered are the underlying assumptions of the "measurement" models. For example, factor and IRT models usually assume that the observations obtained from multiple individuals are *independent and identically distributed*. Similarly, when calculating and using an intraindividual standard deviation, it is assumed that the repeated measures obtained from each individual are independent and identically distributed. This assumption may often run counter to basic ideas regarding individuals' occasion-to-occasion continuity (Baltes, Lindenberger, & Staudinger, 2006). Precise application of all of the measures demonstrated with our example data rests on assumptions that the order of responses is immaterial (i.e., that there are no within-person time-related trends), and that behavior at any occasion t is not affected by or related to the behavior at $t-1$ or at any other prior or future occasion. Such dependencies in the data, which we have described elsewhere as *time-structured intraindividual variability*, should be removed, and dispersion measures should be calculated on the remaining or residual *net intraindividual variability* (Ram & Gerstorf, 2009).

In our data, preliminary inspections of the time-series data did not reveal systematic time-related trends or lags (see Craigmile, Perrugia, & Van Zandt, 2010; Shumway & Stoffer, 2006). However, the data preprocessing steps needed to ensure that the data meet the model assumptions were constrained by the very data they were being applied to. For example, the single-subject time series may simply have been too short and thus did not provide enough power to identify systematic patterns of change (e.g., autocorrelation). Similarly, the measurement instruments and response scales may have been too granular (binary-, 5-, or 7-point vs. truly continuous response scales) and thus were not sensitive enough to capture subtle patterns of change.

Data: Considerations for Study Design

In many of the EMA studies conducted to date, it is likely that the data collection designs have similarly constrained our ability to identify and study the nuances of time-structured variability. It is for this very reason that we have explored and promote the potential that quantifications of *net* intraindividual variability (or data treated as net) hold for examination of individuals' dynamic characteristics. Data always put constraints on and provide affordances for particular kinds of examinations. The data used here provide opportunities to examine dynamic characteristics. As researchers integrate technological advances into their data collections, there will likely be more opportunities and greater power to identify/model time-structured intraindividual variability and to investigate the dynamic processes embedded there (Ebner-Priemer, Eid, Kleindienst, Stabenow, & Trull, 2009; Mehl & Conner, 2012; Shiffman et al., 2008; Walls & Schafer, 2006). We highlight two aspects of design that have become increasingly relevant as more and more data collections incorporate and make use of real-time digital technology.

Response scales. Self-report instruments have typically used multi-item scales and Likert-type response scales. The dataset used here, for instance, assessed pleasant and unpleasant feeling states using a total of 20 items with 7-point response scales. Subtle occasion-to-occasion changes may be lost during the construction of summary scales (averaging across items) or never obtained because of the granularity of the response scale. For example, when occasion-to-occasion changes are not so large as to prompt individuals to move their response to the next higher or lower category, the granularity of the response scale may be inadvertently imposing a limit on what constitutes "meaningful" change. Digital technologies allow for implementation and automated scoring of visual analogue response scales, the benefits of which are well known (Latti, Guthrie, & Ward, 2010; Wewers & Lowe, 1990). Obtained on a continuous response scale, the resulting scores provide additional opportunities for separating stability and error, identifying subtle patterns of change, and obtaining fine-grained quantifications of both time-structured and net intraindividual variability (including the precise shape of the underlying distributions that feed into indices of dispersion). Furthermore, there do not seem to be any substantial costs associated with moving from Likert-type multicategory response options to the continuous scale. The scores, which are only constrained by screen resolution and sensitivities, can be "degraded" in resolution (e.g., a 0–100 scale can be reduced to a 0–10 or 1–5 scale) Programming costs are no more or less than implementations of other types of response formats. Following the lead of other proponents of EMA approaches (see, e.g., Shiffman et al., 2008), we suggest that, as researchers adapt their items for use in intensive repeated-measures studies, they consider visual "digital" scales as truly viable alternatives to the 5-, 7-, and even 10+-point scales that were used in measures' original construction.

Persons/occasions tradeoff. A glance at the literature suggests that diary and EMA designs are obtaining more and more measurements from their participants. Certainly the within-person tracking of social-network communications and Internet browsing activity done by Facebook, Google, and other institutions is producing incredible streams of intraindividual data. The power of such designs is housed in the repeated measurements—the sampling of the same person's behavior across many contexts and on many occasions. Primary concerns for generalizeability are shifting from descriptions of the prototypical or average behavior toward "personalized" experiences and behavior (e.g., personalized medicine). In the PSU AMIB study, we began by obtaining 8 days of reports from a rather homogenous sample of 190 persons incentivized by course credit. Thirty participants were then invited to provide an additional 14 days of data for a modest monetary reward. Several benefits may be derived from such a "planned missingness" design. Between-person power and generalizability across persons is derived from the 190-person sample. Within-person power and generalizability across contexts and occasions is derived from the relatively longer time-series data obtained from the 30-person subsample. Put together, the data are useful for assessing the generalizability across both persons and occasions. For example, using bootstrapping principles, we can make an informed assessment about the reliability of our intraindividual variability measures by comparing the scores calculated from a relatively smaller set of observations obtained over random subsets of observations with those calculated from the relatively larger set of observations.

Considered and pushed further it is likely that some optimal tradeoffs can be made between the much less costly participants that provide valuable information about between-person differences and the relatively more expensive participants that provide valuable information about within-person changes over time and across contexts (see Collins, 2006; Nesselroade & Jones, 1991). Given many researchers' access to large psychology student or similarly structured participant pools, we suggest further use and elaboration of how these staged designs may be optimized for obtaining findings that generalize both across persons and across occasions (and across measures) at very reasonable costs. There are fantastic opportunities for such studies (even on rather homogeneous samples) to contribute to a honing of our still rather exploratory examinations of individuals' dynamic characteristics. Much can be learned from the systematic integration of between- and within-person-oriented designs and investigations.

As the study of intraindividual variability expands, we look forward to the many discoveries that may result from precise tethering of dynamic theories, methods of analysis, and intensive repeated-measures data.

ACKNOWLEDGMENTS

We gratefully acknowledge the support provided by the National Institute on Aging (Grant Nos. RC1 AG035645 and R21 AG032379) and the Penn State Social Science Research Institute.

REFERENCES

American Psychiatric Association. (2000). *Diagnostic and statistical manual of mental disorders* (revised 4th ed.). Washington, DC: Author.

Anestis, M. D., Selby, E. A., Crosby, R. D., Wonderlich, S. A., Engel, S. G., & Joiner, T. E. (2010). A comparison of retrospective self-report versus ecological momentary assessment measures of affective lability in the examination of its relationship with bulimic symptomology. *Behaviour Research and Therapy, 48,* 607–613.

Baltes, P. B., Lindenberger, U., & Staudinger, U. M. (2006). Lifespan theory in developmental psychology. In R. M. Lerner (Ed.), *Handbook of child psychology:*

Vol. 1. Theoretical models of human development (6th ed., pp. 569–664). New York: Wiley.

Blatt, S. J., Auerbach, J. S., & Levy, K. N. (1997). Mental representations in personality development, psychopathology, and the therapeutic process. *Review of General Psychology, 1,* 351–374.

Bolger, N., Davis, A., & Rafaeli, E. (2003). Diary methods: Capturing life as it is lived. *Annual Review of Psychology, 54,* 579–616.

Bretherton, I., & Munholland, K. A. (2008). Internal working models in attachment relationships: Elaborating a central construct in attachment theory. In J. Cassidy & P. R. Shaver (Eds.), *Handbook of attachment: Theory, research, and clinical applications* (2nd ed., pp. 102–127). New York: Guilford Press.

Brose, A., & Ram, N. (2012). Within-person factor analysis: Modeling how the individual fluctuates and changes across time. In M. R. Mehl & T. S. Conner (Eds.), *Handbook of research methods for studying daily life.* New York: Guilford Press.

Buss, A. H. (1989). Personality as traits. *American Psychologist, 44,* 1378–1388.

Carstensen, L. L., Pasupathi, M., Mayr, U., & Nesselroade, J. R. (2000). Emotional experience in everyday life across the adult lifespan. *Journal of Personality and Social Psychology, 79,* 644–655.

Carstensen, L. L., Turan, B., Scheibe, S., Ram, N., Ersner-Hershfield, H., Samanez-Larkin, G. R., et al. (2011). Emotional experience improves with age: Evidence based on over 10 years of experience sampling. *Psychology and Aging, 26,* 21–33.

Cassidy, J. (1999). The nature of the child's ties. In J. Cassidy & P. R. Shaver (Eds.), *Handbook of attachment: Theory, research, and clinical applications* (pp. 3–20). New York: Guilford Press.

Cattell, R. B. (1966). Patterns of change: Measurement in relation to state-dimension, trait change, lability, and process concepts. In R. B. Cattell (Ed.), *Handbook of multivariate experimental psychology* (pp. 355–402). Chicago: Rand McNally.

Cattell, R. B., Cattell, A. K. S., & Rhymer, R. M. (1947). P-technique demonstrated in determining psychophysical source traits in a normal individual. *Psychometrika, 12,* 267–288.

Clarkin, J. F., Yeomans, F. E., & Kernberg, O. F. (2006). *Psychotherapy for borderline personality disorder: Focusing on object relations.* Arlington, VA: American Psychiatric Publishing.

Collins, L. M. (2006). Analysis of longitudinal data: The integration of theoretical model, temporal design, and statistical model. *Annual Review of Psychology, 57,* 505–528.

Craigmile, P. F., Perrugia, M., & Van Zandt, T. (2010). Detrending response time series. In S. M. Chow, E. Ferrer, & F. Hsieh (Eds.), *Statistical models for modeling human dynamics: An interdisciplinary dialogue* (pp. 213–240). New York: Routledge.

Csikszentmihalyi, M., & Larson, R. (1987). Validity and reliability of the experience-sampling method. *Journal of Nervous and Mental Disease, 175,* 526–536.

Dvorak, R. D., & Simons, J. S. (2008). Affective differences among daily tobacco users, occasional users, and non-users. *Addictive Behaviors, 33,* 211–216.

Ebner-Priemer, U. W., Eid, M., Kleindienst, N., Stabenow, S., & Trull, T. J. (2009). Analytic strategies for understanding affective (in)stability and other dynamic processes in psychopathology. *Journal of Abnormal Psychology, 188,* 195–202.

Eid, M., & Diener, E. (1999). Intraindividual variability in affect: Reliability, validity, and personality correlates. *Journal of Personality and Social Psychology, 76,* 662–676.

Fair, D. A., Cohen, A. L., Dosenbach, N. U., Church, J. A., Miezin, F. M., & Barch, D. M. (2008). The maturing architecture of the brain's default network. *Proceedings of the National Academy of Science, 105,* 4028–4032.

Feldman Barrett, L., & Russell, J. A. (1999a). Independence and bipolarity in the structure of current affect. *Journal of Personality and Social Psychology, 74,* 967–984.

Feldman Barrett, L., & Russell, J. A. (1999b). The structure of current affect: Controversies and emerging consensus. *Current Directions in Psychological Science, 8,* 10–14.

Fiske, D. W., & Rice, L. (1955). Intra-individual response variability. *Psychological Bulletin, 52,* 217–250.

Gorsuch, R. L. (1983). *Factor analysis* (2nd ed.). Hillsdale, NJ: Erlbaum.

Guttman, L. (1954). Some necessary conditions for common-factor analysis. *Psychometrika, 19,* 149–161.

Harter, S. (2006). Self processes and developmental psychopathology. In D. Cicchetti & D. J. Cohen (Eds.), *Developmental psychopathology: Vol. 1. Theory and method* (2nd ed., pp. 370–418). Hoboken, NJ: Wiley.

Hopwood, C. J., Pincus, A. L., DeMoor, R. M., & Koonce, E. A. (2008). Psychometric characteristics of the Inventory of Personal Problems—Short Circumplex (IIIP-SC) with college students. *Journal of Personality Assessment, 90,* 615–618.

Horowitz, L. M. (2004). *Interpersonal foundations of psychopathology.* Washington, DC: American Psychological Association.

Jahng, S., Wood, P. K., & Trull, T. J. (2008). Analysis of affective stability in ecological momentary assessment: Indices using successive difference and group comparison using multilevel modeling. *Psychological Methods, 13,* 354–375.

Kernberg, O. F. (1984). *Severe personality disorders: Psychotherapeutic strategies.* New Haven, CT: Yale University Press.

Kuppens, P., Van Mechelen, I., Nezlek, J. B., Dossche, D., & Timmermans, T. (2007). Individual differences in core affect variability and their relationship to personality and adjustment. *Emotion, 7,* 262–274.

Latti, C., Guthrie, L. C., & Ward, M. M. (2010). Comparison of the construct validity and sensitivity to change of the visual analog scale and a modified rating scale as measures of patient global assessment in rheumatoid arthritis. Journal of Rheumatology, 37, 717–722.

Lukowitsky, M. R., & Pincus, A. L. (in press). The pantheoretical nature of mental representations and their ability to predict interpersonal adjustment in a nonclinical sample. *Psychoanalytic Psychology.*

Luyten, P., & Blatt, S. J. (2011). Integrating theory-driven and empirically-derived models of personality development and psychopathology: A proposal for DSM V. *Clinical Psychology Review, 31,* 52–68.

MacDonald, S. W. S., Hultsch, D. F., & Dixon, R. A. (2008). Predicting impending death: Inconsistency in speed is a selective and early marker. *Psychology and Aging, 23,* 595–607.

Mahler, M. S., Pine, F., & Bergman, A. (1975). *The psychological birth of the human infant: Symbiosis and individuation.* New York: Basic Books.

Mardia, K. V. (1972). *Statistics of directional data.* New York: Academic Press.

Mehl, M. R., & Conner T. S. (Eds.). (2012). *Handbook of research methods for studying daily life.* New York: Guilford Press.

Morin, P. J. (1999). *Community ecology.* Malden, MA: Blackwell.

Moskowitz, D. S. (1994). Cross-situational generality and the interpersonal circumplex. *Journal of Personality and Social Psychology, 66,* 921–933.

Moskowitz, D. S., & Zuroff, D. C. (2004). Flux, pulse, and spin: Dynamic additions to the personality lexicon. *Journal of Personality and Social Psychology, 86,* 880–893.

Moskowitz, D. S., & Zuroff, D. C. (2005). Robust predictors of flux, pulse, and spin. *Journal of Research in Personality, 39,* 130–147.

Nesselroade, J. R. (1991). The warp and woof of the developmental fabric. In R. Downs, L. Liben, & D. Palermo (Eds.), *Visions of development, the environment, and aesthetics: The legacy of Joachim F. Wohlwill* (pp. 213–240). Hillsdale, NJ: Erlbaum.

Nesselroade, J. R., & Jones, C. J. (1991). Multi-modal selection effects in the study if adult development: A perspective on multivariate, replicated, single-subject, repeated measures designs. *Experimental Aging Research, 17,* 21–27.

Newell, K. M., & Hancock, P. A. (1984). Forgotten moments: A note on skewness and kurtosis as influential factors in inferences extrapolated from response distributions. *Journal of Motor Behavior, 16,* 320–335.

Pincus, A. L., Ansell, E. B., Pimentel, C. A., Cain, N. M., Wright, A. G., & Levy, K. N. (2009). Initial construction and validation of the pathological narcissism inventory. *Psychological Assessment, 21,* 365–379.

Pincus, A. L., & Gurtman, M. B. (2003). Interpersonal assessment. In J. S. Wiggins (Ed.), *Paradigms of personality assessment* (pp. 246–261). New York: Guilford Press.

Pincus, A. L., & Wilson, K. R. (2001). Interpersonal variability in dependent personality. *Journal of Personality, 69,* 223–251.

Posner, J., Russell, J. A., & Peterson, B. S. (2005). The circumplex model of affect: An integrative approach to affective neuroscience, cognitive development, and psychopathology. *Development and Psychopathology, 17,* 715–734.

Ram, N., & Gerstorf, D. (2009). Time-structured and net intraindividual variability: Tools for examining the aging of dynamic characteristics and processes. *Psychology and Aging, 24,* 778–791.

Ram, N., Gerstorf, D., Lindenberger, U., & Smith, J. (2011). Developmental change and intraindividual variability: Relating cognitive aging to cognitive plasticity, cardiovascular lability, and emotional diversity. *Psychology and Aging, 26,* 363–371.

Ram, N., Rabbitt, P., Stollery, B., & Nesselroade, J. R. (2005). Cognitive performance inconsistency: Intraindividual change and variability. *Psychology and Aging, 20,* 623–633.

Rammstedt, B., & John, O. P. (2007). Measuring personality in one minute or less: A 10-item short version of the Big Five Inventory in English and German. *Journal of Research in Personality, 41,* 203–212.

Russell, J. A., & Carroll, J. M. (1999). On the bipolarity of positive and negative affect. *Psychological Bulletin, 125,* 3–30.

Russell, J. A., Weiss, A., & Mendelsohn, G. A. (1989). Affect grid: A single-item scale of pleasure and arousal. *Journal of Personality and Social Psychology, 57,* 493–502.

Schwartz, J. E., & Stone, A. A. (2007). The analysis of real-time momentary data: A practical guide. In A. A. Stone, S. Shiffman, A. A. Atienza, & L. Nebeling (Eds.), *The science of real-time data capture: Self-reports in health research* (pp. 76–116). New York: Oxford University Press.

Shannon, C. E. (1950). Prediction and entropy of printed English, *Bell System Technical Journal, 30,* 50–64.

Shiffman, S., Stone, A. A., & Hufford, M. R. (2008). Ecological momentary assessment. *Annual Review of Clinical Psychology, 4,* 1–32.

Shumway, R. H., & Stoffer, D. S. (2006). *Time series analysis and its applications* (2nd ed.). New York: Springer.

Simons, J. S., & Carey, K. B. (2006). An affective and cognitive model of marijuana and alcohol problems. *Addictive Behaviors, 31,* 1578–1592.

Trull, T. J., Solhan, M. B., Tragesser, S. L., Jahng, S., Wood, P. K., Piasecki, T. M., et al. (2008). Affective instability: Measuring a core feature of borderline personality disorder with ecological momentary assessment. *Journal of Abnormal Psychology, 117,* 647–661.

Walls, T. A., & Schafer, J. L. (Eds.). (2006). *Models for intensive longitudinal data.* New York: Oxford University Press.

Warr, P., Barter, J., & Brownbridge, G. (1983). On the independence of positive and negative affect. *Journal of Personality and Social Psychology, 44,* 644–651.

Wei, M., Russel, D. W., Mallinckrodt, B., & Vogel, D. L. (2007). The Experiences in Close Relationship scale (ECR)—Short Form: Reliability, validity, and factor structure. *Journal of Personality Assessment, 88,* 187–204.

Weiner, B. (2007). Examining emotional diversity in the classroom: An attribution theorist considers the moral emotions. In P. A. Schutz & R. Pekrun (Eds.), *Emotions and education* (pp. 75–88). San Diego, CA: Elsevier.

Weinstein, S. M., Mermelstein, R., Shiffman, S., & Flay, B. (2008). Mood variability and cigarette smoking escalation among adolescents. *Psychology of Addictive Behaviors, 22,* 504–513.

Wessman, A. E., & Ricks, D. F. (1966). *Mood and personality.* New York: Holt, Rinehart, and Winston.

Wewers, M. E., & Lowe N. K. (1990). A critical review of visual analogue scales in the measurement of clinical phenomena. *Research on Nursing Health, 13,* 227–236.

Wilcox, A. R. (1973). Indices of qualitative variation and political measurement. *Western Political Quarterly, 26,* 325–343.

Winkler, D., Pjrek, E., Heiden, A., Wiesegger, G., Klein, N., Konstantinidis, A., et al. (2004). Gender differences in the psychopathology of depressed inpatients. *European Archives of Psychiatry and Clinical Neuroscience, 254,* 209–214.

Yung, Y.-F., & Chang, W. (1999). Statistical analyses using bootstrapping: Concepts and implementation. In R. H. Hoyle (Ed.), *Statistical strategies for small sample research* (pp. 81–105). Thousand Oaks, CA: Sage.

Zautra, A. J., Affleck, G. G., Tennen, H., Reich, J. W., & Davis, M. C. (2005). Dynamic approaches to emotions and stress in everyday life: Bolger and Zuckerman reloaded with positive as well as negative affects. *Journal of Personality, 73,* 1511–1538.

CHAPTER 5

DYNAMIC SYSTEMS ANALYSIS OF AFFECTIVE PROCESSES IN DYADIC INTERACTIONS USING DIFFERENTIAL EQUATIONS

Emilio Ferrer
University of California

Joel Steele
Portland State University

INTRODUCTION

Dyadic interactions involve the interrelations of two interdependent units in a system (e.g., teacher-student, husband-wife) as the system unfolds over time. To model dyadic interactions accurately, techniques are needed that can capture such interrelations and their time sequence. Differential equation models (DEMs) are one such technique. DEMs are powerful tools to examine change that occurs in a continuous fashion. Although DEMs are the common language in most scientific disciplines, their use in the social

Advances in Longitudinal Methods in the Social and Behavioral Sciences, pages 111–134
Copyright © 2012 by Information Age Publishing
All rights of reproduction in any form reserved.

and behavioral sciences is not as widespread. In this chapter we apply differential equations to model the affect dynamics of individuals in couples. The chapter is organized as follows. First, we describe dyadic interactions and approaches typically used to model such interactions. Second, we provide a brief overview of DEMs and indicate some of the advantages of this technique. Third, we fit a number of systems of DEMs to empirical time-series data from couples. We finish the chapter with a summary of results and a discussion of implications for future research.

MODELS FOR DYADIC INTERACTIONS

Many methods are now available for the analyses of dyadic interactions to fit the researcher's data and questions. Some pioneering techniques, developed in the 1970s, include sequential methods (Bobbitt, Gourevitch, Miller, & Jensen, 1969; Castellan, 1979; Goodman, 1970; Gottman, 1979; Sackett, 1979). More advanced approaches have been created recently to accommodate various types of data and research designs. For example, a popular technique is hierarchical linear modeling. This technique considers the nested structure of the data (e.g., individuals within dyads, repeated observations within individuals) and has been applied to dyadic interactions using both cross-sectional (Campbell & Kashy, 2002; Kashy & Kenny, 2000; Kenny, Kashy, & Cook, 2006) and longitudinal data (Butner, Diamond, & Hicks, 2007; Laurenceau, Troy, & Carver, 2005; Newsom, 2002; Raudenbush, Brennan, & Barnett, 1995; Thomson & Bolger, 1999).

In the case of data consisting of multiple variables showing systematic fluctuations, relevant approaches are dynamic factor analysis (Molenaar, 1985) as well as a general modeling framework termed "state-space models." Dynamic factor analysis, for example, integrates time-series models with factor analysis and is suited for dyadic interactions data. In this context, it can reveal the factorial structure of multiple observed variables together with the dynamics of the latent factors over time. This technique has been applied to examine the dynamics of affective processes in dyads (Ferrer & Nesselroade, 2003; Ferrer & Widaman, 2008; Ferrer & Zhang, 2009). Similarly, state-space models have been used with longitudinal data consisting of affect reports from dyads using filtering procedures (Chow, Ferrer, & Nesselroade, 2007; Song & Ferrer, 2009), and auto-regressive models (Hamaker, Zhang, & van der Maas, 2009).

Although not as widely used, another approach for analyzing dyadic interactions consists of exploratory models. These techniques are typically based on visualization methods, pattern recognition, and computational modeling. Although lacking a theoretical specification, these techniques can serve as an important tool that informs further analyses. Examples of such exploratory models applied to dyadic interactions include hierarchical segmentation, a nonparametric technique used to identify time periods of coherence between the affect of two individuals in dyads (Ferrer, Chen, Chow, & Hsieh, 2010; Hsieh, Ferrer, Chen, & Chow, 2010); fixations, a technique for examining affective dynamics based on patterns of variability (Ferrer, Steele, & Hsieh, 2012); and recurrence plots (e.g., Marwan & Kurths, 2002).

Differential Equation Models

One common feature among the approaches described previously is that they are suited for data measured at discrete intervals. When the data are measured continuously, however, other techniques are needed. One such technique that can be applied to the analysis of dyadic interactions is differential equation modeling (DEM). Although DEM is a common tool in most of the physical sciences, its use in the social and behavioral sciences is less widespread. This is due, in part, to a lack of statistical approaches that are available for many researchers, but also because continuous data are not the standard type of data in these disciplines.

DEMs have been applied to social behavior in several contexts (Tuma & Hannan, 1984), including the study of interaction in a group (Simon, 1957), arms races (Rapaport, 1960), and network effects on social influence (Friedkin, 1998). In the context of dyadic interactions, DEMs have been used as a theoretical framework to investigate predictive trajectories of different types of dyads (Felmlee, 2006; Felmlee & Greenberg, 1999) but also as an analytic method to model turn-taking in conversations (Buder, 1991; Newtson, 1993), types of social relationships and marriages (Baron, Amazeen, & Beek, 1994), emotional interactions and breakup in couples (Gottman, Murray, Swanson, Tyson, & Swanson, 2002), intimacy and disclosure in married couples (Boker & Laurenceau, 2006), affect coregulation between romantic partners (Butner et al., 2007), and the dynamics of affective processes between individuals in close relationships (Chow et al., 2007; Steele & Ferrer, in press).

DEMs are particularly useful as a technique for examining dyadic interactions, as these models explicitly consider the two members of a dyad as an interdependent system. Moreover, they directly model the changes in the system—or each of its units—as a continuous process. In this chapter, we consider a system of two differential equations, such as

$$\frac{dx}{dt} = f(x,y), \text{ and}$$

$$\frac{dy}{dt} = f(y,x),$$

where dx/dt and dy/dt represent the instantaneous rate of change over time (t) of two individuals' behavior x and y, respectively. In this system of equations, such changes are expressed as a function of both the actor and the partner. This general expression can be modified to accommodate specific hypotheses. For example, such hypotheses could specify changes as a function of either an individual component (e.g., an individual is influenced by his or her own behavior), a system component (e.g., one individual's behavior influences the other), or both individual and system components. In this general expression, time is unspecified and could represent any interval of time (e.g., years, months, days) pertinent to the type of behavior under study. Traits such as attitudes, for example, might change relatively slowly and, in that case, time, t, might represent months or years. The frequency of nonverbal cues exchanged between a pair, on the other hand, could shift by the minute. Even faster exchanges are possible such as changes in physiological signals, which may vary by the millisecond.

DYADIC INTERACTIONS BASED ON INDIVIDUAL GOALS AND DYADIC INFLUENCES

The DEMs that we propose in this chapter are based on a theoretical model proposed to study interactions between couples (Felmlee, 2006; Felmlee & Greenberg, 1999). This general model can be written as a system of linear differential equations, as

$$\frac{dx}{dt} = a_1(x^* - x) + a_2(y - x), \text{ and}$$

$$\frac{dy}{dt} = b_1(y^* - y) + b_2(x - y) \tag{5.1}$$

where x and y represent the behavior—or any other dependent variable—of two actors measured at any time t; a and b are parameters to be estimated from the data; and x^* and y^* refer to ideal types of behavior (e.g., goals) that each person seeks out. In this specification, changes in each person's behavior over time are a function of individual factors (first term; i.e., oneself) as well as the system factors (second term; i.e., the other person). The individual factor considers how far the person's current behavior is from the ideal behavior, and this is quantified by the coefficients a_1 and b_1, for persons x and y, respectively. The system factor considers how far the person's current behavior is from the other person's behavior, and this is quantified by the coefficients a_2 and b_2, for persons x and y, respectively. If all the coefficients are positive, the model represents a dyadic system in which both members are cooperative, as each individual will attempt to approach his or her goals as well as the partner's behavior.

This general model for dyadic interactions is grounded in a number of assumptions (see Felmlee & Greenberg, 1999). First, dyads form dynamic and interactive systems. That is, the relationship changes over time and the two individuals in the couple influence each other. Second, change takes place in a continuous manner—as opposed to, say, at discrete intervals. Finally, the model coefficients are constant over time (but this restriction could be relaxed, as we discuss in the discussion section). For a detailed discussion of the analytic equilibrium solution for the model and its derivation, see Felmlee and Greenberg (1999).

There are numerous variations of this basic model that have a range of implications for the long-term activity of the dyadic system (Felmlee, 2006), varying from predictions that the couple's interaction patterns smoothly approach an equilibrium over time, to those where unstable, separate partner paths are expected to emerge. In addition to this cooperative system, we consider four other specifications. The first variation represents a system in which both members are independent from each other. This specification can be written as

$$\frac{dx}{dt} = a_1(x^* - x), \text{ and}$$

$$\frac{dy}{dt} = b_1(y^* - y). \quad (5.2)$$

Equation 5.2 represents a system in which the changes in each person's behavior are only a function of him- or herself, but not the other person in the dyad. The next specification considers both members in the dyad as contrarians, and can be expressed as

$$\frac{dx}{dt} = -a_2(y - x), \text{ and}$$

$$\frac{dy}{dt} = -b_2(x - y), \quad (5.3)$$

where the negative sign before coefficients a_2 and b_2 indicate that each person's behavior will tend to move away from that of the partner.

A final specification that we consider is that in which one member of the dyad is uncooperative whereas the other member is dependent. We consider two variations of this model in which the male and female are specified as the uncooperative and the dependent member, respectively. This model can be written as

$$\frac{dx}{dt} = a_1(x^* - x) - a_2(y - x), \text{ and}$$

$$\frac{dy}{dt} = b_2(x - y) \qquad (5.4)$$

where x and y represent the uncooperative and the dependent member, respectively. In this model, person x's behavior will tend to approach his or her goals as well as move away from the partner's behavior (i.e., increase the difference between both behaviors). The behavior of person y, however, is cooperative and will tend to approach that of person x (i.e., shorten the distance between both behaviors). Furthermore, the first member in the dyad is influenced by personal goals, x^*, whereas the behavior of the second partner is affected only by that of her or his partner.

To illustrate some possibilities of this model, consider the intimacy expressed by both members of the couple. Imagine that the first person's expressions of intimacy are a reaction to those of the other person, perhaps due to an avoidant attachment style. Thus, the more intimacy expressed by the partner, the more this person avoids such behaviors. On the other hand, the partner always makes an effort to harmonize his or her level of intimacy to that of the first person; perhaps this person has a secure attachment style. Based on the model, we would expect that the couple could develop a repeated, cyclical pattern of approach and avoidance. For certain parameter values, this "on again-off again" relationship pattern could become routine and sustainable, according to the theoretical model.

Each of the model specifications has a dynamic solution with different predictions of the couple's behavior over time. That is, the parameter constraints that define each unique specification can be incorporated into the analytic solution to investigate the couple's behavior over time.[1] For example, the trajectories for each person in the couple from Model 1 are expected to approach each other, given reasonable initial conditions (i.e., behavior for each person at an initial time point). For Model 2, however, such trajectories are expected to be separate from each other and remain as such uniformly over time, whereas those for Model 3 are expected to increasingly repel each other over time. Finally, the trajectories from the dynamic solution of Model 4 are expected to show cyclical oscillations that either approach stability for some period of time or are unstable and explode. Specific details of each of these models as well as their dynamic solutions are described elsewhere (Felmlee, 2006; Felmlee & Greenberg, 1999).

METHOD

Participants

The data used in this chapter are part of the Dynamics of Dyadic Interactions Project (DDIP), an ongoing project at the University of California, Davis, focused on the development of models to analyze dyadic interactions (see, e.g., Ferrer & Widaman, 2008). Participants in the DDIP include couples involved in a romantic relationship. As part of the overall project, all participants were asked to complete a daily questionnaire about their affect for up to 90 consecutive days. In this report we present data from 112 couples who had from 50 days to 98 days of complete data.[2] The age of participants ranged from 19.1 to 74.11 years ($M = 34.5$; $SD = 12.6$). The time that they had been involved in the relationship ranged from 0.8 to 35.1 years ($M = 9.80$; $SD = 9.31$). Of the 112 dyads, four (3.6%) were dating casually, 86 (77%) were living together, six (5%) were engaged, and 16 (14.4%) were married.

Measures

The daily questionnaire was intended to examine day-to-day fluctuations in affect. As part of this questionnaire, a set of 18 items was intended to tap into the participants' positive and negative emotional experiences specific to their relationship. Participants were asked to complete these items responding to the instructions "Indicate to what extent you have felt this way about your relationship today." The nine positive items included "emotionally intimate," "trusted," "committed," "physically intimate," "free," "loved," "happy," "loving," and "socially supported," whereas the nine negative mood items included "sad," "blue," "trapped," "argumentative," "discouraged," "doubtful," "lonely," "angry," and "deceived."

For all items, participants were asked to respond using a 5-point Likert-type scale ranging from 1 (very slightly or not at all) to 5 (extremely). To examine the precision of the measurement of systematic change of persons across days, we computed the reliability of change within-person using generalizability analysis (Cranford et al., 2006). The resulting reliability coefficients for positive and negative affect were .85 and .87 (for females) and

.82 and .85 (for males). For all analyses, we created unit-weight composites for positive and negative affect, for each person, using all the items in the scales. Figure 5.1 displays plots of these composites for four dyads. These plots suggest substantial differences in the emotional experiences among the dyads. Such differences are apparent with regard to the levels of affect (i.e., high vs. low), fluctuation and stability, and apparent coupling between the affect of the two members in the dyad.

For the subsequent analyses, we constructed a ratio of positive affect in relation to all affect [*positive* / (*positive* + *negative*)]. Our choice was motivated by the Balanced State of Mind model (BSOM; Schwartz, 1997), an integrative model of positive and negative affect. Research using this approach has shown that different ratios can describe various states of affect, ranging from psychopathological, normal, and optimal states. In particular, ratios of about .70 to .80 have been found to indicate normal and optimal functioning in individuals (Schwartz et al., 2002) and couples (Gottman, 1994). In our models, we use .80 as the ideal types of behavior x^* and y^* in the models.[3]

Estimation of Differential Equation Models

There are multiple approaches to estimate DEMs. One of the most traditional methods is to pool cross-section and time-series data and use weighted generalized least squares. Another approach is to use filtering procedures such as the Kalman filter (e.g., Julier, Uhlmann, & Durrant-Whyte, 1995). This procedure has been used successfully to fit both linear and nonlinear models in behavioral science research (Chow et al., 2007; Hamaker, Dolan, & Molenaar, 2005). There are also toolboxes in software packages that allow fitting linear and nonlinear dynamical system models directly to the data. One such toolbox is the package ReBEL in Matlab (Recursive Bayesian Estimation Library; Van der Merwe, 2003). Other programs such as R and SAS include procedures for ordinary differential equations. In the analyses reported here, we used the procedure MODEL in SAS. The Appendix includes an example script of PROC MODEL.

MODEL is a procedure to analyze models in which the relations among the variables comprise a system of one or more nonlinear equations. Some of the principal uses of the procedure include estimation, simulation, and forecasting of simultaneous equation models. This procedure includes various possibilities with regard to methods for parameter estimation, including ordinary least squares, two-stage least squares, seemingly unrelated regression and iterative seemingly unrelated regression, and three-stage least squares. For the analyses reported here we used full information maximum likelihood (FIML). FIML assumes that the equation errors have a multivari-

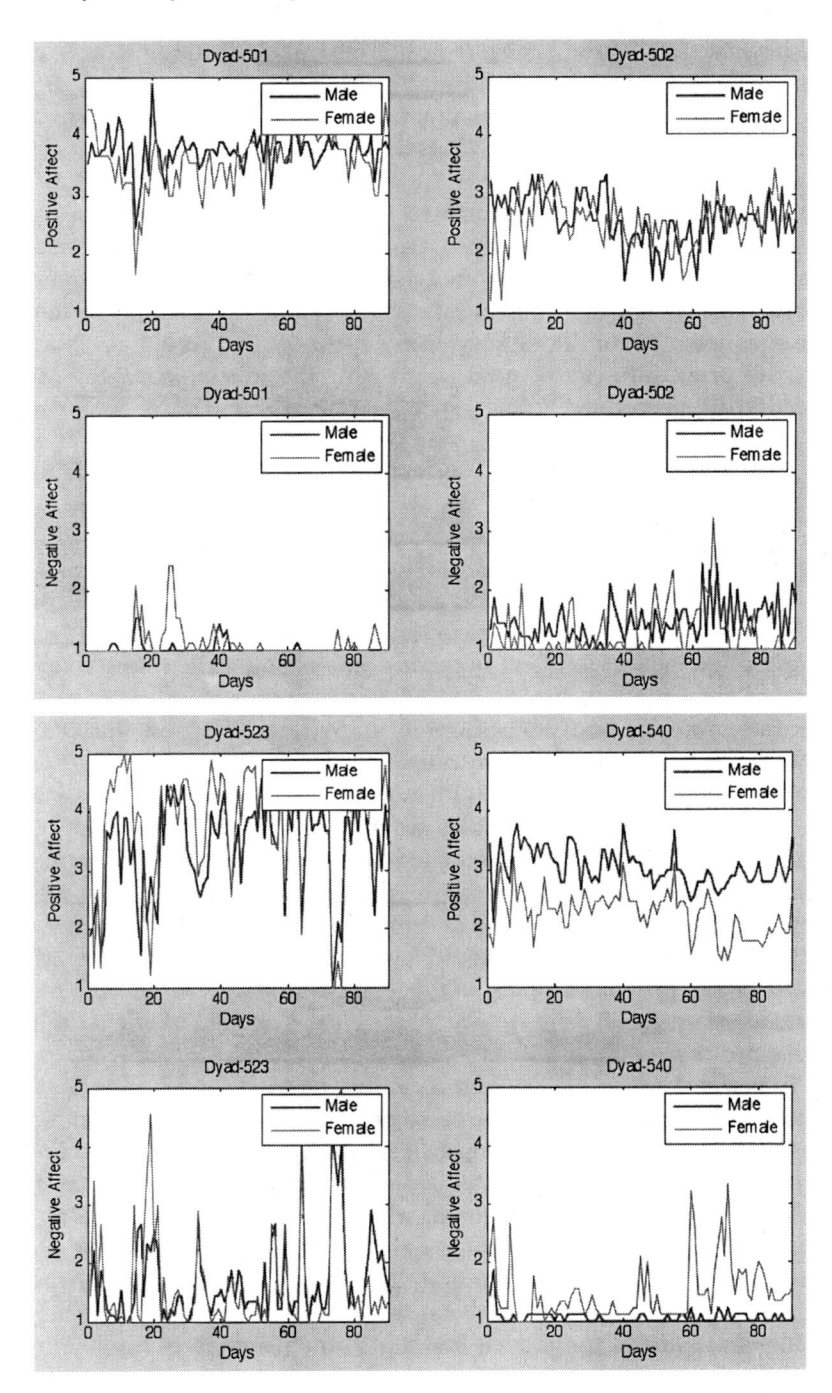

Dynamic Systems Analysis of Affective Processes in Dyadic Interactions ▪ **119**

Figure 5.1 Positive and negative affect over time for four dyads.

ate normal distribution, which is not unreasonable in these data, even if our proposed model is deterministic. Furthermore, FIML helps to deal with the so-called "simultaneous equation bias problem" inherent in systems of equations that are dependent. Cross-dependency in these equations leads to a violation of independence in the errors (Pindyck & Rubinfeld, 1981). FIML is known to overcome or at least reasonably attenuate this bias (Amemiya, 1977; Gallant & Holly, 1980). In addition to the estimation features, the MODEL procedure can be used to forecast. When the specified model has variables that enter linearly, forecasting can be done simply by solving the equations. When the variables enter the model in a nonlinear way, an iterative procedure can be used by invoking the subcommand SOLVE in the MODEL procedure.

RESULTS

Data-Analytic Steps and Classification Procedure

The goals of our analyses were to represent theoretical predictions about couples' interaction in affect over time and examine the numerical solutions of the different models, as well as the predicted trajectories of affect over time for both individuals in the system. For these analyses, we followed several steps. First, we fitted the described five models to each dyad separately. The five models included: Model 1, both members are cooperative; Model 2, both members are independent; Model 3, both members are contrarian; Model 4a, female is uncooperative, male is dependent; and Model 4b, male is uncooperative, female is dependent. In the second step, we evaluated the fit of the different models for each dyad separately with the goal of assigning each dyad to one of the five models representing prototypes of dynamic systems. In the final step, we summarized the model parameters across all dyads to characterize the dynamics of affect for each of the prototypes.

To evaluate model fit, we used a number of criteria, including the sum of squared error (SSE), mean squared error (MSE), root mean squared error (RMSE), R square (Rsq), adjusted R square (AdjR), and log-likelihood (LL). Because model fit can differ between the two members of the couple, we looked for dyads showing agreement in model fit for the two individuals. This procedure resulted in a large number of couples showing no dyadic agreement on which model was best. In addition, the parameter estimates for some of the models were beyond reasonable values, indicating the possibility that some of the models had unrealistic restrictions, leading to difficulties in our attempt to classify the dyads. Because of these limitations, we decided to fit an unrestrictive model and perform the classification based on the parameter estimates. Thus, we fitted Model 1 without any restrictions to each of the dyads separately. Of the 112 dyads, 14 did not converge or converged to biased estimates that were not reliable. For each of the 98 remaining dyads, we saved the individual estimates and evaluated the parameter estimate to standard error ratios in order to determine the likelihood of each of the parameters. We considered reliable estimates those exceeding 1.96 in absolute values. We used this information to classify the dyads into classes or dyadic prototypes.

Our classification scheme was meant to mimic the theoretical models described previously. Thus, if the two parameters indicating co-regulation in the model (i.e., a_2 and b_2) were positive, as in Model 1, the dyad was assigned to the "interdependent" (or cooperative) class. If both a_2 and b_2 were zero, the dyad was assigned to the "independent" class. If a_2 was positive and b_2 was zero, the dyad was assigned to the "female dependent" class. In contrast, if a_2 was zero and b_2 was positive, the dyad was assigned to the "male dependent" class. If a_2 was negative, the dyad was assigned to the "female contrarian" class. If b_2 was negative, the dyad was assigned to the "male contrarian" class. If all four parameters in the model were zero, the dyad was assigned to the "unregulated" class.

Dyadic Systems Prototypes

The procedure described previously resulted in the following classification: one dyad was represented as interdependent (or cooperative), 43 as independent, 15 as a dyadic prototype in which the female is dependent, 10 dyads as a prototype in which the male is dependent, two dyads as a prototype in which the female is contrarian, and 27 dyads as unregulated. Table 5.1 includes the frequencies of the different dyadic prototypes together with the classification scheme.

Table 5.2 includes the descriptive statistics of the parameter estimates of each of the dyadic prototypes. For example, the coefficients representative of self-regulation in Model 1 (i.e., "interdependent") are $a_1 = 0$ and $b_1 = .319$, for the female and male, respectively. The coefficients representing co-regulation are $a_2 = .608$ and $b_2 = .397$, for the female and male, respectively. For the "independent" dyadic class, the only nonzero parameters were $a_1 = .467$ and $b_1 = .559$, indicating no co-regulation in those couples. Figure 5.2 displays the predicted trajectories of affect versus the observed data for couples representative of the various dyadic prototypes. For each model, we include representative couples with the largest R-square values. An inspection of these plots reveals that, for most couples, the predictions match the observed data quite well.

TABLE 5.1 Dyadic Model Class Frequencies and Classification Rules

Model class	Freq.	a_1	b_1	a_2	b_2
Interdependent	1			> 0	> 0
Independent	43	$(> 0$ $(\geq 0$	AND $\geq 0)_1$ AND $> 0)_2$	$= 0$	$= 0$
Female dependent	15			> 0	$= 0$
Male dependent	10			$= 0$	> 0
Female contrarian	2			< 0	≥ 0
Male contrarian	0			≥ 0	< 0
Unregulated	27	$= 0$	$= 0$	$= 0$	$= 0$
Total	98				

Note: Subscripts 1 and 2 represent alternate conditional pairs for the *Independent* dyad classification. $N = 98$ dyads.

TABLE 5.2 Descriptive Statistics for Parameter Estimates Across Dyadic Prototypes

Model/parameter	Mean	SD	Min	Max
Interdependent ($N = 1$)				
a_1	0.000	—	0.000	0.000
b_1	0.319	—	0.319	0.319
a_2	0.608	—	0.608	0.608
b_2	0.397	—	0.397	0.397
Independent ($N = 43$)				
a_1	0.467	0.514	0.000	1.756
b_1	0.559	0.630	0.000	2.287
a_2	0.000	—	—	—
b_2	0.000	—	—	—
Female Dependent ($N = 15$)				
a_1	0.399	0.522	−0.740	1.281
b_1	0.099	0.175	0.000	0.497
a_2	0.678	0.424	0.176	1.432
b_2	0.000	—	—	—
Male Dependent ($N = 10$)				
a_1	0.093	0.220	0.000	0.676
b_1	0.408	0.381	0.000	0.919
a_2	0.000	—	—	—
b_2	0.516	0.218	0.302	0.940
Female Contrarian ($N = 2$)				
a_1	0.254	0.359	0.000	0.507
b_1	0.350	0.495	0.000	0.701
a_2	−0.395	0.380	−0.663	−0.126
b_2	1.170	1.654	0.000	2.340

Dynamic Systems Analysis of Affective Processes in Dyadic Interactions ▪ **123**

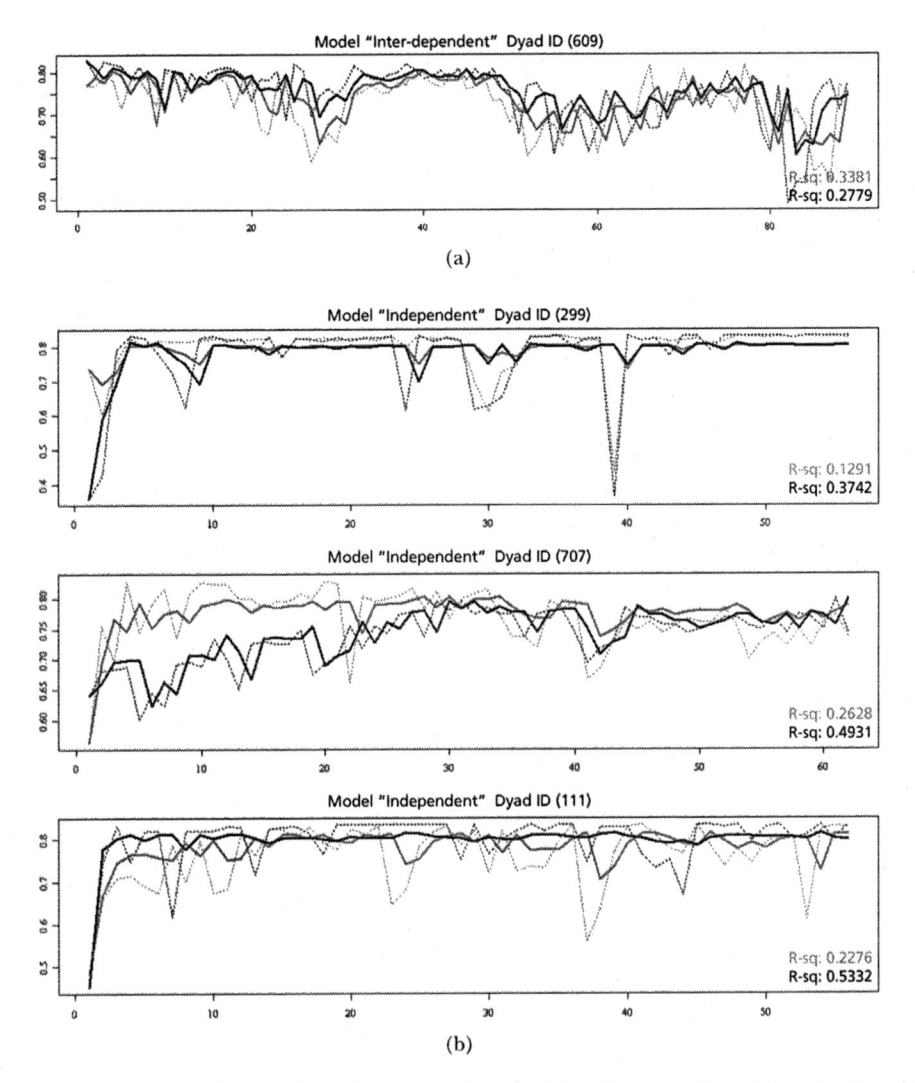

(a)

(b)

Figure 5.2 Predicted trajectories versus observed data for three best-fitting dyads across dyadic prototypes. Panel (a), "interdependent" class; panel (b), "independent" class.

(continued)

Model "Female Dependent" Dyad ID (505)

R-sq: 0.2179
R-sq: 0.0841

Model "Female Dependent" Dyad ID (650)

R-sq: 0.1307
R-sq: 0.4539

Model "Female Dependent" Dyad ID (650)

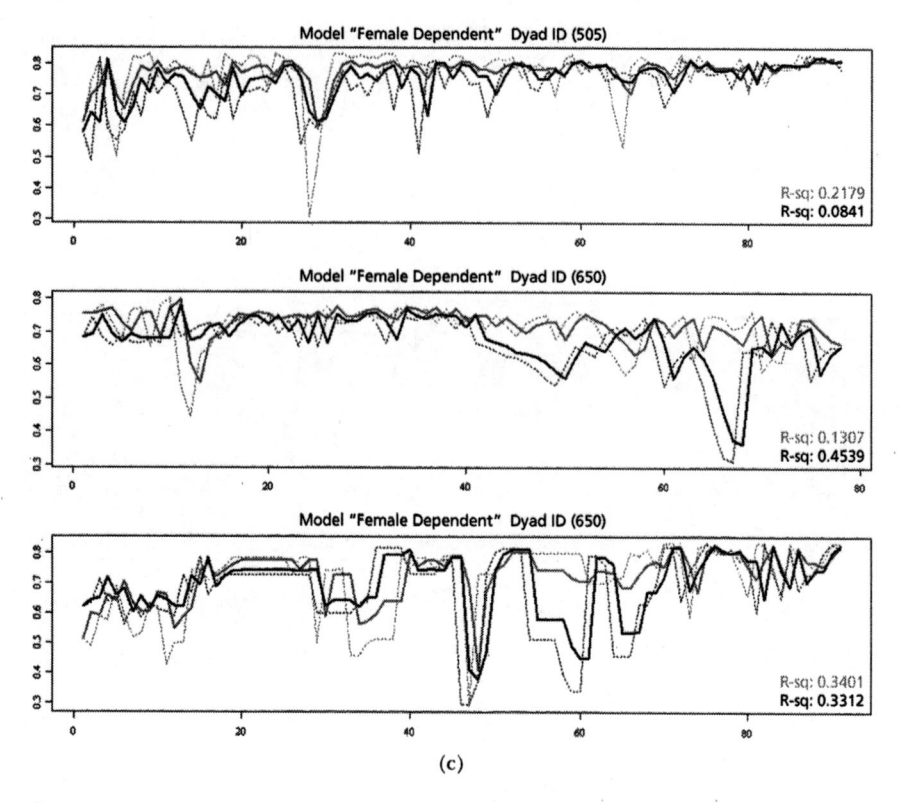

R-sq: 0.3401
R-sq: 0.3312

(c)

Figure 5.2 (continued) Predicted trajectories versus observed data for three best-fitting dyads across dyadic prototypes. Panel (c), "female dependent" class.

DISCUSSION

Summary of Results

In this chapter we presented a dynamic systems analysis of affective processes in dyads using differential equations. We followed theoretical models of dyadic interactions developed for couples (Felmlee & Greenberg, 1999). These models represented ideal types of dyadic interactions. We used differential equations for fitting such models to empirical data of daily affect from dyads. We fitted each of the theoretical models to each dyad separately and then compared the fit among the models to assign each dyad to one of the ideal types. Following this procedure we were able to classify all the dyads into possible types of dyadic interaction.

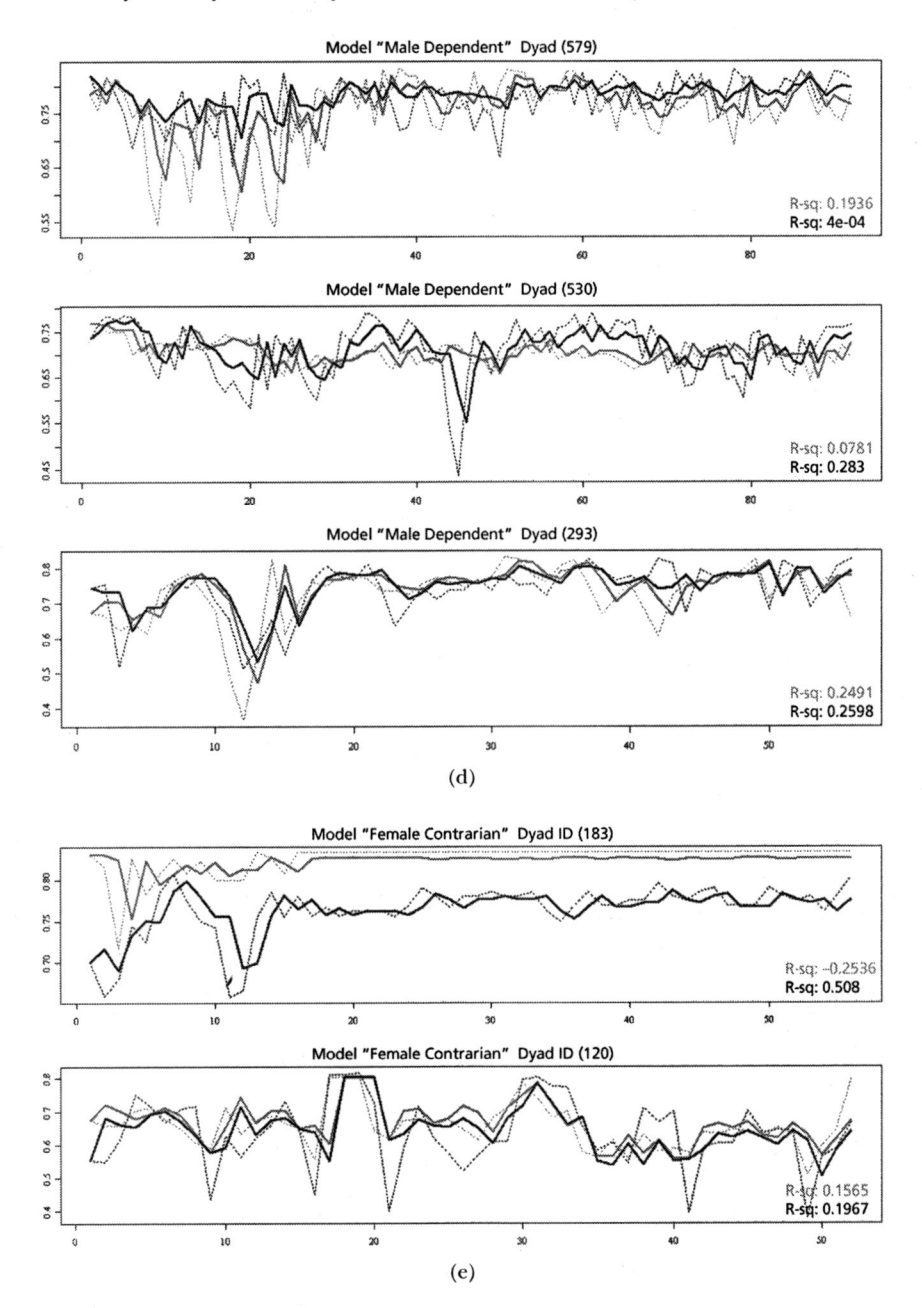

Figure 5.2 (continued) Predicted trajectories versus observed data for three best-fitting dyads across dyadic prototypes. Panel (d), "male dependent" class; panel (e), "female contrarian" class; panel. *(continued)*

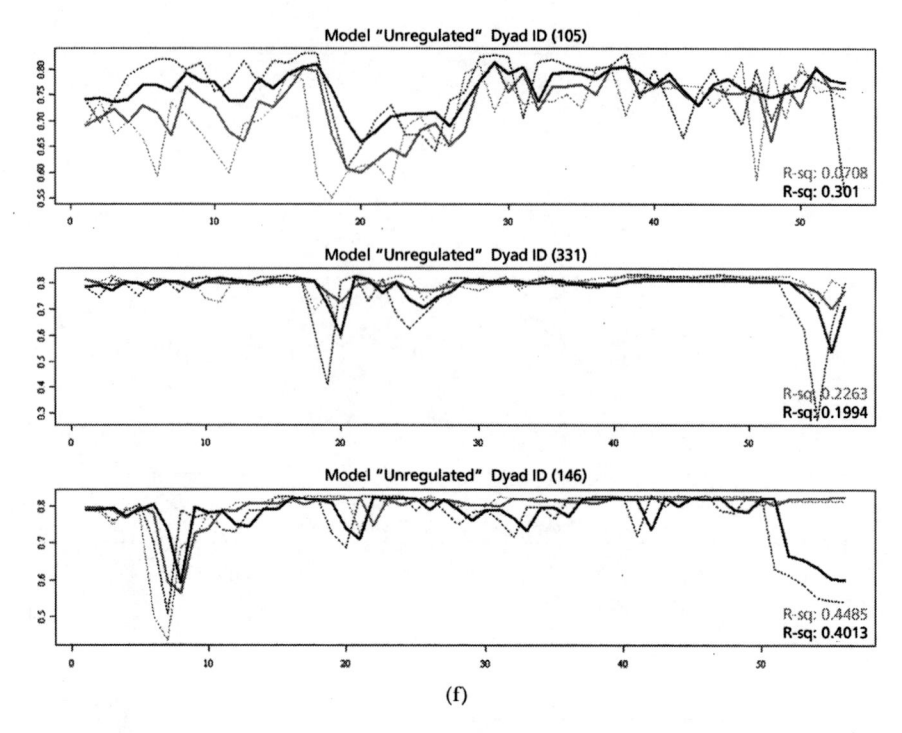

[Figure: Three panels showing "Model 'Unregulated' Dyad ID" for IDs 105, 331, and 146, with R-sq values: 0.0708/0.301, 0.2263/0.1994, and 0.4485/0.4013 respectively.]

(f)

Figure 5.2 (continued) Predicted trajectories versus observed data for three best-fitting dyads across dyadic prototypes. Panel (f), "unregulated" class.

The results from our analyses indicate that most of the classified dyads were best characterized as "independent" or "un-regulated." According to the former model, the only influences of the affective dynamics in the system were those of self-regulation. In other words, the daily variability of affect for each individual of the dyad was a function of his or her affect, but not that of the other person in the dyad. This self-regulatory mechanism worked by making one person's current affect change as a function of the distance from his or her own ideal affective state.

A second type of dyadic model that seemed to characterize a large number of couples was that in which all four parameters were not different from zero. In this model, the affect of the two individuals in the dyads would not be regulated by any mechanism related to themselves or their partners, but rather by random shocks. These shocks could be due to external sources (e.g., weather, jobs) or to the individuals themselves (e.g., sickness) but they are not related to the measured data. A third type of dyadic model that showed relative frequency was that in which the female was dependent. According to this model, her affect would be governed by a co-regulatory mechanism whereby she would try to get close to her partner's affect. For some of these couples, the females' affect would also be regulated by their own ideal affective state, but in all cases, the male's affect was not related to the female's. An opposite type of dyadic behavior was also observed with relative frequency. That was the case for dyads in which the male was dependent and the females independent. In other words, the males' affect was related to their partner's affective state, but the opposite was not the case.

Two types of the predicted dyadic models were only observed by very few couples. The first of these two models was a dyadic behavior in which the females were "contrarian" and their daily affect moved away from that of their male partners. The males' affect, in contrast, was positively related to the females' affect, in an attempt to move close to theirs. Only two couples were characterized as following this model. Finally, the general model predicting interdependence (or cooperation) between the affect of both dyadic members was only observed for one couple.

Methodological Issues

The results from these analyses are informative about affective dynamics in the population. These analyses were guided by theoretical models. Without any theoretical guidelines, deciding on analyses is a difficult task, especially for modeling procedures such as those used here that require detailed specifications for model fitting. One limitation of these guidelines, however, is that they might not represent the data properly. In our previous attempts to classify the dyads, some of them could not be assigned to any given prototype of dyadic interaction, primarily because there was not agreement about which model best fitted the time series of two individuals in the couple. In addition, the fitted model did not converge or yield reliable estimates for 14 couples. One immediate question is, then, what type of dyadic interaction do these couples follow? To answer this question, other model specifications could be tested as well. To keep our analyses focused, such competing models were not implemented in this chapter.

One possible approach to modify the dyadic specifications in our analyses is using alternative theoretical models. The models that we used were theoretical models of dyadic interactions based on ideal types of behavior (Felmlee, 2006; Felmlee & Greenberg, 1999). For our purposes, such an ideal type represented an affective state, in terms of a positive/negative affect ratio. Although this approach seems reasonable, it is plausible that it did not accurately characterize the daily affect for many couples. Such an ideal type might be better represented using individual information such as the mean across all days or general affect, not related to the relationship. Alternatively, other theoretical models are also possible such as Gottman's nonlinear dynamical systems for dyadic interactions (Gottman et al., 2002), coupled oscillator models of self- and co-regulatory systems (e.g., Boker & Laurenceau, 2006), models based on thresholds of behavior or affect (Hamaker et al., 2009), and, of course, other general models of dyadic interactions not specific to affect or couples (e.g., Steenbeek & van Geert, 2007). In addition to testing other theoretical hypotheses, these alternative models could very well fit our data much better than the models used in our analyses.

Another possible approach for characterizing the types of dyadic interactions in our couples is the use of exploratory procedures such as visualization methods, pattern recognition, and computational modeling. Although lacking of theoretical basis, exploratory approaches can provide valuable information about hidden patterns in the data and can be helpful to develop further analyses. This can be particularly valuable in situations seeking to preserve idiosyncratic information of the individual or the dyad. For example, we have applied such exploratory methods to examine the dynamics of affective processes using nonparametric approaches based on hierarchical segmentation and stochastic transition networks (Ferrer et al., 2010; Hsieh et al., 2010). With hierarchical segmentation we were able to detect periods of time in which time series of affect from dyadic members show synchronized patterns of variability. With the use of small-world networks, we were able to visualize and describe daily transitions in affect for dyads. In addition, we have used pattern recognition methods for examining affective dynamics in couples based on intraindividual and intradyad variability (Ferrer et al., 2012). Other methods such as cross-recurrence plots can be useful to extract patterns of interrelations from time series of couples without having to rely on assumptions of stationarity or linearity (Marwan & Kurths, 2002).

In our analyses, each of the theoretical models was fitted to each dyad separately and then summaries were generated based on the information that would pertain to groups of couples. That is, we wanted to start from the dyad—our unit of analysis—and build up to the population. Our approach was useful but not completely satisfactory or conclusive. For example, the resulting dyadic types did not show obvious features that could distinguish dyads among the various classes. Even though the theoretical predictions from the models were unambiguous, leading to unique trajectories over time, when applied to the empirical data, those trajectories were not unique or distinctive. This made it difficult to generate common types of dyadic interactions in practice. One possible way to circumvent this issue could be via mixed models with random components. These models could be used in a second step as a confirmatory approach. That is, the original models could be fitted to each dyad separately—as applied here—and then use mixed models with random components to extract variability in the dynamic parameters across the selected dyads. Using this approach would also be consistent with the view against aggregating data from individuals to identify interindividual changes over time, as it may mischaracterize how each person changes over time (Hamaker et al., 2005; Molenaar, 2004; Molenaar & Valsiner, 2005; Nesselroade, 2001; 2002).

Extensions and Future Directions

There are multiple ways in which the current analyses can be extended. For example, our models based on differential equations assumed that change occurred in a continuous fashion. But this assumption might not be entirely tenable in our data. Instead, change might be discontinuous, with multiple equilibrium points and nonstationarity. In those situations other models may be needed. Similarly, our specifications assumed the couples to be closed systems, without any input from forces outside the system (e.g., events external to the dyads). In previous work with these types of data, we have found that random shocks to the system (e.g., external events, unrelated to the affective processes) can account for nontrivial amounts of variability. Hence, it may be important to model such random shocks explicitly.

Of course, the data-generating process underlying our time series could be more complex than the models included here, so our approach is inherently limited. For example, individuals and dyads could have multiple emotional set points, with distinct periods of synchrony and other periods of independence. For this, we would need more complex models that could capture such interactions and nonlinearities. Some families of very flexible approaches that could be useful in these situations include state-space models (e.g., Ho, Shumway, & Ombao, 2006; Shumway & Stoffer, 2006), and functional data analyses (Ramsay & Silverman, 2005). In general, simulation studies would be beneficial to determine to what extent and under what conditions these models—as well as the ones used in our analyses—can accurately recover the parameters. This point is particularly salient considering our results. For example, most couples in our data were best characterized by a dyadic model of independent or unregulated members. A pertinent question is whether this was a true characterization of the dyadic interactions in the data or the result of a poor specification of the dynamics in the model. In other words, were the parameters in the model correctly specified as to capture the dyadic interactions in the data? Simulation work is needed to answer this question in full detail.

A possible third extension of the current analyses concerns the use of external variables that may be related to the dynamics. For example, the type of affective exchange implied by the theoretical models used in our analyses may be related to relationship satisfaction or relationship stability in the future (see, e.g., Ferrer et al., 2012). If that is the case, information about the dynamic parameters for each couple could be used to make predictions about quality and stability of the couples at some distal point.

Concluding Remarks

The results we present in this chapter are exploratory but, we believe, they can serve to inform new analyses, develop alternative models, and refine our theoretical notions of dyadic interactions. We used theoretically based models applied to individual dyads and combined this approach with exploratory techniques to classify all dyads and summary information about dynamics. We believe this combination of confirmatory and exploratory methods is a fruitful and promising approach. More importantly, we based all of our analyses on the assumption that individuals in dyads form a dynamic system with interdependent forces between both members. We hope this idea serves to illustrate the possibilities of modeling interactions in dyads as dynamic systems.

ACKNOWLEDGMENTS

This work was supported in part by grants from the National Science Foundation (Nos. BCS-05-27766 and BCS-08-27021) and the National Institutes of Health-National Institute of Neurological Disorders and Stroke (No. R01 NS057146-01) to Emilio Ferrer.

We appreciate the help and comments by Fushing Hsieh, Diane Felmlee, David Greenberg, Dave Sbarra, Kevin Grimm, Hairong Song, Jonathan Helm, Laura Castro-Schilo, Michael McAssey, Keith Widaman, and the members of the DDIP Lab.

NOTES

1. Because the system of equations is linear, there exists an analytic solution that represents the integral form of the equation. From these solutions, one can compute the eigenvalues and determine if the system is asymptotically stable (tending toward an equilibrium, or state of no change) or diverging over time. Since the submodels are specified using inequality constraints on the parameters of the system, they are not really different models with regard to the form of the analytic solution. This analytic solution stays the same for the equation, with differences only in the constrained coefficients (e.g., positive, negative, or strictly zero) during estimation. Moreover, the equilibrium solu-

tion is dependent on the x^* and y^* values as well, so these are not really model dependent as much as they are dyad-by-dyad dependent.
2. All analyses presented here were carried out with complete data. This choice was motivated by the many and complex patterns of missing data, within and across dyads. However, analysis with missing data is also possible.
3. We chose values of .80 to represent theoretically meaningful ratios of positive to negative affect, as theoretically determined by Schwartz (1997). Alternative values for these parameters are also possible. For example, they can be specified as the mean of the series or, alternatively, estimated from the data (see Steele, Ferrer, & Nesselroade, 2011).

APPENDIX

Sample Script of PROC MODEL Used for the Analyses

```
TITLE 'Model 1: Cooperative system (.80 ideal)';
PROC MODEL DATA = paff_ode_inits;
    BY dyad_id;

    PARM a1=.1 a2=.1 b1=.1 b2=.1;
    RESTRICT a1 > 0;
    RESTRICT b1 > 0;
    RESTRICT a2 > 0;
    RESTRICT b2 > 0;

    dert.faf = a1*(.80-faf) + a2*(maf-faf);
    dert.maf = b1*(.80-maf) + b2*(faf-maf);

    FIT faf maf / FIML
    OUT = dypos_m1_out
    OUTALL OUTEST = dypos_m1_est;
RUN;
```

REFERENCES

Amemiya, T. (1977). The Maximum Likelihood estimator and the nonlinear Three-Stage Least Squares estimator in the general nonlinear simultaneous equation model. *Econometrica, 45,* 955–968.

Baron, R. M., Amazeen, P. G., & Beek, P. J. (1994). Local and global dynamics of social relations. In R. R. Vallacher & A. Nowak (Eds.), *Dynamical systems in social psychology* (pp. 111–138). San Diego, CA: Academic Press.

Bobbitt, R. A., Gourevitch, V. P., Miller, L. E., & Jensen, G. D. (1969). Dynamics of social interactive behavior: A computerized procedure for analyzing trends, patterns, and sequences. *Psychological Bulletin, 71,* 110–121.

Boker, S. M., & Laurenceau, J-P. (2006). Dynamical systems modeling: An application to the regulation of intimacy and disclosure in marriage. In T. A. Walls & J. L. Schafer (Eds.), *Models for intensive longitudinal data* (pp. 195–218). New York: Oxford University Press.

Buder, E. H. (1991). A nonlinear dynamic model of social interaction. *Communication Research, 18*, 174–198.

Butner, J., Diamond, L. M., & Hicks, A. M. (2007). Attachment styles and two forms of affect coregulation between romantic partners. *Personal Relationships, 14*, 431–455.

Campbell, L., & Kashy, D. A. (2002). Estimating actor, partner, and interaction effects for dyadic data using PROC MIXED and HLM: A guided tour. *Personal Relationships, 9*, 327–342.

Castellan, N. (1979). The analysis of behavior sequences. In R. Cairns (Ed.), *The analysis of social interactions: Methods, issues, and illustrations* (pp. 81–116). Hillsdale, NJ: Erlbaum.

Chow, S-M., Ferrer, E., & Nesselroade, J. R. (2007). An unscented Kalman filter approach to the estimation of nonlinear dynamical systems models. *Multivariate Behavioral Research, 42*, 283–321.

Cranford, J. A., Shrout, P. E., Iida, M., Rafaeli, E., Yip, T., & Bolger, N. (2006). A procedure for evaluating sensitivity to within-person change: Can mood measures in diary studies detect change reliably? *Personality and Social Psychology Bulletin, 32*, 917–929.

Felmlee, D. H. (2006). Application of dynamic systems analysis to dyadic interactions. In A. D. Ong & M. van Dulmen (Eds.), *Handbook of methods in positive psychology* (pp. 409–422). New York: Oxford University Press.

Felmlee, D. H., & Greenberg, D. F. (1999). A dynamic systems model of dyadic interaction. *Journal of Mathematical Sociology, 23*, 155–180.

Ferrer, E., Chen, S., Chow, S.-M., & Hsieh, F. (2010). Exploring intra-individual, inter-individual and inter-variable dynamics in dyadic interactions. In S.-M. Chow, E. Ferrer, & F. Hsieh (Eds.), *Statistical methods for modeling human dynamics: An interdisciplinary dialogue* (pp. 381–411). New York: Taylor & Francis.

Ferrer, E., & Nesselroade, J. R. (2003). Modeling affective processes in dyadic relations via dynamic factor analysis. *Emotion, 3*, 344–360.

Ferrer, E., Steele, J., & Hsieh, F. (2012). Analyzing dynamics of affective dyadic interactions using patterns of intra- and inter-individual variability. *Multivariate Behavioral Research, 47*, 136–171.

Ferrer, E., & Widaman, K. F. (2008). Dynamic factor analysis of dyadic affective processes with inter-group differences. In N. A. Card, J. P. Selig, & T. D. Little (Eds.), *Modeling dyadic and interdependent data in the developmental and behavioral sciences* (pp. 107–137). Hillsdale, NJ: Psychology Press.

Ferrer, E., & Zhang, G. (2009). Time series models for examining psychological processes: Applications and new developments. In R. E. Millsap, & A. Maydeu-Olivares (Eds.), *Handbook of quantitative methods in psychology* (pp. 637–657). London: Sage.

Friedkin, N. E. (1998). *A structural theory of social influence.* New York: Cambridge University Press.

Gallant, A. R., & Holly, A. (1980). Statistical inference in an implicit, nonlinear, simultaneous equation model in the context of maximum likelihood estimation. *Econometrica, 48,* 697–720.

Goodman, L. (1970). The multivariate analysis of qualitative data: Interactions among multiple classifications. *Journal of the American Statistical Association, 65,* 226–256.

Gottman, J. (1979). Detecting cyclicity in social interaction. *Psychological Bulletin, 86,* 338–348.

Gottman, J. M. (1994). *What predicts divorce?: The relationship between marital processes and marital outcomes.* Hillsdale, NJ: Erlbaum.

Gottman, J., Murray, J., Swanson, C., Tyson, R., & Swanson, K. (2002). *The mathematics of marriage: Dynamic nonlinear models.* Cambridge, MA: MIT Press.

Hamaker, E. L., Dolan, C. V., & Molenaar, P. C. M. (2005). Statistical modeling of the individual: Rationale and application of multivariate stationary time series analysis. *Multivariate Behavioral Research, 40,* 207–233.

Hamaker, E. L., Zhang, Z., & van der Maas, H. I. J. (2009). Using threshold autoregressive models to study dyadic interactions. *Psychometrika, 74,* 727–745.

Ho, R. M., Shumway, R., & Ombao, H. (2006). The state-space approach to modeling dynamical processes. In T. A. Walls & J. L. Schafer (Eds.), *Models for intensive longitudinal data* (pp. 148–175). New York: Oxford University Press.

Hsieh, F., Ferrer, E., Chen, S., & Chow, S.-M. (2010). Exploring nonstationary dynamics in dyadic interactions via hierarchical segmentation. *Psychometrika, 75,* 351–372.

Julier, S. J., Uhlmann, J. K., & Durrant-Whyte, H. F. (1995). A new approach for filtering nonlinear systems. In *Proceedings of the American Control Conference* (pp. 1628–1632). Seattle, WA: IEEE Press.

Kashy, D., & Kenny, D. (2000). The analysis of data from dyads and groups. In H. Reiss & C. Judd (Eds.), *Handbook of research methods in social psychology* (pp. 451–477). New York: Cambridge University Press.

Kenny, D. A., Kashy, D. A., & Cook, W. L. (2006). Dyadic data analysis. In D. A. Kenny (Ed.), *Methodology in the social sciences.* New York: Guilford Press.

Laurenceau, J., Troy, A. B., & Carver, C. S. (2005). Two distinct emotional experiences in romantic relationships: Effects of perceptions regarding approach of intimacy and avoidance of conflict. *Personality and Social Psychology Bulletin, 31,* 1123–1133.

Marwan, N., & Kurths, J. (2002). Nonlinear analysis of bivariate data with cross recurrence plots. *Physics Letters A, 302,* 299–307.

Molenaar, P. C. M. (1985). A dynamic factor model for the analysis of multivariate time series. *Psychometrika, 50,* 181–202.

Molenaar, P. C. M. (2004). A manifesto on psychology as idiographic science: Bringing the person back into scientific psychology—this time forever. *Measurement, 2,* 201–218.

Molenaar, P. C. M., & Valsiner, J. (2005). How generalization works through the single case: A simple idiographic process analysis of an individual psychotherapy. *International Journal of Idiographic Science,* Article 1. Retrieved October 18, 2005, from *www.valsiner.com/articles/molenvals.htm.*

Nesselroade, J. R. (2001). Intraindividual variability in development within and between individuals. *European Psychologist, 6,* 187–193.

Nesselroade, J. R. (2002). Elaborating the differential in differential psychology. *Multivariate Behavioral Research, 37,* 543–561.

Newsom, J. (2002). A multilevel structural equation model for dyadic data. *Structural Equation Modeling: A Multidisciplinary Journal, 9,* 431–447.

Newtson, D. (1993). The dynamics of action and interaction. In L. B. Smith & E. Thelen (Eds.), *A dynamic systems approach to development: Applications* (pp. 241–264). Cambridge, MA: MIT Press.

Pindyck, R. S., & Rubinfeld, D. L. (1981). *Econometric models and economic forecasts* (2nd ed.). New York: McGraw-Hill.

Ramsay, J. O., & Silverman, B. W. (2005). *Functional data analysis.* New York: Springer.

Rapaport, A. (1960). *Fights, games and debates.* Ann Arbor: University of Michigan Press.

Raudenbush, S. W., Brennan, R. T., & Barnett, R. C. (1995). A multivariate hierarchical model for studying psychological change within married couples. *Journal of Family Psychology, 9,* 161–174.

Sackett, G. (1979). The lag sequential analysis of contingency and cyclicity in behavioral interaction research. In J. Osofsky (Ed.), *Handbook of infant development.* New York: Wiley.

Schwartz, R. M. (1997). Consider the simple screw: cognitive science, quality improvement, and psychotherapy. *Journal of Consulting and Clinical Psychology, 65,* 970–983.

Schwartz, R. M., Reynolds III, C. F., Thase, M. E., Frank, E., Fasiczka, A. L., & Haaga, D. A. F. (2002). Optimal and normal affect balance in psychotherapy of major depression: Evaluation of the balanced states of mind model. *Behavioural and Cognitive Psychotherapy, 30,* 439–450.

Shumway, R., & Stoffer, D. (2006). *Time series analysis and its applications: With R examples.* New York: Springer.

Simon, H. (1957). *Models of man.* New York: Wiley.

Song, H., & Ferrer, E. (2009). State-space modeling of dynamic psychological processes via the Kalman smoother algorithm: Rationale, finite sample properties, and applications. *Structural Equation Modeling: A Multidisciplinary Journal, 16,* 338–363.

Steele, J., & Ferrer, E. (in press). Latent differential equation modeling of self-regulatory and coregulatory affective processes. *Multivariate Behavioral Research.*

Steele, J., & Ferrer, E., & Nesselroade, J.R. (2011). *Dyadographic analysis: An idiographic approach to estimating models of dyadic interactions with differential equations.* Manuscript submitted for publication.

Steenbeek, H. W., & van Geert, P. L. C. (2007). A theory and dynamic model of dyadic interaction: Concerns, appraisals, and contagiousness in a developmental context. *Developmental Review, 27,* 1–40.

Thomson, A., & Bolger, N. (1999). Emotional transmission in couples under stress. *Journal of Marriage & the Family, 61,* 38–48.

Tuma, N. B., & Hannan, M. T. (1984). *Social dynamics: Models and methods.* Orlando, FL: Academic Press.

Van der Merwe, R. (2003). *ReBEL: Recursive Bayesian Estimation Library.* ReBEL online documentation.

PART II

DRAWING VALID INFERENCES: LONGITUDINAL DESIGN CONSIDERATIONS AND MODEL ASSUMPTIONS

CHAPTER 6

SENSITIVITY ANALYSIS OF MIXED-EFFECTS MODELS WHEN LONGITUDINAL DATA ARE INCOMPLETE

Shelley A. Blozis
University of California, Davis

INTRODUCTION

Mixed-effects models have become a widely adopted approach to the analysis of longitudinal data. Key aspects of the methodology that make mixed-effects models well suited for longitudinal data analysis are that models may be specified to handle different types of response distributions, different mathematical functions to describe the growth trajectory, individual-specific times of measurement, and missing data (Skrondal & Rabe-Hesketh, 2004). With regard to missing data in particular, statistical inference of a mixed-effects model is considered valid when data are missing completely at random (MCAR) or missing at random (MAR). Data are MCAR whether or not data are missing (known as missingness) is independent of the missing and observed data, such as if missing data are planned in advance of data collection (see, e.g., Graham, Taylor, Olchowski, & Cumsille,

2006). Data are MAR if the missingness is related to the observed data but is independent of the missing data, such as if the probability of missing data is related to measured covariates (e.g., participant's gender) but not to the missing data (e.g., life satisfaction measures) (Little & Rubin, 2002). Thus, mixed-effects models provide a more flexible approach in terms of the assumptions about missing data compared to methods that require complete data and so also require that data are MCAR (e.g., repeated-measures ANOVA).

Mixed-effects models have gained popularity as a major approach to the study of longitudinal data in part because some of the challenges in dealing with missing data common to longitudinal studies may be met by this method. As a general statistical framework, mixed-effects models may be specified so that person-specific data collection patterns, such as unique times of measurement for each individual, may be handled. Furthermore, individuals need not be observed the same number of times, and so missing data are also allowed.

Data are MAR if the missingness is independent of the missing data. Under MAR, whether or not data are missing may depend on the observed data, such as measures taken prior to the time of participant dropout, including both observed measures of the longitudinal response and covariates that may also be included in a model, but is not dependent on the missing data otherwise. In this case, the missing data process may be ignored and a mixed-effects model may be applied (see, e.g., Laird, 1988). That is, there is no need to address the missing data process as would be done, for instance, in a model that assumed data are not missing at random (MNAR) (see the discussion to follow) (Molenberghs & Kenward, 2007). In sum, data are MAR if the missingness, conditional on the observed data, is independent of the missing data. In this situation the missing data mechanism need not be taken into account in the analysis for making valid statistical inference.

Although mixed-effects models offer some flexibility with regard to the assumptions about missing data (i.e., statistical inference is considered valid when data are MCAR or MAR), a difficulty arises in the evaluation of the assumptions. Specifically, given that the missing data are not available for study, nor is the mechanism giving rise to the missing data typically known (e.g., whether some or all data are MAR or not is not often known), it is not possible to test the assumption that the missingness and missing data are independent. Consequently, researchers may apply a mixed-effects model to incomplete data, although the validity of statistical inference may not be fully evaluated in light of the true missing data process and the missing data. Indeed, even methods that specifically address a MNAR mechanism must rely on the observed data.

A less restrictive assumption about missing data is one in which the missingness, conditional on the observed data, is dependent on the missing data. In such cases, data are said to be MNAR, such as if the missing data of individuals who drop from a study are related to the probability of dropout even after accounting for the relationship between dropout and the observed data (such as scores observed at the start of a study). In a different example, data are MNAR in a study of life satisfaction if individuals who tend to have poorer life satisfaction tend also not to respond to survey questions pertaining to life satisfaction. If data are MNAR, the missing data process should not be ignored under a mixed-effects model. Indeed, statistical inference of a mixed-effects model may be invalid if data are MNAR and the missing data mechanism is not addressed in the analysis (Molenberghs & Kenward, 2007). For longitudinal data in particular, the missing data process may be complex, such as if the missingness is related to the observed longitudinal response and possibly covariates, in addition to the missing data (conditional on the observed data). In these situations, the missing data may be in part MAR and MNAR. Whether data are MAR or MNAR or are due to a combination of the two, neither assumption can be empirically tested, however, because the missing data are not available.

Sensitivity analysis may be used in the study of missing data under a mixed-effects model if data are MNAR to demonstrate that by also including a model for the missing data process, such as allowing the missing data upon dropout to depend on previously observed scores, a different set of parameter estimates result for the model of substantive interest (Molenberghs & Kenward, 2007). Sensitivity analysis in general is an approach to assessing how a change in data or a model may influence the statistical inference of a model. Sensitivity analysis may be used, for instance, to study how the data of a particular individual in a sample may influence the parameter estimates of a model. Here, sensitivity analysis is considered in the context of fitting mixed-effects models to longitudinal data that are incomplete, and it is of interest to study the sensitivity of the parameter estimates of a longitudinal model under different assumptions about the missing data. That is, given a model of substantive interest, in particular a mixed-effects model, the model is fitted under a variety of conditions in which different missing data processes are considered. Sensitivity analysis involves a comparison of parameter estimates of the model of interest that result from the various models fitted. Important discrepancies, such as meaningful differences in effect size estimates or statistical test results, resulting from the model of primary interest assuming MAR and those that also serve to address the missing data process may suggest that data are MNAR.

This chapter considers a sensitivity analysis of a mixed-effects model for longitudinal data under two frameworks that have been proposed for the study of longitudinal data that are incomplete. These include a selection model and a pattern-mixture random-effects model. In practice, the mechanism underlying the missing data process of a given set of data is not typically known. Thus, exactly how a missing data process should be specified to operate in any given situation can be a difficult decision. By considering multiple frameworks for the missing data process, complete reliance on any single method is avoided. Furthermore, within each framework, variations of how the missing data process operates may also be considered.

The patterns of missing data in a longitudinal dataset may be varied. Missing data in longitudinal studies are often due to participant dropout in which data are no longer observed from the time of dropout. Intermittent patterns of missing data, such as cases in which an individual misses one or more waves of data collection but completes the final wave of assessment and thus is not considered to have dropped from the study, are also possible. The focus here is on missing data that are due to participant dropout. Intermittent missing data patterns are not treated but rather are assumed to represent data that are MAR (see, e.g., Diggle & Kenward, 1994). It may be that in some situations this is not a valid assumption about intermittently missing data and a different modeling strategy ought to be adopted.

The remainder of this chapter is organized as follows. To start, a brief description of a mixed-effects model is provided. The two frameworks considered here for the analysis of longitudinal data under a mixed-effects model if the missing data process is not ignorable are reviewed. An example is provided, and suggestions for future work are discussed.

MIXED-EFFECTS MODELS FOR LONGITUDINAL DATA

A mixed-effects model for a normally distributed variable may be expressed in a way that allows for a range of possibilities in terms of the functional form of a response as it is measured over time, as well as the manner in which fixed and random coefficients enter the model. A more general description of mixed-effects models that allows for a range of response distributions beyond the normal distribution may be found in Skrondal and Rabe-Hesketh (2004). Linear mixed-effects models are those in which the unknown coefficients, fixed or random, of the growth function enter the model linearly, such as in a linear growth model (Laird & Ware, 1982). Measures of time, however, may enter the model in a linear or nonlinear manner. In a linear growth model, for instance, the values of time enter linearly. Conversely, in a quadratic growth model, the values of time are squared and so enter nonlinearly. Nonlinear mixed-effects models involve unknown coefficients, fixed or random, that may enter the model linearly or nonlinearly (Davidian & Giltinan, 1995).

Let y_{ij} denote a response for individual i on the jth occasion, where $\mathbf{y}_i = (y_{i1}, \ldots, y_{in_i})'$ is a set of responses across n_i occasions for the individual. The particular number of observations and times at which an individual is observed may vary between individuals, as denoted by the subscript i for n_i. Under a mixed-effects model, the longitudinal response set is assumed to follow a model, presented here in a general form:

$$\mathbf{y}_i = f_i(\mathbf{X}_i, \boldsymbol{\beta}, \mathbf{b}_i) + \boldsymbol{\varepsilon}_i \qquad (6.1)$$

where $f_i(\cdot)$ is a vector-valued function of a set of known variables $\mathbf{X}_i = (X_{i0}, \ldots, X_{ip})'$ whose values may vary by time (within-subject variables) or be constant across the study period (between-subject variables), a fixed and unknown coefficient vector $\boldsymbol{\beta} = (\beta_0, \ldots, \beta_p)'$, and a random coefficient vector $\mathbf{b}_i = (b_{0i}, \ldots, b_{pi})'$. The fixed coefficients in $\boldsymbol{\beta}$ are the corresponding common effects of the variables in $\mathbf{X}_i$. The random coefficients typically relate directly to the fixed coefficients, that is, a fixed effect often has a corresponding random effect. The random coefficients allow the effects of variables to vary between individuals. The occasion-specific errors are denoted by the set $\boldsymbol{\varepsilon}_i = (\varepsilon_{i1}, \ldots, \varepsilon_{in_i})'$.

Variations of a mixed-effects model are possible. Under a fully nonlinear mixed-effects model, elements of both the fixed and random coefficient vectors in (6.1) may enter the model in a linear or nonlinear manner (Davidian & Giltinan, 1995). A coefficient enters a model in a linear manner when it enters in an additive way, such as in a linear growth function. A coefficient enters a model in a nonlinear manner when it enters in a nonadditive manner, such as a coefficient that appears in an exponent or in the denominator of a fraction. A special case of a nonlinear mixed-effects model is a partially nonlinear mixed-effects model in which the random coefficients may only enter the model linearly, whereas the fixed coefficients may enter linearly or nonlinearly (Blozis & Cudeck, 1999; Davidian & Giltinan, 1995). Under a linear mixed-effects model, elements of both the fixed and random coefficient vectors enter the model in a strictly linear manner.

Maximum likelihood (ML) estimation of a linear or partially nonlinear mixed-effects model may proceed using procedures commonly used to estimate strictly linear models, such as the Newton-Raphson or quasi-Newton Raphson algorithm (Blozis & Cudeck, 1999; Jennrich & Schluchter, 1986). Estimation may be carried out using one of several commercially available software packages. SPSS and SAS PROC MIXED, for instance, may be used to estimate linear mixed-effects models. LISREL, beginning with LISREL 8.80 for Windows, may be used to estimate partially nonlinear mixed-effects models if data are complete (Blozis, Harring, & Mels, 2008). Mx may be used to estimate partially nonlinear mixed-effects models if data are complete or incomplete (Blozis, 2007). ML estimation of a fully nonlinear mixed-effects model must follow alternative procedures given that a closed-form solution is not possible, except in special circumstances (see Davidian & Giltinan, 1995). Estimation of fully nonlinear mixed-effects models if some data are missing may be carried out using SAS PROC NL-MIXED, for instance. In any case where there are missing data, the data are assumed to be MAR.

MISSING DATA FRAMEWORKS FOR DATA THAT ARE MNAR

Under a mixed-effects model that is applied to a longitudinal response, if the missing data process is ignorable such that the missingness provides no added information about the response beyond the fitted model, then there is no need to address the missing data process in the analysis and statistical inference is considered to be valid. In such cases the missingness is noninformative. If data are MNAR, however, the missing data process should not be ignored when drawing inference from a mixed-effects model and information concerning the missingness should be incorporated into the analysis of the longitudinal response for valid inference. Thus, in these cases the missingness is said to be informative. A failure to address the missing data process if it is an important feature of a longitudinal process may result in misleading conclusions about the longitudinal response (see Molenberghs & Kenward, 2007).

Assuming the missingness is informative, a full response set Y_i for the individual in a population is defined in which some observations are observed and some are missing:

$$Y_i = \{(Y_i^o)', (Y_i^m)'\}'$$

where, for individual i, Y_i^o is a set of observed responses, and Y_i^m is a set of missing responses. A variable R is used to denote the missingness, such that $R = 1$ if Y is observed and $R = 0$ if Y is missing. If the missingness is informative, Y and R may be considered together in a model.

For a given observed dataset, a data analysis that is carried out under the assumption that the missingness is informative involves the joint density of the longitudinal response y_i, where some values of y_i in a sample may be missing due to, for instance, participant dropout, and a set of missing data indicators r_i, where r_i is a set of m indicator variables that reflect particular patterns of missing data in the sample. Values in r_i are equal to 1 if the individual is missing data for a variable and are equal to 0 otherwise. Assuming the longitudinal response follows a mixed-effects model, individuals also vary with respect to one or more of the random coefficients b_i of the longitudinal model. Then, the data analysis is based on the joint density of the longitudinal response, the random coefficients, and the missing data indicators, denoted by $f_i(\mathbf{y}_i, \mathbf{r}_i, \mathbf{b}_i)$, which may be expressed as

$$f(\mathbf{y}_i, \mathbf{r}_i, \mathbf{b}_i \mid \mathbf{X}_i, \theta, \psi)$$

where $\mathbf{y}_i$, $\mathbf{r}_i$, and $\mathbf{b}_i$ are conditional on $\mathbf{X}_i$, θ, and ψ, as dictated by a given model. Relating to the longitudinal response is $\mathbf{X}_i$, a fixed and known matrix that typically contains information about the times of measurement for $\mathbf{y}_i$, in addition to other variables that may also be measured. It is assumed that no data are missing in $\mathbf{X}_i$. A set of fixed parameters in θ characterize the longitudinal response as a function of $\mathbf{X}_i$. A set of fixed parameters in ψ describe the missing data process.

Several approaches have been proposed in specifying a mixed-effects model for longitudinal data that also include information about a missing data process. In practice, the mechanism leading to the missing data is typically unknown, presenting a challenge in specifying the missing data process. Given this and that several approaches are available for specifying the missing data process, one recommendation is to consider multiple strategies, rather than to rely on any one method (Little & Rubin, 2002; Molenberghs & Kenward, 2007). Two frameworks are considered here for specification of a mixed-effects model if the missingness is not ignorable. These are a selection model and a pattern-mixture random-effects model.

Selection Model

Under a selection model for longitudinal data that assumes data are MNAR, indicators of the missing data (such as participant dropout) are assumed to depend on the longitudinal response. Diggle and Kenward (1994) consider a selection model based on a linear mixed-effects model for data that are MNAR. In their application, the joint distribution of a longitudinal response and an indicator of dropout is assumed to follow a model based on a linear mixed-effects model for the longitudinal response and a logistic regression model for the probability of dropout that depends on the longitudinal response. Specifically, for individual i, D_i is used to denote the occasion at which dropout occurs, which may then depend on the longitudinal response observed prior to dropout and possibly the missing response at the time of dropout for those who drop from the study. For those with complete data, D_i depends on the observed longitudinal response. In any case, the probability of dropout does not depend on future responses. This process may be represented by a regression of the logit of the probability of dropout at occasion j on the longitudinal response as:

$$logit[P(D_i = j \mid D_i \geq j)] = \psi_0 + \psi_1 y_{i,j-1} + \psi_2 y_{ij}$$

where ψ_0 is the intercept of the regression, ψ_1 is the effect of the longitudinal response prior to dropout, and ψ_2 is the effect of the possibly unobserved longitudinal response at the time of dropout. This work was extended in Xu and Blozis (2011) to allow for a partially nonlinear mixed-effects model, as well as a structured latent curve model, for the longitudinal response and a logistic regression model for indicators of the missing data. In their application, a longitudinal response may follow a growth model that includes unknown growth coefficients that enter the model in a nonlinear but fixed manner.

Another formulation of a selection model is a shared parameter model in which the missingness depends on the random coefficients of the longitudinal model (Wu & Carroll, 1988). For example, dropout may be considered to be due to an individual's intercept and slope. In this formulation of a selection model, a mixed-effects model is assumed to address the longitudinal response, such as using a linear growth model with a random intercept and slope that is unique to the individual:

$$y_{ij} = \beta_{0i} + \beta_{1i}\text{time}_{ij} + \varepsilon_{ij}$$

where β_{0i} and β_{1i} are the person-specific intercept and linear time effect, time_{ij} is a measure of time at occasion j for the individual, and ε_{ij} is the individual's time-specific error at occasion j. A logit model may then be used to regress the probability of dropout on the random effects of the longitudinal model:

$$logit[P(D_i = j \mid D_i \geq j)] = \psi_0 + \psi_1 \beta_{0i} + \psi_2 \beta_{1i},$$

where ψ_1 and ψ_2 are the effects of the intercept and slope, respectively, on the log odds of dropout. The two models, that for the longitudinal responses as a function of time and that for dropout, are estimated simultaneously.

Pattern-Mixture Random-Effects Model

A pattern-mixture random-effects model for longitudinal data assumes that a longitudinal response depends in part on indicators of the missing data (Little, 1995; Little & Rubin, 2002). Hedeker and Gibbons (1997) describe a pattern-mixture random-effects model in which an indicator of missing data depends on the random coefficients of a linear mixed-effects model that define particular features of change in a longitudinal response (Little & Rubin, 2002). This formulation of a model allows for the study of how individual-specific coefficients that describe change in a longitudinal response may vary according to patterns of missing data, such as whether or not an individual completes a study. Individuals who drop from a study may have, for instance, relatively poor ratings on a clinical inventory at the beginning of a treatment program relative to those who complete the program.

In addition to allowing for variation in coefficients that characterize a longitudinal response to depend on patterns of missing data, it is possible to obtain population-level coefficients of the longitudinal process that are a weighted average of the coefficients across missing data patterns. This averaging takes into account the proportion of individuals having a particular pattern of missing data. In this way, the model may provide a more realistic representation of the population-level longitudinal profile as a weighted average across individuals who complete a study and those who do not.

Estimation

Parameter estimation can be problematic as a result of missing data. Although data may be MAR, model parameters may not be identified, such as if particular parameters cannot be estimated as a result of the missing data. In a longitudinal study, for instance, a model may specify a covariance between a longitudinal response at two particular time points, but in a given sample there may be no individuals for whom the measures were taken at the two time points. In this case, the covariance is not identified because there are no data available to estimate the covariance.

Estimation of a selection model is complicated due to the dependence of the missing data indicators on the missing data, but several strategies for dealing with this problem have been proposed (see, e.g., Molenberghs & Kenward, 2007). ML estimation of a linear mixed-effects model based on a selection framework for data that are MNAR may be carried out using procedures described in Diggle and Kenward (1994) and Dmitrienko, Offen, Faries, Chuang-Stein, and Molenberghs (2005). Similar procedures for fitting a partially nonlinear mixed-effects model and structured latent curve model based on a selection model are described in Xu and Blozis (2011).

ML estimation of a pattern-mixture random-effects model may follow procedures that are used to carry out estimation of a linear or nonlinear mixed-effects model that includes between-subject covariates that relate to the random coefficients of the latent growth model. Specifically, ML estimates of the effects of missing data indicators on the individual growth parameters is analogous to estimating the effects of other person-level covariates, such as gender (e.g., Hedeker & Gibbons, 1997).

EXAMPLE: LONGITUDINAL ANALYSIS OF ILLNESS SEVERITY RATINGS

Data from the National Institute of Mental Health Schizophrenia Collaborative Study are presented here (see Hedeker & Gibbons, 1997, and references therein). Data are available for $N = 437$ psychiatric patients randomly assigned to either a placebo ($n = 108$) or psychiatric medication ($n = 329$) group. A 7-point ordinal-scaled illness severity rating (IMPS97), where a value of 1 denoted normal functioning and the highest score of 7 indicated the most severe illness rating, were available weekly for up to six weeks following the study's onset. Here, ratings are treated as continuous measures. Following Hedeker and Gibbons, an indicator of participant dropout, denoted here as *Dropout*, was defined as whether or not a patient dropped by the final measurement wave. *Dropout* was equal to 1 if a patient dropped from the study and was equal to 0 otherwise. Of those assigned to the placebo group, 70 (65%) completed the study. Of those assigned to the medication group, 265 (81%) completed the study. Intermittent patterns of missing data were assumed to be ignorable.

Longitudinal Model

Plots of an arbitrarily selected subsample of individual trajectories are shown in Figure 6.1 with data from those assigned to the placebo and medication groups shown separately. From the plots, individual differences in responses are apparent. Scores generally seem to decrease with time. A set of growth models were fitted to the responses, ranging from a model that assumed no growth to one that assumed growth followed by an exponential function. Time was centered to the first wave of data collection. For each model fitted, the time-specific errors were assumed to be independent between waves with constant variance σ^2, and the growth coefficients were assumed to vary at random across individuals. The individual growth coefficients of each model were allowed to covary with one another and assumed to be independent of the time-specific errors. Model fit among the set of models was evaluated using deviance tests and comparing values of the Akaike information criterion (AIC). Between any two models smaller values of the AIC suggest a better-fitting model while taking into account model parsimony. Estimation was carried out using SAS (version 9.2) PROC NLMIXED with ML estimation. The particular growth models that were fitted are summarized in Table 6.1.

For the model that assumed exponential growth, a structured latent curve model was applied (Browne, 1993; Browne & du Toit, 1991). A structured latent curve model is a nonlinear latent growth model in which a

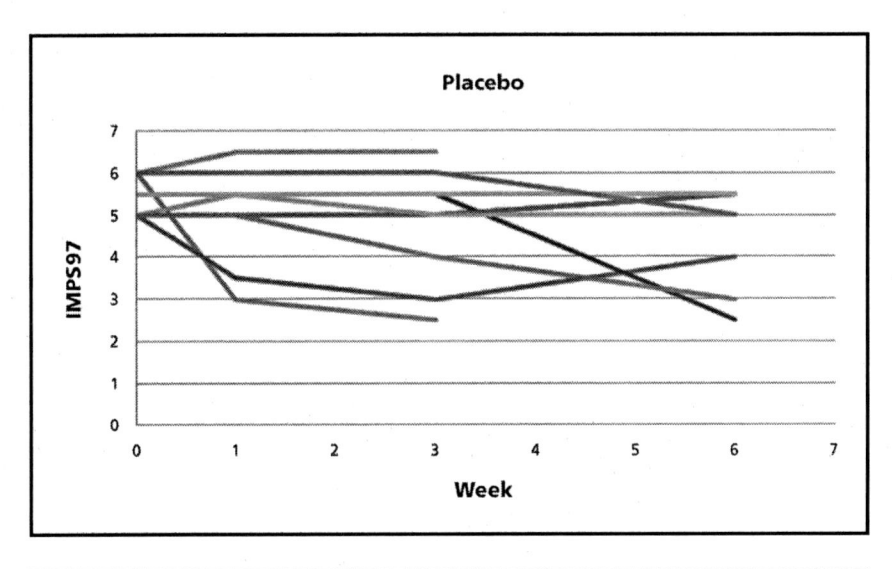

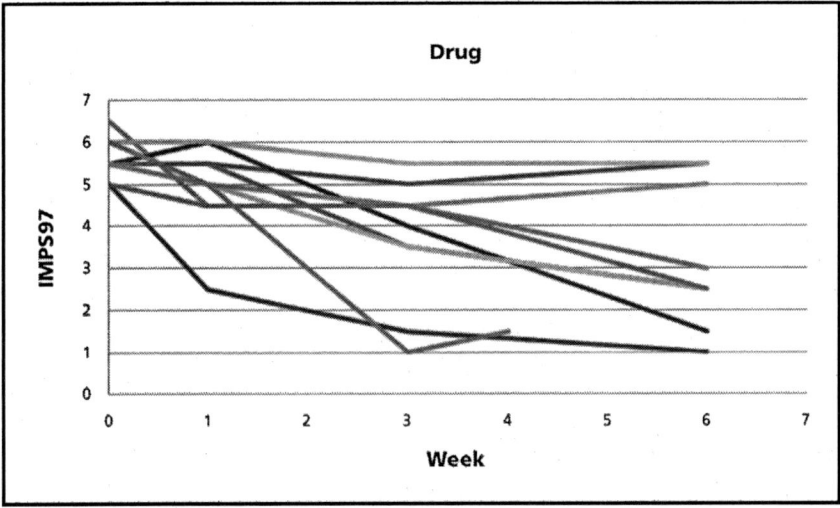

Figure 6.1 Arbitrary subsamples of individual observed trajectories, with data shown separately for those assigned to the placebo (upper figure) and medication groups (lower figure).

target function, a function that describes growth at the population level, may be nonlinear in its parameters. The response at the individual level is assumed to be due to a Taylor polynomial based on the target function. Specifically, an individual's response is assumed to be a sum of the target function plus a weighted sum of a set of basis functions that are defined by the first-order partial derivatives of the target function taken with respect to

TABLE 6.1 Indices of Model Fit for Illness Ratings (N = 437)

Growth description	Growth model	−2lnL	q	AIC
No growth	$y_{ij} = \beta_{0i} + \varepsilon_{ij}$	5668	3	5674
Linear	$y_{ij} = \beta_{0i} + \beta_{1i}t_{ij} + \varepsilon_{ij}$	4874	6	4886
Quadratic	$y_{ij} = \beta_{0i} + \beta_{1i}t_{ij} + \beta_{2i}t_{ij} + \varepsilon_{ij}$	4700	10	4720
Exponential	$y_{ij} = \Lambda_{ij}\alpha + \beta_{0i}f'_{0ij} + \beta_{1i}f'_{1ij} + \beta_{2i}f'_{2ij} + \varepsilon_{ij}$	4668	10	4688

Note: −2ln*L* is the −2 log likelihood function value, *q* is the number of model parameters, and *AIC* is Akaike Information Criterion. For the exponential function, the matrix of first-order partial derivatives Λ_{ij} and the vectors of first-order partial derivatives, f'_{0ij}, f'_{1ij}, and f'_{2ij}, are evaluated at $t = j$ for individual i.

the growth coefficients. The weights that are applied to the basis functions vary at random across individuals. Although limited to functions that satisfy a condition in which the target function is invariant to a constant scaling factor (see Browne, 1993, p. 177), the functions that may be considered under this framework are often relevant in many behavioral studies.

An exponential function was applied to illness severity ratings using a structured latent curve model. The function included an intercept β_0 defined as the response level at the first wave of measurement due to the centering of time at the first wave, a lower asymptote β_1, and a nonlinear change parameter β_2. Specifically, the target function at occasion j for the population response μ_j was specified as

$$\mu_j = f(\beta, t_j) = \beta_1 - (\beta_1 - \beta_0)\exp\{-\beta_2 t_j\} \quad (6.2)$$

where t_j is a centered value of time, for $t = 0, \ldots, 6$.

For the individual, the response is based on a Taylor polynomial. Analytic first-order partial derivatives of the exponential function in equation 6.2 are provided in Browne (1993). An individual's response set y_i is assumed to be due to a sum of the target function, expressed as a linear combination of a matrix of basis functions Λ_i weighted by a fixed coefficient vector α, and a weighted sum of the first-order partial derivatives, $b_{0i}f'_0 + b_{1i}f'_1 + b_{2i}f'_2$, plus a set of time-specific errors ε_i:

$$y_i = \Lambda_i\alpha + b_{0i}f'_0 + b_{1i}f'_1 + b_{2i}f'_2 + \varepsilon_i$$

where α is obtained by solving a set of linear equations, such that $f(\beta, t_i) = \Lambda_i\alpha$, where $f(\beta, t_i)$ is a vector-valued function of $t_i = (t_{i1}, \ldots, t_{in_i})'$, with n_i denoting the last occasion of measurement for individual i (see Blozis, 2004). For a structured latent curve model based on the exponential function in equation 6.2, for instance, solving for α results in $\alpha = (\beta_0, \beta_1, 0)'$. The derivatives, f'_0, f'_1, and f'_2, are evaluated according to values of t_i.

RESULTS

Values of the −2 log-likelihood function values and AIC values are provided in Table 6.1. Among the models fitted, the exponential growth model provided the best overall fit, as evidenced by the AIC value being lowest for this model. Additionally, a deviance test comparing the fit of the model that assumed no change in illness ratings to that for the exponential function suggested that the latter was preferable ($\chi^2(7\ df) = 1000$, $p < .001$).

To account for individual differences due to treatment assignment, an indicator variable denoting treatment status for the individual, $Drug_i$, was added to the model as a moderator of the three growth coefficients at the second level of the exponential growth model:

$$\beta_{0i} = \beta_{00} + \beta_{01} Drug_i + r_{0i}$$

$$\beta_{1i} = \beta_{10} + \beta_{11} Drug_i + r_{1i}$$

$$\beta_{2i} = \beta_{20} + \beta_{21} Drug_i + r_{2i}$$

where β_{00}, β_{10}, and β_{20} are the expected values of the respective growth coefficients for those patients assigned to receive the placebo. The coefficients β_{01}, β_{11}, and β_{21} are the expected differences in the respective growth coefficients between those assigned to receive the placebo and those assigned to receive a medication. The random errors of the three regression equations, r_{0i}, r_{1i}, and r_{2i}, are the discrepancies between the individual growth coefficients and the expected values after accounting for group membership. The estimated 95% confidence intervals for the estimated effects of $Drug$ on each of the growth coefficients suggested a difference in the asymptote between those receiving the placebo and those who did not but did not suggest group differences in the remaining two growth coefficients. The model was simplified by dropping the moderating effect of $Drug$ on the intercept and change rate. A deviance test comparing the fit of this model and the more complex model supported the lack of a need for these two group effects ($\chi^2(2\ df) = 0.8$, $p = 0.67$). ML estimates from the simplified model in which $Drug$ moderated only the asymptote are provided in Table 6.2. ML estimates are assumed to be valid if the missing data mechanism is ignorable.

Models for Data That Are MNAR

A selection model that assumed exponential growth in illness ratings, with the random asymptote assumed to be moderated by the grouping variable $Drug$ as described in the previous analysis, was fitted in which dropout was assumed to depend on the illness ratings. Specifically, the logit of the

TABLE 6.2 Maximum Likelihood Estimates of an Exponential Growth Model with Drug ($N = 437$)

Mean structure

Parameter	MLE (SE)	95% CI
β_{00}, Intercept	5.32 (0.04)	(5.24, 5.40)
β_{10}, Asymptote	4.37 (0.18)	(4.02, 4.72)
β_{11}, Asymptote*$Drug_i$	−1.68 (0.20)	(−2.08, −1.28)
β_{20}, Rate	0.35 (0.04)	(0.28, 0.42)

Covariance structure

$$\text{Level 2: } \hat{\Phi} = \begin{bmatrix} 2.3 & -0.10 & 0.42 \\ -0.080 & 0.30 & -0.51 \\ 0.74 & -0.33 & 1.3 \end{bmatrix} \quad \text{Level 1: } \hat{\sigma}^2 = 0.469$$

Note: MLE is the maximum likelihood estimate with corresponding standard error (SE). 95% CI is an estimated 95% confidence interval for the corresponding parameter. The estimated covariance matrix at the individual level is given by $\hat{\Phi}$, where variances appear along the diagonal and covariances in the off-diagonal. Corresponding correlations are given in the upper diagonal. ML estimates assume missing data are MAR.

probability that a patient dropped from the study at occasion j was assumed to depend on the illness rating prior to dropout ($y_{i,j-1}$), assuming the patient was observed prior to dropout, as well as possibly the unobserved illness rating at the time of dropout (y_{ij}):

$$\text{logit}[P(Dropout_i = j \mid Dropout_i \geq j)] = \psi_0 + \psi_1 y_{i,j-1} + \psi_2 y_{ij}$$

where ψ_0 is the intercept of the logit regression, and the coefficients ψ_1 and ψ_2 are the effects on the logit of the response prior to and at the time of dropout, respectively. Under this model, if the true values of ψ_1 and ψ_2 are equal to zero, then the missingness is independent of both the observed and missing illness ratings, and the data are MCAR. If ψ_2 but not ψ_1 is equal to zero, then the missingness depends on the observed illness ratings but not the unobserved responses, and the data are MAR. In either of these cases, the missing data mechanism is ignorable under a mixed-effects model. If, however, ψ_2 is not equal to zero, then the missingness depends on the unobserved responses, and the data are MNAR. In this case, the model should address the missing data mechanism so that inference of the ML estimates of the longitudinal model is valid. Other formulations of a missing data model are possible, such as allowing the missingness to depend on only the initial response (e.g., Xu & Blozis, 2011).

ML estimates of model parameters and −2 log-likelihood function values for three selection models that differed with regard to their assumptions about the missing data process are provided in Table 6.3. Specifically, Model 1 assumed both ψ_1 and ψ_2 were equal to zero so that the missingness did not depend on either the responses observed prior to dropout or the missing responses at the time of dropout. Model 2 assumed that ψ_2 was equal to zero so that the missingness could depend on only the observed responses prior to dropout but not the missing values at the time of dropout. Model 3 set no constraints on either ψ_1 or ψ_2 so that the missingness could depend on the responses observed prior to dropout and the missing responses at the time of dropout. It should be noted that although Model 1 specifies a missing data process in which dropout depends on the observed data, the model for the longitudinal response is based on a mixed-effects model that assumes data are MAR. Thus, estimates from Models 1 and 2 for the longitudinal model component are expected to be the same (see Table 6.3).

A deviance test comparing the fit between Model 1 and 2 suggested that the missingness was dependent on the illness ratings prior to dropout ($\chi^2(1\ df) = 15.5$, $p < .001$). A similar comparison between Models 2 and 3 using a deviance test should not be made, however, because the test is not reliable (Jansen et al., 2006; Molenberghs & Kenward, 2007, Section 19.6). Specifically, the estimate of ψ_2 represents the effect of the missing data on the probability of dropout and so is based on relatively little information and has been shown to be very sensitive to changes in data or a model. Similarly, evaluation of the estimate of ψ_2 relative to its standard error is also not considered to be reliable.

In comparing the models that assume MAR versus MNAR, a sensitivity analysis may be then performed to assess the need to include a model for the missing data process. A sensitivity analysis was performed here by comparing parameter estimates from Models 2 and 3. Possibly the most remarkable differences between the point estimates of parameters for Models 2 and 3 concern the asymptote and the moderating effect of *Drug* on the asymptote. Specifically, the estimated asymptote is relatively high when assuming MNAR versus MAR, which suggests that improvement was not as great as might be concluded when assuming MAR. The estimated moderating effect of *Drug* on the asymptote is relatively strong when assuming MNAR versus MAR, which suggests that the effect of *Drug* may be underestimated if data are assumed to be MAR. Although these differences are noted, the clinical significance of these differences is left for interpretation. Differences in estimates also involve the variances and covariances of the random effects at the second level, which may also suggest differences in the extent to which individuals vary with regard to the model coefficients. Overall, these results suggest some sensitivity of parameter estimates to as-

TABLE 6.3 Maximum Likelihood Estimates of an Exponential Growth Model with Drug under Different Selection Models for Missing Data (N = 437)

	Model 1		Model 2		Model 3	
Parameter	MLE (SE)	95% CI	MLE (SE)	95% CI	MLE (SE)	95% CI
β_{00}, Intercept	5.32 (0.04)	(5.24, 5.40)	5.32 (0.04)	(5.24, 5.40)	5.30 (0.04)	(5.22, 5.38)
β_{10}, Asymptote	4.37 (0.18)	(4.02, 4.72)	4.37 (0.18)	(4.02, 4.72)	4.77 (0.20)	(4.38, 5.16)
β_{11}, Asymptote*$Drug_i$	−1.68 (0.20)	(−2.07, −1.29)	−1.68 (0.20)	(−2.07, −1.29)	−1.87 (0.22)	(−2.30, −1.44)
β_{20}, Rate	0.35 (0.04)	(0.27, 0.43)	0.35 (0.04)	(0.27, 0.43)	0.35 (0.04)	(0.27, 0.43)
Φ	$\begin{bmatrix} 2.3 & -0.10 & 0.42 \\ -0.080 & 0.30 & -0.51 \\ 0.74 & -0.33 & 1.3 \end{bmatrix}$		$\begin{bmatrix} 2.3 & -0.10 & 0.42 \\ -0.080 & 0.30 & -0.51 \\ 0.74 & -0.33 & 1.3 \end{bmatrix}$		$\begin{bmatrix} 1.9 & -0.15 & 0.08 \\ -0.16 & 0.61 & -0.57 \\ 0.20 & -0.78 & 3.1 \end{bmatrix}$	
σ^2	0.47 (0.03)		0.47 (0.03)		0.58 (0.07)	
ψ_0	−2.44 (0.10)		−1.17 (0.32)		−2.84 (0.95)	
ψ_1			−0.29 (0.07)		−1.58 (0.43)	
ψ_2					1.64 (0.54)	
$-2\ln L$	7315.54		7300.02		7273.28	

sumptions about the missing data process, and so the missing data mechanism may not be ignorable.

Similar to conclusions drawn from estimating any statistical model, such as those that concern estimated effect sizes or statistical test results, conclusions drawn from the results of a sensitivity analysis are based on the importance placed on such results by the researcher. A sensitivity analysis that leads to a statistically significant treatment effect when assuming data are MAR but not when assuming data are MNAR, for instance, would likely be taken as evidence that data are MNAR and that the missing data process ought to be addressed. In a different example, a sensitivity analysis that resulted in a weakened effect size when assuming data were MNAR may be considered important in planning future studies with regard to sample size estimation because a larger sample size may be necessary to detect meaningful effects.

Next, a pattern-mixture random-effects model was fitted to the illness ratings. In this model, the exponential growth model was extended to include moderating effects of *Dropout* on the three growth coefficients. At the second level of the model, the three growth coefficients were assumed to be due to dropout status and, in addition, the asymptote was assumed to also vary according to $Drug_i$ as specified in the selection models considered previously:

$$\beta_{0i} = \beta_{00} + \beta_{02} Dropout_i + r_{0i}$$
$$\beta_{1i} = \beta_{10} + \beta_{11} Drug_i + \beta_{12} Dropout_i + r_{1i}$$
$$\beta_{2i} = \beta_{20} + \beta_{22} Dropout_i + r_{2i},$$

where β_{00} and β_{20} are the expected values of the intercept and change rate, respectively, for those patients who completed the study. The coefficients β_{02} and β_{22} are the expected differences in the intercept and change rate, respectively, for those patients who completed the study and those who did not. The coefficient β_{10} is the expected value of the asymptote for those patients who completed the study and were assigned to the placebo condition. The coefficient β_{11} is the expected difference in the asymptote between those assigned to receive the placebo and those assigned to receive a medication, holding constant the effect of *Dropout*. The coefficient β_{12} is the expected difference in the asymptote between those who completed the study and those who did not, holding constant the effect of *Drug*. The random errors of the three regression equations, r_{0i}, r_{1i}, and r_{2i}, are the discrepancies between the individual growth coefficients and the expected values after accounting for *Dropout*, and for the asymptote, the added effect of *Drug*.

Estimated 95% CI of *Dropout* on each of the growth coefficients suggested a difference in the asymptote and change rate between those who

TABLE 6.4 Maximum Likelihood Estimates of an Exponential Growth, Pattern-Mixture Model (N = 437)

Mean structure

Parameter	MLE (SE)	95% CI
β_{00}, Intercept	5.32 (0.04)	(5.24, 5.40)
β_{10}, Asymptote	4.31 (0.19)	(3.93, 4.68)
β_{11}, Asymptote*Drug	−1.65 (0.20)	(−2.05, −1.25)
β_{12}, Asymptote*Dropout	0.60 (0.26)	(0.09, 1.10)
β_{20}, Rate	0.31 (0.03)	(0.24, 0.37)
β_{22}, Rate*Dropout	0.53 (0.12)	(0.29, 0.78)

Covariance structure

$$\text{Level 2: } \hat{\Phi} = \begin{bmatrix} 3.1 & -0.04 & 0.53 \\ -0.04 & 0.32 & -0.54 \\ 0.86 & -0.28 & 0.87 \end{bmatrix} \quad \text{Level 1: } \hat{\sigma}^2 = 0.47$$

Note: MLE is the maximum likelihood estimate with corresponding standard error (SE). 95% CI is an estimated 95% confidence interval for the corresponding parameter. The estimated covariance matrix at the individual level is given by $\hat{\Phi}$, where variances appear along the diagonal and covariances in the off-diagonal. Corresponding correlations are given in the upper diagonal.

completed the study and those who had dropped. Conversely, the estimated 95% CI of *Dropout* on the intercept included zero as an interior point. The model was simplified by dropping the moderating effect of *Dropout* on the intercept. A deviance test comparing the fit of this model and the more complex model supported the lack of a need for this effect of dropout ($\chi^2(2\ df) = 1.2$, $p = 0.27$). ML estimates from a simplified model in which *Dropout* moderated the asymptote and change rate are provided in Table 6.4. Specifically, ML estimates, standard errors, and 95% confidence intervals (CIs) for the simplified pattern-mixture random-effects model are given. The estimated variances and covariances of the conditional random effects at the second level and the estimated time-specific variance are also provided. These results suggest that those who dropped from the study had on average poorer measured outcome levels toward the end of the study period and a faster rate of change. Similar to the results from the analyses based on selection models, these results suggest that *Dropout* may be important in the interpretation of the measured outcome and that perhaps additional steps should be taken to better understand its effect on the longitudinal measures.

DISCUSSION

If data are missing, as is often the case in longitudinal investigations, statistical inference of a mixed-effects model is valid (with regard to the missing data process) if the mechanism that gives rise to the missing data is ignorable. There is no need, for example, to incorporate into the longitudinal model of primary interest a separate model for the missing data process. The missingness is ignorable under a mixed-effects model if data are MAR. Assuming data are MAR, the missingness may depend on the observed data, including the longitudinal response observed prior to dropout, as well as other covariates that are included in the model. Under MAR the missingness is, however, assumed to be independent of the missing data, even after taking into account dependencies of the missingness on the observed data.

In situations where missingness is dependent on the missing data, the data are said to be MNAR. In this case, even after taking into account the longitudinal response observed prior to participant dropout, in addition to other model covariates, the missingness remains dependent on the missing data. Maximum likelihood estimates based on a model that assumes the missing data process is ignorable when data are actually MNAR will be biased if the missing data process is not addressed by the analysis.

Several approaches have been proposed to incorporate a model for the missing data process when data are MNAR. Two common frameworks for longitudinal data include a joint model based on a selection model for the missing data process and a random-effects model for the longitudinal data, and a pattern-mixture random-effects model that directly specifies that the longitudinal response depends on patterns of missing data. A variety of applications of each framework have been considered. A general recommendation is to consider multiple model formulations in any given application. This is due to the fact that the assumption that data are MNAR cannot be directly tested but one may study the behavior of parameter estimates under different plausible scenarios that may explain the missing data process. Thus, it is advisable to consider both multiple frameworks (e.g., selection models and pattern-mixture models) and different formulations of a missing data process within a given framework.

As described earlier, mixed-effects models for longitudinal data assume the missing data process is ignorable such that the missingness need not be addressed in the analysis. Important to the assumption that data are MAR is that the missingness cannot depend on the missing data but can depend on the observed data. In practice, this means that if correlates of the missing data can be observed prior to participant dropout, these correlates may be incorporated into a data model. Indeed, studies have shown that including variables that are related to the missingness may help to improve parameter estimates (Collins, Schafer, & Kam, 2001; Graham, 2003). Thus, there may be great benefit in careful planning of a longitudinal study to anticipate participant dropout and those correlates of the missingness.

REFERENCES

Blozis, S. A. (2004). Structured latent curve models for the study of change in multivariate repeated measures. *Psychological Methods, 9,* 334–353.

Blozis, S. A. (2007). A Newton procedure for a conditionally linear mixed-effects model. *Behavior Research Methods, 39,* 695–708.

Blozis, S. A., & Cudeck, R. (1999). Conditionally linear mixed-effects models with latent variable covariates. *Journal of Educational and Behavioral Statistics, 24,* 245–270.

Blozis, S. A., Harring, J. R., & Mels, G. (2008). Using LISREL to fit nonlinear latent curve models. *Structural Equation Modeling, 15,* 356–379.

Browne, M. (1993). Structured latent curve models. In C. M. Cuadras & C. R. Rao (Eds.), *Multivariate analysis: Future directions 2* (pp. 171–198). Amsterdam: North-Holland.

Browne, M. W., & du Toit, S. H. C. (1991). Models for learning data. In L. M. Collins & J. L. Horn (Eds.), *Best methods for the analysis of change* (pp. 47–68). Washington: American Psychological Association.

Collins, L. M., Schafer, J. L., & Kam, C.-H. (2001). A comparison of inclusive and restrictive strategies in modern missing data procedures. *Psychological Methods, 6,* 330–351.

Davidian, M., & Giltinan, D. M. (1995). *Nonlinear models for repeated measurement data.* London: Chapman & Hall.

Diggle, P. J., & Kenward, M. G. (1994). Informative drop-out in longitudinal data analysis (with discussion). *Applied Statistics, 43,* 49–93.

Dmitrienko, A., Offen, W. W., Faries, D., Chuang-Stein, C., & Molenberghs, G. (2005). *Analysis of clinical trial data using the SAS System.* Cary, NC: SAS Publishing.

Graham, J. W. (2003). Adding missing-data-relevant variables to FIML-based structural equation models. *Structural Equation Modeling, 10,* 80–100.

Graham, J. W., Taylor, B. J., Olchowski, A. E., & Cumsille, P. E. (2006). Planned missing data designs in psychological research. *Psychological Methods, 11,* 323–343.

Hedeker, D., & Gibbons, R. D. (1997). Application of random-effects pattern-mixture models for missing data in longitudinal studies. *Psychological Methods, 2,* 64–78.

Jansen, I., Hens, N., Molenberghs, G., Aerts, M., Verbeke, G., & Kenward, M. G. (2006). The nature of sensitivity in missing not at random models. *Computational Statistics and Data Analysis, 50,* 830–858.

Jennrich, R. I., & Schluchter, M. D. (1986). Unbalanced repeated-measures models with structured covariance matrices. *Biometrics, 42,* 805–820.

Laird, N. M. (1988). Missing data in longitudinal studies. *Statistics in Medicine, 7,* 305–315.

Laird, N. M., & Ware, J. H. (1982). Random-effects models for longitudinal data. *Biometrics, 38,* 963–974.

Little, R. J. A. (1995). Modeling the drop-out mechanism in repeated measures studies. *Journal of the American Statistical Association, 90,* 1112–1121.

Little, R. J. A., & Rubin, D. B. (2002). *Statistical analysis with missing data* (2nd ed.). New York: Wiley.

Molenberghs, G., & Kenward, M. G. (2007). *Missing data in clinical studies.* West Sussex, UK: Wiley.

Schafer, J. L., & Graham, J, W. (2002). Missing data: Our view of the state of the art. *Psychological Methods, 7,* 147–177.

Skrondal, A., & Rabe-Hesketh, S. (2004). *Generalized latent variable modeling.* London: Chapman & Hall/CRC.

Wu, M. C., & Carroll, R. J. (1988). Estimation and comparison of changes in the presence of informative right censoring by modeling the censoring process. *Biometrics, 44,* 175–188.

Xu, S., & Blozis, S. A. (2011). Sensitivity analysis of mixed models for incomplete longitudinal data. *Journal of Education and Behavioral Statistics, 36,* 237–256.

CHAPTER 7

FINITE MIXTURES OF NONLINEAR MIXED-EFFECTS MODELS

Jeffrey R. Harring
University of Maryland

Nonlinear patterns of change arise frequently in the analysis of repeated measures from longitudinal studies in the behavioral and social sciences and, as a consequence, practitioners have begun turning with more frequency to methods that can incorporate intrinsically nonlinear functions into an analysis. In contrast to linear processes, which assume steady incremental change across time or other condition, the cornerstone of nonlinear development is that change occurs more quickly in some periods than in others. Furthermore, there is often an implicit understanding that a nonlinear function can be identified—either grounded in theory, derived empirically from an initial exploration of the data, or both—that effectively summarizes the repeated measures and whose parameters capture important facets of the underlying process. The nonlinear mixed-effects (NLME) model (Davidian & Giltinan, 1995; Pinheiro & Bates, 2000) has become a popular platform for the analysis of continuous repeated-measures data with these notable characteristics where primary interest focuses on individual-level change.

The NLME model is particularly well suited for situations in which (1) the time-response pattern is comparable across subjects yet individual differences are clearly apparent; (2) individual trajectories follow the generic curvilinear time-response pattern that characterizes the behavior, but vary on particular salient features (i.e., decreases are more gradual or steeper) that are linked directly to model parameters; (3) substantial within-subject variability is evident in the relation between response and time across individuals; (4) subjects might be measured at different time points, or observed at a different number of occasions; and (5) they are missing at random. As Cudeck and Harring (2007) pointed out, the analytic method should satisfactorily accommodate all of these features: nonlinear trajectories, imbalanced designs and missing data, consequential within- and between-subject variability, and, above all, individual differences in the response. Fortunately, these data and design considerations are easily managed within a subject-specific model, like the NLME model.

Once a mathematical function for the repeated measures has been decided upon—a valuable activity in its own right—additional insights into the behavior captured by the repeated measures can be garnered when relations between individual attributes and regression coefficients are posited to account for the response. In a standard analysis where group attributes are well defined, group membership is often used to sharpen an understanding of the repeated measures. For example, gender or treatment condition may be used to help explain differences in initial status or potential performance of a longitudinal outcome (Blozis, 2004). Unfortunately, in some instances manifest groups are unknown yet genuinely distinctive clusters of change exist, but are embedded within individuals' growth patterns. When unobservable heterogeneity of this type is suspected, latent classes might be inferred from characteristics of the within-subject profiles. In short, finite mixture models could be incorporated to aid in uncovering these latent classes of different longitudinal trajectories.

Although finite mixture models have been extended recently in a number of interesting ways across diverse research areas (see, e.g., Hancock & Samuelsen, 2008, for a convenient summary of some of these extensions), several statistical methods and models for longitudinal data analysis have been successfully integrated with finite mixture models to address the analytic situation where within-subject correlation and subpopulation heterogeneity exist simultaneously. These include linear mixed-effects mixture models (LMM; Verbeke & Lesaffre, 1996; Verbeke & Molenberghs, 2000), growth mixture models (GMM; Muthén, 2001a, 2001b, 2002, 2004; Muthén & Shedden, 1999), and generalized mixed-effects mixture models (Hall & Wang, 2005).

Continued advances in the area of mixture models notwithstanding, methodological progress appears to be connected to the development and implementation of computational algorithms that can keep pace with myriad interesting innovations (Leisch, 2004). This is certainly true for the aforementioned mixtures of statistical models for the analysis of longitudinal data, a methodological domain in which inherently nonlinear response functions are noticeably absent from the literature. Accordingly, a logical progression in the context of modeling population heterogeneity for nonlinear repeated-measures data would dictate deriving a finite mixture model able to accommodate functions with at least one coefficient that enters nonlinearly.

Thus, the goal of this chapter is to describe an extended finite mixture model that combines features of two well-known statistical models: nonlinear mixed-effects (NLME) models and latent class or finite mixture models. This hybrid model, which will be referred to throughout the chapter as a nonlinear mixed-effects mixture (NLMM) model, broadens the existing LMM and GMM structures to intrinsically nonlinear functions. Analysis of this model is carried out using maximum likelihood estimation with the expectation-maximization (EM) algorithm. Technical aspects of implementing the EM algorithm and computing standard errors are addressed in the Appendix. Utility of the general model is illustrated with two specific examples.

The remainder of the chapter unfolds in the following way. The chapter begins with a brief overview of the NLME model outlining important analytic decision points in a standard analysis. This overview is followed by a detailed explication of the NLMM model. In a subsequent section, two examples using learning data are provided to underscore the efficacy and utility of the mixture approach in summarizing nonlinear growth with unobservable population heterogeneity. As will become obvious in upcoming sections, the data used in both examples exhibit characteristics for which this type of modeling makes sense. The chapter concludes with a discussion of the technical aspects of the estimation of the NLMM model as well as some of the model's limitations.

OVERVIEW OF THE NONLINEAR MIXED-EFFECTS MODEL

The following is a cursory review of the NLME model for continuous repeated-measures data (for advanced applications, methodological overviews, and advancements, see, e.g., Cudeck, 1996; Cudeck & Harring, 2007, 2010; Davidian & Giltinan, 2003; Pinheiro & Bates, 1995; or for book-length treatments, see, e.g., Davidian & Giltinan, 1995; Pinheiro & Bates, 2000; Vonesh & Chinchilli, 1997). The basic model consists of three interconnected components. The first is the nonlinear function that describes change over time in the repeated measures. This function is defined for individual subjects and employs subject-specific coefficients, all of which may or may not vary across individuals.[1] The second element is the within-subject covariance structure of the residuals. The third is the set of models for the regression coefficients that summarize differences among individuals.

Subject-Specific Model for Nonlinear Change

Unless theoretically derived, the functional form characterizing the within-subject behavior is commonly determined empirically through an initial exploration of the data.[2] Let the jth observation of the response for the ith subject, y_{ij}, be modeled as

$$y_{ij} = f(x_{ij}, \beta_{1i}, \ldots, \beta_{pi}) + e_{ij} \qquad i = 1, \ldots, M; \; j = 1, \ldots, n_i \qquad (7.1)$$

where f is an arbitrary nonlinear function governing within-individual behavior depending on p subject-specific regression parameters, $\beta_{1i}, \ldots, \beta_{pi}$, and predictor, x_{ij}, typically taken as the elapsed time from the beginning of an experiment to the jth assessment or the age of the subject at occasion j. Allowing x_{ij} to differ for each participant permits the greatest flexibility from a design standpoint. M is the total number of subjects.

In contrast to the structured latent curve model (Browne, 1993), where individual trajectories need not follow the same form as the function for the mean vector, the algebraic function used for the NLME model is understood to be the same for all, but because coefficients vary across subjects the actual fitted trajectories may be strikingly dissimilar.

Covariance Structure for the Residuals

The residuals in equation 7.1, e_{ij}, are random intraindividual deviations $e_{ij} = y_{ij} - f(x_{ij}, \beta_{1i}, \ldots, \beta_{pi})$ reflecting uncertainty in the response of the ith individual at the jth design point and are assumed to satisfy $E[e_{ij} | \beta_{1i}, \ldots, \beta_{pi}] = 0$ for all i and j. Covariation in the residuals within an individual is captured through the within-subject, or level 1, covariance structure, $\Gamma_i(\gamma)$, which may depend on parameter vector, γ. These residuals are assumed to be normally distributed. When coupled with random effects, the residuals are often assumed to have a simple structure depending on a small number of parameters, such as mutual independence with equal variances:

$$\text{var}(e_{ij}) = \sigma^2 \text{ for all } j, \; \text{cov}(e_{ij}, e_{ik}) = 0 \text{ for all } j \neq k.$$

Alternatively, when serial correlation is suspected and measurements are taken at equally spaced time points, the residuals may satisfy a first-order autoregressive process so that the jkth element of $\Gamma_i(\gamma)$ is given by

$$[\Gamma]_{jk} = \sigma^2 \rho^{|j-k|}$$

where vector γ contains the first-order error autocorrelation, ρ, and the common error variance, σ^2. More complex covariance structures can be specified as well (Davidian & Giltinan, 1995, Sec. 2) in which variances and covariances are uncoupled, allowing each parameter type to have a distinct systematic relation that could very well depend on functional parameters, design points, x_{ij}, and additional covariates. As Davidian and Giltinan (1995) pointed out, how one models within-subject covariation may have consequential effects on inference. Thus, it is recommended that the choice of residual structure be based on a sound rationale and appraised empirically.

Individual Coefficients and the Between-Subject Covariance Structure

For the model specified on the right-hand side in equation 7.1, random variation occurring among individuals is accounted for through the subject-specific parameters, β_{qi}, of nonlinear function f. These regression coefficients symbolize interesting, scientifically important aspects of the phenomenon manifest in the associated underlying change process. As such, a primary goal of an analysis is to understand individual differences on these variables. Toward that end, a standard approach is to specify a submodel for each. Characteristics of the data, the availability of individual-level covariates, and the nature of research hypotheses will almost always dictate the degree of complexity of the submodels.

A basic form of the model for the regression coefficients is

$$\beta_{qi} = \beta_q + b_{qi}. \tag{7.2}$$

In this configuration, the qth individual coefficient is comprised of a population parameter, β_q, and a subject-specific effect, b_{qi}, known as a *fixed* and *random* effect, respectively. The most general specification of an individual's coefficients, β_i, models interindividual variation as a function of fixed growth parameters (β), random effects (b_i), regression coefficients (ω), and individual attributes (z_i) in the following way:

$$\beta_i = g(\omega, z_i, \beta, b_i). \tag{7.3}$$

Here, **g** is a d-dimensional vector-valued function, where each element of **g** is associated with a corresponding element of β_j, so that the functional relation may be of a different form for each coefficient, β_{qi}. For example, consider the situation in which the functions for two individual regression coefficients both consist of a fixed effect and single covariate, but only one coefficient incorporates a random effect. Then,

$$\beta_{1i} = \beta_1 + \omega_1 z_i + b_{1i}$$
$$\beta_{2i} = \beta_2 + \omega_2 z_i.$$

In the population of subjects, it is generally assumed that the random effects are normally distributed with mean zero and covariance matrix, Φ. That is,

$$\mathbf{b}_i \sim N(\mathbf{0}, \Phi),$$

where $\mathbf{b}_i$ is a $(r \times 1)$ vector of random effects. This is called the between-subject or level-2 covariance structure. If an exploratory analysis were to show that the normality assumption was untenable, then another distributional form for the random effects could be employed, such as a multivariate t distribution, or a nonparametric alternative. Even group structures may be implemented if there was empirical evidence or a theoretic rationale (for examples of various level-2 structures, see, e.g., Beal & Sheiner, 1992; Davidian & Gallant, 1993; Wakefield, 1995).

To make this idea concrete, the covariance matrix among the random effects for the particular situation in which $r = 3$ is

$$\text{cov}(\mathbf{b}_i) = \Phi = \begin{pmatrix} \text{var}(b_{1i}) & & \\ \text{cov}(b_{2i}, b_{1i}) & \text{var}(b_{2i}) & \\ \text{cov}(b_{3i}, b_{1i}) & \text{cov}(b_{3i}, b_{2i}) & \text{var}(b_{3i}) \end{pmatrix} = \begin{pmatrix} \varphi_{11} & & \\ \varphi_{21} & \varphi_{22} & \\ \varphi_{31} & \varphi_{32} & \varphi_{33} \end{pmatrix},$$

where the diagonal elements of Φ are variance components that summarize the degree of dispersion of each random effect around zero and, while the off-diagonal elements quantify the extent to which the random effects are linearly associated.

Marginal Distribution of y_i and the Loglikelihood

Inference within NLME models is often carried out on the marginal distribution of $\mathbf{y}_i$ via maximum likelihood estimation. Let the conditional density of $\mathbf{y}_i$ given $\mathbf{b}_i$ be $p_{y|b}(\mathbf{y}_i | \mathbf{b}_i)$ and the density of $\mathbf{b}_i$ be $p_b(\mathbf{b}_i)$, then the marginal distribution of $\mathbf{y}_i$ is given by

$$h(\mathbf{y}_i) = \int p_{y|b}(\mathbf{y}_i | \mathbf{b}_i) p_b(\mathbf{b}_i) d\mathbf{b}_i.$$

For linear growth models, where random effects enter the function linearly, the fact that $p_{y|b}(\mathbf{y}_i | \mathbf{b}_i)$ and $p_b(\mathbf{b}_i)$ may be multivariate normal densities necessarily implies that the marginal density $h(\mathbf{y}_i)$ will also be normal. When the random effects enter the function in a nonlinear manner this arrangement no longer holds, and in the vast majority of circumstances the integral will be analytically intractable. Let $\xi = vech(\Phi)' = (\varphi_{11}, \varphi_{21}, \varphi_{22}, \ldots, \varphi_{rr})$, where the $vech(\cdot)$ operator creates a column vector of a symmetric matrix (i.e., Φ) by stacking successive row-wise elements of the lower triangle below one another. Combining the unknown, nonstochastic parameters into one vector, θ where $\theta = (\beta', \gamma', \xi, \omega')'$, maximum likelihood estimates for θ can be found by maximizing the loglikelihood in θ

$$l(\theta) = \ln L(\theta) = \ln \prod_{i=1}^{M} \int p_{y|b}(\mathbf{y}_i | \mathbf{b}_i) p_b(\mathbf{b}_i) d\mathbf{b}_i \qquad (7.4)$$

$$= \sum_{i=1}^{M} \ln \int p_{y|b}(\mathbf{y}_i | \mathbf{b}_i) p_b(\mathbf{b}_i) d\mathbf{b}_i.$$

The multidimensional integral of this function cannot be computed in closed form when the model function f is nonlinear in $\mathbf{b}_i$. Several estimation schemes have been proposed to overcome this obstacle (for convenient summaries of current, mainstream methods, see, e.g., Davidian & Giltinan, 1993; Pinheiro & Bates, 1995).

Analytic Decision Points

In a typical application, there are three main decisions regarding the repeated-measures submodel. First and foremost is the choice of response function. As Blozis and Cudeck (1999) argued, because competing models can be equally justifiable based on similar performance of fit and parameter interpretability, specifying a particular nonlinear function can be difficult. Second is the choice of the between-subject covariance structure—determining whether all coefficients should be stochastic (or fixed) and if coefficients ought to covary. Finally, the choice of a level-1 covariance structure for the repeated measures must be decided upon. In the two examples later in the chapter, provisional NLME analyses are presented that are effective in summarizing the data and seem suitable for the context as a precursor to incorporating mixtures. Drawing inferences in many applications is based on maximum likelihood estimation, which itself relies on large sample theory (see, e.g., Davidian & Giltinan, 2003, for an overview summarizing specific details). The quality of inferences is dependent not only on large sample size, but also on distributional assumptions, correct specification of the mean function, and the form of the model-implied covariance structure. As Blozis and Cudeck (1999) pointed out, due to the interconnected nature of these components as a part of the entire system, in practice caution must be used when computing confidence intervals and carrying out hypothesis tests.

THE NONLINEAR MIXED-EFFECTS MIXTURE MODEL

In subject-specific models, such as the NLME model, regression parameters are allowed to vary across individuals, resulting in differing within-subject profiles. In part, this heterogeneity can be effectively captured through the random effects. Yet, a basic tenet for the model in equation 7.1 is that the random effects have a mean of zero, which translates into assuming that all individuals have been sampled from a single population with common population parameters. A finite mixture model (Everitt & Hand, 1981; Titterington, Smith, & Makov, 1985), like the one introduced in this section, relaxes the single population assumption to allow for parameter differences across unobserved subpopulations. The form of the densities in each of these subpopulations is often specified in advance and typically of the same parametric family, with parameters that are allowed to differ across components or latent classes (McLachlan & Peel, 2000). This type of modeling may be needed when more fundamental individual differences are present. Such differences in development can be described by latent trajectory classes, where each class potentially has a different NLME model. Operationally, mixture modeling captures this population heterogeneity through an unobservable categorical variable. In the context of NLME models, the main inferential goals are: (1) to decompose the sample into its mixture components and (2) to estimate the mixture probabilities and the unknown class parameters (e.g., class-specific regression, variance, and covariance parameters).

The following NLMM model incorporates the ideas presented for the NLME model in the previous section. Consider observed variables for the ith individual, $\mathbf{y}_i$, $\mathbf{x}_i$, and $\mathbf{z}_i$ where $\mathbf{y}_i$ denotes the n_i measurements on the response variable y; $\mathbf{x}_i$ is an n_i-dimensional vector of elapsed time from the beginning of the experiment, of age or of some other longitudinal design condition; and $\mathbf{z}_i$ is a q-dimensional vector of individual attributes. Vector $\mathbf{c}_i = (c_{i1}, c_{i2}, \ldots, c_{iK})'$ denotes a latent categorical variable with K classes, where $c_{ik} = 1$ if the ith individual belongs to class k of the mixture and zero otherwise. It immediately follows that

$$\Pr(c_{ik}=1) = \mathrm{E}[c_{ik}] = \pi_k,$$

which is commonly referred to as the *prior probability* of belonging to class k. It is assumed that the mixing probabilities satisfy two conditions:

$$0 \leq \pi_k \leq 1 \text{ and } \sum_{k=1}^{K}\pi_k = 1.$$

Multivariate normality is assumed for $\mathbf{y}_i$ conditional on $\mathbf{x}_i$, β_i, and class k; then the NLMM model can be defined hierarchically as

$$\mathbf{y}_i = f(\mathbf{x}_i, \beta_i) + \mathbf{e}_i \tag{7.5}$$

$$\beta_i = \mathbf{g}(\beta_k, \omega_k, \mathbf{z}_i, \mathbf{b}_i) \tag{7.6}$$

where f is any arbitrary intrinsically nonlinear function, the $(n_i \times 1)$ residual vector $\mathbf{e}_i$ is $N(\mathbf{0}, \Gamma_i(\gamma_k))$, and the $(r \times 1)$ vector of random effects, $\mathbf{b}_i$, is $N(\mathbf{0}, \Phi_k)$, both assumed to be uncorrelated with other variables. Here, regression parameters in β_k vary across classes to capture different types of nonlinear change. If no covariates are utilized, the regression coefficients β are simply the means of the growth characteristics associated with function f for class k. Parameter vector, ω_k, allows class differences in how covariates in $\mathbf{z}_i$ influence individuals' growth parameters. In the upcoming applications, the functional form of β_i will be variants of a simple linear regression specification.

Estimation

The NLMM model can be estimated via maximum likelihood. The joint density for $\mathbf{y}_i$ can expressed as

$$h(\mathbf{y}_i) = \int p_{y|b}(\mathbf{y}_i \mid \mathbf{b}_i) p_b(\mathbf{b}_i) d\mathbf{b}_i \tag{7.7}$$

$$= \int \sum_{k=1}^{K} \pi_k g_{y|b}^k(\mathbf{y}_i \mid \mathbf{b}_i) g_b^k(\mathbf{b}_i) d\mathbf{b}_i$$

$$= \sum_{k=1}^{K} \pi_k \int g_{y|b}^k(\mathbf{y}_i \mid \mathbf{b}_i) g_b^k(\mathbf{b}_i) d\mathbf{b}_i$$

$$= \sum_{k=1}^{K} \pi_k h_{ik}(\mathbf{y}_i),$$

where $g_{y|b}^k$ is the conditional distribution of **y** given **b** for class k, while g_b^k is the marginal distribution of **b** for class k. These are both assumed to have multivariate normal densities. In this form, the marginal density of $\mathbf{y}_i$ comes from a mixture of densities with class probabilities $\pi_1, \ldots, \pi_k$ and class-specific densities $h_{ik}(\mathbf{y}_i)$. Expressing the likelihood function involves vectorizing all model parameters. Given the equality constraint that the probabilities have to sum to 1, let $\pi = (\pi_1, \ldots, \pi_{k-1})'$ be the $(1 \times k-1)$ vector of class probabilities; furthermore, $\beta = (\beta_1', \ldots, \beta_K')'$, $\omega = (\omega_1', \ldots, \omega_K')'$, $\gamma = (\gamma_1', \ldots, \gamma_K')'$, and $\delta = (vech(\Phi_1)', \ldots, vech(\Phi_K)')'$. Finally, let $\theta = (\pi', \xi')'$ be the vector of all model parameters where $\xi = (\beta', \omega', \gamma', \delta')'$. The likelihood function can now be defined as

$$L(\theta) = \prod_{i=1}^{M} h(\mathbf{y}_i \mid \theta),$$

from which the loglikelihood can be expressed as

$$l(\theta) = \ln\left(\prod_{i=1}^{M} h(\mathbf{y}_i \mid \theta)\right) \quad (7.8)$$

$$= \ln\left(\prod_{i=1}^{M} \sum_{k=1}^{K} \pi_k h_{ik}(\mathbf{y}_i \mid \theta_k)\right)$$

$$= \sum_{i=1}^{M} \ln\left(\sum_{k=1}^{K} \pi_k h_{ik}(\mathbf{y}_i \mid \theta_k)\right).$$

Maximizing the loglikelihood in equation 7.8 can be accomplished using the EM algorithm. This is particularly salient for mixture problems, which can often be configured as a missing data problem. Details of the implementation of the EM algorithm can be found in the Appendix.

Classification

Once the estimation algorithm has converged to a plausible solution, the posterior probability that the ith individual belongs to class k is estimated as

$$\Pr(k \mid \mathbf{y}, \hat{\theta}) = \hat{\pi}_{ik} = \frac{\hat{\pi}_k h_{ik}(\mathbf{y}_i \mid \hat{\theta})}{\sum_{k=1}^{K} \hat{\pi}_k h_{ik}(\mathbf{y}_i \mid \hat{\theta})}.$$

These probabilities can be used to categorize an individual into the class that he or she most likely belongs. The quality of a mixture model can be assessed, in part, on the precision of this classification. That is, an individual's posterior probability of belonging to a particular class ought to be high, whereas the posterior probabilities for belonging to any other class should be small.

REPRESENTATIVE EXAMPLES

In this section, to illustrate the main features of the NLMM model, two empirical datasets are introduced. Both utilize repeated measures, but their designs are quite different. The first dataset examines speech errors in young children whose ages range from 2 to 8 years old (Burchinal & Appelbaum, 1991). In this study, the ages at time of measurement varied across the subjects, an occurrence that is common in longitudinal studies but often difficult to handle statistically. There are a variety of patterns of observed and missing data as well. The second study involves repeated-measures data obtained from a learning experiment to assess verbal skill acquisition.

In this study, the data are balanced and complete. However, a small complication is that the pattern of variances for the residuals appears to be nonlinear. In the first example, an independent rating of overall speech intelligibility was made based on a structured interview, with scores ranging from 0 for unintelligible to 6 for good. This rating will serve as a covariate to help explain differences among children in the pattern of change in the repeated measures of speech errors, and will be allowed to vary across latent classes. In the second example, no covariates are included in the analysis.

Speech Error in Children

When young children speak, they make an assortment of syntactical and grammatical errors communicating in everyday language, at least initially. As they become older these errors decrease rapidly and eventually cease. In a study of language development (Burchinal & Appelbaum, 1991), data were obtained on a sample of 43 children between the ages of 2 and 8 years old. Speech errors were recorded using a standardized instrument of language proficiency. A maximum number of six repeated measures were taken and ages at the time of testing differed for each child. A plot of nonlinear repeated-measures data, as seen in Figure 7.1, clearly represents the facets of change for which the NLME model is undeniably appropriate.

The primary feature in this example is the prominent individual differences in the longitudinal profiles. The number of assessments as well as the

170 ▪ J. R. HARRING

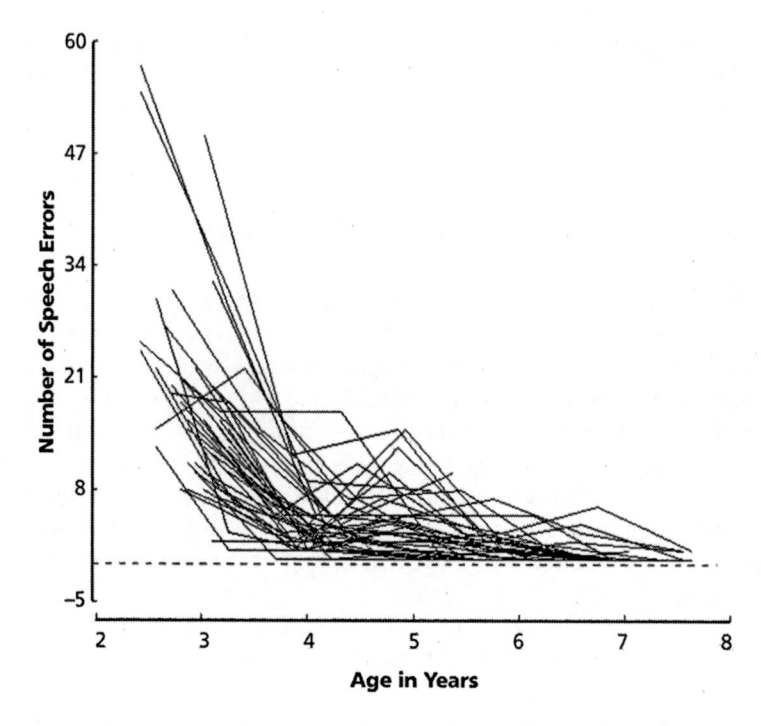

Figure 7.1 Individual learning curves for 43 young children, ages 2–8.

ages of the children at the times of assessment differed so that the data are neither balanced nor complete. To make clear, data from three children are shown in Table 7.1, where x_{ij} = *age* in years-months, and $n_1 = 6$, $n_{21} = 5$, and $n_{33} = 4$. The speech intelligibility rating for each of the three children, z_i, is given as well.

TABLE 7.1 Speech Errors, Ages, and Intelligibility Ratings for Three Children

Case	x_1	x_2	x_3	x_4	x_5	x_6	
1	3–1	4–0	4–11	6–1	7–2	8–3	
21	3–6	4–5	5–4	6–7	7–6	—	
33	3–2	4–5	5–5	6–7	—	—	

Case	y_1	y_2	y_3	y_4	y_5	y_6	z_i
1	22	6	2	1	0	0	5
21	7	3	3	1	0	—	4
33	10	2	0	0	—	—	4

Note: Missing data is denoted by —.

It is clear from Figure 7.1 that individuals' profiles are distinctly nonlinear. In contrast to a linear process where speech errors decline at a constant rate, the rate of decrease in errors here is different at different ages—declining sharply between ages 3 and 4, and then improving more steadily for every child in the sample until age 7 or 8 when errors effectively disappear. Some young children may have developmental trajectories in which speech errors cease within an acceptable age range, while for other children cessation occurs later. The primary objective in many developmental studies is to understand how the behavior develops, which is essential in understanding critical periods of change that should inform *when* an intervention might show the greatest impact.

Verbal Skill Acquisition

The second example involves data from a learning experimental study in which researchers were interested in skill acquisition. As one part of a more comprehensive battery, the outcome variable here represents performance on a procedural task created and developed for the assessment of verbal skill acquisition. Quantitative and spatial skills acquisition were also evaluated. For each task, study participants were required to learn a set of declarative rules for assessing attributes of visual stimuli presented in series. Tasks were given together in blocks, with order of administration varied within blocks. There were 24 trial blocks for each task, and each trial block is the mean of 16 individual trials. Thus, each task actually had 24 × 16 = 384 basic trials. Both response times and accuracy scores were recorded. Data for a restricted sample of 214 individuals whose average accuracy score across trial blocks was 85% or better is considered here. Blozis (2004) also analyzed these data and pointed out that the sample was restricted to only individuals with higher accuracy to reduce any effect of an accuracy/speed trade-off in response time. The median time to respond for the procedural task was computed as an aggregate for each set of 32 trials in 12 separate blocks. Sample means and covariances are given in Table 7.2.

ANALYSIS OF SPEECH ERRORS DATA

NLME Model Analysis

Learning data tend to follow nonlinear monotonic trajectories that level off at later measurement occasions. Consequently, subjects' learning profiles can be effectively modeled and may differ in initial status, asymptotic

TABLE 7.2 Sample Mean Vector and Covariance Matrix for the Verbal Procedural Learning Task Data ($M = 214$)

Trial block	1	2	3	4	5	6	7	8	9	10	11	12
1	95.32											
2	54.51	48.35										
3	28.90	26.02	19.76									
4	17.59	15.60	10.87	7.37								
5	13.16	11.68	7.37	5.72	5.22							
6	9.31	8.09	5.27	4.18	3.58	3.25						
7	6.68	6.42	4.23	3.48	2.99	2.43	2.36					
8	5.90	5.15	3.59	2.90	2.54	2.13	1.91	1.98				
9	5.46	4.31	3.21	2.74	2.20	1.84	1.70	1.63	1.84			
10	4.32	3.54	2.45	2.09	1.84	1.53	1.41	1.35	1.29	1.28		
11	4.30	3.48	2.47	2.22	1.91	1.58	1.52	1.41	1.46	1.23	1.54	
12	3.48	3.04	2.32	1.97	1.64	1.42	1.38	1.31	1.33	1.13	1.25	1.29
Mean	21.7	14.1	10.8	9.1	8.2	7.5	7.2	7.0	6.8	6.6	6.5	6.4

behavior, or rate of change. Due to the declining nature of speech errors coupled with a leveling-off at later ages, Burchinal and Appelbaum (1991) suggested a two-parameter exponential model with random effects to characterize the within-subject nonlinear change. The model used here is also an exponential model, equivalent in fit to that employed by Burchinal and Appelbaum, but whose coefficient governing rate of change has been reparameterized. The adopted exponential function is specified as

$$f(\beta_{1i}, \beta_{2i}, x_{ij}) = \beta_{1i} \cdot 2^{[-(x_{ij}-3)/(\beta_{2i}-3)]}, \quad \beta_{2i} > 3, \tag{7.9}$$

where x_{ij} is age at the jth occasion. The trajectory of this model is similar for all of the children. The function exhibits steep decline to zero errors by age 8. By including the difference $(x_{ij} - 3)$ in the exponent, the intercept, β_{1i}, is interpreted as the number of speech errors at age 3 years (the approximate mean at the first assessment). When $x_{ij} = \beta_{2i}$, then $f_{ij} = \frac{1}{2}\beta_{1i}$. Thus, the second coefficient, β_{2i}, is the age at which a child's speech errors are reduced by half relative to the number of speech errors at age 3 (*half age*).

The model for the coefficients is

$$\beta_{1i} = g_1(\beta_1, b_{1i}, \omega_1, z_i) \qquad \beta_{2i} = g_2(\beta_2, b_{2i}, \omega_2, z_i)$$
$$= \beta_1 + \omega_1(z_i - \bar{z}) + b_{1i} \qquad = \beta_2 + \omega_2(z_i - \bar{z}) + b_{2i}.$$

Both individual coefficients depend on a fixed coefficient (β_1 or β_2), a fixed coefficient for z_i (ω_1 or ω_2), and a random effect (b_{1i} or b_{2i}). The covariate was mean-centered to facilitate interpretation of the fixed effects. The structure of residuals is posited as independent and homogeneous (i.e., $\Gamma_i(\gamma) = \sigma^2 I_{n_i}$).

Various models can be compared by calculating the Akaike (1974) information criterion (AIC). This index penalizes models with many (rather than too few) free parameters and is defined as

$$AIC = -2 \ln L + 2m,$$

where $\ln L$ is the natural log of the likelihood function value and m is the number of parameters in the model. In this form of the index, the modeling yielding the smallest relative value is preferred. For the full version of the model previously outlined, $AIC_{Full} = 1233.4$. Maximum likelihood parameter estimates[3] with standard error estimates in parentheses are provided for the full model in Table 7.3.

Prior to parameter interpretation, a couple of observations regarding the results are warranted. The covariance between the random effects as well as the coefficient of the covariate are small compared to their standard errors, $\hat{\phi}_{21} = -0.15$ ($se = 0.35$) and $\hat{\omega}_2 = -0.05$ ($se = 0.03$). The implication of the former is that there is no detectable linear association between initial numbers of speech errors and half age, while the latter suggests that z_i does not account for individual differences in half age. A second version of the model was fit constraining these parameters to zero. These modifications improved the fit with $AIC_{Reduced} = 1229.8$. Maximum likelihood estimates of the revised model are also provided in Table 7.3.

By way of interpretation, in the reduced model the estimated number of speech errors for a child at age 3 with an average intelligibility rating is $\hat{\beta}_1 = 18.5$. Intelligibility is an effective predictor of the intercept.

TABLE 7.3 Maximum Likelihood Estimates and Standard Errors for Both the Full Version and Reduced Version of the Nonlinear Mixed-Effects Model for the Speech Error Data

Model	$\hat{\beta}_1$	$\hat{\beta}_2$	$\hat{\omega}_1$	$\hat{\omega}_2$	$\hat{\Phi}$	$\hat{\sigma}^2$
Full model	19.2 (1.2)	3.7 (0.1)	-2.8 (0.9)	-0.05 (.03)	68.3 (15.6) -.15 (0.35) 0.06 (0.02)	9.3 (1.1)
Reduced model	18.5 (1.3)	3.7 (0.1)	-2.9 (0.9)		62.9 (15.9) 0.04 (0.01)	9.4 (1.1)

Note: Standard errors are in parentheses.

For every one unit increase in z_i, the number of errors at age 3 decreases by 2.9 ($\hat{\omega}_1 = -2.9$). The age at which half of the number of errors is reached is $\hat{\beta}_2 = 3.7$, or at approximately 3 years and 8 months. This means that the typical child cuts his or her number of speech errors in half within the first year or two of speech development. There appears to be sizeable variability of both intercepts and half age: $\hat{\varphi}_{11} = 62.9$ and $\hat{\varphi}_{22} = 0.04$, respectively. Children who experience difficulties in speech development may demonstrate trajectory characteristics that are different than children with what might be deemed as normal development. Identifying these children may result in the planning, timing, and implementation of some intervention that may aid in their progress. Fitting the same nonlinear mixed-effects model as a finite mixture may aid in uncovering just who these children are, as seen next.

NLMM Model Analysis

A generally accepted modeling framework is to perform a conventional NLME analysis to get a sense of the extent to which individual regression coefficients vary as well as to assess a reasonable covariance structure for the repeated measures. The final parameter estimates for the mean and covariance structures determined from the "one-class" analysis can be used as starting values for multiple class analyses. The next step in the analysis is to try to account for heterogeneity in speech development using finite mixtures of NLME models. An initial task is to decide on the number of unobservable trajectory classes. Each class could have its own set of regression coefficients as well as class-specific variance-covariance parameters. To assess the number of classes, Muthén (2001) suggested setting the level-2 covariance matrix, Φ, to zero, thereby suppressing within-class between-subject variation, yet allowing within-subject variance to be estimated. This coincides with the latent class mixture (LCM) modeling proposed originally by Nagin (1999), but for intrinsically nonlinear functions.

Fit of models with a distinct number of classes can be evaluated using an index of model fit such as BIC. The Bayesian information criteria (BIC; Schwarz, 1978) penalizes overparameterized models and takes into account sample size, and is given as

$$\text{BIC} = -2\ln L + m\ln(M),$$

where p is the number of free parameters and M is the sample size. A plot of these BIC values can steer the researcher's decision as to how many components are likely to be embedded in the longitudinal profiles, with the model corresponding to the lowest BIC value preferred. Class-specific regression parameters of the typical individual from the final model can then be used as starting values to explore within-class variability by allowing the random effects covariance matrix to be freely estimated. That was the strategy employed here.

Figure 7.2 shows the plot of the BIC values for the speech error data, using one to four classes. BIC values are shown for both the LCM model and the NLMM model.

The one-class BIC value is for the standard NLME model. Clearly, BIC values improved by using more than one class and two classes seem optimal in the NLMM modeling context. Not surprisingly because of the small sample size, the four-class solution did not converge. The BIC values obtained from the LCM models are markedly worse for any given number of classes. Evidently, between-subject variation is essential for this application, and the question of whether different level-2 covariance matrices (i.e., Φ_k) must still be addressed. Further exploration into this issue supported the invariance of the level-2 covariance matrix, Φ [i.e., $\Phi_1 = \cdots = \Phi_k = \Phi$: BIC (class-invariant) = 1208.2; BIC (class-variant) = 1215.6]. The parameter estimates, standard errors,[4] and class proportions for the two-class solution are summarized in Table 7.4. The solid lines in Figure 7.3 are the curves

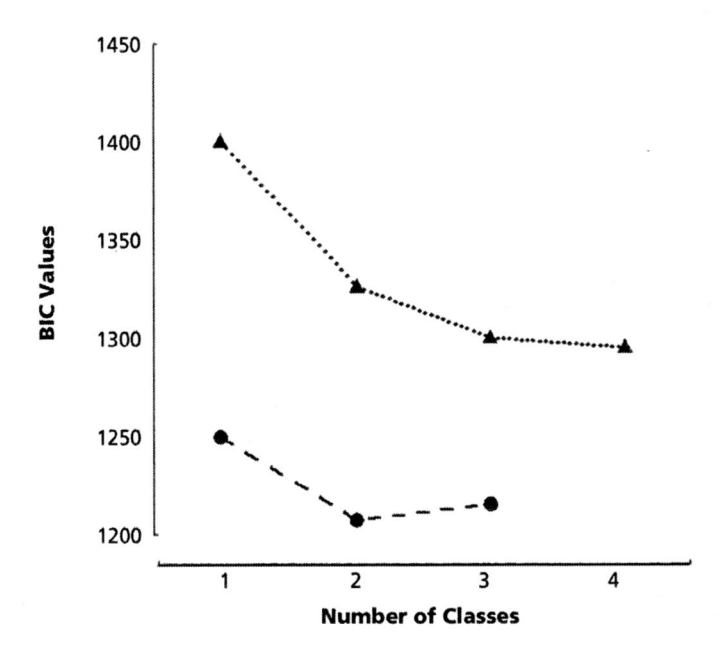

Figure 7.2 BIC values for the speech error data. No within-class variation (·····), within-class variation (– – –).

TABLE 7.4 Maximum Likelihood Estimates for the Two-Class Exponential Model for the Speech Error Data (*M* = 43)

Class-specific regression coefficents $\hat{\beta}_k$	Class-specific covariate estimates $\hat{\omega}_k$	Class-specific covariate estimates $\hat{\Phi}_k = \hat{\Phi}$	Class-specific residual variance $\hat{\sigma}_k^2 = \hat{\sigma}^2$
$\begin{pmatrix} 12.66\ (0.07) \\ 3.42\ (0.03) \end{pmatrix}$ $\hat{\pi}_1 = 0.35\ (0.06)$	$\hat{\omega}_1 = -3.83\ (0.23)$	$\begin{pmatrix} 50.58 \\ (0.82) \\ 0.29 \\ (0.03) \end{pmatrix}$	3.58 (0.46)
$\begin{pmatrix} 20.00\ (0.50) \\ 3.97\ (0.03) \end{pmatrix}$ $\hat{\pi}_2 = 0.65$	$\hat{\omega}_2 = -4.41\ (0.42)$		

Note: Gaussian-Hermite quadrature was used with *Q* = 20 quadrature points. Standard errors are in parentheses.

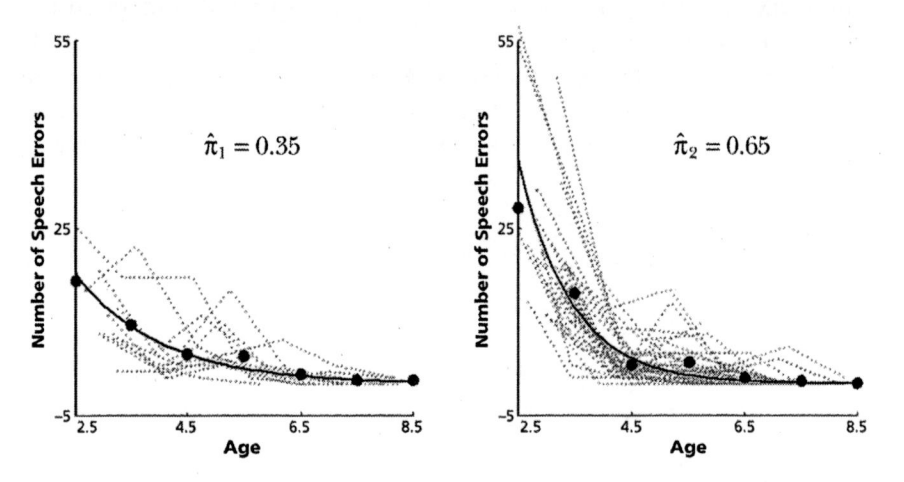

Figure 7.3 Class mean trajectories superimposed on individual data assigned to that class for the speech error data.

corresponding to the estimated typical values in each class, in this case for a child with an average intelligibility score for that class.

The two-component mixture model clearly subdivided the children into two groups. The first is characterized by a smaller initial number of speech errors at age 3 coupled with a younger age at which half of the number of speech errors disappear. Children whose speech errors vanish earlier are children who begin with fewer speech errors. The second group ostensibly began with greater numbers of speech errors at age 3 whose errors were halved at an older age. It also appears that intelligibility ratings have a class-specific effect on intercepts. For the first class, each unit increase in intelligibility rating results in a decrease in speech errors at age 3 of approximately 3.8 errors, while for subjects in class 2, speech errors decrease by almost 4.5 errors.

Individual Coefficients

Once all parameters θ in a NLMM model have been estimated, focus shifts to estimating individual fitted functions. To compute individual regression coefficients, estimates of random effects vector $\mathbf{b}_i$ must be obtained. Typically, empirical Bayes estimates are defined as the mode of

$$p(\mathbf{b}_i \mid \mathbf{y}_i, \theta) \propto p(\mathbf{y}_i \mid \mathbf{b}_i, \theta) p(\mathbf{b}_i), \quad (7.10)$$

the posterior distribution of the random effects, conditional on $\mathbf{y}_i$. However, due to the possible multimodality of the random effects distribution under the NLMM model, this definition is no longer suitable. Under the NLMM model, the posterior distribution of $\mathbf{b}_i$ can also be written as

$$p(\mathbf{b}_i \mid \mathbf{y}_i, \theta) \propto \sum_{k=1}^{K} \pi_{ik} p_{ik}(\mathbf{b}_i \mid \mathbf{y}_i, \theta_k),$$

where $p_{ik}(\mathbf{b}_i \mid \mathbf{y}_i, \theta_k)$ is the posterior density function of $\mathbf{b}_i$, conditional on the fact that it was sampled from the kth component in the mixture. Therefore, the empirical Bayes estimates can be defined as

$$\hat{\mathbf{b}}_i = \sum_{k=1}^{K} \pi_{ik}(\hat{\theta}) \hat{\mathbf{b}}_i^{(k)},$$

where $\hat{\mathbf{b}}_i^{(k)}$ is the empirical Bayes estimate of the random effect for the subject i in the kth class.

Individual fitted functions for eight of the 43 total subjects are shown in Figure 7.4—four subjects from each class. These graphs give an indication of the range of patterns and the extent of the individual differences that are present.

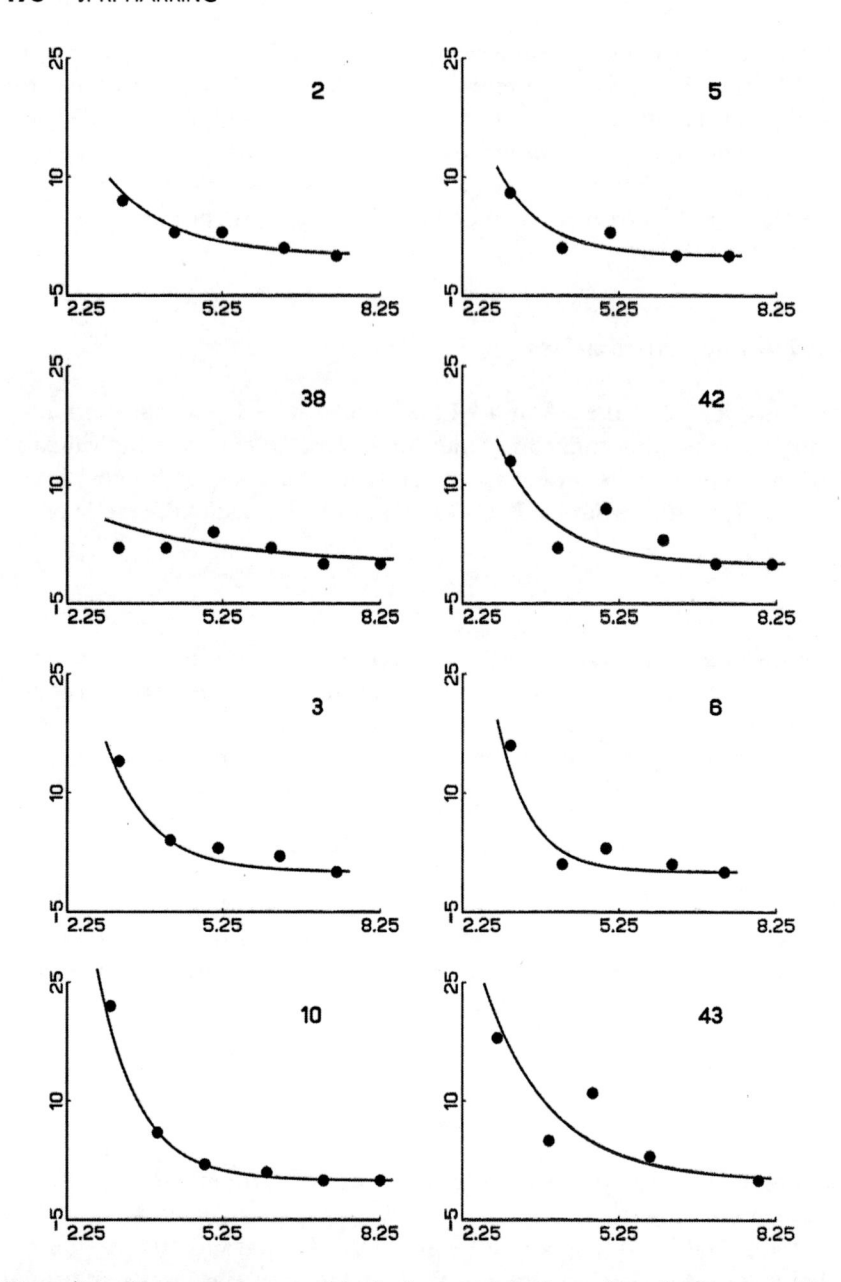

Figure 7.4 The top two rows of the lattice panel displays selected subject-specific curves from class 1 of a two-class mixture for the speech error data. The bottom two rows in the lattice panel displays selected subject-specific curves from class 2 of the mixture.

ANALYSIS OF VERBAL SKILL ACQUISITION DATA

NLME Model Analysis

Visual exploration of the repeated-measures data, as a preliminary step to an analysis, is critical. This can be carried out by plotting individuals' observed data or fitted curves with competing nonlinear functions. The former type of graphic, a spaghetti plot, provides information about interesting features of the data (i.e., asymptotic behavior) for which a particular nonlinear function is best suited. It also indicates both degree and structure of within- and between-subject variability. Data from a 15% random sample of individuals are shown in Figure 7.5.

In developing and eventually deciding on a model, the objective is to find a version that performs well in terms of data-model fit and that pro-

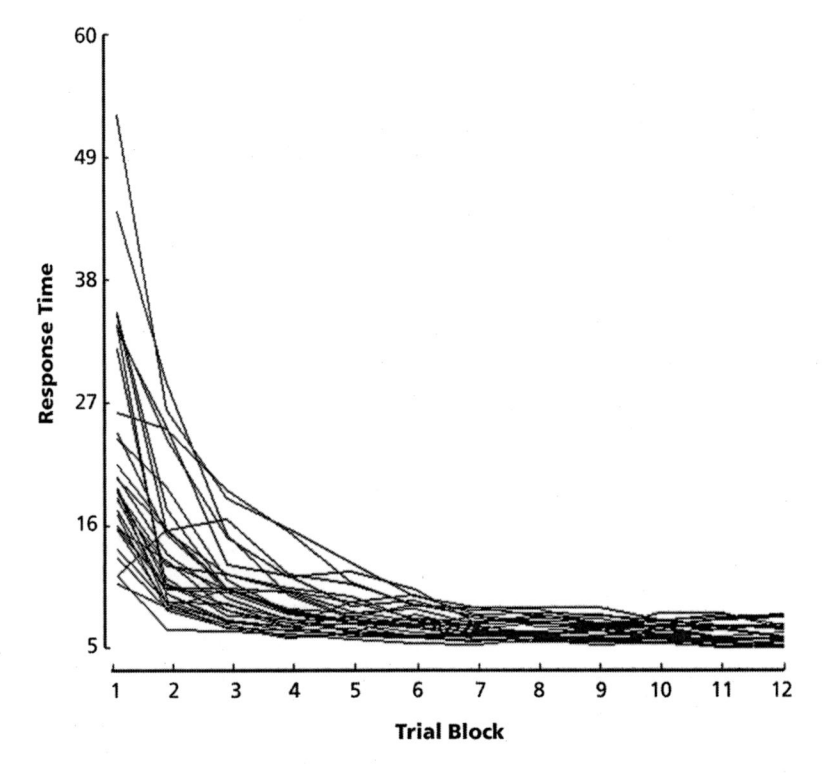

Figure 7.5 Random 15% subsample of repeated response time scores on the verbal procedural learning task.

duces information about the process being studied that is different from the measurements actually obtained (Cudeck & Harring, 2007). It is the model parameters that give new information. As was pointed out by Cudeck and Harring (2010), the model is formulated so that parameters embody features of individual change that can be utilized to address questions that are difficult to answer without the model. The data displayed in Figure 7.5 suggest a rapid decline in response from a high starting value down to an individual plateau and is not expected to rebound. An exponential function has been frequently used for data exhibiting these change pattern characteristics (see, e.g., Blozis, 2004; Browne, 1993; Grimm & Ram, 2009; Harring, Cudeck, & du Toit, 2006). The predicted value of the response for individual i at occasion j under the exponential function is written as

$$f_{ij} = \beta_{2i} - (\beta_{2i} - \beta_{1i})\exp(\beta_{3i}(x_j - 1)), \quad \beta_{3i} \leq 0, \qquad (7.11)$$

with the 12 trials numbered $\mathbf{x} = (1, 2, \ldots, 12)'$ for all i and j. In this form, at $x_j = 1$, the function reduces to $f_{ij} = \beta_{1i}$ and is considered the initial response time score at the beginning of the study; later, after several trials when j is large, the function is $f_{ij} \to \beta_{2i}$. Consequently, β_{2i} is potential performance corresponding to later trials, a model-based estimate of quickest response time scores. The coefficient, β_{3i} (the rate parameter), governs how rapidly the function proceeds from β_{1i} to β_{2i} as x_j increases, with strong negative values indicating steeper rate of decline.

In this example, individuals' coefficients in equation 7.11 are posited to be the sum of fixed parameters and random effects

$$\beta_{1i} = \beta_1 + b_{1i} \quad \beta_{2i} = \beta_2 + b_{2i} \quad \beta_{3i} = \beta_3 + b_{3i},$$

where β_1, β_2, and β_3 are fixed population parameters and b_{1i}, b_{2i}, and b_{3i} are random effects unique to individual i. The random effects are assumed to be normally distributed with zero means and covariance matrix, Φ. Fitting the model in equation 7.11 with an unstructured level-2 covariance matrix Φ and an independent, constant covariance structure for level 1 (i.e., $\Gamma_i(\gamma) = \sigma^2 \mathbf{I}_{n_i}$) revealed that all parameters, regression coefficients, and level-1 and level-2 covariance parameters, were statistically significant ($p < 0.05$). Maximum likelihood parameter estimates for the NLME model analysis are

$$\hat{\beta} = \begin{pmatrix} 20.5\ (0.7) \\ 6.7\ (0.1) \\ -0.8\ (0.02) \end{pmatrix} \quad \hat{\sigma}^2 = 1.1\ (0.03) \quad \hat{\Phi} = \begin{pmatrix} 94.9\ (9.4) & & \\ 4.8\ (0.9) & 1.4\ (0.2) & \\ -1.9\ (0.5) & -0.2\ (0.06) & 0.4\ (0.06) \end{pmatrix}.$$

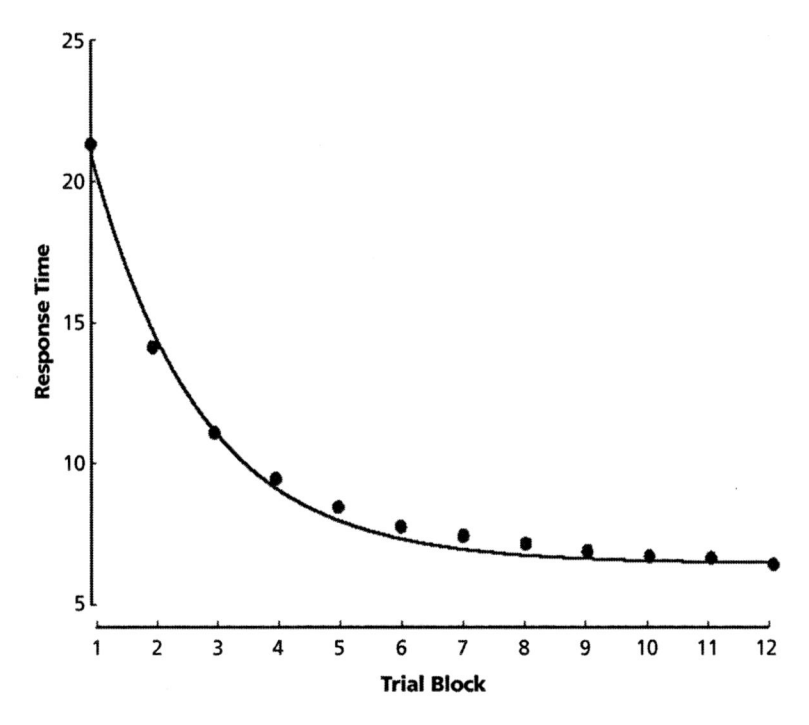

Finite Mixtures of Nonlinear Mixed-Effects Models • 181

Figure 7.6 Empirical means of the response time scores with the fitted exponential function for the typical subject superimposed.

Figure 7.6 presents the fitted exponential function for the typical individual superimposed on the empirical means. Mean response time scores for the verbal task was a little more than 20, $\hat{\beta}_1 = 20.5$. Potential response time score for the typical subject is $\hat{\beta}_2 = 6.7$. The rate of decrease is $\hat{\beta}_3 = -0.8$. As a result, the fitted function for the typical subject is given by the equation

$$\hat{\mu}_j = 6.7 - (6.7 - 20.5)\exp\{-0.8 \cdot (x_j - 1)\}.$$

Individual differences in the three aspects of response-time relation for the verbal task can be investigated by examination of the variance components of Φ. Both their size and statistical significance suggest that individual differences in these change characteristics do indeed exist. The covariance between change characteristics can be assessed by the off-diagonal elements. However, to facilitate interpretation of these parameters, Φ can be rescaled so that off-diagonal elements represent correlations:

$$\Phi = \mathbf{D}^{1/2}\mathbf{P}\mathbf{D}^{1/2} = \begin{pmatrix} 9.48 & & \\ & .63 & \\ & & .44 \end{pmatrix} \begin{pmatrix} 1 & & \\ .63 & 1 & \\ -.14 & -.35 & 1 \end{pmatrix} \begin{pmatrix} 9.48 & & \\ & .63 & \\ & & .44 \end{pmatrix}$$

where $\mathbf{D}$ is a diagonal matrix of variances and $\mathbf{P}$ is a matrix of correlations. It appears that initial and potential performance are moderately positively correlated such that individuals who begin with higher response time scores will have higher response time scores at the end of the study. Rate of change and potential scores are negatively correlated, $\hat{\rho}_{32} = -.35$, indicating that individuals who ended with higher response time scores declined at a slower rate than those who finished with lower scores.

NLMM Model

Using parameter estimates from the one-class NLME model as starting values for the mixture modeling, two-, three-, and four-class NLMM models were fit to the data allowing for class differences in regression coefficients and within-subject covariance parameters. There was no compelling evidence in the initial exploration to suggest that parameters in Φ are allowed to differ across classes; therefore, they were set equal (i.e., $\Phi_1 = \cdots = \Phi_K = \Phi$ for all k). However, variability for the intraindividual errors was allowed to differ by classes (i.e., $\Gamma_{ik} = \sigma_k^2 \mathbf{I}_{n_i}$). Based on BIC values, entropy, and subjects' posterior probability separation, a two-class NLMM model was chosen as the final model.[5] Visually, the two-class NLMM model shows distinct separation between the groups. The fitted exponential curve for the typical subject in each class is shown in Figure 7.7.

Classes 1 and 2 have class probabilities 0.30 and 0.70, respectively. Average posterior probabilities from the two-class model displayed in Table 7.5 are used to show, in part, the quality of the classification. The estimated model is given in Table 7.6.

The two class results suggest class 1 ($\hat{\pi}_1 = 0.30$) is characterized by subjects who initially have higher response time scores ($\hat{\beta}_1^{(1)} = 33.02$) while ending with higher response time scores ($\hat{\beta}_2^{(1)} = 7.17$) at later trial blocks. Subjects in class 1 also decline more rapidly ($\hat{\beta}_3^{(1)} = -0.91$) than subjects in class 2. Subjects in class 2 ($\hat{\pi}_2 = 0.70$) performed better on the procedural task, at least initially ($\hat{\beta}_1^{(2)} = 15.06$), ending with lower response time scores ($\hat{\beta}_2^{(2)} = 6.47$), and subsequently improved at a slower rate ($\hat{\beta}_3^{(2)} = -0.67$). In addition, after accounting for within-class between-subject variability (which was specified to be equal across classes), the regression errors are

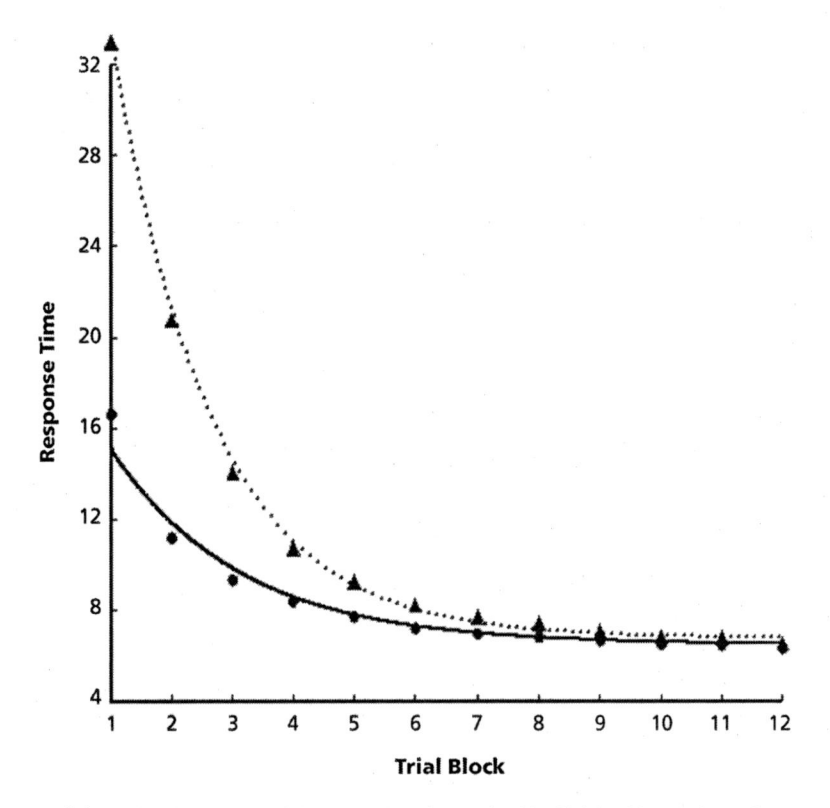

Finite Mixtures of Nonlinear Mixed-Effects Models ▪ **183**

Figure 7.7 Fitted exponential curves for the typical individual in each of the two classes for the verbal procedural learning task. Class 1 (·····) and Class 2 (——).

TABLE 7.5 Average Posterior Probabilities from the Two-Class Model

	Class 1 ($\hat{\pi}_1 = 0.30$)	Class 2 ($\hat{\pi}_2 = 0.70$)
Class 1	0.920	0.080
Class 2	0.048	0.952

not as variable in class 1 as they are in class 2 ($\hat{\sigma}_1^2 = 0.21$ vs. $\hat{\sigma}_2^2 = 1.09$). While leveling-off occurs in both subpopulations, further investigation to uncover those subject-specific characteristics that differentiate pertinent growth characteristics would be warranted.

TABLE 7.6 Maximum Likelihood Estimates for the Two-Class Exponential Model with an Exponential Model for the Variances of the Level-1 Covariance Structure ($M = 214$)

Parameter	Class 1 (30%) Estimate (SE)	Class 2 (70%) Estimate (SE)
π	0.30 (0.04)	
β_1	33.02 (1.50)	15.06 (0.72)
β_2	7.17 (0.18)	6.47 (0.11)
β_3	−0.91 (0.02)	−0.67 (0.03)
$\hat{\varphi}_{11}$	38.93 (5.17)	38.93 (5.17)
$\hat{\varphi}_{21}$	2.61 (0.66)	2.61 (0.66)
$\hat{\varphi}_{22}$	1.22 (0.13)	1.22 (0.13)
$\hat{\varphi}_{31}$	−0.78 (0.32)	−0.78 (0.32)
$\hat{\varphi}_{32}$	−0.11 (0.04)	−0.11 (0.04)
$\hat{\varphi}_{33}$	0.22 (0.05)	0.22 (0.05)
$\hat{\sigma}^2$	0.21 (0.04)	1.09 (0.10)

Note: Gaussian-Hermite quadrature was used with $Q = 20$ quadrature points. Standard errors are in parentheses.

DISCUSSION AND CONCLUSIONS

The area of finite mixture models is sufficiently large and well established, cutting across numerous research domains, as a viable method for explaining relations in observed data.

This research considers a finite mixture of nonlinear mixed-effects models for describing nonlinear change that may be different for each of potentially different latent subpopulations. The proposed NLMM model extends the linear mixed-effects mixture model and growth mixture modeling framework and is specifically designed for individual profiles, which can be described by intrinsically nonlinear functions (e.g., a monotonically increasing, decelerating exponential function). The necessity for NLMM models arises when groups of nonlinear growth patterns vary in idiosyncratic ways, but because manifest class membership is unidentified a priori, latent classes must be inferred from attributes of within-subject profiles. Latent class models can provide insight about behavioral characteristics as sources of population heterogeneity of various response-time dynamics—characteristic of learning and developmental longitudinal data—by reducing the high dimensionality and making clear the major components of the underlying structure of the data in terms of the unobservable latent variables.

Two examples using learning data were presented to demonstrate the utility of this longitudinal clustering model. Considerable time is spent initially to determine empirically which model parameters will be stochastic and which ones might be fixed. The mixture analysis also begins with a preliminary investigation. The primary goals to begin with are (1) to settle on how many latent classes are theoretically justifiable and empirically supported; (2) to determine which parts of the NLME model will be class-specific; and (3) to produce plausible starting values for estimating the multiple component models. All of this "up front" work is essential if subsequent analyses are to be completed successfully.

Arguably, modeling manifest class information would help sharpen an understanding of the repeated measures (e.g., treatment condition, gender). In the absence of critical categorical information, NLMM models are statistical tools that can be effectively used for clustering individuals based on differences in functional characteristics of their nonlinear growth patterns. In sum, the NLMM model allows researchers to capture different nonlinear change processes of group membership that cannot be determined in advance.

APPENDIX

The EM algorithm is an iterative optimization strategy motivated by a notion of missingness and by consideration of the conditional distribution of what is missing given what has been observed. While EM-based ideas have been around since the late 1950s, the strategy's statistical foundations and effectiveness in a variety of statistical problems were demonstrated in a seminal paper by Dempster, Laird, and Rubin (1977). Several book-length treatments devoted to the development, implementation, and application of the EM algorithm are currently available (e.g., Little & Rubin, 2002; McLachlan & Krishnan, 1997). One glaring deficit inherent in the EM algorithm is speed of convergence, specifically a lack thereof. Yet, the popularity and usefulness of the EM algorithm stems from its seemingly simple implementation and how reliably it can ascertain a global optimum through stable, uphill steps.

The implementation of the EM algorithm for NLMM models in this iteration follows the framework discussed in Aitkin and Rubin (1985), McLachlan and Peel (2000), and McLachlan and Krishnan (1997). Modifications to the basic algorithmic structure will be pointed out as subsequent technical details unfold.

Incomplete and Complete Data

In practice, maximization of the loglikelihood function in equation 7.8 is difficult using standard optimization procedures such as Newton's method, although advances in computing have made this a realistic possibility.[6] Fitting mixture models by maximum likelihood (ML) is an example of a problem that is considerably simplified through EM's conceptual unification of ML estimation of data that can be viewed as being incomplete. Response vectors y_i along with unobserved population indicators c_i can be thought of constituting complete data, whereas vectors y_i alone can be viewed as incomplete data since information containing population classification is missing. As a consequence, the loglikelihood function in (7.8) corresponds to the incomplete data. To see this finite mixture problem as one of incomplete data, define an unobservable or missing data vector $c = \{c_1', \ldots, c_M'\}'$, where c_k is a j-dimensional vector of zero-one indicator variables and where

$$c_{ik} = \begin{cases} 1 & \text{if the } i\text{th subject belongs to class } k \\ 0 & \text{otherwise} \end{cases} \quad i=1,\ldots,M \quad k=1,\ldots,K$$

The likelihood function that would have been obtained if population indicator values $c = \{c_1', \ldots, c_M'\}'$ had actually been observed is then

$$L(\theta | y_i, c_i) = \prod_{i=1}^{M} \prod_{k=1}^{K} \left[\pi_k h_{ik}(y_i | \theta_k) \right]^{c_{ik}}.$$

The *complete* loglikelihood for the observed measurements y and the vector of unobserved data c_{ik} can be expressed as

$$l(\theta | y, c) = \sum_{i=1}^{M} l_i(\theta | y_i, c_i) = \sum_{i=1}^{M} \sum_{k=1}^{K} c_{ik} \left\{ \ln(\pi_k) + \ln\left[h_{ik}(y_i | \theta_k) \right] \right\}.$$

Maximizing the complete loglikelihood depends on unknown indicator variables, c_{ik}. Therefore, this reduces to a problem of maximizing the expected value of $l(\theta | y, c)$, conditional on y, and provides a jumping-off point to introduce the EM algorithm in some detail.

Implementation of the EM Algorithm

The EM algorithm approaches the problem of solving the incomplete data loglikelihood, $l(\theta | y)$, indirectly by proceeding iteratively in terms of the complete-data loglikelihood function, $l(\theta|y,c)$. Since it is unobservable, the complete-data loglikelihood equation is replaced by its conditional expectation function given y, using the current iteration of θ. In particular, let θ^w be the value of θ at iteration w. Then on the next iteration, the expectation-step (E-step), the conditional expected value of the loglikelihood, referred to in the literature as the Q function (McLachlan & Krishnan, 1997), is calculated. That is,

$$Q(\theta|\theta^w) = E[l(\theta|y,c)|y,\theta^w]$$
$$= \sum_{i=1}^{M}\sum_{k=1}^{K} E[c_{ik}|y,\theta^w]\{\ln(\pi_k) + \ln[h_{ik}(y_i|\theta_k)]\}$$

where

$$E[c_{ik}|y,\theta^w] = \left.\frac{\pi_k^w h_{ik}(y_i|\theta^w)}{\sum_{k=1}^{K}\pi_k^w h_{ik}(y_i|\theta^w)}\right|_{\theta^w}$$
$$= \pi_{ik}(\theta^w)$$

The expression $\pi_{ik}(\theta^w)$ is the posterior probability of the ith subject belonging to the kth population. The E-step reduces to computing the posterior probabilities with respect to parameter values at the wth iteration. The second step of the algorithm, the maximization step (M-step), consists of maximizing the objective function $Q(\theta|\theta^w)$ with respect to θ to obtain the updated parameter vector, $\theta^{(w+1)}$. Thus, the objective function to be maximized is

$$Q(\theta|\theta^w) = \sum_{i=1}^{M}\sum_{k=1}^{K}\pi_{ik}\{\ln(\pi_k) + \ln[h_{ik}(y_i|\theta_k)]\}$$

In this form of the objective function, maximization can be carried out by parsing $Q(\theta|\theta^w)$ into two smaller, more manageable quantities and summing their contributions. The objective function can be written as the sum of two parts

$$Q(\theta|\theta^w) = Q_1(\pi|\theta^w) + Q_2(\theta_k|\theta^w)$$
$$= \sum_{i=1}^{M}\sum_{k=1}^{K}\pi_{ik}\ln(\pi_k) + \sum_{i=1}^{M}\sum_{k=1}^{K}\pi_{ik}\ln[h_{ik}(y_i|\theta_k)].$$

Maximizing Q_1 results in updating the component probabilities in the following way

$$\pi_k^{w+1} = M^{-1}\sum_{i=1}^{M}\pi_{ik}(\theta^w).$$

The second part, $Q_2(\theta_k|\theta^w)$, can be maximized but requires a numerical optimization procedure such as Newton-Raphson or Fisher's Scoring.

Dempster et al. (1977) defined a generalized EM algorithm (GEM) for which the M-step requires θ^{w+1} to be chosen such that

$$Q(\theta^{w+1};\theta^w) \geq Q(\theta^w;\theta^w)$$

holds. That is, choose θ^{w+1} to increase the Q-function over its value at $\theta = \theta^w$, rather than maximize it over all θ in the parameter space. Dempster et al. demonstrated that the condition on θ^{w+1} was sufficient to ensure that $l(\theta^{w+1}) \geq l(\theta^w)$. The implication in practice is that on each M-step a parameter vector θ^{w+1} need only increase the Q-function—not maximize it. Because it is not essential that θ^{w+1} actually maximizes the Q-function for the likelihood to increase, iterative optimization procedures such as quasi-Newton, Fisher's Scoring, or Newton-Raphson algorithms can be used without the computational burden that would accompany reaching an optimum value.

ACKNOWLEDGMENTS

I would like to thank Margaret Burchinal and Mark Appelbaum for use of the speech error data and Robert Cudeck and Shelley Blozis for use of the verbal procedural task data.

NOTES

1. In contrast to the NLME model described herein, where some coefficients of the function are stochastic while others can be fixed, there exists the random coefficient model (see, e.g., Fitzmaurice, Laird, & Ware, 2004; Hand & Crowder, 1996), a subclass of the more flexible NLME model in which all regression coefficients vary across individuals.
2. Frequently, this is accomplished by plotting random samples of individuals via a spaghetti plot and fitting candidate functions to individuals using nonlinear least squares estimation. Bates and Watts (1988, Sec. 3) recommend three criteria to evaluate competing candidate functions: (1) the ability of the function to fit the sample data, (2) the interpretability of the parameters, and (3) the characteristics of the function—its shape and parameterization—imitate the underlying process in significant ways.
3. Each NLME model was fit with SAS PROC NLMIXED using Gaussian-Hermite quadrature with $Q = 20$ points.

4. Standard errors for NLMM models can be computed in a number of ways, including bootstrapping or using an approximation of the observed information matrix (see, e.g., Louis, 1982). For these analyses, standard errors for the NLMM models were computed by using a direct maximization of equation 7.8 at convergence using the EM algorithm. Standard errors can be obtained directly from the diagonal elements of the Hessian matrix at convergence.
5. BIC values for the two-, three-, and four-class solutions were 8510.3, 8515.1, and 8545.8, respectively. Entropy, as defined in M*plus*:

$$E_K = 1 - \frac{\sum_{i=1}^{M}\sum_{k=1}^{K}(-\hat{\pi}_{ik}\ln\hat{\pi}_{ik})}{M\ln K}$$

for the two-class solution is 0.882. An entropy value of 1 indicates perfect classification.
6. SAS PROC NLMIXED has been used with the general likelihood specification feature for mixture problems of univariate normal distributions.

REFERENCES

Aitkin, M., & Rubin, D. B. (1985). Estimation and hypothesis testing in finite mixture models. *Journal of the Royal Statistical Society, Series B, 47,* 67–75.

Bates, D. M., & Watts, D. G. (1988). *Nonlinear regression and its applications.* New York: Wiley.

Beal, S. L., & Sheiner, L. B. (1992). *NONMEM user's guides.* San Francisco: NONMEM Project Group, University of California, San Francisco.

Blozis, S. A. (2004). Structured latent curve models for the study of change in multivariate repeated measures data. *Psychological Methods, 9,* 334–353.

Browne, M. W. (1993). Structured latent curve models. In C. M. Cuadras & C. R. Rao (Eds.), *Multivariate analysis: Future directions 2* (pp. 171–197). Amsterdam: Elsevier Science.

Burchinal, M., & Appelbaum, M. I. (1991). Estimating individual developmental functions: Methods and their assumptions. *Child Development, 62,* 23–34.

Cudeck, R. (1996). Mixed-effects models in the study of individual differences with repeated measures data. *Multivariate Behavioral Research, 31,* 371–403.

Cudeck, R., & Harring, J. R. (2007). The analysis of nonlinear patterns of change with random coefficient models. *Annual Review of Psychology, 58,* 615–637.

Cudeck, R., & Harring, J. R. (2010). Developing a random coefficient model for nonlinear repeated measures data. In S.-M. Chow, E. Ferrer, & F. Hsieh (Eds.), *Statistical methods for modeling human dynamics: An interdisciplinary dialogue.* New York: Routledge.

Davidian, M., & Gallant, A. R. (1993). The nonlinear mixed effects model with a smooth random effects density. *Biometrika, 80,* 475–488.

Davidian, M., & Giltinan, D. M. (1993). Some general estimation methods for nonlinear mixed effects models. *Journal of Biopharmaceutical Statistics, 3,* 23–55.

Davidian, M., & Giltinan, D. M. (1995). *Nonlinear models for repeated measurement data.* London: Chapman & Hall.

Davidian, M. & Giltinan, D. M. (2003). Nonlinear models for repeated measurements: An overview and update. *Journal of Agricultural, Biological, and Environmental Statistics, 8,* 387–419.

Dempster, A. P., Laird, N. M., & Rubin, D. B. (1977). Maximum likelihood estimation from incomplete data via the EM algorithm. *Journal of the Royal Statistical Society, Series B, 39,* 1–38.

Everitt, B. S., & Hand, D. J. (1981). *Finite mixture distributions.* New York: Chapman & Hall.

Fitzmaurice, G. M., Laird, N. M., & Ware, J. H. (2004). *Applied longitudinal analysis.* New York: Wiley.

Grimm, K. J., & Ram, N. (2009). Nonlinear growth models in M*plus* and SAS. *Structural Equation Modeling, A Multidisciplinary Journal, 16,* 676–701.

Hall, D. B., & Wang, L. (2005). Two-component mixtures of generalized linear mixed effects models for cluster correlated data. *Statistical Modelling, 5,* 21–37.

Hancock, G. R., & Samuelsen, K. M. (Eds.). (2008). *Advances in latent variable mixture models.* Charlotte, NC: Information Age Publishing.

Hand, D., & Crowder, M. (1996). *Practical longitudinal data analysis.* London: Chapman & Hall.

Harring, J. R., Cudeck, R., & du Toit, S. H. C. (2006). Fitting partially nonlinear random coefficient models as SEMs. *Multivariate Behavioral Research, 41,* 579–596.

Leisch, F. (2004). FlexMix: A general framework for finite mixture models and latent class regression in R. *Journal of Statistical Software, 11,* 1–18.

Little, R. J. A., & Rubin, D. B. (2002). *Statistical analysis with missing data* (2nd ed.). Hoboken, NJ: Wiley.

Louis, T. A. (1982). Finding the observed information matrix when using the EM algorithm. *Journal of the Royal Statistical Society, Series B, 44,* 226–233.

McLachlan, G. J., & Krishnan, T. (1997). *The EM algorithm and extensions.* New York: Wiley.

McLachlan, G. J., & Peel, D. (2000). *Finite mixture models.* New York: Wiley.

Muthén, B. (2001a). Latent variable mixture modeling. In G. A. Marcoulides & R. E. Schumacker (Eds.), *New developments and techniques in structural equation modeling* (pp. 1–33). Mahwah, NJ: Erlbaum.

Muthén, B. (2001b). Second-generation structural equation modeling with a combination of categorical and continuous latent variables: New opportunities for latent class-latent growth modeling. In L. M. Collins & A. Sayer (Eds.), *New methods for the analysis of change* (pp. 291–322). Washington, DC: American Psychological Association.

Muthén, B. (2002). Beyond SEM: General latent variable modeling. *Behaviormetrika, 29,* 81–117.

Muthén, B. (2004). Latent variable analysis: Growth mixture modeling and related techniques for longitudinal data. In D. Kaplan (Ed.), *Handbook of quantitative methodology for the social sciences.* Newbury Park, CA: Sage.

Muthén, B., & Shedden, K. (1999). Finite mixture modeling with mixture outcomes using the EM-algorithm. *Biometrics, 55,* 463–469.

Pinheiro, J. C., & Bates, D. M. (1995). Approximations to the loglikelihood function in the nonlinear mixed effects model. *Journal of Computational and Graphical Statistics, 4,* 12–35.

Pinheiro, J. C., & Bates, D. M. (2000). *Mixed-effects models in S and S-PLUS.* New York: Springer-Verlag.

Titterington, D. M., Smith, A. F. M., & Makov, U. E. (1985). *Statistical analysis of finite mixture distributions.* Chichester, UK: Wiley.

Verbeke, G., & Lesaffre, E. (1996). A linear mixed-effects model with heterogeneity in the random effects population. *Journal of the American Statistical Association, 91,* 217–221.

Verbeke, G., & Molenberghs, G. (2000). *Linear mixed models for longitudinal data.* New York: Springer-Verlag.

Vonesh, E. F., & Chinchilli, V. M. (1997). *Linear and nonlinear models for the analysis of repeated measurements.* New York: Marcel Dekker.

Wakefield, J. C. (1995). The Bayesian analysis of population pharmacokinetics models. *Journal of the American Statistical Association, 88,* 171–178.

CHAPTER 8

GROWTH MIXTURE MODELING AND CAUSAL INFERENCE

Booil Jo
Stanford University

INTRODUCTION

In randomized controlled trials or in field experiments, comparing outcomes across groups as originally randomized is considered the gold standard of inference. This analysis principle, referred to as intention to treat (ITT) analysis, guarantees strong causal inference based on random assignment, which results in unbiased distribution of confounding variables across randomized groups. Given this comparability, we interpret the difference in the outcome across randomized groups as caused by treatment assignment.

From the ITT analysis, it is common to find a moderate or small treatment effect, especially in universal intervention trials, which we focus on in this chapter. When intervention trials are conducted including everyone (e.g., everyone in the recruited schools), the overall treatment effect estimate is not only unlikely to be substantial, but also unlikely be very informative either in identifying individuals who would benefit the most or

Advances in Longitudinal Methods in the Social and Behavioral Sciences, pages 193–214
Copyright © 2012 by Information Age Publishing
All rights of reproduction in any form reserved.

in designing/improving future intervention trials. In this case, identifying heterogeneous subpopulations that respond differently to the treatment would be of great importance. However, identifying subpopulations that may benefit differently from the intervention is in general not an easy task, especially in the context of preventive interventions. For example, in a school setting, conducting intervention trials targeting students who are at risk at baseline may pose ethical and practical problems. Identifying a high-risk group may not be an easy task when prevention interventions are given to young children before some of them start exhibiting noticeable levels of problem behaviors. The assessment of risk will then be mostly based on family socioeconomic status and home environment (which could be stigmatizing), which may not even well predict children's later problem behaviors such as substance use. In this chapter, we focus specifically on the longitudinal outcome development as a basis for identifying heterogeneous subpopulations and as a source of heterogeneity in treatment response. We believe this strategy will improve our inferential practice by identifying subpopulations taking into account outcome information (e.g., conduct problems, substance use) instead of based only on baseline characteristics and by utilizing richer information from repeatedly measured outcomes.

When outcomes are measured repeatedly over time in randomized intervention trials, we have a unique opportunity of observing longitudinal outcome development or prognosis. One natural question that arises in the presence of this information is whether there are distinctive groups of individuals that manifest themselves in the form of heterogeneous trajectory strata. Another question that arises given this heterogeneity is whether individuals in different trajectory strata benefit differently from the treatment. For example, in a longitudinal substance abuse intervention trial, researchers would be particularly interested in learning how individuals who develop an undesirable trajectory course (e.g., constantly increasing level of substance use) in the absence of intervention would benefit from being assigned to the intervention condition. Figure 8.1 illustrates this hypothetical situation.

The problem with this inference is that it requires outcome information under both the intervention and control conditions for each trajectory class of interest, which is unattainable from the observed data given that individuals cannot be assigned to both conditions. In growth mixture modeling (GMM; Muthén, 2001; Muthén & Shedden, 1999), this seemingly impossible identification problem is solved by using empirical model fitting. GMM has been increasingly used in the context of intervention trials (e.g., Kellam et al., 2008; Stulz, Thase, Klein, Manber, & Crits-Christoph, 2010; van Lier, Muthén, van der Sar, & Crijnen, 2004). However, little study has been conducted so far about the possibility of formal causal interpretation of the treatment effect estimates in this framework.

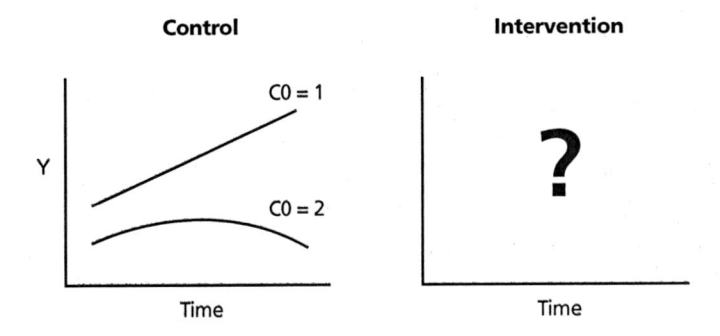

Figure 8.1 What would happen to C0=1 and C0=2 trajectory classes if assigned to the intervention condition?

This remainder of this chapter is organized as follows. First, we briefly review GMM and principal stratification, which is one of the causal modeling frameworks most similar to GMM. Then, feasibility of causal inference in the GMM framework is examined. Specifically, we go over a list of candidate identifying assumptions and evaluation standards that can be used for causal interpretation of the results in the GMM framework. Based on Monte Carlo simulations, feasibility of using these assumptions and evaluation standards for causal inference are assessed. Finally, the chapter concludes with discussion on remaining challenges and possible future directions.

Growth Mixture Modeling

GMM utilizes a general latent variable modeling framework where continuous latent variables capture growth trajectories (continuous heterogeneity) as in conventional mixed-effects modeling, and categorical latent variables capture subpopulation classes (discrete heterogeneity) as in latent class analysis. GMM has been developed to identify subpopulations that manifest themselves in the form of heterogeneous trajectory strata. In principle, GMM can simultaneously utilize all available information, including treatment response, to effectively divide individuals into latent trajectory classes. Therefore, in the context of randomized intervention/treatment studies, this method can be used to identify heterogeneous treatment effects for these latent subpopulations (Muthén et al., 2002; Muthén & Brown, 2009). In this method, heterogeneous outcome trajectory classes can be identified utilizing observed outcome information from both the treatment and control conditions. As a by-product of this latent classification, differential treatment effects can also be identified for these latent trajectory classes. In this approach, identification of latent trajectory classes and their corresponding treatment effects is possible on the basis of empirical model fitting (for further discussion, see, e.g., Jo, Wang, & Ialongo, 2009). Figure 8.2 illustrates a general form of GMM. A similar example (but without a treatment variable Z) can also be found in Example 8.1 (GMM for a continuous outcome) in the *Mplus User's Guide* (version 6; Muthén & Muthén, 1998–2011). In the model shown in Figure 8.2, *Y* stands for outcome, *X* stands for baseline covariates, *Z* stands for treatment assignment, and *I* and *S* are random effects that capture a linear longitudinal development of *Y*; individuals are classified (probabilistically) into a few discrete groups (*C*) based on their longitudinal outcome development. The key parameter here is the effect of treatment on the slope (*S* on *Z*), which may vary depending on the trajectory class membership *C* (i.e., *C* impacts the effect of *Z* on *S*). In other words, through this model we are interested in learning how heterogeneity (across *C*) impacts treatment effectiveness.

Identifying heterogeneous subpopulations based on longitudinal developments of actual outcomes is very appealing in the context of prevention intervention. Universal interventions are usually chosen in conducting early prevention interventions before the emergence of problem behaviors that will undermine children's development to healthy adulthood. Catego-

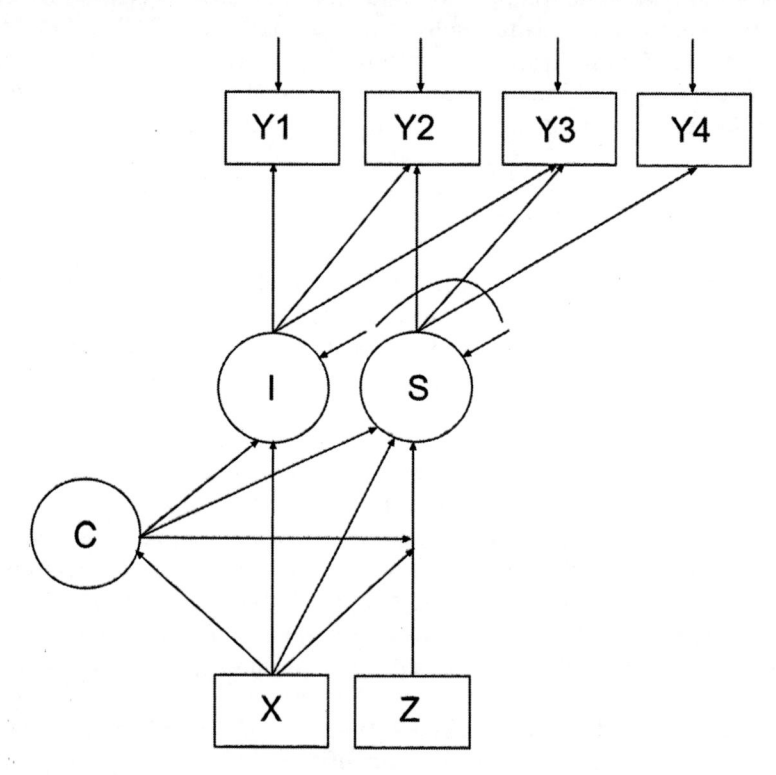

Figure 8.2 A general example of GMM.

rizing children at this young age into high- and low-risk groups based on background characteristics other than actual problem behaviors (e.g., substance use) would pose ethical and practical problems. Furthermore, these background variables may not even be especially predictive of future outcome patterns. In this situation, actual longitudinal outcome patterns provide important information as we try to better identify heterogeneous groups. GMM seems to be a promising method of identifying differential intervention effects for these heterogeneous trajectory strata. If successful, these results may be used to better evaluate the impact of the current intervention program and to improve future intervention trials. In universal interventions, a particular behavioral intervention program may not be effective for everyone, but may be very effective for individuals with a certain type of longitudinal outcome development. For example, in a substance abuse prevention program, the intervention may not have much impact on children who will be consistently at low risk or children who will improve themselves over time even without the intervention. However, the intervention can be a great help for another group of children who will develop a high-risk development pattern and also suffer from a lack of parental involvement and social support.

GMM utilizes longitudinal outcome measures including posttreatment measures that are affected by treatment assignment. However, the latent trajectory class membership in GMM is an intrinsic characteristic that is unaffected by treatment assignment. In other words, the latent trajectory class membership (C in Figure 8.2) is more like a moderator variable (i.e., a baseline variable that affects the effect of treatment on the outcome) even though latent trajectory classes are derived from posttreatment outcome measures. This is, in fact, a central property of latent trajectory class variables, which provide a foundation for causal interpretation of stratum-specific treatment effects. A very similar concept can be found in a causal modeling approach called *principal stratification* (Frangakis & Rubin, 2002), as described next.

Principal Stratification

Causal modeling, in a very broad sense, refers to a method of causal inference that focuses on the clarification of assumptions that makes causal interpretation possible, often by facilitating the concept of potential outcomes (e.g., Angrist, Imbens, & Rubin, 1996; Frangakis & Rubin, 2002; Holland, 1986; Neyman, 1923; Robins, 1986; Rosenbaum & Rubin, 1983; Rubin, 1974, 1978, 1980, 2005). Based on these assumptions that identify causal effects, sensitivity of causal effect estimates can then be examined considering plausible conditions. This framework of causal inference has not been practiced in GMM and latent variable modeling in general. Given that GMM is heavily dependent on empirical model fitting, typical strategies of contemporary causal modeling may not directly apply to causal inference using GMM. Nonetheless, the broad framework—defining identifying assumptions and conducting sensitivity analyses based on these assumptions—may well apply to causal inference using GMM.

One causal modeling approach that is especially similar to GMM in terms of its interest in heterogeneous, discrete, latent subpopulations is called *principal stratification* (Frangakis & Rubin, 2002). Among several possible causal modeling traditions, we focus on principal stratification in this chapter. Principal stratification means stratifying individuals based on potential values of a posttreatment intermediate outcome under all treatment conditions that are compared. As a result, the principal stratum membership is independent of treatment assignment just like pretreatment baseline covariates. In each principal stratum, the outcome of interest can be compared across treatment conditions. This effect is called the *principal effect*. Any principal effect is a causal effect. Similarly, in GMM, the latent trajectory class membership is unaffected by treatment assignment and, therefore, in each trajectory stratum, the treatment effect can be interpreted as a causal effect. For example, in Figure 8.1, the two classes $C0=1$ and $C0=2$ are intrinsic latent trajectory strata that are not affected by treatment assignment. In practice, if the class membership ($C0$) is correctly identified among individuals assigned to both the control and intervention conditions, the difference between the two conditions in terms of longitudinal outcome development can also be identified and interpreted as a causal effect in each trajectory stratum. A more detailed nontechnical introduction to principal stratification can be found in Jo (2008), and the relationship between GMM and principal stratification can be found in Jo et al. (2009).

Despite their conceptual similarity, principal stratification and GMM are quite different in terms of their strategies for identifying causal treatment effects. A widely known example of the principal stratification approach can be found in Angrist et al. (1996), where the treatment receipt status is an intermediate variable affected by treatment assignment. In this example, individuals are randomly assigned either to the treatment or to the control condition where they either receive or do not receive the treatment. The key idea is that every individual has a potential treatment receipt behavior under each treatment condition, which will be revealed under the condition she or he is actually assigned to and latent or missing under the other conditions. Because there are two possible treatment conditions and two possible treatment receipt behaviors in this example, all individuals belong to only one of the four possible latent compliance types. *Compliers* are individuals who receive treatment only if they are assigned to the treatment condition. *Never-takers* are individuals who do not receive the treatment even if they are assigned to the treatment condition. *Defiers* are individuals who do the opposite of what they are assigned to do. *Always-takers* are individuals who always receive the treatment no matter which condition they are assigned to. However, in practice, from the observed data, these four latent classes (principal strata) cannot be separated because treatment receipt status under only one treatment condition is observed for everyone. Given partially observed stratum information and predetermined classification rules (i.e., two possible treatment assignment statuses × two possible treatment receipt statuses = four possible principal strata), explicit identifying assumptions can be established. These assumptions make up for missing information and help identify causal effects. Therefore, parametric model fitting can be used, but, in general, does not play a central role in identifying causal effects.

FEASIBILITY OF CAUSAL INFERENCE IN THE GMM FRAMEWORK

In GMM, trajectory strata are formulated based on empirical model fitting, and as such trajectory information is completely latent or missing under all treatment conditions until model fitting is completed. In other words, we do not have partially observed strata membership, nor do we have prespecified theoretical strata. In the absence of trajectory strata information, one way to identify causal treatment effects for heterogeneous trajectory strata is to use a one-step approach, where both the trajectory strata and treatment effects for these strata are simultaneously identified based on empirical model fitting (Muthén et al., 2002; Muthén & Brown, 2009). The model choice itself depends on empirical fitting, although experts' opinion may be incorporated in the process to some extent. In that sense, identification strategies used in the GMM approach are largely exploratory compared to those used in the principal stratification approach. There has been little discussion on whether causal modeling is an applicable and practical option in the GMM framework.

The most critical first task in causal modeling is to clarify conditions (assumptions) that support causal interpretation of effect estimates. Given its emphasis on empirical model fitting, defining conditions necessary for causal inference has not been a key component in GMM and latent variable modeling in general. It is not an easy task to define these conditions even in the principal stratification framework, but we at least have clear prespecified theoretical strata that can be used as a basis for formulating possible identifying assumptions. Clarifying assumptions necessary to identify stratum-specific causal treatment effects in GMM is a quite different and more difficult task since there are no theoretical strata (and therefore no partial observation of the strata). One natural starting point for this investigation would be to carefully identify conditions under which GMM is likely to successfully capture the true trajectory strata. Based on this general information, we can start building more customized assumptions depending on specific situations. This is a big task that requires much collaborative work among intervention researchers, causal modelers, and latent variable modelers. This chapter explores the possibilities in this future development.

Assumptions to Support Causal Inference in GMM

In principal stratification models, identifying assumptions can be built on the basis of known theoretical strata and partially observed individual strata membership. For example, in the four-stratum example discussed by Angrist et al. (1996), it is assumed that there are no defiers (monotonicity) and that there is no effect of treatment assignment for never-takers and always-takers (exclusion restriction). This kind of clear formulation of assumptions is difficult in the GMM framework because there are neither known theoretical strata nor partially observed strata membership among individuals. In the absence of theoretical strata, the goal of GMM is to successfully recover true trajectory strata in the targeted population. As the difference between outcome trajectories under different conditions within a particular trajectory class is a treatment effect, if trajectory strata are estimated correctly then the resulting stratum-specific treatment effects will also be estimated correctly. Given that GMM relies on empirical model fitting, there are some general conditions that are likely to help GMM successfully recover true trajectory strata. Additional and potentially more effective conditions can be identified as we further investigate possible candidate assumptions. The following can be considered a tentative list of identifying assumptions that are likely to help identification of stratum-specific causal treatment effects in the GMM framework.

1. *Model specifications are correct.* Model specifications correctly capture heterogeneous growth trajectories within each stratum and correctly capture differences across strata. In principle, all model specifications need to be correct. Because we are working with models that are parametrically identified, causal effect estimates can be quite sensitive to any minor model misspecifications (such as restrictions on residual variances and covariate effects within and across strata). Extensive sensitivity analyses seem necessary in this regard.
2. *Parametric assumptions hold.* In the GMM framework, parametric assumptions such as normality are a key driving force in separating trajectory strata. Both the estimation of strata and stratum-specific

treatment effects can be very sensitive to deviations from parametric assumptions. Sensitivity analysis seems important, but at the same time it is unclear how sensitivity analysis should be conducted considering various possibilities of deviations from parametric assumptions.

3. *The sample is large enough to provide sufficient power to detect all heterogeneous strata.* Even if the two previous assumptions hold, we still may not be able to recover the true trajectory strata if the sample size is too small. The choice of model mainly relies on empirical fitting and, therefore, with insufficient power, we may end up with too few strata and may miss small but important trajectory classes.

4. *Trajectory strata are well separated.* Given that GMM relies heavily on parametric assumptions, the distances among trajectory strata constitute a key factor for a successful separation of the strata. As these distances increase, it is more likely that the true strata will be successfully recovered. How large the distance should be could depend on several factors such as how well the normality assumption holds and whether we have strong auxiliary information that predicts strata membership.

5. *Within each trajectory stratum, potential trajectories under different treatment conditions are close to each other.* In the GMM framework, the differences between outcome trajectories under different conditions within trajectory strata are treatment effects. For successful identification of these effects based on empirical fitting, trajectory strata need to be far apart from one another, but at the same time within each trajectory stratum the trajectory under the treatment and the trajectory under the control condition need to be close to each other. In other words, the distance between trajectories across different strata needs to be larger than the distance between trajectories (i.e., trajectories of treatment conditions) within strata. Otherwise, the potential outcome trajectories under the treatment condition will be poorly connected to those under the control condition, which will directly lead to a failure in correctly identifying stratum-specific causal treatment effects. The connection of trajectories between treatment conditions can be greatly strengthened by imposing model restrictions described below.

6. *Study designs allow model restricting assumptions.* To satisfy Condition 1 above, model specifications need to be general enough to properly capture heterogeneity across trajectory strata. At the same time, having too many free parameters is likely to lead to poor recovery of trajectory strata, low precision, and convergence problems. Study designs may provide useful information that can be used to formulate model restricting assumptions. For example, in randomized intervention trials that have prerandomization outcome measures we can

impose baseline equality of the outcome across treatment groups on the basis of random assignment. As is shown in the simulation study in this chapter, design-based model restrictions can play a critical role in improving the quality of causal effect estimation in the GMM framework.

7. *The data provide auxiliary information.* When the data have strong auxiliary information, such as from covariates that are good predictors of trajectory strata membership, we are more likely to successfully recover the true trajectory strata. This information can be critical in terms of increasing power and reducing bias (this has been shown in nonlongitudinal settings in Jo, 2002a, 2002b).

Evaluation Standards

In the absence of theoretical strata, the goal of GMM is to successfully recover true trajectory strata in the targeted population. This is the highest standard in evaluating the quality of causal effect estimation. In practice, it would often be difficult to reach this standard. Furthermore, because we do not have known theoretical strata, evaluating the quality of strata and stratum-specific treatment effect estimates will have to depend on sensitivity analyses and model diagnostics. In Monte Carlo simulations, however, we know the true trajectory strata and their true treatment effects, and therefore we may apply the following criteria in evaluating the results.

1. *True population trajectory strata and true stratum-specific treatment effects are well recovered.* This is the highest standard in evaluating the quality of causal effect estimation. Well recovered is based on typical criteria such as nominal 95% coverage rate with average bias close to zero and small root mean square error.

2. *True population trajectory strata are reasonably coarsened or partitioned.* Neighboring trajectories may be coarsened or partitioned. Trajectory strata may also be partitioned into adjacent multiple trajectory strata, resulting in mixing of different trajectory strata. In practice, we may not have enough statistical power to recover all trajectory classes, in particular smaller ones, and therefore trajectory strata with small numbers of individuals are likely to be partitioned into adjacent major trajectory strata. As a result of this partitioning, we may fail to detect a large treatment effect for a small trajectory class. This may still be considered a successful result if we take the conservative side and focus on avoiding Type I error. However, this may be considered a failure when the trial's interest is in identifying

a trajectory stratum that benefits the most from the treatment even though its size is small.
3. *No misleading results that are far from the truth are provided.* This is closely related to Standard 2. If coarsening, partitioning, or mixing of trajectory strata occur, maintaining the connection within trajectory strata (i.e., trajectories under the treatment and control conditions are still well bound), we are unlikely to end up with largely misleading results. However, if the connection within trajectory strata is not maintained in this process, we may end up with artificial results, for example, with very large desirable or undesirable effects of the treatment while they do not really exist (i.e., serious Type I error). The situation may get exacerbated when combined with deviations from parametric assumptions and/or model misspecifications.

SIMULATION STUDY

A Monte Carlo simulation study was conducted under two likely scenarios in prevention intervention research practice. In principle, we should examine how all seven conditions (and more as they become identified) interplay in determining the quality of causal effect estimation in the GMM framework. This is indeed an overwhelming task that should be carefully conducted in future studies. In this section, we look at scenarios where Conditions 1–3 hold, but Conditions 4 and 7 do not hold. Under these scenarios, we focus on examining how Conditions 5 and 6 interplay in identifying trajectory strata and their treatment effects.

The first three of the seven conditions discussed earlier are assumed to hold in these simulations. First, the data were generated and analyzed using a linear trend for all trajectory strata. Second, we assumed multivariate normality both at level 1 and level 2 and both in data generation and analyses. Third, we used a sample size of 500 with a balanced design (random assignment to two conditions with equal probability). This sample size was chosen considering typical numbers of subjects in psychosocial intervention studies. Another reason was to have a large enough sample in each stratum. All of the trajectory strata have 20–30% of the total sample, and therefore the smallest strata still have around 100 subjects. For Condition 4, we assumed moderate distances separating trajectory strata with maximum distances of 0.4–2.0 standard deviations (based on standard deviation at baseline) across assessment points. In a previous simulation study reported in Muthén and Brown (2009), a minimum distance of 3–4 standard deviations was used, which resulted in a good separation of trajectory strata. In the current study, we focus on less than ideal but more realistic situations in terms of Condition 4. Condition 5 is not well satisfied in one scenario, but is relatively well satisfied in the other scenario. Conditions 5 and 6 are closely related in the current simulation setting. That is, for Condition 6, on the basis of random assignment to treatment conditions, the equality across treatment conditions at baseline within each trajectory class approximately holds, which results in a better condition for Condition 5. This baseline equality holds in one scenario and does not hold in the other so that we can contrast the results. In terms of Condition 7, we do not introduce any covariates, which may further improve the quality of causal effect estimation, but, at the same time, could introduce model specification issues regarding the covariate effects.

Scenario 1: Four Strata with Unequal Intercepts Across Treatment Conditions

The first scenario we consider is based on a randomized substance abuse intervention trial where the universal prevention intervention is given during the first grade. All students in the participating schools are assigned either to the intervention or to the control condition. Because substance use is very unlikely in early years, the outcome is measured from the sixth grade. The assumption here is that there is no variation in terms of substance use during the first grade (i.e., all zero). From a growth modeling perspective, this situation means that we cannot assume equal intercepts across the two conditions. In other words, the effect of treatment assignment cannot be assumed to be zero at the first assessment (grade 6) even though the treatment assignment was randomized. In fact, the effect of the treatment could be the largest at this first assessment, which is the closest from the time of intervention.

Figure 8.3 shows the true trajectory strata assumed for Scenario 1. It is shown that trajectory Class 1 (20%) would benefit considerably at the first posttreatment assessment at grade 6 (effect size = 1.3), although the effect diminishes somewhat over time. Class 2 (30%) would be hardly affected by treatment assignment. Individuals in class 3 (30%) would be somewhat negatively affected by being assigned to the intervention condition at grade 6, but the effect of intervention would turn out to be somewhat positive as they get older. Class 4 (20%) represents a group of people who are consistently at low risk. The intervention assignment has little impact on this trajectory class. In this hypothetical universal intervention trial, correctly identifying a sizable intervention effect on a particular trajectory class (i.e., Class 1) would be considered a successful result.

For data generation, a linear trend was assumed for all four strata under both treatment conditions. Here we assume that randomization takes place right after the baseline ($t = 1$) assessment. A continuous outcome Y for individual i in the trajectory class j at time point t, where $i = 1, 2, \ldots, N$,

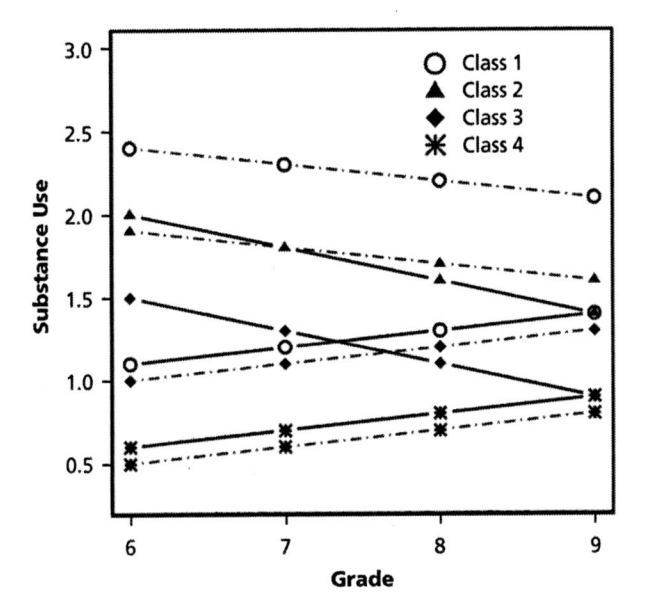

Growth Mixture Modeling and Causal Inference ▪ 205

Figure 8.3 Scenario 1: True trajectory strata (solid lines are trajectory strata under the treatment condition and dashed lines are under the control condition).

$j = 1, 2, \ldots, J$, and $t = 1, 2, \ldots, T$ (in the current setting, $J = 4$ and $T = 4$), can be expressed as

$$y_{it} = \eta_{Iij} + \eta_{Sij} W_t + \varepsilon_{it} \tag{8.1}$$

$$\eta_{Iij} = \alpha_{Ij} + \gamma_{Ij} Z_i + \zeta_{Ii} \tag{8.2}$$

$$\eta_{Sij} = \alpha_{Sj} + \gamma_{Sj} Z_i + \zeta_{Si} \tag{8.3}$$

where W_t is a time score at time point t, Z is the treatment assignment status ($Z = 1$ if assigned to the treatment, $Z = 0$ if assigned to the control condition), γ_{Ij} is the effect of treatment assignment on the intercept, and γ_{Sj} is the effect of treatment assignment on the linear slope both for the jth trajectory class. The two random effects, the initial status (η_{Iij}) and the linear growth (η_{Sij}), vary across J trajectory strata. The effects of treatment on these random effects, γ_{Ij} and γ_{Sj}, also vary across J strata. It is assumed that $\varepsilon_i \sim \text{MVN}(0, \Sigma_\varepsilon)$ and that $\zeta_i \sim \text{MVN}(0, \Sigma_\zeta)$. In this study, these two covariance structures are held constant across J strata for both data generation and analysis for simplicity. However, in principle, they can be allowed to vary across strata. The level-1 residual variance is 0.36 at $t = 1$, 0.49 at $t = 2$, 0.64 at $t = 3$, and 1.0 at $t = 4$, with more variation at later time points. The level-2 residual variance is 1.0 for the initial status and 0.25 for the linear growth. The true trajectory shapes and treatment effects vary across simulation settings and can be found in Tables 8.1–8.6 and Figures 8.3 and 8.4.

The probability π_i for a person i to belong to a certain latent class ($C_i = j$) can be expressed as a multinomial logit model,

$$\text{logit}(\pi_i) = \beta_{00}, \quad (8.4)$$

where the intercept, β_{00}, is a $J-1$ dimensional vector of multinomial logit intercepts. The probability π_i is a $J-1$ dimensional vector of $(\pi_{i1}, \pi_{i2}, \ldots, \pi_{i(J-1)})$, where $\pi_{ij} = \Pr(C_i = j)$ and $\text{logit}(\pi_i) = (\log[\pi_{i1}/\pi_{iJ}], \log[\pi_{i2}/\pi_{iJ}], \ldots, \log[\pi_{i(J-1)}/\pi_{iJ}])$.

The data were generated based on Scenario 1 in Figure 8.3 and equations 8.1–8.4. For all simulation settings, 500 datasets were generated. These data were analyzed using the same growth mixture model described in equations 8.1–8.4. In practice, we cannot know the true parameter values and the true number of classes. Given the moderate sample size ($N = 500$), we assumed that the number of classes chosen for analyses in practice is most likely to be between one and four. Three different sets of starting values were used to examine stability of the analysis results in practice. For the estimation of growth mixture models, maximum likelihood (ML) estimation using the expectation-maximization (EM) algorithm, implemented in Mplus (Muthén & Muthén, 1998–2011), was employed. Details on ML estimation via the algorithm of common growth mixture models are provided in Jo et al. (2009).

The Monte Carlo simulation results under Scenario 1 are summarized in Tables 8.1–8.3. Because the outcome is substance use, negative estimates

TABLE 8.1 Scenario 1: Simulation Results with Four-Class Model with Three Different Sets of Starting Values (SV1, SV2, SV3)

Class	Parameter	True value	Estimate (SV1)	Estimate (SV2)	Estimate (SV3)
1	Class%	20.0	14.1	20.8	19.1
	γ_I	-1.3	-1.762	-0.402	-0.774
	γ_S	0.2	0.233	-0.063	-0.065
2	Class%	30.0	37.5	26.1	12.4
	γ_I	0.1	0.154	-0.046	0.009
	γ_S	-0.1	-0.059	-0.086	-0.022
3	Class%	20.0	11.9	29.5	37.3
	γ_I	0.5	0.236	0.173	0.197
	γ_S	-0.3	-0.382	-0.038	-0.048
4	Class%	30.0	36.6	23.6	31.2
	γ_I	0.1	0.233	-0.226	-0.139
	γ_S	0.0	-0.048	-0.034	-0.034

TABLE 8.2 Scenario 1: Simulation Results with Three-Class Model with Three Different Sets of Starting Values (SV1, SV2, SV3)

Class	Parameter	True value	Estimate (SV1)	Estimate (SV2)	Estimate (SV3)
1	Class%	20.0	14.6	45.2	26.7
	γ_I	−1.3	−1.756	−0.399	−0.433
	γ_S	0.2	0.178	−0.048	−0.048
2	Class%	30.0	45.9	27.8	33.2
	γ_I	0.1	0.163	0.041	−0.179
	γ_S	−0.1	−0.092	−0.079	−0.031
3	Class%	20.0	39.5	27.0	40.1
	γ_I	0.5	0.247	0.228	0.244
	γ_S	−0.3	−0.099	−0.051	−0.076
4	Class%	30.0			
	γ_I	0.1			
	γ_S	0.0			

TABLE 8.3 Scenario 1: Simulation Results with Two-Class Model with Three Different Sets of Starting Values (SV1, SV2, SV3)

Class	Parameter	True value	Estimate (SV1)	Estimate (SV2)	Estimate (SV3)
1	Class%	20.0	48.0	65.6	50.1
	γ_I	−1.3	−1.330	−0.358	−0.437
	γ_S	0.2	0.093	−0.047	−0.051
2	Class%	30.0			
	γ_I	0.1			
	γ_S	−0.1			
3	Class%	20.0	52.0	34.4	49.9
	γ_I	0.5	1.027	0.352	0.272
	γ_S	−0.3	−0.191	−0.082	−0.073
4	Class%	30.0			
	γ_I	0.1			
	γ_S	0.0			

of γ_I and γ_S indicate positive effects of the intervention. Stratum-specific parameter estimates are summarized under the true trajectory classes with best-matching true parameter values. However, this matching should not be taken seriously, especially for the analyses assuming numbers of classes fewer than four. The results show that trajectory strata proportions and stratum-specific treatment effects are poorly estimated even with the correct analysis model with the correct number of trajectory strata. To rule out the possibility that the poor results may be due to lack of power, the same simulation analyses were repeated with a much larger sample size ($N = 10,000$), although this made little improvement in the results. These results suggest that correct model specifications, good normality conditions, and large sample sizes (Conditions 1–3) are not sufficient to guarantee unbiased estimates of stratum-specific causal treatment effects using GMM.

The results shown in Tables 8.1–8.3 are quite unstable across analyses using different sets of starting values. Depending on the choice of starting values, both treatment effect estimates and mixing proportions can seriously deviate from the true values. In the four- and the three-class models, we may fail to detect the large treatment effect for Class 1 (see Figure 8.3). That is, the intervention effect for Class 1 at grade 6 ranges from moderate (–0.4) to very large (–1.8), depending on starting values (Tables 8.1 and 8.2). Using the two-class model (Table 8.3), we may underestimate the large desirable effect of the intervention on Class 1 (ranges from –0.4 to –1.3), and at the same time, may overestimate the moderate harmful effect on Class 3 (ranges from 0.3 to 1.6).

Scenario 2: Four Strata with Equal Intercepts Across Treatment Conditions

The second scenario to be considered is a randomized school intervention trial focusing on reduction of attention deficit. As in the first scenario, the universal prevention intervention is given during the first grade. All students in the participating schools are assigned either to the intervention or to the control condition. The outcome is measured at baseline (i.e., first grade) and three more times after the intervention. Because the outcome is measured for everyone during the first grade before the intervention, we can assume that the intercepts are the same under the two conditions on the basis of random assignment. In other words, the effect of treatment assignment can be assumed to be zero at the first assessment (Grade 1).

Figure 8.4 shows the true trajectory strata assumed for Scenario 2. It is shown that trajectory Class 1 (30%) would benefit considerably as they get older (effect size is about 1 at grade 4). Class 2 (20%) would be hardly affected by treatment assignment. Individuals in Class 3 (20%) would somewhat benefit from being assigned to the intervention condition, especially as they get older. Class 4 (20%) represents a group of people who are consistently at low risk. The intervention assignment has little impact on this trajectory class. In this hypothetical universal intervention trial, correctly identifying a sizable intervention effect on a particular trajectory class (i.e., Class 1) would be considered a successful result.

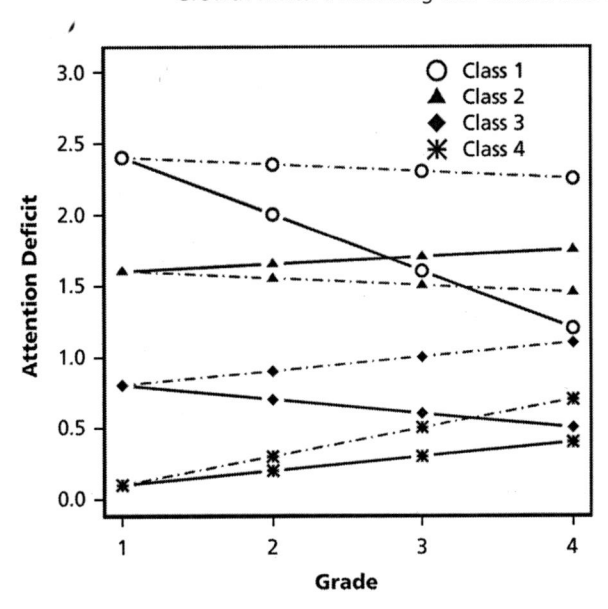

Growth Mixture Modeling and Causal Inference ▪ 209

Figure 8.4 Scenario 2: True trajectory strata (solid lines are trajectory strata under the treatment condition and dashed lines are under the control condition).

The data were generated based on Scenario 2 shown in Figure 8.4 and Equations 8.1–8.4 and were analyzed using the same GMM described in these same equations. The only difference under Scenario 2 is that the effect of treatment assignment (γ_I) is fixed at zero both in the data generation and in the analyses for all four strata on the basis of randomization. Analyses were conducted assuming two to four classes. Three different sets of starting values were used to examine stability of the analysis results in practice.

The Monte Carlo simulation results under Scenario 2 are summarized in Tables 8.4–8.6. Because the outcome is attention deficit, negative estimates of γ_S indicate positive effects of the intervention. Stratum-specific parameter estimates are summarized under the true trajectory classes with best-matching true parameter values. The results show that both treatment effect estimates and mixing proportions can still be somewhat biased and unstable depending on starting values and the number of classes chosen. However, in comparison to the results under Scenario 1, the results (especially treatment effect estimates) under Scenario 2 are much more stable. Serious Type I or II error is also much less likely under Scenario 2. For example, the effect size for Class 1 at Grade 4 is around 1 regardless of the choice of starting values, meaning that serious Type II error is unlikely. For the other trajectory classes with small to moderate effect sizes, there is no indication of extreme positive or negative effects, meaning that serious Type I error is unlikely. As the number of classes in the model decreases,

TABLE 8.4 Scenario 2: Simulation Results with Four-Class Model with Three Different Sets of Starting Values (SV1, SV2, SV3)

Class	Parameter	True value	Estimate (SV1)	Estimate (SV2)	Estimate (SV3)
1	Class%	30.0	12.2	19.0	13.6
	γ_s	−0.35	−0.403	−0.309	−0.300
2	Class%	20.0	15.1	24.4	11.7
	γ_s	−0.20	−0.314	−0.132	−0.298
3	Class%	20.0	44.2	35.0	47.4
	γ_s	0.10	−0.083	−0.120	−0.125
4	Class%	30.0	28.5	21.6	27.3
	γ_s	−0.10	−0.166	−0.177	−0.149

TABLE 8.5 Scenario 2: Simulation Results with Three-Class Model with Three Different Sets of Starting Values (SV1, SV2, SV3)

Class	Parameter	True value	Estimate (SV1)	Estimate (SV2)	Estimate (SV3)
1	Class%	30.0	15.9	37.4	21.1
	γ_s	−0.35	−0.318	−0.294	−0.321
2	Class%	20.0	31.4	33.1	30.3
	γ_s	−0.20	−0.199	−0.116	−0.141
3	Class%	20.0			
	γ_s	0.10			
4	Class%	30.0	52.7	29.6	48.6
	γ_s	−0.10	−0.106	−0.087	−0.103

TABLE 8.6 Scenario 2: Simulation Results with Two-Class Model with Three Different Sets of Starting Values (SV1, SV2, SV3)

Class	Parameter	True value	Estimate (SV1)	Estimate (SV2)	Estimate (SV3)
1	Class%	30.0	35.7	50.7	40.5
	γ_s	−0.35	−0.291	−0.266	−0.291
2	Class%	20.0			
	γ_s	−0.20			
3	Class%	20.0			
	γ_s	0.10			
4	Class%	30.0	64.3	49.3	59.5
	γ_s	−0.10	−0.102	−0.090	−0.091

treatment effects seem to get combined reasonably well without generating seriously misleading estimates. The practical implication here is that these errors are unlikely to be serious enough to change our evaluation of the intervention and therefore to lead our clinical or policy decisions to a wrong direction. Of course, how serious is serious enough would change depending on the context.

The results under Scenario 2 suggest that Conditions 4–6 are critical in generating unbiased estimates of stratum-specific causal treatment effects using GMM. Whereas Condition 4 is not something we can observe or control, Condition 5 can be better understood by examining the study design features. By utilizing information embedded in the study design, Condition 6 can be strengthened. The results also suggest that correctly recovering trajectory strata and stratum-specific treatment effects would still be difficult unless strata are extremely well separated (Condition 4: all strata are at least 3–4 standard deviations apart). However, the quality of trajectory strata and stratum-specific treatment effect estimates in GMM is likely to further improve as we include more model-restricting assumptions and/or good auxiliary information such as from covariates.

CONCLUSIONS

As in any causal modeling approach, the first task in causal inference using GMM is to clarify assumptions necessary for causal interpretation. Based on these assumptions, causal interpretation is possible and good sensitivity analysis methods can be developed. This study showed some feasibility of causal inference in the GMM framework. As a first step, the study focused on identifying conditions under which GMM is likely to successfully recover true trajectory strata in the targeted population. The investigation conducted in this study is limited in its scope, and much work is ahead to establish a good foundation for causal modeling in the GMM framework.

Monte Carlo simulation results showed that correct model specifications, good normality conditions, and large sample sizes are not sufficient to guarantee unbiased estimates of stratum-specific causal treatment effects using GMM. The results suggested that correctly recovering trajectory strata and stratum-specific treatment effects would be difficult unless strata are extremely well separated. However, even under less than ideal conditions, the quality of trajectory strata and stratum-specific treatment effect estimates in GMM are still likely to improve in the presence of model-restricting assumptions based on study designs. Given GMM's reliance on parametric assumptions, the larger the distance between trajectory strata and the narrower the distance within strata across treatment conditions, identification of causal treatment effects is more likely to be successful. Whereas the distance between trajectory strata is beyond our control, the connection between treatment arms within strata can be predicted and enforced in the analyses under certain conditions. For example, when prerandomization outcome measure is available in randomized trials, it is reasonable to assume the baseline equality on the basis of random assignment. In a previous simulation study of GMM presented in Muthén and Brown (2009), two prerandomization measures and 10 postrandomization measures were considered, which greatly enhanced binding between treatment arms within strata.

Identifying causal treatment effects in GMM mainly relies on empirical model fitting and parametric assumptions in the absence of predetermined theoretical strata and partially observed stratum membership. Therefore, establishing sensitivity analysis strategies is a particularly difficult task in the GMM framework. As we discussed in the chapter, there are many conditions that may interact and jointly affect the quality of causal effect estimation in the GMM framework. In this study, Monte Carlo simulations were conducted assuming that some of the central conditions such as parametric assumptions hold. Extensive simulation studies are necessary in future studies to fully examine sensitivity of causal effect estimates under various conditions, which will provide critical information in developing good sensitivity analysis methods for real data analyses.

In addition to developing identifying assumptions and sensitivity analysis methods, it is also critical to investigate the feasibility of causal inference at the conceptual level. In this study, principal stratification was considered as the potential causal modeling framework for GMM. However, it is not clear whether we will benefit from fully adopting the conceptual framework of principal stratification. Principal stratification means stratifying individuals based on potential values of a mediator under all treatment conditions that are compared. This idea of cross-classification based on potential outcomes under the treatment and under the control condition is clearly helpful in the presence of theoretical strata. There has been little discussion regarding whether or not cross-classification helps interpretation of treatment effects in the GMM context, where strata are derived based on empirical fitting (i.e., no predetermined theoretical strata). The conceptual framework of causal modeling in the GMM framework needs to be further refined considering the similarities and differences between GMM and causal modeling approaches including principal stratification.

One approach of causal inference using GMM that has not been discussed in this chapter is a two-step approach proposed by Jo et al. (2009). In this approach, only one treatment condition (reference condition) is used to identify heterogeneous trajectory strata (reference strata) and then treatment effects for these strata are identified using the entire sample treating the trajectory strata membership estimated using the reference condition as known for those who are assigned to the reference condition and missing for those who are assigned to different conditions. The first step of identifying trajectory strata under the reference condition still relies on empirical model fitting. However, in the second step of identifying stratum-specific causal treatment effects, we can apply the same identification strategies used in principal stratification. The advantage of this approach is that we rely less on empirical fitting and parametric assumptions in identifying stratum-specific causal treatment effects. The drawback of this approach is that the trajectory strata identified using data from only one treatment condition may not fully capture heterogeneous subpopulations. Using both this two-step approach and the one-step approach focused on in this study is likely to strengthen causal inference in the GMM framework. Further study is needed to examine the relation between the two and to examine effective ways of jointly using the two methods.

REFERENCES

Angrist, J. D., Imbens, G. W., & Rubin, D. B. (1996). Identification of causal effects using instrumental variables. *Journal of the American Statistical Association, 91,* 444–455.

Frangakis, C. E., & Rubin, D. B. (2002). Principal stratification in causal inference. *Biometrics, 58,* 21–29.

Holland, P. W. (1986). Statistics and causal inference. *Journal of the American Statistical Association, 81,* 945–960.

Jo, B. (2002a). Model misspecification sensitivity analysis in estimating causal effects of interventions with noncompliance. *Statistics in Medicine, 21,* 3161–3181.

Jo, B. (2002b). Statistical power in randomized intervention studies with noncompliance. *Psychological Methods, 7,* 178–193.

Jo, B. (2008). Causal inference in randomized experiments with mediational processes. *Psychological Methods, 13,* 314–336.

Jo, B., Wang, C-P., & Ialongo, N. S. (2009). Using latent outcome trajectory classes in causal inference. *Statistics and Its Interface, 2,* 403–412.

Kellam, S. G., Brown, C. H., Poduska, J. M, Ialongo, N. S., Wang, W., Toyinbo, P., et al. (2008). Effects of a universal classroom behavior management program in first and second grades on young adult behavioral, psychiatric, and social outcomes. *Drug and Alcohol Dependence, 95,* S5-S28.

Muthén, B. O. (2001). Second-generation structural equation modeling with a combination of categorical and continuous latent variables: New opportunities for latent class/latent growth modeling. In L. M. Collins & A. G. Sayer (Eds.), *New methods for the analysis of change* (pp. 291–322). Washington, DC: American Psychological Association.

Muthén, B. O., & Brown, C. H. (2009). Estimating drug effects in the presence of placebo response: Causal inference using growth mixture modeling. *Statistics in Medicine, 28,* 3363–3385.

Muthén, B. O., Brown, C. H., Masyn, K., Jo, B., Khoo, S. T., Yang, C. C., et al. (2002). General growth mixture modeling for randomized preventive interventions. *Biostatistics, 3,* 459–475.

Muthén, B. O., & Shedden, K. (1999). Finite mixture modeling with mixture outcomes using the EM algorithm. *Biometrics, 55,* 463–469.

Muthén, L. K., & Muthén, B. O. (1998–2011). *Mplus user's guide.* Los Angeles: Authors.

Neyman, J. (1923). On the application of probability theory to agricultural experiments. Essay on principles. *Section 9 translated in Statistical Science, 5,* 465–480.

Robins, J. M. (1986). A new approach to causal inference in mortality studies with sustained exposure periods-application to control of the healthy worker survivor effect. *Mathematical Modeling, 7,* 1393–1512.

Rosenbaum, P. R., & Rubin, D. B. (1983). The central role of the propensity score in observational studies for causal effects. *Biometrika, 70,* 41–55.

Rubin, D. B. (1974). Estimating causal effects of treatments in randomized and nonrandomized studies. *Journal of Educational Psychology, 66,* 688–701.

Rubin, D. B. (1978). Bayesian inference for causal effects: The role of randomization. *Annals of Statistics, 6,* 34–58.

Rubin, D. B. (1980). Discussion of "Randomization analysis of experimental data in the Fisher randomization test" by D. Basu. *Journal of the American Statistical Association, 75,* 591–593.

Rubin, D. B. (2005). Causal inference using potential outcomes: Design, modeling, decisions. *Journal of the American Statistical Association, 100,* 322–331.

Stulz, N., Thase, M. E., Klein, D. N., Manber, R., & Crits-Christoph, P. (2010). Differential effects of treatments for chronic depression: a latent growth model reanalysis. *Journal of Consulting and Clinical Psychology, 78,* 409–419.

van Lier, P. A. C., Muthén, B. O., van der Sar, R. M. & Crijnen, A. A. M. (2004). Preventing disruptive behavior in elementary schoolchildren: Impact of a universal classroom-based intervention. *Journal of Consulting and Clinical Psychology, 72,* 467–478.

PART III

THE ROLE OF MEASUREMENT IN MODELING
WITHIN-SUBJECT AND BETWEEN-SUBJECT EFFECTS

CHAPTER 9

DISAGGREGATING WITHIN-PERSON AND BETWEEN-PERSON EFFECTS IN MULTILEVEL AND STRUCTURAL EQUATION GROWTH MODELS

Patrick J. Curran
University of North Carolina at Chapel Hill

Taehun Lee
University of California, Los Angeles

Andrea L. Howard
University of North Carolina at Chapel Hill

Stephanie Lane
University of North Carolina at Chapel Hill

Robert MacCallum
University of North Carolina at Chapel Hill

Growth models are being used to study interindividual differences in intraindividual change at a rapidly increasing rate in the social sciences. These are most often estimated as either a structural equation model (SEM) or as a multilevel linear model (MLM), although other estimation methods are available (e.g., fixed effects growth, general estimating equations, etc.). Regardless of approach, the core concept behind a growth model is to use a set of repeated measures to infer the existence of one or more parameters that define an unobserved (or latent) trajectory over time. The functional form of the trajectories might be flat with respect to time (e.g., an intercept-only model), they might be linearly increasing or decreasing, or they might be some complex nonlinear function. Whatever the form, growth models typically estimate the fixed and random effects associated with stability and change over time. The fixed effects capture the mean of the trajectory pooling over all of the individuals within the sample and the random effects reflect individual variability around the mean trajectory. Smaller random effects suggest greater similarity in growth across individuals; larger random effects suggest greater individual heterogeneity in change over time.

It is common to include one or more exogenous predictors in a growth model. Measures that directly predict the growth trajectories are often called time-invariant covariates (or TICs) because these are believed to be unrelated to the passage of time. Examples of covariates that are truly time-invariant include biological sex, birth order, country of origin, race, and certain genetic markers. In principle, a truly time-invariant covariate can be assessed at any point in time given that the measure is independent of time. A related type of TIC is a measure that might be expected to vary as a function of time but only the initial assessment of the measure is included in the model. For example, although adolescent deviant peer affiliations might theoretically vary over time, an application might only consider a single measure of deviant peer affiliations taken at the initial assessment period (e.g., Chassin, Curran, Hussong, & Colder, 1996). Regardless of type, one or more TICs are used to predict variability in the parameters that define the trajectory over time.

Although not always explicitly recognized in many substantive applications, the inclusion of TICs as predictors of growth provide for direct tests of *between-person* differences in growth. These between-person differences are captured in the estimated regression parameters that reflect a shift in the conditional means of the distribution of trajectory parameters as a function of a shift in the mean of the TICs. For example, boys might report significantly higher initial values relative to girls, or individuals in a treatment condition might report significantly steeper increases in an outcome over time relative to individuals in a control condition. TICs are thus person-specific measures that are constant over time and capture between-person effects by directly predicting the trajectory parameters.

However, there is another important component of individual change that has received much less attention in the estimation of many growth models, and this is the systematic study of *within-person* influences on change over time. Whereas the estimation of between-person differences is based on measures taken at a single point in time (i.e., TICs), the estimation of within-person differences involves measures taken repeatedly over time; as such, these measures are referred to as time-varying covariates, or TVCs. Unlike TICs (which directly influence the random growth parameters), the TVCs directly influence the repeated assessments of the outcome measure *net* the influence of underlying growth in the outcome. Whereas the between-person TIC effect reflects a mean shift in the parameters defining growth pooling across the sample of individuals, the within-person TVC effect reflects a mean shift in the time-specific outcome measure as a function of the relative distribution of the TVCs *within* each individual. More colloquially, TICs provide insights regarding "for whom" an effect exists and TVCs provide insights regarding "at what time" an effect exists. TVCs are thus person- and time-specific measures that capture within-person effects by directly predicting the repeated measures above and beyond systematic growth in the outcome over time.

There is an added complexity to the within-person and between-person distinction that is better known in the quantitative literature but is much less evident in substantive research applications. Specifically, it is possible that a person- and time-specific TVC simultaneously exerts *both* a within-person and a between-person effect. The within-person effect is captured in the relation between the person- and time-specific measure of the TVC and the person- and time-specific measure of the outcome; the between-person effect is captured in the relation between the person-specific (and thus time invariant) *mean* of the TVC and the growth trajectories. Either confounding or misattributing these two levels of effects can lead to potentially significant errors of inference (see Curran & Bauer, 2011, for a recent review). Only by simultaneously considering these two types of influences can the full nature of the relation between a TVC and the outcome be understood (Raudenbush & Bryk, 2002; Schwartz & Stone, 1998; Singer & Willett, 2003).

As a reflection of the potentially complex nature of these relations, a TVC might exert a between-person effect but not a within-person effect. For example, Hoffman and Stawski (2009) studied the relation between negative mood, stress, and physical symptoms in a sample of younger and older adults. One key finding was that there was support for a significant positive between-person effect between daily negative mood and daily physical symptoms, but there was no support for a within-person effect between the same two measures (Hoffman & Stawski, 2009, Figure 2). In other words, individuals reporting greater overall negative mood tended to report higher overall physical symptomatology; however, there was no relation between a time-specific elevation of negative mood relative to the individual's overall baseline in the prediction of an associated time-specific elevation of physical symptoms.

Alternatively, a TVC might exert a within-person effect but not a between-person effect. For example, Rodebaugh, Curran, and Chambless (2002) studied the relation between daily anxiety and panic expectancy. Individuals reporting higher levels of expectancy of panic relative to their overall baseline in the evening were more likely to report experiencing a panic attack the following day (Rodebaugh et al., 2002, Figure 2). However, there was no support for a meaningful between-person effect on the same measures. In other words, individuals reporting elevations in expectancy relative to their norm on one day tended to report higher incidents of panic the following day; however, there was not a systematic relation between the overall person-specific levels of expectancies and person-specific panic pooling over all repeated measures across individuals.

It is thus possible that a TVC exerts only a between-person effect, only a within-person effect, neither, or both. Examining only one level of influence can meaningfully alter substantive conclusions about the true structural relation between the TVC and the outcome. One might miss an effect that actually exists, or one might mistakenly obtain an aggregate effect that reflects neither the between-person nor within-person relation. It is thus critical that these influences be appropriately disaggregated, evaluated, and interpreted.

However, as we describe in detail later, the MLM and SEM approaches to growth modeling incorporate and evaluate these TVC effects in quite different ways. Indeed, what initially appear to be identically parameterized models result in very different estimates of between-person and within-person effects. These differences may in turn have a significant impact on how TVC-relevant hypotheses are tested and interpreted in practice. As we demonstrate later, different conclusions could be drawn about the nature of a relation depending on whether an SEM or MLM approach was fitted to the same measures. Despite the potential importance, we believe these issues have not been fully explicated, either analytically or substantively. Our motivating goal here is to both conceptually and statistically compare how TVC effects are estimated within the MLM and SEM growth modeling traditions, particularly with respect to the disaggregation of the within- and between-person effects of the TVC on the outcome.

We begin with a review of the standard growth model estimated within the MLM framework and demonstrate that both the within- and between-person effects of the TVC can be directly obtained using well-established methods, at least when certain underlying assumptions are met. Next, we review the standard growth model estimated within the SEM framework and demonstrate that only the within-person effect of a TVC can be directly obtained. We then show that the same methods used to disaggregate effects in the MLM cannot be applied within the SEM and we analytically explicate precisely how the SEM and MLM approaches incorporate TVCs in quite different ways. We then explore several options for obtaining disaggregated estimates within the SEM and we propose a new approach that disattenuates the estimate of the between-person effect for sampling variability in the person-mean. We conclude with current limitations of our approach and offer recommendations for the use of these techniques in applied research.

THE MULTILEVEL GROWTH MODEL

The growth model within the MLM framework is motivated by the fact that multiple repeated measures are nested within individual, and this results in a natural two-level hierarchical data structure (e.g., Bryk & Raudenbush, 1987; Raudenbush & Bryk, 2002; Singer & Willett, 2003). As we will see, although there are many similarities between the SEM and MLM growth models, there are several critically important points of divergence (e.g., Bauer, 2003; Curran, 2003; Raudenbush, 2001; Willett & Sayer, 1994). Given the many differences in the parameterization of the same model within the SEM and MLM, we use a notation scheme that is consistent with the MLM tradition.

To begin, we define y_{ti} to represent an observed repeated measure on construct y at time point t for individual i. For a linear growth model, the observed repeated measure can be expressed as a function of an individually varying intercept and slope weighted by time. This is given as

$$y_{ti} = \beta_{0i} + \beta_{1i} time_{ti} + e_{ti} \quad (9.1)$$

where β_{0i} and β_{1i} represent the intercept and linear slope for individual i, respectively; $time_{ti}$ is the observed value of time at assessment t for individual i; and e_{ti} is the time- and individual-specific residual. Note that for comparison to SEMs we describe later, time enters the MLM as a numeric level-1 predictor variable (i.e., $time_{ti}$).

An important characteristic of the growth model is that the intercept and slope values are treated as random variables. In other words, these are governed by a bivariate probability distribution and can thus be expressed as

$$\begin{aligned} \beta_{0i} &= \gamma_{00} + u_{0i} \\ \beta_{1i} &= \gamma_{10} + u_{1i} \end{aligned} \quad (9.2)$$

where γ_{00} and γ_{10} are the overall mean intercept and slope, respectively, and u_{0i} and u_{ai} are the individual-specific deviations from these means, respectively. Finally, equation 9.2 can be substituted into equation 9.1 to define the reduced form expression of the model:

$$y_{ti} = (\gamma_{00} + \gamma_{10} time_{ti}) + (u_{0i} + u_{1i} time_{ti} + e_{ti}) \qquad (9.3)$$

where the first parenthetical term reflects the fixed effects for the model, and the second parenthetical term reflects the random effects and all is defined as before.

The parameters that define the MLM described in equations 9.1 and 9.2 are $E(\beta_{0i}) = \gamma_{00}$, $E(\beta_{1i}) = \gamma_{10}$, $\text{var}(u_{0i}) = \tau_{00}$, $\text{var}(u_{1i}) = \tau_{11}$, and $\text{var}(e_{ti}) = \sigma_t^2$. The covariance between random effects is commonly estimated as part of this model as well (e.g., $\text{cov}[u_{0i}, u_{1i}] = \tau_{10}$). Finally, although there are a number of alternative possible structures for σ_t^2, here we assume the residuals are independent and homoscedastic over time (i.e., $\sigma_t^2 = \sigma^2$ for all t). This is a simplifying restriction that does not impact any of our later developments.

This model can be expanded to include one or more time-invariant covariates (TICs), and these enter into the level-2 equations. For a single TIC, denoted w_i, equation 9.2 would be expanded so that

$$\beta_{0i} = \gamma_{00} + \gamma_{01} w_i + u_{0i}$$
$$\beta_{1i} = \gamma_{10} + \gamma_{11} w_i + u_{1i} \qquad (9.4)$$

where γ_{01} and γ_{11} represent the fixed-effect regression of the intercept and slope factors on the TIC, respectively. It is clear from the subscripting that w_i is a time-invariant covariate given that the value is unique to individual i but does not vary as a function of time point t. As such, the regression coefficients associated with the TIC are explicit estimates of the between-person effects.

Additionally, one or more TVCs can be incorporated into the level-1 equation. Whereas the TICs enter into the level-2 equations, the TVCs enter into the level-1 equations. For example, for a single TVC denoted z_{ti}, the level-1 equation is given as

$$y_{ti} = \beta_{0i} + \beta_{1i} time_{ti} + \beta_{2i} z_{ti} + e_{ti} \qquad (9.5)$$

where z_{ti} represents the time-varying covariate z at time t for individual i, and all else is defined as above.

Although the influence of the TVC (i.e., β_{2i}) can be defined as random (Raudenbush & Bryk, 2002, equation 6.21), we focus our discussion here on the TVC defined as having only a fixed effect; this implies that the magnitude of the relation between the TVC and the outcome is constant across individuals. We do this to allow for more direct comparisons between the MLM and the SEM, the latter of which does not easily allow for the estimation of random effects for the TVCs.[1] The level-2 equations are thus

$$\beta_{0i} = \gamma_{00} + u_{0i}$$
$$\beta_{1i} = \gamma_{10} + u_{1i} \quad (9.6)$$
$$\beta_{2i} = \gamma_{20}$$

with reduced form

$$y_{ti} = \left(\gamma_{00} + \gamma_{10} time_{ti} + \gamma_{20} z_{ti}\right) + \left(u_{0i} + u_{1i} time_{ti} + e_{ti}\right). \quad (9.7)$$

As before, the first parenthetical term contains the fixed effects and the second contains the random effects. Importantly, the regression of the outcome on the TVC (i.e., γ_{20}) captures the shift in the conditional mean of y_{ti} per unit shift in z_{ti}, net the effect of the underlying trajectory. However, as we will see next, this is an aggregate effect that inextricably combines the within- and between-person components of the relation between the TVC and the outcome. We must take additional steps to disaggregate these two influences, and it is to this we now turn.

DISAGGREGATING BETWEEN- AND WITHIN-PERSON EFFECTS

It is well known that, under certain assumptions, within- and between-person effects can be efficiently and unambiguously disaggregated within the MLM using the strategy of person-mean centering (e.g., Hofmann & Gavin, 1998; Kreft, de Leeuw, & Aiken, 1995; Raudenbush & Bryk, 2002, p. 183). Traditionally, the term *centering* is typically used to describe the rescaling of a random variable by deviating the observed values around the mean of the variable (e.g., Aiken & West, 1991, pp. 28–48). For example, within the standard fixed-effects regression model, a predictor x_i is centered via $x'_i = x_i - \bar{x}$, where $\bar{x}$ is the observed mean of x_i and x'_i is the mean-deviated rescaling of x_i (see, e.g., Cohen, Cohen, West, & Aiken, 2003, p. 261). By definition, the mean of a centered variable is equal to zero, and this property offers both interpretational and sometimes computational advantages in a number of modeling applications.

However, centering becomes more complex when considering TVCs. This is because multiple repeated measures are nested within each individual, and there are thus two means to consider: the grand mean of the TVC pooling over all time points and all individuals, and each person-specific mean pooling over all time points *within* individuals. To better see this, reconsider equation 9.7, in which we defined the TVC to be z_{ti}. There are two ways that we can center the TVC.

First, we can deviate the TVC around the grand mean pooling over all individuals. Here, $\ddot{z}_{ti} = z_{ti} - \bar{z}$, where $\ddot{z}_{ti}$ represents the grand-mean-centered TVC, z_{ti} is the observed TVC, and $\bar{z}$ is the grand mean of z_{ti} pooling over all individuals and all time points. Second, we can deviate the TVC around the person-specific mean of the TVC unique to each individual. Specifically, $\dot{z}_{ti} = z_{ti} - \bar{z}_i$, where $\dot{z}_{ti}$ represents the person-mean-centered TVC, z_{ti} is again the observed TVC, and $\bar{z}_i$ is the person-specific mean for individual i. Either z_{ti}, $\dot{z}_{ti}$, or $\ddot{z}_{ti}$ can be used as the level-1 predictor in equation 9.7. Importantly, all three scalings of the TVC will result in precisely the same model fit (i.e., in terms of deviance and all deviance-based measures); however, the associated regression parameters and variance components offer different interpretations, sometimes markedly so (see, e.g., Raudenbush & Bryk, 2002, Table 5.10).

Although the between- and within-person effects can be disaggregated using any of the three scalings of the TVC, these effects can be most efficiently obtained within the multilevel model using the person-mean-centered TVC at level 1 (i.e., $\dot{z}_{ti}$) and the person-specific mean at level 2 (i.e., $\bar{z}_i$). The level-1 equation is given as

$$y_{ti} = \beta_{0i} + \beta_{1i} time_{ti} + \beta_{2i} \dot{z}_{ti} + e_{ti} \quad (9.8)$$

the level-2 equation as

$$\beta_{0i} = \gamma_{00} + \gamma_{01} \bar{z}_i + u_{0i}$$

$$\beta_{1i} = \gamma_{10} + \gamma_{11} \bar{z}_i + u_{1i} \quad (9.9)$$

$$\beta_{2i} = \gamma_{20}$$

and the reduced-form equation as

$$y_{ti} = \left(\gamma_{00} + \gamma_{10} time_{ti} + \gamma_{20} \dot{z}_{ti} + \gamma_{01} \bar{z}_i + \gamma_{11} \bar{z}_i time_{ti} \right) + \left(u_{0i} + u_{1i} time_{ti} + e_{ti} \right) \quad (9.10)$$

where γ_{00} is the intercept, γ_{10} is the fixed effect of time, γ_{20} is a direct estimate of the within-person effect, γ_{01} is a direct estimate of the between-person effect, and γ_{11} is the cross-level interaction between the person-specific mean and time.[2] As before, the within-person and between-person effects are net the contribution of the linear effect of time.

Although these methods for disaggregating effects are well established and widely used, there are also several assumptions that must hold for these techniques to work properly; we explore these assumptions in detail in Curran and Bauer (2011). Of key interest to our discussion here is the assumption that the within-person variability among the set of repeated measures of the TVCs is equal to zero; in other words, it is assumed that the person-specific mean is assessed with perfect reliability. This can most clearly be seen in that the person-specific mean of the TVCs is computed and used as a level-2 predictor, but the within-person standard deviation of the TVCs around the person-specific mean is discarded. Omitting this important source of within-person sampling variability leads to bias in the estimation of the true variance of the person-specific mean and in turn attenuates the estimate of the between-person effect; see Lüdtke et al. (2008) for an excellent recent discussion of this issue.

As a concrete example, consider two individuals who have precisely the same mean value among a set of TVCs, say $\bar{z}_1 = \bar{z}_2 = 5.00$. This reflects that the overall level of the TVC is equal for these two individuals and each obtains the same value for the analysis. However, say that the standard deviations for the two individuals were $sd_1 = .50$ and $sd_2 = 2.50$, respectively; these standard deviations capture the within-person variability of the repeated measures around the person-specific mean. The difference in magnitude of these standard deviations reflects that the repeated assessments of the TVC are much more tightly clustered around the mean for the first individual compared to that of the second. Yet when using the person-mean as a manifest predictor of the random intercept of y_{ti}, the between-person differences in within-person variability are not introduced into the model; indeed, both are assumed to be zero and these two individuals would be treated as identical with respect to the TVC.

Within both the MLM and SEM, exogenous covariates are assumed to be fixed and known and thus error free. Although within-person sampling variability among the TVCs is not measurement error in the traditional psychometric sense of the term (e.g., as in measurement error in classical test theory), the MLM and SEM assume this source of variability to be zero. It is well known within the general linear model that violating the assumption of perfectly reliable exogenous covariates tends to attenuate the associated regression coefficient (see Bollen, 1989, pp. 151–175, and Lüdtke et al., 2008). With respect to our work here, we expect that omitting within-person variability would drive down the sample estimate of the between-person effect, potentially significantly so (Lüdtke et al., 2008, Figure 1). Given this, we pay particular attention to the potential attenuating effects of omitting within-person variability when estimating the between-person effect in both the MLM and SEM.

To demonstrate the use of existing methods for disaggregating effects within the MLM and to subsequently compare these to the SEM, we next use computer simulation methodology to fit the model defined in equation 9.10 to artificially generated data with known population structure.

SIMULATED DATA

We begin our evaluation of the MLM using computer simulation methodology that allows us to draw unambiguous conclusions about the relative accuracy of parameter estimation given the known population structure. We drew upon recent published applications of growth models along with our collective experience to define a population model that we felt was both realistic and constructed in a way as to highlight the differences between within-person and between-person effects of the TVC. We based our population model on a hypothetical relation between anxiety symptoms and alcohol use. The positive between-person effect reflects that, on average, individuals who are characterized by higher overall levels of anxiety tend to drink at higher levels (e.g., possibly due to drinking alcohol to lessen anxiety symptoms; Kassel et al., 2010). The negative within-person effect reflects that, on average, individuals tend to drink less when anxiety symptoms are elevated relative to their own baseline (e.g., when anxious they avoid social situations where alcohol is available; Kaplow, Curran, & Costello, 2001). Thus, whereas individuals who are more anxious tend to drink more (the positive between-person effect), individuals tend to drink less on days where they are experiencing higher anxiety (the negative within-person effect).[3]

Consistent with this hypothetical example we defined the population-generating model to be a growth model with both a random intercept and a random positive linear slope of time as well as main effects of the within- and between-person TVC.[4] Of key interest to us here are the fixed effects of the within- and between-person effects of the TVC on the outcome. The population value of the within-person effect was set to $-.25$, indicating that higher values of the time-specific TVC are associated with lower values on the outcome. The population value of the between-person effect was set to .75, indicating that higher values of the person-specific overall level of the TVC are associated with higher values on the outcome. We generated data in SAS Version 9.2 based on $T = 5$ repeated measures assessed on $N = 250$ individuals and we created $R = 1{,}000$ data replications.[5] All tabled values present the means and standard deviations of the parameter estimates pooling over the 1,000 replications.

Fitting the MLM

We fitted a number of different models to precisely the same artificial data that in turn allows us to directly compare the MLM to the SEMs that we will define in a moment. We began by fitting a standard linear growth model without the inclusion of any other predictors (i.e., equation 9.3); these results are labeled *Model 1* in the first column of Table 9.1. The mean intercept over the 1,000 replications was 22.496 ($SD = .127$) and the mean slope was 1.998 ($SD = .071$). Thus the model-implied starting point was approximately 22.5 and this increased at approximately two units per unit-time.

We then expanded this growth model to include just the main effect of the uncentered TVC (i.e., z_{ti}); more specifically, we fitted the model

$$y_{ti} = (\gamma_{00} + \gamma_{10} time_{ti} + \gamma_{20} z_{ti}) + (u_{0i} + u_{1i} time_{ti} + e_{ti}) \quad (9.11)$$

TABLE 9.1 Means and Standard Deviations of Parameter Estimates for Multilevel Model Summarized over 1,000 Replications at Sample Size $N = 250$

Parameter	Model 1 Growth only	Model 2 Growth plus uncentered TVC	Model 3 Growth plus centered TVC	Model 4 Growth plus centered TVC plus person-mean
Intercept ($\hat{\gamma}_{00}$)	22.496	22.262	22.495	17.841
	(.127)	(.368)	(.126)	(1.047)
Time ($\hat{\gamma}_{10}$)	1.998	1.999	1.999	2.020
	(.071)	(.070)	(.070)	(.589)
TVC ($\hat{\gamma}_{20}$)	—	−.177	−.250	−.250
		(.034)	(.035)	(.035)
Mean ($\hat{\gamma}_{01}$)	—	—	—	.465
				(.103)
Interaction ($\hat{\gamma}_{11}$)	—	—	—	−.002
				(.059)
$\hat{\tau}$	2.537	2.832	2.564	2.248
	(.351)	(.375)	(.346)	(.318)
$\hat{\tau}_{01}$	−.197	−.198	−.197	−.193
	(.143)	(.147)	(.141)	(.134)
$\hat{\tau}_{11}$	1.009	1.009	1.009	1.004
	(.108)	(.107)	(.107)	(.107)
$\hat{\sigma}^2$	2.128	2.011	2.000	2.000
	(.110)	(.103)	(.102)	(.102)

Note: First number is mean and number in parentheses is standard deviation; dashes indicate that the corresponding value was not estimated as part of the associated model.

to the 1,000 simulated samples of size $n = 250$. The model results are presented under *Model 2* in Table 9.1. Most important to our discussion here, the mean of the 1,000 sample estimates of the main effect of the uncentered TVC was equal to $-.177$ ($SD = .034$). As expected, because in this model the TVC is in the raw scale metric, this effect represents the *aggregate* relation between the TVC and the outcome. Given that the population within-person effect is $-.25$ and the population between-person effect is $.75$, this aggregate effect reflects neither the within-person nor between-person effects (Raudenbush & Bryk, 2002, equation 5.38). However, we can use the methods described above to disaggregate these two levels of effect.

To accomplish this we fitted the same model as above to the same 1,000 simulated samples but this time we used the person-mean-centered scaling of the TVC (i.e., $\dot{z}_{ti}$); these results are summarized under *Model 3* in Table 9.1. Again, most important to our discussion here, the mean of the 1,000 sample estimates of the main effect of the person-mean-centered TVC was equal to $-.25$ ($SD = .037$). Given that we are using the person-mean-centered scaling of the TVC, this represents a direct estimate of the within-person effect; indeed, the obtained mean of the sample estimates is precisely equal to the population-generating value. However, we still have no information regarding the between-person effect; we can incorporate the person-mean as a level-2 predictor to obtain this effect.

To obtain estimates of both the within-person and between-person effects, we expanded the prior model to include the person-specific mean as a level-2 predictor of the random intercept.[6] Thus the model fitted to the 1,000 simulated samples corresponds to equation 9.10; the results are summarized under *Model 4* in Table 9.1. The mean of the 1,000 within-person estimates was $-.25$ ($SD = .035$) and of the between-person estimates was $.465$ ($SD = .103$). Note that whereas the within-person effect is accurate with respect to the population model, the between-person effect is substantially attenuated relative to the corresponding population value (see Lüdtke et al., 2008, for a clear description of why this attenuation occurs). Given that the population value is $.75$ and obtained value is $.47$, the sample estimate of the between-person effect is underestimated by nearly 40% within the MLM.

This brings us to our first observation:

> *As expected from existing analytic theory, the within- and between-person effects can be simultaneously and unambiguously disaggregated within the MLM by incorporating the person-centered TVC as a level-1 predictor and the person-mean as a level-2 predictor; however, the between-person effect is attenuated due to the omission of within-person variability around the person-specific mean.*

To clarify, we have yet to offer any new developments thus far and have primarily reviewed and demonstrated existing knowledge in this area. However, we now turn to a closer examination of how these same effects are obtained within the SEM, a topic that in our opinion is much less well understood.

THE STRUCTURAL EQUATION GROWTH MODEL

The growth model is conceptualized in the MLM framework as modeling a hierarchical data structure that is induced by the nesting of multiple repeated observations within each individual. In contrast, the growth model is conceptualized in the SEM framework as modeling multiple observed repeated measures as manifest indicators that define an underlying latent growth process (e.g., Bollen & Curran, 2006; McArdle, 1988, 1989, 1991; McArdle & Epstein, 1987; Meredith & Tisak, 1984, 1990). Switching notation to stay consistent with the SEM framework, we begin by considering a linear growth model in which the measurement equation is defined as

$$y_{ti} = \alpha_i + \lambda_{ti}\beta_i + \varepsilon_{ti} \tag{9.12}$$

where y_{ti} is the observed outcome for individual i at time point t, α_i and β_i are the person-specific intercept and slope components for the linear trajectory for individual i, λ_{ti} is the numerical value of time at time point t, and ε_{ti} is the residual term for individual i at time point t. Because we conceptualize the intercept and slope components as random variates (e.g., realizations randomly drawn from a bivariate probability distribution), we can write structural equations for these terms as

$$\alpha_i = \mu_\alpha + \zeta_{\alpha_i}$$
$$\beta_i = \mu_\beta + \zeta_{\beta_i} \tag{9.13}$$

where μ_α and μ_β are the mean intercept and slope components, respectively, and $\zeta_{\alpha i}$ and $\zeta_{\beta i}$ are the individual-specific deviations around these mean values for individual i. Finally, the structural equation can be substituted into the measurement equation to produce the reduced form equation as

$$y_{ti} = \left(\mu_\alpha + \lambda_{ti}\mu_\beta\right) + \left(\zeta_{\alpha_i} + \lambda_{ti}\zeta_{\beta_i} + \varepsilon_{ti}\right) \tag{9.14}$$

where all terms are defined as above.

Because we are working within the framework of the general SEM, the time-specific measures of the outcome y_{ti} are treated as observed manifest

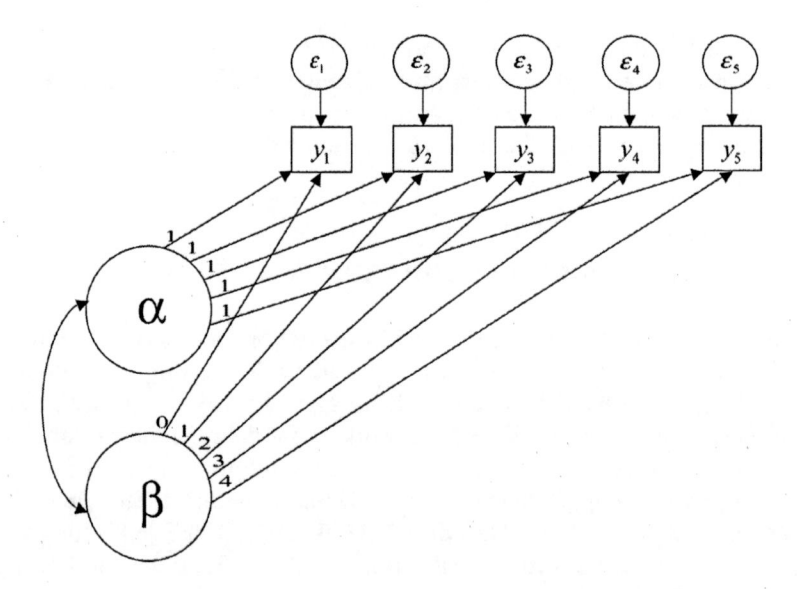

Figure 9.1 Path diagram for a five-time-point unconditional linear SEM growth model.

variables. As such, each trajectory component is defined as an unobserved latent variable with a mean (i.e., the fixed effect) and a variance (i.e., the random effect). Finally, the numerical values of time are fixed factor loadings that relate the observed variables to the latent variables. A path diagram for this model is presented in Figure 9.1.

This linear growth model is defined by two fixed effects (i.e., $E(\alpha_i) = \mu_\alpha$ and $E(\beta_i) = \mu_\beta$) and three random effects (i.e., $\text{var}(\zeta_{\alpha_i}) = \psi_{\alpha\alpha}$, $\text{var}(\zeta_{\beta_i}) = \psi_{\beta\beta}$, and $\text{var}(\varepsilon_{ti}) = \sigma_t^2$). The covariance between the two random effects (i.e., $\text{cov}(\zeta_{\alpha_i}, \zeta_{\beta_i}) = \psi_{\alpha\beta}$) is typically estimated as part of the model. Furthermore, the time-specific residual variance (i.e., σ_t^2) can either vary as a function of time t or can be held constant over time; to remain consistent with the MLM defined earlier, we retain the assumption of homoscedasticity (i.e., $\sigma_t^2 = \sigma^2$ for all t).

The SEM can easily incorporate one or more predictors either within the measurement equation, the structural equations, or both. TICs are denoted by w_i and enter directly into the structural equations

$$\alpha_i = \mu_\alpha + \gamma_\alpha w_i + \zeta_{\alpha_i}$$
$$\beta_i = \mu_\beta + \gamma_\beta w_i + \zeta_{\beta_i}$$
(9.15)

where γ_α and γ_β represent the fixed effect of the TIC on the random intercepts and slopes, respectively. These fixed effects capture between-person differences in the prediction of within-person change as a function of w_i. However, the focus of our work here is on the estimation and interpretation of effects of the TVCs.

We continue to denote the TVCs as z_{ti} to reflect that the obtained value varies as a function of time point t for individual i; this is in contrast to the TIC where w_i reflected that the obtained value only varies as a function i but not t. We can thus incorporate a TVC directly into the measurement equation as

$$y_{ti} = \alpha_i + \lambda_{ti}\beta_i + \gamma_t z_{ti} + \varepsilon_{ti} \qquad (9.16)$$

where z_{ti} is the TVC for individual i at time point t, and γ_t is the fixed effect of the TVC on the outcome at time point t. The SEM allows the value of γ_t to take on unique values at each time point t; here we make the assumption that γ is constant over t to better make direct comparisons back to the MLM, although this in no way limits our later developments.[7] Because the TVC does not vary over individual, the structural equations remain defined as in equation 9.13, and the resulting reduced-form equation is

$$y_{ti} = (\mu_\alpha + \lambda_{ti}\mu_\beta + \gamma z_{ti}) + (\zeta_{\alpha_i} + \lambda_{ti}\zeta_{\beta_i} + \varepsilon_{ti}) \qquad (9.17)$$

where all terms are defined as before. A path diagram of this model is presented in Figure 9.2. We now briefly demonstrate this model using the 1,000 samples of artificially generated data.

Fitting the SEM

We fit a series of SEMs to the same simulated data as we used earlier. We begin by fitting an unconditional growth model (i.e., the model presented in Figure 9.1) and, as expected, we obtain precisely the same parameter estimates as those obtained for the equivalently parameterized multilevel growth models. These results are summarized under *Model 1* in Table 9.2. We next extended this model to include the main effect of the uncentered TVC.

Descriptively, this is a random intercept and random linear slope growth model with z_{ti} as the single time-varying covariate, the magnitude of which is held constant over time. Consistent with the structure of the population model, we restricted the time-specific residual variance to be homoscedastic over time (i.e., $\text{var}(\varepsilon_{ti}) = \sigma^2$). Furthermore, consistent with the standard parameterization of SEMs, all exogenous variables were allowed to freely covary (i.e., all TVCs covaried with one another and with the random intercept). Finally, we used standard normal theory maximum likelihood estimation to obtain parameter estimates and standard errors.

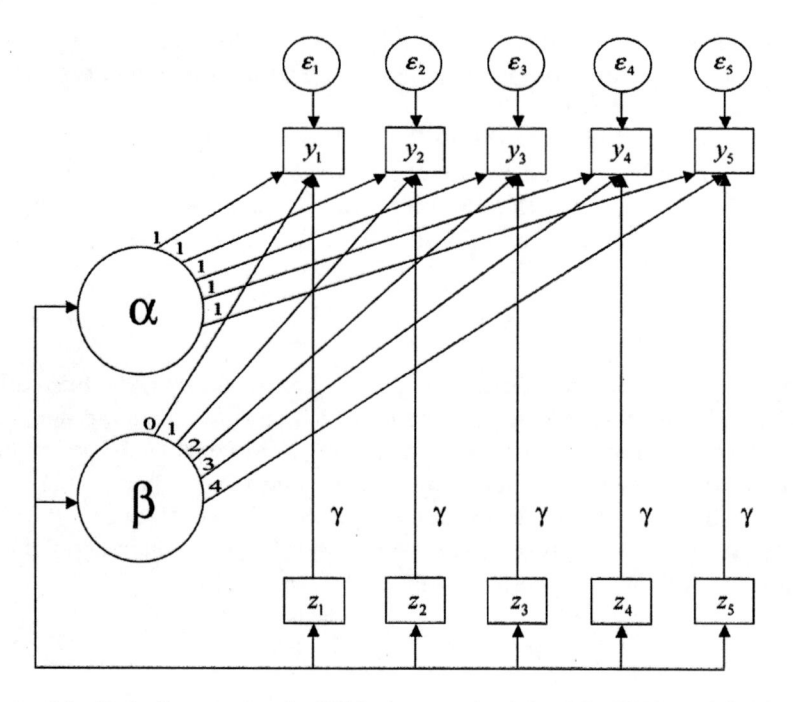

Figure 9.2 Path diagram for the SEM parameterization of the TVC model. All factor loadings and single-headed arrows from residuals are fixed to 1.0; single-headed arrows from z to y are regression coefficients; connected double-headed arrows represent all possible covariances.

The model results are summarized under *Model 2* in Table 9.2. The mean of the 1,000 sample estimates of the uncentered TVC was equal to −.25 (*SD* = .037). This is identical to the population within-person effect of −.25 and the sample point estimate is precisely equal to those obtained from the MLM using the person-specific mean-centered TVCs (compare *Model 3* in Table 9.1 with *Model 2* in Table 9.2). Quite interestingly, in direct contrast to the MLM, the inclusion of the TVC kept in its original scale (i.e., z_{ti}) in the measurement equation of the SEM accurately captured the *within-person* relation between the measure of z_{ti} and the outcome y_{ti}. Furthermore, note that there is no information available about the potential *between-person* relation between the TVC and the outcome. Recall that the structure of the artificial data includes a large and positive between-person relation (i.e., .75), yet no evidence of this between-person effect is obtained from these SEM results. Given our knowledge of the population-generating model, this is a salient omission from the SEM.

TABLE 9.2 Means and Standard Deviations of Parameter Estimates and Model Fit Statistics for Structural Equation Model Summarized over 1,000 Replications at Sample Size $N = 250$

	Model 1 Growth only	Model 2 Growth plus uncentered TVC	Model 3 Growth plus uncentered TVC and zero covs	Model 4 Growth plus latent TVC factor	Population-generating values
Intercept ($\hat{\mu}_\alpha$)	22.496 (.127)	24.992 (.391)	24.263 (.368)	14.901 (1.553)	15.0
Time ($\hat{\mu}_\beta$)	1.998 (.071)	1.999 (.070)	1.999 (.070)	2.029 (.829)	2.0
$\hat{\gamma}$	—	-.250 (.037)	-.177 (.034)	-.250 (.035)	-.25
$\hat{\gamma}_\alpha$	—	—	—	.759 (.154)	.75
$\hat{\gamma}_\beta$	—	—	—	-.003 (.083)	0
$\hat{\delta}_0$	—	.999 (.153)	—	—	1.0
$\hat{\delta}_1$	—	-.003 (.082)	—	—	0
$\hat{\psi}_{\alpha\alpha}$	2.537 (.351)	2.987 (.389)	2.832 (.375)	1.952 (.332)	2.0
$\hat{\psi}_{\alpha\beta}$	-.197 (.143)	-.199 (.149)	-.198 (.147)	-.191 (.135)	-.20
$\hat{\psi}_{\beta\beta}$	1.009 (.108)	1.010 (.107)	1.009 (.107)	1.003 (.107)	1.0
$\hat{\sigma}^2$	2.128 (.110)	2.000 (.102)	2.011 (.103)	2.000 (.102)	2.0
χ^2	13.718 (5.145)	28.146 (7.437)	286.717 (38.823)	53.253 (10.367)	53
df	14	28	48	53	53

Note: First number is mean and number in parentheses is standard deviation; dashes indicate that the corresponding value was not estimated as part of the associated model.

This brings us to our second observation:

The inclusion of an uncentered time-varying covariate in a standard SEM provides an accurate estimate of the within-person effect of the TVC on the outcome, but no information is available about the potential between-person effect of the TVC.

We view this as an important observation for two reasons. First, we conducted an extensive literature review of TVCs within the SEM and did not find a single instance in which a TVC effect was unequivocally interpreted as a within-person effect. This includes our own work on this same topic. For example, Bollen and Curran (2006) present results from an SEM growth model in which math ability is the dependent measure and reading ability is the TVC. The relation between the TVC and the outcome is described as "...a significant and positive prediction of math ability from the contemporaneous influence of reading ability ($\hat{\gamma} = .41$, $p < .0001$)" (p. 197). This is not an incorrect interpretation, but it is an imprecise interpretation. As a within-person effect, the more precise interpretation of the TVC is that higher reading scores *relative to the individual's baseline reading skills* are associated with higher math scores *relative to the individual's baseline math skills*. It is thus not an aggregate interpretation (e.g., overall reading predicting overall math), but a more precise relation of time-specific standing relative to a person-specific baseline. Given the lack of attention currently paid to the distinction of within-person and between-person effects within the SEM, it is likely that TVC effects within the SEM are not commonly interpreted in as precise and accurate a way as is otherwise possible.

A second concern that is highlighted by our artificial data results is that, despite the existence of a large and positive between-person effect that exists in the population model, there is no evidence of this effect in the SEM sample results. As such, a significant characteristic of the data structure is not captured in this model and this could in turn lead to limited or even misleading conclusions about the processes under study. Returning to the example presented in Bollen and Curran (2006, p. 197), no comment is made regarding potential between-person differences in the relation between reading and math ability; an aggregate interpretation was provided regarding the TVC effect and nothing more was said. This is a universal interpretation of TVC models estimated within the SEM, and a major component of the over-time relation between the TVC and the outcome is being ignored.

Returning to our simulated data, we have obtained a direct estimate of the within-person effect in the SEM via the uncentered TVC, but we have no information about the corresponding between-person effect. Given that the SEM and MLM are being fitted to precisely the same data, it seems logical that the well-established strategies used to disaggregate between- and within-person effects in the MLM could equivalently be applied to the SEM to obtain these same estimates. However, two critical problems are encountered when attempting to do this.

To begin, even though we demonstrated that the within-effect can be obtained in the SEM using the raw scale TVC (i.e., z_{ti}), we consider an SEM in which the person-mean-centered TVC is used instead (i.e., $\dot{z}_{ti}$). We do this to directly compare the SEM and MLM results when using the same scaling for the TVC.[8] However, we immediately encounter a significant problem: the standard SEM is not estimable under maximum likelihood (ML) estimation when using the person-centered TVC. The reason is that, within the framework of the SEM, the person-centered TVC is an *ipsative* measure (Cattell, 1944; Clemans, 1966). An ipsative measure is defined as one in which the sum of a set of items for a given individual is equal across all individuals within the sample. Because by definition $\Sigma \dot{z}_{ti} = 0$ over all t within i, $\dot{z}_{ti}$ is ipsative.

There is a long history in the development and application of statistical methods to ipsative measures (e.g., Cattell, 1944; Chan & Bentler, 1996; Dunlap & Cornwell, 1994). However, there is a particular characteristic of ipsative measures that is salient to our discussion here. Namely, the elements within any row or column of the covariance matrix among the set of ipsative items must sum to zero. As such, the matrix is singular and has a zero determinant. This poses a fatal problem for standard ML estimation within the SEM given the requirement that the log of the determinant of the sample covariance matrix be calculated during optimization (e.g., Bollen, 1989, equation 4.67). Although there are potential *ad hoc* ways to address this problem (e.g., ridge estimation, unweighted least squares), these are generally not acceptable given that these estimators can be biased and none result in true ML estimates of model parameters (e.g., Greene, 2000).

This leads us to our third observation:

The SEM is not estimable under standard maximum likelihood when using person-mean-centered TVCs because the TVCs are ipsative and the sample covariance matrix is singular.

To be clear, although we are not able to include the person-mean-centered TVC within the SEM, this is not problematic from a practical standpoint since we can obtain direct estimates of the within-person effect using the raw scaled TVCs. However, the ipsative nature of the person-mean-centered TVC highlights a distinct difference in how the TVCs are being incorporated into the MLM and SEM. More importantly, for the moment we remain unable to obtain a direct estimate of the between-person effect within the SEM.[9] Continuing to draw on the established strategies used in the MLM, we next consider incorporating the person-mean as a predictor to obtain these between-person effects.

Between-Person Effects within the SEM

We continue to follow the recommended strategy for use within the MLM to disaggregate between- and within-person effects; that is, we can extend the SEM expression for the TVC model to include the person-mean as a predictor of the random intercept. The measurement equation remains unchanged

$$y_{ti} = \alpha_i + \lambda_{ti}\beta_i + \gamma z_{ti} + \varepsilon_{ti} \tag{9.18}$$

but the structural equations are now

$$\alpha_i = \mu_\alpha + \gamma_\alpha \bar{z}_i + \zeta_{\alpha_i}$$
$$\beta_i = \mu_\beta + \gamma_\beta \bar{z}_i + \zeta_{\beta_i} \tag{9.19}$$

with reduced form

$$y_{ti} = (\mu_\alpha + \lambda_{ti}\mu_\beta + \gamma z_{ti} + \gamma_\alpha \bar{z}_i + \gamma_\beta \lambda_{ti}\bar{z}_i) + (\zeta_{\alpha_i} + \lambda_{ti}\zeta_{\beta_i} + \varepsilon_{ti}) \tag{9.20}$$

where $\bar{z}_i$ is the person-specific mean of the TVC for individual i pooling over all time points t, γ_α and γ_β are the between-person effects of the TVC on the outcome, and all else is as defined before.

Despite the importance of including the person-mean as a predictor within the MLM, this same model defined in equation 9.20 is not estimable within the SEM framework. There is a remarkably simple reason: the covariance matrix of the TVCs (i.e., z_{ti}) and the person-specific mean ($\bar{z}_i$) is singular, again making optimization impossible under ML estimation. Interestingly, this indeterminacy has a markedly different source than the one we previously encountered. Whereas the prior indeterminacy arose from the ipsative nature of the person-mean-centered TVCs (i.e., $\dot{z}_{ti}$), here the singularity is due to the fact that there is a direct linear dependency between the set of uncentered scores z_{ti} and the person-mean $\bar{z}_i$. Indeed, this is precisely the example we commonly use when teaching introductory statistics as to why the degrees-of-freedom for computing the sample variance is $n-1$: namely, that knowledge of the sample mean restricts one dimension of variability in the data. As such, there is a column dependency, the determinant of the sample covariance matrix is zero, and ML estimation is again not possible.

This brings us to our fourth observation:

It is not possible to obtain an estimate of the between-person effect in the SEM by using the person-mean as an exogenous predictor because of the linear dependency between the person-mean and the TVCs in the covariance matrix.

Given this observation, there is not a method for simultaneously estimating the within-person effect and the between-person effect using the person-mean within the SEM. This is in direct contrast to the established strategies that are widely used within the MLM and leaves us with two logical questions. First, exactly what accounts for the differences between the MLM and SEM approaches to the TVC model? And second, is there a way to estimate the between-person effect within the SEM that does not rely on the inclusion of the person-mean as an exogenous predictor? We address each of these issues in turn.

THE SOURCE OF THE DISCREPANCY

The source of the discrepancy between the MLM and SEM estimates of the TVC effect relates to precisely how the two modeling approaches parameterize the covariance structure among the TVCs and the random intercept. In the Appendix we present the analytic derivations that explicate the relation between the SEM and MLM growth modeling frameworks. Here we augment these derivations with a more descriptive discussion of the two underlying models.

Consider the reduced-form expressions for a random intercept model with one TVC for the MLM

$$y_{ti} = (\gamma_{00} + \gamma_{10}time_{ti} + \gamma_{20}z_{ti}) + (u_{0i} + time_{ti}u_{1i} + e_{ti}) \qquad (9.21)$$

and for the SEM

$$y_{ti} = (\mu_\alpha + \lambda_{ti}\mu_\beta + \gamma z_{ti}) + (\zeta_{\alpha_i} + \lambda_{ti}\zeta_{\beta_i} + \varepsilon_{ti}). \qquad (9.22)$$

Despite the apparent structural similarities between these two equations, fundamentally different assumptions underlie each expression. In the MLM it is explicitly assumed that the predictors (i.e., z_{ti}) are uncorrelated with the random effects (u_{0i} and e_{ti}). More formally, $\text{cov}(z_{ti}, u_{0i}) = 0$ for all t and all i. Although an explicit assumption of the model (e.g., Raudenbush & Bryk, 2002, p. 255, point #6), in a very real sense these covariances do not even exist in the MLM; that is, these parameters are not a formal part of the model, which is why assumptions are required that these covariances equal zero in the population.

In contrast, in the SEM these same covariances are an explicit part of the model. More formally, $\text{cov}(z_{ti}, \zeta_{\alpha_i}) = \psi_{z_t,\alpha}$ for $t = 1, 2, \ldots, T$. In other words, the model allows for the estimation of covariances between the random intercept and all time-specific TVCs (this can be seen in the double-headed arrows between the TVCs and the intercept factor in the path diagram presented in Figure 9.2). Furthermore, these covariances can be freely estimated or fixed to zero in any given application. Thus, in the MLM the covariances between the TVCs and the random intercept are assumed to be zero; in the SEM these covariances may be freely estimated as part of the growth model. This is precisely where the difference in the estimation of the between- and within-person effects lies.

Let us first consider the MLM. As described in Raudenbush and Bryk (2002, p. 256, point #6), the assumption that predictors at one level are uncorrelated with random effects at the other level implies that biases are not introduced by the omission of relevant predictors at either level. However, if the uncentered TVC (i.e., z_{ti}) is used as a level-1 predictor, and no other predictors are included at level 2, there will be a nonzero covariance induced between the TVCs and the random intercept (assuming an intraclass correlation for the TVCs that is greater than zero; see Raudenbush & Bryk, 2002).

The reason is that the uncentered measure of the TVC contains information about *both* within-person differences *and* between-person differences. Specifically, the TVC can be expressed as

$$z_{ti} = \bar{z}_i + \varepsilon_{z_{ti}} \tag{9.23}$$

where the first term varies *between* individuals (i.e., the person-specific mean $\bar{z}_i$) and the second term varies *within* individuals (i.e., the person-specific and time-specific residual $\varepsilon_{z_{ti}}$). When using the raw-scaled TVC there is thus a between-person component embedded within the TVCs that has been omitted from the model, and this in turn induces a cross-level correlation, a correlation that the MLM assumes to be zero.

However, this model misspecification can be circumvented in one of two ways. First, the TVC can be person-mean centered, thus making the within- and between-person effects orthogonal and meeting the assumption of zero covariance. Second, the person-specific mean can be included as a level-2 covariate, thus incorporating the previously omitted predictor and correcting for the bias (Raudenbush & Bryk, 2002, pp. 261–262). Both of these approaches are often used in many MLM applications.

In contrast, in the SEM the covariance structure between the TVCs and the random intercept enters directly into the model formulation. As such, this allows for the random intercept effect to be estimated *net* the TVC effects and, most important to our discussion here, the TVC effects are *net* the influence of the random intercept. As such, the uncentered TVCs capture the within-person effect because these effects are unique to the influence of the random intercept. That is, the saturated covariance structure among the TVCs and the random intercept "absorbs" the omitted predictor, precisely as is possible in the general linear model. This is why all exogenous predictors freely covary in the multiple regression model (e.g., Greene, 2000).

To summarize, because the MLM assumes the covariance between the TVC and the random intercept to be zero, modifications must be made either directly to the data (via centering) or to the model (via inclusion of the person-mean) to address this issue. In contrast, because the SEM can explicitly incorporate these same covariances as part of the model, these cross-level relations can be directly modeled and the data need not be manually modified via data management outside of the analysis.

To briefly demonstrate the impact of the exogenous covariance structure, we reestimated the SEM using the uncentered TVC but we fixed the covariances between the TVCs and the random intercept to be zero (thus corresponding to the standard MLM parameterization). Consistent with expectations, the resulting TVC effect represented precisely the same aggregate effect as the MLM estimated to the uncentered TVC earlier; specifically, compare *Model 2* in Table 9.1 with *Model 3* in Table 9.2. Thus in the SEM the uncentered TVC results in a direct estimate of the *within*-person effect when the TVCs freely covary with the random intercept but results in an estimate of the *aggregate* effect when these covariances are held to zero.

To better explicate the critical role the exogenous covariances play in the SEM, we can capitalize on the information that is contained in the covariance structure between the TVCs and the random intercept and slope within the SEM to derive an estimate of the between-person effect. Consider again the reduced form of the SEM described above

$$y_{ti} = (\mu_\alpha + \lambda_{ti}\mu_\beta + \gamma z_{ti}) + (\zeta_{\alpha_i} + \lambda_{ti}\zeta_{\beta_i} + \varepsilon_{ti}) \quad (9.24)$$

in which γ represents a direct estimate of the within-person effect. Furthermore, define δ_0 to be the difference between the within- and between-person effects for the random intercept[10]; this is consistent with the compositional effect of Raudenbush and Bryk (2002, equation 5.42). Because the compositional effect is the difference between the between-person effect and the within-person effect, we can obtain an estimate of the between-person effect based solely on the within-person effect and the compositional effect; in other words, the between-person effect is the sum of the within-person effect and the compositional effect.

As we detail in the Appendix, a sample estimate of the compositional effect can be derived based solely on parameter estimates drawn from the

SEM TVC model defined in equation 9.24. Specifically, the compositional effect is given as

$$\delta_0 = \frac{\frac{1}{T}\sum_{t=1}^{T}\text{cov}(z_{ti},\zeta_{\alpha i}^{*})}{\frac{1}{T^2}\left\{\sum_{t=1}^{T}\text{var}(z_{ti})+\sum_{t\neq t'}^{T}\text{cov}(z_{ti},z_{t'i}')\right\}} \quad (9.25)$$

where $t = 1, 2, \ldots, T$, $t \neq t'$, $z \neq z'$, and all else is defined as above. In other words, the estimate δ_0 is the ratio of the mean of the covariances between each TVC and the random intercept (the numerator) to the scaled summation of the variance of each TVC and the covariance of each TVC with all other TVCs (the denominator). Although the compositional effect is of substantive interest in some applications (e.g., Raudenbush & Bryk, 2002, pp. 139–141), here we only use this to obtain the between-person effect. More specifically, when δ_0 is added to the within-person effect, we obtain a direct estimate of the between-person effect even though we have no explicit information about between-person variability in the model (i.e., we have no information about $\bar{z}_i$ anywhere in the model).

To demonstrate the information contained in δ_0, we applied equation 9.25 to the results obtained from our earlier TVC model fitted to the 1,000 replications of sample size 250 within the SEM. Recall that our within-person effect was –.25. Applying equation 9.25 to the results from this SEM, we obtain a mean estimate for the compositional effect of $\hat{\delta}_0 = 1.0$. Thus our between-person effect is obtained as $\hat{\delta}_0 + \hat{\gamma} = 1.0 + (-.25) = .75$, which is precisely equal to the population between-person effect.

This brings us to our fifth observation:

Within the SEM, sufficient information is contained in the covariance structure among the TVCs and the random intercept to allow for the estimation of the between-person effect without requiring the inclusion of the person-specific mean as an exogenous predictor; furthermore, the between-person estimate is not attenuated given that the calculation does not rely on the person-specific mean.

This observation highlights exactly why the within-person effect is obtained from the uncentered TVC in the SEM but the aggregate effect is obtained from the uncentered TVC in the MLM. We can next consider what options the SEM might provide to move beyond the standard methods of disaggregation currently used in the MLM. Although the MLM is of course characterized by myriad significant strengths, embedding the TVC model within the SEM allows for a number of model expansions that are not currently available within the MLM (just as the MLM offers a number of model expansions that are not currently available within the SEM). Although there are a variety of interesting ways in which these models can be expanded within the SEM, here we focus on one important example: the estimation of the person-specific mean of the TVCs using a latent variable methodology to explicitly incorporate information about within-person sampling variability. It is to this we now turn.

ESTIMATING THE PERSON-MEAN VIA A LATENT FACTOR

We earlier demonstrated why the person-specific mean cannot be included in the SEM given the linear dependency between the person-mean and the TVCs. In contrast, the person-mean can be incorporated into the MLM to provide a direct estimate of the between-person effect of the TVC on the outcome. However, it is important to keep in mind that the person-mean that is used to predict the random intercept in the MLM is an exogenous manifest measure and, as such, is assumed to be error free (e.g., Bollen, 1989; Raudenbush & Bryk, 2002). The assumption of perfect reliability is widely known to be often dubious, the violation of which can yield biased parameter estimates and standard errors (e.g., Lüdtke et al., 2008). However, one of the key strengths of the SEM is that multiple indicator latent factors can be used to estimate the true score variance associated with a set of measures that in turn avoids the strong assumption of error-free predictors. We conclude by exploring how a latent variable approach can be used to explicitly include information about within-person sampling variability in the disaggregation of within- and between-person effects.

Earlier we described the potential importance of incorporating information about within-person variability when computing the person-specific mean of the TVC. We can draw on the developments of Rogosa and Saner (1995) to formalize these issues. We can express the TVC z_{ti} as an additive function of a person-specific mean and a time-specific deviation from that mean such that

$$z_{ti} = \bar{z}_i + \varepsilon_{z_{ti}} \quad (9.26)$$

where $\bar{z}_i$ is the mean for person i and $\varepsilon_{z_{ti}}$ is the time-specific deviation around this mean. The standard approach within the MLM is to use the person-specific mean as a level-2 predictor but to discard $\varepsilon_{z_{ti}}$. However, additional information is embedded in this term, specifically the variance of these time-specific deviations from the person-specific mean. This is simply given as $\text{var}(\varepsilon_{z_{ti}}) = \hat{\sigma}^2_{z_i}$ and represents the within-person variance of the TVC over time.

Given the above, the grand mean of the set of N person-specific means is

$$\bar{z}_{\bar{z}} = \frac{\sum_{i=1}^{N} \bar{z}_i}{N} \quad (9.27)$$

and the grand mean of the set of N person-specific variances is

$$\hat{\sigma}_z^2 = \frac{\sum_{i=1}^N \hat{\sigma}_{zi}^2}{N}. \qquad (9.28)$$

We can now modify Rogosa and Saner's (1995) expressions for this simple case to define the true score variance of the sample means as

$$\hat{\psi}_{\alpha_z\alpha_z} = \text{var}(\bar{z}_i) - \frac{\hat{\sigma}_z^2}{T} \qquad (9.29)$$

where $\hat{\psi}_{\alpha_z\alpha_z}$ represents the estimate of true score variance, $\text{var}(\bar{z}_i)$ represents the variance of the individual person-specific means, $\hat{\sigma}_z^2$ represents the mean of the individual person-specific variances, and T represents the total number of repeated assessments.[11]

Equation 9.29 demonstrates that the variance of the person-specific means is overestimated by an amount equal to $\hat{\sigma}_z^2 / T$. Thus, using the sample mean as a predictor of the random intercept implicitly (and unrealistically) assumes that $\hat{\sigma}_z^2 / T = 0$ for all i; that is, there is no error of estimation, and each within-person time-specific measure of the TVC is equal to the person-specific mean of the set TVCs.

However, we can simultaneously estimate both the true score variance and the residual variance in a straightforward manner within the SEM. Just as we earlier defined a random intercept factor for the outcome y_{ti}, we define a second random intercept factor for the TVC z_{ti}. We now write the reduced-form equation for the TVCs as

$$z_{ti} = \mu_{\alpha_z} + \zeta_{\alpha_{zi}} + \varepsilon_{z_{ti}} \qquad (9.30)$$

where $E(z_{ti}) = \mu_{\alpha_z}$, $\text{var}(z_{ti}) = \text{var}(\zeta_{\alpha_{zi}} + \varepsilon_{z_{ti}}) = \psi_{\alpha_z\alpha_z} + \sigma_z^2$. We have now included a subscript z to distinguish these values from similar expressions for y in equation 9.17. Importantly, note the estimation of two variance components, one estimating true score variance ($\psi_{\alpha_z\alpha_z}$) and the other within-person residual variance (σ_z^2). We are thus able to disaggregate these two variance components associated with the TVC by defining a latent factor intercept for the TVCs.

We will use the random intercept latent factor for the TVC as defined in equation 9.30 as a predictor of the random intercept latent factor of the outcome y in order to incorporate this variance component into the model. Although this is quite straightforward (and is really nothing more than a second random intercept in a multivariate growth model), we encounter one final complexity that we must address. Because our goal is to obtain *simultaneous* estimates of the between- and within-person effects, we must re-

Disaggregating Within-Person and Between-Person Effects ▪ 243

tain our regression of outcome y_{ti} on the TVC z_{ti}. However, because we have defined a random intercept for z_{ti}, we must not regress y_{ti} directly on z_{ti} as we have done thus far in the SEM. Doing so will result in an *aggregate* effect of the TVC on the outcome.[12] Instead, we must estimate a nonstandard effect in which we regress y_{ti} on the time-specific *residual* of z_{ti}, specifically $\varepsilon_{z_{ti}}$. The motivation for this is that the time-specific residuals represent the deviation of each observation from the true mean of the TVC (e.g., see equation 9.30). We are thus mean-deviating each time-specific TVC through the parameterization of the latent factor as opposed to manually mean-deviating the observed scores as is done in the MLM. This parameterization allows for the simultaneous estimation of both the within- and between-person effects based solely on the inclusion of the raw-scaled TVC.

We present this final model in diagrammatic form in Figure 9.3.[13] We fitted this model to our artificially generated 1,000 datasets of $N = 250$ and obtained a mean within-person effect of −.25 ($SD = .035$) and a mean between-person effect of .759 ($SD = .154$); see Model 4 in Table 9.2 for com-

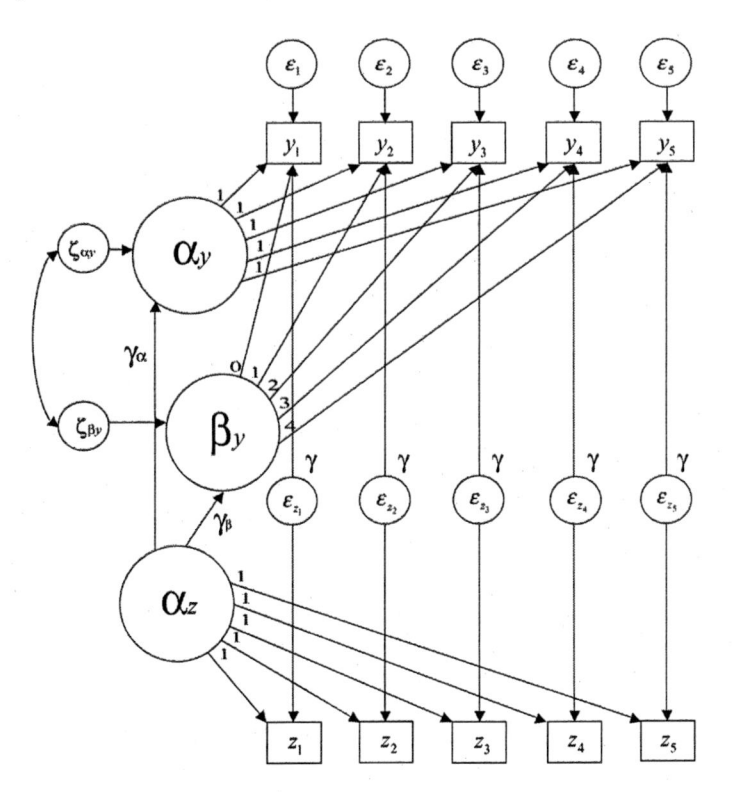

Figure 9.3 Final structural equation model for disaggregating within-person (denoted γ_1) and between-person (denoted γ_2) effects of the TVC on the criterion.

plete results. Importantly, note that the between effect is captured in the regression of the intercept factor for the outcome on the intercept factor for the TVCs. The within-person effect remains unchanged from before; this result was expected given that we are simply person-mean centering the TVCs through the parameterization of the model as opposed to manually calculating these outside of the analysis. However, the between-person effect is almost identical to the population-generating parameter that considers within-person variability around the person-specific mean. Furthermore, this obtained estimate is nearly 65% larger than that obtained from the MLM estimate of the within-person effect obtained that ignore within-person variability. This finding is directly consistent with expectations given that sampling variability in a predictor tends to negatively bias associated regression coefficients (Lüdtke et al., 2008). Because we have disaggregated true score variance and sampling variance, the between-person effect has been subsequently disattenuated for sampling variability and is thus a more accurate estimate of the corresponding population effect.

This brings us to our sixth and final observation:

The within-person and between-person effects of the TVC can be simultaneously disaggregated through the alternative parameterization of the SEM, and the between-person effect has been disattenuated by correcting for within-person sampling variability in the estimation of the person-mean.

CONCLUSION

We have explored a large number of topics with the goal of highlighting five specific issues related to the disaggregation of within-person and between-person effects in TVC growth models.

1. A multilevel model estimated with an uncentered TVC and no person-specific mean at level 2 will result in an aggregation of between- and within-person effects. Inclusion of the person-specific mean centered TVC at level 1 and the person-mean of the TVC at level 2 will result in direct estimates of the within- and between person effects, respectively. However, the between-person effect is attenuated due to the violated assumption of perfect reliability of the person-specific mean.
2. A standard SEM estimated under ML with a person-specific mean-centered TVC is not estimable due to the singularity of the covariance matrix, regardless of whether the person-specific means are included. Thus neither a within-person nor between-person effect can be obtained from inclusion of the person-specific mean-centered TVC in the SEM.

3. A standard SEM estimated with an uncentered TVC and no person-specific mean will result in a direct estimate of the within-person effect. Inclusion of the person-specific mean as a predictor of the intercept factor yields a model that is not estimable due to the singularity of the covariance matrix. Thus no between-person effect can be directly obtained from the SEM that only includes the uncentered TVC.
4. The between-person effect can be analytically computed based on the weighted combination of parameter estimates obtained from the standard SEM estimated with the uncentered TVC. This between-person effect is not attenuated given that the calculation does not rely on the inclusion of the person-specific mean.
5. An SEM estimated with an uncentered TVC and (a) a latent intercept factor estimated for the TVC, (b) the latent intercept of the outcome regressed on the latent intercept of the TVC, and (c) the repeated measures of the outcome regressed directly on the residuals of the TVC will result in direct estimates of both the between- and within-person effects. These estimates are unbiased and the between-person effect has been disattenuated for within-person sampling variability around the person-specific mean.

We have presented no novel developments in terms of the traditional methods used to disaggregate within- and between-person effects within the multilevel model. However, we believe that much less attention has been paid to the attenuating effects of estimating the between-person effect using the person-specific mean related to the omission of information about within-person variability among the set of TVCs (but see Lüdtke et al., 2008, for a discussion of the related topic of individuals nested within groups). More importantly, we are aware of no prior discussions of the many issues that are encountered when attempting to disaggregate effects within the SEM. Indeed, we were unable to identify a single published instance in which a TVC effect within the SEM was interpreted explicitly in terms of within-person effects; nor were we able to identify any prior discussions of estimating a between-person effect of a TVC within the SEM. This includes our own joint collection of work on this topic. As such, much potentially important information is omitted from these models and results are routinely imprecisely interpreted.

Yet, as we demonstrated above, obtaining a direct estimate of the between-person effect in the SEM is not a trivial issue. We cannot use a person-centered TVC because a singularity arises from the ipsative nature of this measure. And we cannot include the person-specific mean as a predictor because a singularity arises from the inclusion of the mean with the TVCs in the same covariance matrix.[14] However, we can obtain these effects through the direct parameterization of the model in which a random intercept is estimated for the TVCs themselves. This not only allows a method to obtain a direct estimate of the between-person effect, but has the added advantage of disaggregating true score variance from within-person sampling variance and is obtained under a true maximum likelihood estimator. Furthermore, once embedded within the SEM framework, many other modeling extensions are possible.

UNRESOLVED ISSUES AND DIRECTIONS FOR FUTURE RESEARCH

Although we believe we have been able to draw a number of general and novel conclusions about the disaggregation of within- and between-person effects in both the MLM and SEM, there are several unresolved issues to bear in mind. First, as we noted earlier, all of our above developments assume that there is not systematic growth in the TVCs over time (Curran & Bauer, 2011). This requirement holds for both the multilevel model using the person-mean at level 2 and the SEM using a latent factor for the TVCs. The reason for this requirement is clear: Deviating the TVCs around the person-mean assumes that the TVCs are not changing systematically over time (e.g., Curran & Bauer, 2011, Figure 9). If some form of a time trend underlies the TVCs, then the person-mean deviated scores that omit this trend are inappropriate. If this situation exists, more complex multivariate models are needed (e.g., Curran & Bollen, 2001; du Toit & Browne, 2001; MacCallum, Kim, Malarkey, & Kiecolt-Glaser, 1997; McArdle & Hamagami, 2001). Further work is needed to better understand precisely how the between- and within-person effects are being manifested within these more complex multivariate models.

Second, we have explored the issues of disaggregation only with respect to continuously distributed TVCs. However, normal distributions need not be a requirement for disaggregation using our proposed methods; assuming the TVCs approximate a continuous distribution, there are several well-developed estimation methods that circumvent the traditional assumption of multivariate normality (or, more precisely, no excessive kurtosis; Browne, 1984) invoked by normal theory ML (e.g., Satorra, 1990). Furthermore, no additional issues arise if the criterion measure is discretely scaled, and all of our developments would generalize to nonlinear link functions and alternative response distributions. However, several intriguing issues arise when the TVC itself is discretely scaled, and particularly when it is dichotomous. For example, the person-mean of the dichotomous TVC represents the proportion of total assessments in which the item was endorsed, and the person-mean-centered TVC would rescale the 0 or 1 around this person-mean. Furthermore, fitting a latent factor to a set of dichotomous indicators requires moving to a nonlinear SEM, thus resulting in a much more complicated model (e.g., Flora & Curran, 2004; Mehta, Neale, & Flay, 2004). Indeed, we typically cannot directly access time-specific residuals in an SEM with discrete dependent measures, yet this is a key component of our proposed latent variable model for the TVC (e.g., Figure 9.3). As such, our general conclusions are primarily restricted to the case of continuously (though not necessarily normally) distributed TVCs. There are thus a number of promising areas for future research both in terms of more precise substantive predictions about the exact nature of individual change as well as the development of new statistical models to capture such change.

It has long been known that there are a large number of advantages to the collection and analysis of repeated-measures data over time. Advantages include increased power, greater ability to study the psychometric properties of measures, and the direct examination of interindividual differences in intraindividual change. However, as we all develop a better understanding of these complex models of change, it is increasingly apparent that one of the most important advantages may well be the ability to disaggregate the between- and within-person influences of a TVC on the outcome variable. Indeed, such a disaggregation is of primary interest to most theories of human behavior (e.g., Curran & Bauer, 2011; Molenaar, 2004; Molenaar & Newell, 2011). Yet, at least in our opinion, insufficient attention has been paid to this disaggregation of effects both within the quantitative and substantive disciplines in the behavioral sciences. We hope that our work here has not only provided some unique insight into how the disaggregation of within- and between-person effects are manifested within the MLM and the SEM but has also chartered several directions in which future developments might proceed. These ongoing quantitative developments can in turn goose us to further refine our substantive theories so that we may better articulate precisely what type of change we posit when making predictions about trajectories of individual stability and change over time.

APPENDIX

Consider a true data generating model for a random intercept and slope with a single time varying covariate; the measurement and structural equations are

$$y_{ti} = \beta_{0i} + \beta_{1i} time_{ti} + \omega(z_{ti} - \bar{z}_i) + \varepsilon_{ti} \tag{9.A1}$$

$$\beta_{0i} = \mu_\beta + (\omega + \delta_0)\bar{z}_i + \zeta_{\alpha i} \tag{9.A2}$$

$$\beta_{1i} = \mu_\beta + (\omega + \delta_1)\bar{z}_i + \zeta_{\beta i} \tag{9.A3}$$

where ω is the within-person effect, $\omega + \delta_0$ is the between-person effect on the intercept, and $\omega + \delta_1$ is the between-person effect on the slope and all else is defined in the manuscript. The reduced form expression of this population model is thus

$$y_{ti} = \mu_\alpha + \mu_\beta^* time_{ti} + \zeta_{\alpha i}^* + \zeta_{\beta i}^* + \omega z_{ti} + \varepsilon_{ti} \tag{9.A4}$$

where $\mu_\beta^* = \mu_\beta + \omega \bar{z}_i$, $\zeta_{\alpha i}^* = \delta_0 \bar{z}_i + \zeta_{\alpha i}$, and $\zeta_{\beta i}^* = \delta_1 \bar{z}_i + \zeta_{\beta i}$.

Importantly, notice that

$$\mathrm{var}(\zeta_{\alpha i}^*) = \delta_0^2 \mathrm{var}(\bar{z}_i) + \psi_{\alpha\alpha} \tag{9.A5}$$

$$\mathrm{var}(\zeta_{\beta i}^*) = \delta_1^2 \mathrm{var}(\bar{z}_i) + \psi_{\beta\beta} \tag{9.A6}$$

$$\mathrm{cov}(\zeta_{\alpha i}^*, \zeta_{\beta i}^*) = \delta_0 \delta_1 \mathrm{var}(\bar{z}_i) + \psi_{\alpha,\beta} \tag{9.A7}$$

$$\mathrm{cov}(\zeta_{\alpha i}^*, \bar{z}_i) = \delta_0 \mathrm{var}(\bar{z}_i) \neq 0 \tag{9.A8}$$

$$\mathrm{cov}(\zeta_{\beta i}^*, \bar{z}_i) = \delta_1 \mathrm{var}(\bar{z}_i) \neq 0 \tag{9.A9}$$

where $\psi_{\alpha\alpha} = \mathrm{var}(\zeta_{\alpha i})$, $\psi_{\beta\beta} = \mathrm{var}(\zeta_{\beta i})$, and $\psi_{\alpha\beta} = \mathrm{cov}(\zeta_{\alpha i}, \zeta_{\beta i})$. Based on this information, we can derive estimates of δ_0 and δ_1 that in turn allows us to obtain direct estimates of the between-person effects. Specifically, δ_0 can be directly obtained by

$$\delta_0 = \frac{\mathrm{cov}(\bar{z}_i, \zeta_{\alpha i}^*)}{\mathrm{var}(\bar{z}_i)} \tag{9.A10}$$

$$= \frac{\frac{1}{T}\sum_{t=1}^{T}\mathrm{cov}(z_{ti}, \zeta_{\alpha i}^*)}{\mathrm{var}\left(\frac{1}{T}\sum_{t=1}^{T}z_{ti}\right)}$$

$$= \frac{\frac{1}{T}\sum_{t=1}^{T}\mathrm{cov}(z_{ti}, \zeta_{\alpha i}^*)}{\frac{1}{T^2}\left\{\sum_{t=1}^{T}\mathrm{var}(z_{ti}) + \sum_{t \neq t'}\mathrm{cov}(z_{ti}, z_{t'i}')\right\}}$$

Following similar logic δ_1 can be computed as

$$\delta_1 = \frac{\frac{1}{T}\sum_{t=1}^{T}\mathrm{cov}(z_{ti}, \zeta_{\beta i}^*)}{\frac{1}{T^2}\left\{\sum_{t=1}^{T}\mathrm{var}(z_{ti}) + \sum_{t \neq t'}\mathrm{cov}(z_{ti}, z_{t'i}')\right\}} \tag{9.A11}$$

As such, sample estimates of both of the contextual effects (i.e., $\hat{\delta}_0$ and $\hat{\delta}_1$) can be calculated using SEM results in equations 9.A10 and 9.A11. Direct estimates for the between-person effects can then be obtained by calculating $\hat{\omega}+\hat{\delta}_0$ and $\hat{\omega}+\hat{\delta}_1$. Standard delta method procedures can be used to obtain an associated standard error for this compound parameter estimate.

To stress, we do not anticipate that the calculation of $\hat{\delta}_0$ and $\hat{\delta}_1$ are likely of use in practice; we show these to explicate precisely how the between- and within-person effects can be analytically obtained from the SEM. We recommend that the latent variable approach for the TVCs be used for disaggregating effects in substantive applications.

ACKNOWLEDGMENT

This research was partially funded by Grant No. DA013148 awarded to the first author and Grant No. DA15398 awarded to the first author and Dr. Andrea Hussong.

REFERENCES

Aiken, L. S., & West, S. G. (1991). *Multiple regression: Testing and interpreting interactions*. Newbury Park, CA: Sage.

Bauer, D. J. (2003). Estimating multilevel linear models as structural equation models. *Journal of Educational and Behavioral Statistics, 28*, 135–167.

Bollen, K. A. (1989). *Structural equations with latent variables*. New York: Wiley.

Bollen, K. A., & Curran, P. J. (2006). *Latent curve models: A structural equation approach*. Hoboken, NJ: Wiley.

Browne, M. W. (1984). Asymptotic distribution free methods in the analysis of covariance structures. *British Journal of Mathematical and Statistical Psychology, 37*, 127–141.

Bryk, A. S., & Raudenbush, S. W. (1987). Application of hierarchical linear models to assessing change. *Psychological Bulletin. 101*, 147–158.

Cattell, R. B. (1944). Psychological measurement: Normative, ipsative, interactive. *Psychological Review, 51*, 292–303.

Chan, W., & Bentler, P. M. (1996). Covariance structure analysis of partially additive ipsative data using restricted maximum likelihood estimation. *Multivariate Behavioral Research, 31*, 289–312.

Chassin, L., Curran, P. J., Hussong, A. M., & Colder, C. R. (1996). The relation of parent alcoholism to adolescent substance use: A longitudinal follow-up study. *Journal of Abnormal Psychology, 105*, 70–80.

Clemans, W. V. (1966). *An analytical and empirical examination of some properties of ipsative measures* (Psychometric Monograph No. 14). Richmond, VA: Psychometric Society. Retrieved from www.psychometrika.org/journal/online/MN14.pdf.

Cohen, J., Cohen, P., West, S., & Aiken, L. (2003). *Applied multiple regression/correlation analysis for the behavioral sciences (3rd ed.).* Hillsdale, NJ: Erlbaum.

Curran, P. J. (2003). Have multilevel models been structural equation models all along? *Multivariate Behavioral Research, 38,* 529–569.

Curran, P. J., & Bauer, D. J. (2011). The disaggregation of within-person and between-person effects in longitudinal models of change. *Annual Review of Psychology, 62,* 583–619.

Curran, P. J., & Bollen, K. A. (2001). The best of both worlds: Combining autoregressive and latent curve models. In L. M. Collins & A. G. Sayer (Eds.), *New methods for the analysis of change* (pp. 105–136). Washington, DC: American Psychological Association.

Dunlap, W. P., & Cornwell, J. J. (1994). Factor analysis of ipsative measures. *Multivariate Behavioral Research, 29,* 115–126.

du Toit, S. H. C., & Browne, M. W. (2001) *The covariance structure of a vector time series.* In R. Cudeck, S. H. C. du Toit, & D. Sörbom (Eds.), *Structural equation modeling: Present and future* (pp. 279–314). Chicago: Scientific Software International.

Flora, D. B., & Curran, P. J. (2004). An empirical evaluation of alternative methods of estimation for confirmatory factor analysis with ordinal data. *Psychological Methods, 9,* 466–491.

Greene, W. H. (2000). *Econometric analysis* (4th ed.). Upper Saddle River, NJ: Prentice Hall.

Hoffman, L., & Stawski, R. (2009). Persons as contexts: Evaluating between-person and within-person effects in longitudinal analysis. *Research in Human Development, 6,* 97–100.

Hofmann, D. A., & Gavin, M. B. (1998). Centering decisions in hierarchical linear models: Theoretical and methodological implications for organizational science. *Journal of Management, 24,* 623–641.

Kaplow, J. B., Curran, P. J., & Costello, E. J. (2001). The prospective relation between dimensions of anxiety and the initiation of adolescent alcohol use. *Journal of Clinical Child Psychology, 30,* 316–326.

Kassel, D. J., Hussong, A. M., Wardle, M. C., Veilleux, J. C., Heinz, A., Greenstein, J. E., et al. (2010). Affective influences in drug use etiology. In L. M. Scheier (Ed.), *Handbook of drug use etiology: Theory, methods and empirical findings* (pp. 183–206). Washington, DC: American Psychological Association.

Kreft, I. G. G., de Leeuw, J., & Aiken, L. S. (1995). The effect of different forms of centering in hierarchical linear models. *Multivariate Behavioral Research, 30,* 1–21.

Lüdtke, O., Marsh, H. W., Robitzsch, A. Trautwein, U., Asparouhov, T., & Muthén, B. (2008). The multilevel latent covariate model: A new, more reliable approach to group-level effects in contextual studies. *Psychological Methods, 13,* 203–229.

MacCallum, R. C., Kim, C., Malarkey, W. B., & Kiecolt-Glaser, J. K. (1997). Studying multivariate change using multilevel models and latent curve models. *Multivariate Behavioral Research, 32,* 215–253.

McArdle, J. J. (1988). Dynamic but structural equation modeling of repeated measures data. In J. R. Nesselroade & R. B. Cattell (Eds.), *Handbook of multivariate experimental psychology* (2nd ed.). New York: Plenum Press.

McArdle, J. J. (1989). Structural modeling experiments using multiple growth functions. In P. Ackerman, R. Kanfer, & R. Cudeck (Eds.), *Learning and individual differences: Abilities, motivation and methodology* (pp. 71–117). Hillsdale, NJ: Erlbaum.

McArdle, J. J. (1991). Structural models of developmental theory in psychology. In P. Van Geert & L. P. Mos (Eds.), *Annals of theoretical psychology, Volume VII* (pp. 139–160). New York: Plenum Press.

McArdle, J. J., & Epstein, D. (1987). Latent growth curves within developmental structural equation models. *Child Development, 58*, 110–133.

McArdle, J. J., & Hamagami, F. (2001). Latent difference score structural models for linear dynamic analyses with incomplete longitudinal data. In L. M. Collins & A. G. Sayer (Eds.), *New methods for the analysis of change* (pp. 137–175). Washington, DC: American Psychological Association.

Mehta, P. D., & Neale, M. C. (2005). People are variables too: Multilevel structural equations modeling. *Psychological Methods, 10*, 259–284.

Mehta, P. D., Neale, M. C., & Flay, B. R. (2004). Squeezing interval change from ordinal panel data: Latent growth curves with ordinal outcomes. *Psychological Methods, 9*, 301–333.

Meredith, W., & Tisak, J. (1984). *"Tuckerizing" curves*. Paper presented at the annual meeting of the Psychometric Society, Santa Barbara, CA.

Meredith, W., & Tisak, J. (1990). Latent curve analysis, *Psychometrika, 55*, 107–122.

Molenaar, P. C. M. (2004). A manifesto on psychology as idiographic science: Bringing the person back into scientific psychology, this time forever. *Measurement: Interdisciplinary Research and Perspective, 2*, 201–218.

Molenaar, P. C. M., & Newell, K. M. (2011). *Individual pathways of change: Statistical models for analyzing learning and development*. Washington, DC: American Psychological Association.

Raudenbush, S. W. (2001). Toward a coherent framework for comparing trajectories of individual change. In L. M. Collins & A. G. Sayer (Eds.), *New methods for the analysis of change* (pp. 35–64). Washington, DC: American Psychological Association.

Raudenbush, S. W., & Bryk, A. S. (2002). *Hierarchical linear models* (2nd ed.). Thousand Oaks, CA: Sage.

Rodebaugh, T., Curran, P., & Chambless, D. (2002). Expectancy of panic in the maintenance of daily anxiety in panic disorder with agoraphobia: A longitudinal test of competing models. *Behavior Therapy, 33*, 315–336.

Rogosa, D. R., & Saner, H. M. (1995). Longitudinal data analysis examples with random coefficient models. *Journal of Educational and Behavioral Statistics, 20*, 149–170.

Satorra, A. (1990). Robustness issues in structural equation modeling: A review of recent developments. *Quality & Quantity, 24*, 367–386.

Schwartz, J. E., & Stone, A. A. (1998). Strategies for analyzing ecological momentary assessment data. *Health Psychology, 17*, 6–16.

Singer, J. D., & Willett, J. B. (2003). *Applied longitudinal data analysis: Modeling change and event occurrence.* New York: Oxford University Press.

Willett, J. B., & Sayer, A. G. (1994). Using covariance structure analysis to detect correlates and predictors of individual change over time. *Psychological Bulletin, 116,* 363–381.

NOTES

1. It is possible under some conditions to estimate random effects for the TVCs within the SEM using definition variables (e.g., Mehta & Neale, 2005), but this is moving well beyond our focus here.
2. To maintain maximum generality we retain the cross-level interaction between the person-specific mean and the measure of time, although in our later simulations we fix this value to zero in order to unambiguously define the main effect of the person-specific mean as the between effect.
3. Formally testing this hypothesis would make an excellent dissertation.
4. All population parameter values are presented in the final column of Table 9.2 using SEM notation that is defined later in the chapter.
5. For simplification, we make the unrealistic assumption of no missing data. However, this imposes no limitations on the developments we present here. Indeed, we reestimated all models with 10% and 20% missing data under MAR mechanisms, and as expected all key conclusions remained unchanged.
6. We include an estimate of the cross-level interaction between the person-specific mean and time, although the value of this effect was fixed to zero in the population.
7. Within the SEM the TVC can take on unique values across time by freely estimating γ at each time point t; in the MLM the same effect can be obtained by entering an interaction between the TVC and the measure of time.
8. It is also possible to grand mean center the TVCs within the SEM, and this strategy offers certain interpretational advantages with respect to the latent variable means. However, grand mean centering does not allow us to obtain direct estimates of the within- and between-person effects of the TVC on the outcome, so we do not pursue this further here.
9. Note that in some cases it might be possible to estimate two separate models, one that contains just the TVC and one that contains just the person-means. The estimates of the within- and between-person effects can then be obtained from each. However, this approach is statistically inefficient, is prone to adverse effects of model misspecification, and limits the estimation of more general models.
10. We can also define a compositional effect for the linear slope component, but here we focus on the more common main effect of the between effect of the TVC predicting the random intercept; see the Appendix for a derivation of the compositional effect for the slope component as well.
11. Here we are assuming that T is constant for all individuals in the sample, but the equations can be adjusted accordingly for unbalanced designs.

12. When the latent factor for the TVC is allowed to covary with that of the outcome (as it is here), the within-person effect is equivalently captured by regressing the repeated measures on either the residual of the TVC or directly on the TVC itself. However, regressing the repeated measures on the residuals is a more general strategy that allows for the estimation of alternative models that we do not detail here.
13. The multivariate equations for this model can be written, but these expressions become tedious in scalar form and requires matrix notation. Given space constraints we do not pursue this further here; see Bollen and Curran (2006, pp. 188–207) for details about these multivariate expressions.
14. It is currently unknown the extent to which these models might be estimable using direct ML estimation that is not based on summary statistics as the unit of analysis; more work is needed to better understand this possibility.

CHAPTER 10

CONSIDERING ALTERNATIVE METRICS OF TIME

Does Anybody Really Know What "Time" Is?

Lesa Hoffman
University of Nebraska-Lincoln

Longitudinal studies (i.e., in which each person is observed at multiple occasions) are a cornerstone of research in psychology and human development and have become increasingly common across fields, such as education and business. Although many developmental questions have initially been addressed using cross-sectional studies, such between-person comparisons of people of different ages at a single point in time are often subject to well-known biases, including cohort effects, self-selection effects, mortality effects, and other problems (for more extended discussion, see Baltes, Cornelius, & Nesselroade, 1979; Baltes & Nesselroade, 1979; Hofer & Sliwinski, 2006; Schaie, 1965, 2008). Longitudinal studies can offer significant advantages over cross-sectional studies, in that not only can they provide cross-sectional, between-person information about interindividual variation (i.e., when the longitudinal study begins as a cross-sectional study of persons at different ages), but because they also provide within-person information about intraindividual change or variation over time (and between-person differences in those within-person changes).

Extensive methodological work has focused on the development of statistical models of change, such as for describing and predicting how scholastic achievement of children grows over time, how job performance of employees changes over time, how marital satisfaction waxes or wanes over time, how physical and cognitive function in older adults declines over time, and so forth. Indeed, much of this book focuses on the development or refinement of longitudinal models to be able to ask and answer questions of increasing complexity. Yet in order to make informed use of such exciting advances for longitudinal models, we must make an important assumption—we presuppose to know exactly what "time" is. That is, what is thought to be the fundamental causal process by which one should index change? Such deliberation on the possible metrics for indexing time (that in turn can reflect different processes) becomes important whenever persons differ at the onset of a study in the time metric of interest (e.g., persons of different ages at baseline). To illustrate, let us consider in more detail three of the examples already given: modeling growth in children' scholastic achievement, increases in employee job performance, and changes in marital satisfaction over time.

Considering Time

First, with respect to growth in children's scholastic achievement over time, we might reasonably assume that learning proceeds as a function of grade in school, given that each child is observed in multiple grades (i.e., there is within-person variation in grade as "time"), even if the children begin the study in different grades (i.e., there is also between-person variation in grade as "time"). Although children in the same grade may still differ in age, to the extent that scholastic achievement is a consequence of instruction (and not biology), then grade in school is likely to be more relevant for indexing learning over time than chronological age. Any effect of age differences between children in the same grade could still be accounted for by including the age at which they entered school as a person-specific covariate. Thus, in this context, what "time" should be seems relatively straightforward (even if more than one option is possible).

Second, in considering employee job performance over time, we might assume that performance improves as a function of years of experience on the job, which we can monitor through repeated performance observations (i.e., "time" represents within-person variation in work experience at their organization). But complications arise because employees often begin their position with different employment histories (i.e., "time" includes between-person variation in work experience also). For instance, consider the process of university promotion and tenure. Whether or not tenure requirements have been met is often evaluated as a function of years of experience (i.e., most candidates will apply for tenure 5–7 years into a tenure-track position), but at what point does the "work experience" that is relevant for promotion and tenure really begin? Does the relevant experience begin only at the entry point into that tenure-track position, or does it begin earlier, at the point of receipt of the doctoral degree, or upon completion of postdoctoral training or internship? What about persons who enter a tenure-track position after completing several years in a similar position at another university? If multiple candidates with different amounts of previous work experience (e.g., only graduate work, postgraduate work, or a previous tenure-track position) apply for tenure at the same time, the expectations for their accomplishments at that point in time may heavily depend on how their relevant "time on the job" is conceptualized and measured. Thus, in this instance, what "time" should be is debatable, but with significant repercussions resulting from each possible alternative.

In other contexts, the best choice for "time" may be even less obvious. For instance, in studying changes in marital satisfaction over time, a logical first choice for time might be "time in marriage" (i.e., marital satisfaction may wax or wane the longer one is married, or due to within-person variation in "time in marriage"), even if couples differ in how long they've been married when they enter the study (i.e., there is also between-person variation in "time in marriage"). However, there is likely to be considerable heterogeneity in how quickly different couples may decide to marry. If one believes that relationship satisfaction progresses as a function of the length of the *overall* relationship (rather than just the length of the marriage), then "time in *relationship*" may more accurately index observed changes in relationship satisfaction than would "time in *marriage*." But some couples may meet and begin dating immediately, whereas others may be friends initially and then later decide to begin dating. In that case, "time in relationship" would need to be further distinguished as "time in *any* relationship" versus "time in a *romantic* relationship." Furthermore, some couples may have more volatile relationships, such that they may break up, but then later decide to get back together (perhaps doing so multiple times). Should any time in between their relationship epochs "count" within whichever time metric is used to index change in relationship satisfaction over time?

In addition, alternative theoretical viewpoints of relationship dynamics may require very different metrics of time for indexing change in relationship satisfaction. What if one believes that relationship satisfaction changes due to changing responsibilities of the spouses or partners (e.g., the transition to parenthood)? If so, how long a couple has been together (however defined) would be less relevant than how long they have been parents together (e.g., the age of their first child). Further still, couples may decide to end their unions at different points in their relationship, and so perhaps declines in satisfaction could be described more parsimoniously by tracking change as a function of a meaningful event, such as beginning counseling, separation, or divorce. In that case, time would be measured backwards in order to describe change over time as a function of the *dissolution* of the relationship instead. That is, couples would be aligned with respect to how soon they will be apart, rather than how long they've been together. Finally, because the couples that are still together after a long relationship are not a random subsample of all couples who had begun a relationship (because they have chosen to stay together), inferences about changes in relationship satisfaction need to be viewed as conditional on this self-selection process. Thus, what "time" should be in this context is anything but clear-cut!

The Focus of This Chapter

The point of the three preceding examples was to illustrate how the decision to index change over time should reflect the theoretical process thought to be responsible for any observed change, and thus how several alternative metrics of time (corresponding to different theoretical orientations) may be useful for tracking change in a given outcome as a result. The purpose of the present work is to thoroughly explore these issues surrounding the choices we make for the specification of time within longitudinal models. The title of this chapter is based on a song recorded by the band Chicago in 1969, in which the lyrics query: "Does anybody really know what time it is?... Does anybody really care (about time)?" I believe that we should indeed care about time (at least when conducting longitudinal analysis), and so the goal of this chapter is to present how often unrecognized assumptions about the treatment of time can have important consequences for subsequent model interpretation. I use a working example examining change in cognitive functioning in older adults as a function of three alternative metrics of time (time since birth, time until death, and time since dementia diagnosis) to address two general issues: (1) what "time" should be and (2) how "time" should be modeled.

What Should Time Be?

It is important to note that the question of what "time" should be is not relevant within persons, in which all metrics for indexing time are indistinguishable. For instance, in the previous relationship example, as each year passes relative to a person's status at the beginning of the study, he or she has been married one year longer, in the relationship one year longer, in the romantic relationship one year longer, has been a parent one year longer, and may be one year closer to separation or divorce. Within persons, these alternative metrics of time cannot be distinguished—within persons, time is just time. Between persons, however, all time metrics are not equivalent—people may begin the study at different points in "time" (e.g., they may have been married longer, have been a parent longer, or may begin the study closer to separation or divorce). As a result, both the amount of interindividual variation in "time" and its relationship with a given outcome are likely to differ depending on what "time" is. Thus, the first question is, given the presence of both between-person and within-person variation in time, from what point should we start counting—how should time be aligned between persons?

How Should Time Be Modeled?

Second, how should our model of change account for the potentially different effects of between- and within-person differences in "time"? Different model specifications (in addition to different time metrics) may result in different conclusions for the description and prediction of change over time. Such considerations have been described more generally for multilevel models as they relate to distinguishing individual effects from contextual effects (e.g., Raudenbush & Bryk, 2002; Snijders & Bosker, 1999), or distinguishing time-specific effects from individual effects of time-varying covariates (e.g., Hedeker & Gibbons, 2006; Hoffman & Stawski, 2009), but relatively little attention has been paid to this issue in the context of indexing time in longitudinal studies, in which the same concerns are also relevant. Thus, the second question is, within a chosen time metric, how should the model be specified to best account for *all* sources of variation in time?

EXAMPLE DATA

Sample

These questions surrounding alternative metrics and models of time are addressed using data from the Octogenarian Twin Study of Aging (as described in Johansson et al., 2004), in which observations were collected longitudinally from same-sex twin pairs. One twin from each pair was randomly selected for use in the current analyses, which included 173 persons (65% women) who were sampled on up to five occasions over an 8-year period (i.e., every 2 years). Other relevant characteristics of the analysis sample are summarized below.

Outcomes

Two cognition outcomes were examined. The Mini-Mental Status Exam (MMSE; Folstein, Folstein, & McHugh, 1975) is a general test of orientation and memory that is often used to identify persons suspected of having dementia. The questions are relatively easy and thus most participants without cognitive impairment score at ceiling. The second outcome was a more sensitive measure of memory, the Memory-in-Reality Object Recall Test (Johansson, 1988), in which participants were asked to place real-life objects in a three-dimensional model of an apartment and were later given a free-recall test for those objects. For ease of interpretation, both outcomes were T-scored to the same scale ($M = 50$, $SD = 10$). Additional information about the original OCTO-Twin sample and these measures of cognition can be found in Johansson et al. (1999, 2004).

Decomposing Variance

Before building longitudinal models, it is useful to decompose the outcome variability into *between-person* variability in the mean level of the outcome over time (i.e., cross-sectional variability representing interindividual differences) and *within-person* variability around a person's mean outcome over time (i.e., longitudinal variability representing intraindividual change and fluctuation). These sources of variation can be quantified by estimating what is called an "empty" longitudinal (multilevel) model, as shown in equation 10.1:

$$\text{Level 1: } y_{ti} = \beta_{0i} + e_{ti} \quad (10.1)$$
$$\text{Level 2: } \beta_{0i} = \gamma_{00} + U_{0i}$$

in which y_{ti} is the outcome at time t for individual i. The level-1 model constructs an outcome at each occasion as a function of an individual intercept, represented by the placeholder β_{0i}, and a time- and individual-specific residual e_{ti}. The level-2 model then describes how each person's intercept is constructed: Here, as a function of the fixed intercept γ_{00}, which is the grand mean of the outcome over time, and the random intercept U_{0i}, which is the deviation from the grand mean of individual i's mean over time. Thus, U_{0i} represents between-person (BP) variation in the person-means (estimated as $\tau_{U_0}^2$) and e_{ti} represents within-person (WP) variation around those person-means (estimated as σ_e^2). We can then form a ratio of these two variance components in order to calculate an intraclass correlation (ICC), as shown in equation 10.2:

$$\text{ICC} = \frac{\text{var}(U_{0i})}{\text{var}(U_{0i}) + \text{var}(e_{ti})} = \frac{\tau_{U_0}^2}{\tau_{U_0}^2 + \sigma_e^2} = \frac{\text{BP variation}}{(\text{BP} + \text{WP}) \text{ variation}} \quad (10.2)$$

in which the ICC is the proportion of variance that is between persons (or equivalently, the average correlation across occasions assuming compound symmetry). In this example, the ICCs for the MMSE and Object Recall outcomes were .50 and .42, respectively, indicating that approximately half of their variance was in mean level over time (between-person, cross-sectional variance).

Accelerated Longitudinal Designs

The example data were collected in an *accelerated longitudinal design* (i.e., overlapping cohort design, cohort sequential design; Bell, 1953; McArdle & Bell, 2000). Accelerated designs are useful for studying human development in a shorter time frame than that in which the development actually occurs. That is, accelerated designs can be useful when one wishes to do a longer-term longitudinal study, but just doesn't have the time. An example of an accelerated design is shown in Figure 10.1, in which the top panel depicts the sampling of different age cohorts (every 5 years from age 50 to 85), each of which is sampled for 10 years. The aim of such an accelerated design would be to capture a general age curve by overlapping the observed age cohorts, as shown in the bottom panel. If the overlapping age cohorts converge onto the same age trajectory, one can then model the developmental trajectory over a larger span of time (i.e., 45 years total in Figure 10.1) than would be directly possible using only longitudinal information (i.e., only 10 years within any person in Figure 10.1).

Choosing amongst Alternative Metrics of Time

The participants analyzed in the current example were selected because they each had known dates of birth, known dates of death, and estimated ages of onset of dementia (including Alzheimer's disease, vascular dementia, or dementia with a mixed or unknown etiology; type of dementia was not distinguished for the purposes of this example). Thus, there are at least three alternative metrics of time that could be used to index change (and thus with which to align between-person variability in "time") in these longitudinal data. Let us consider each in turn.

Age as Time

First, we could index change as a function of age, or *time since birth*, given that participants ranged from age 79 to 100 years of age ($M = 84$ years,

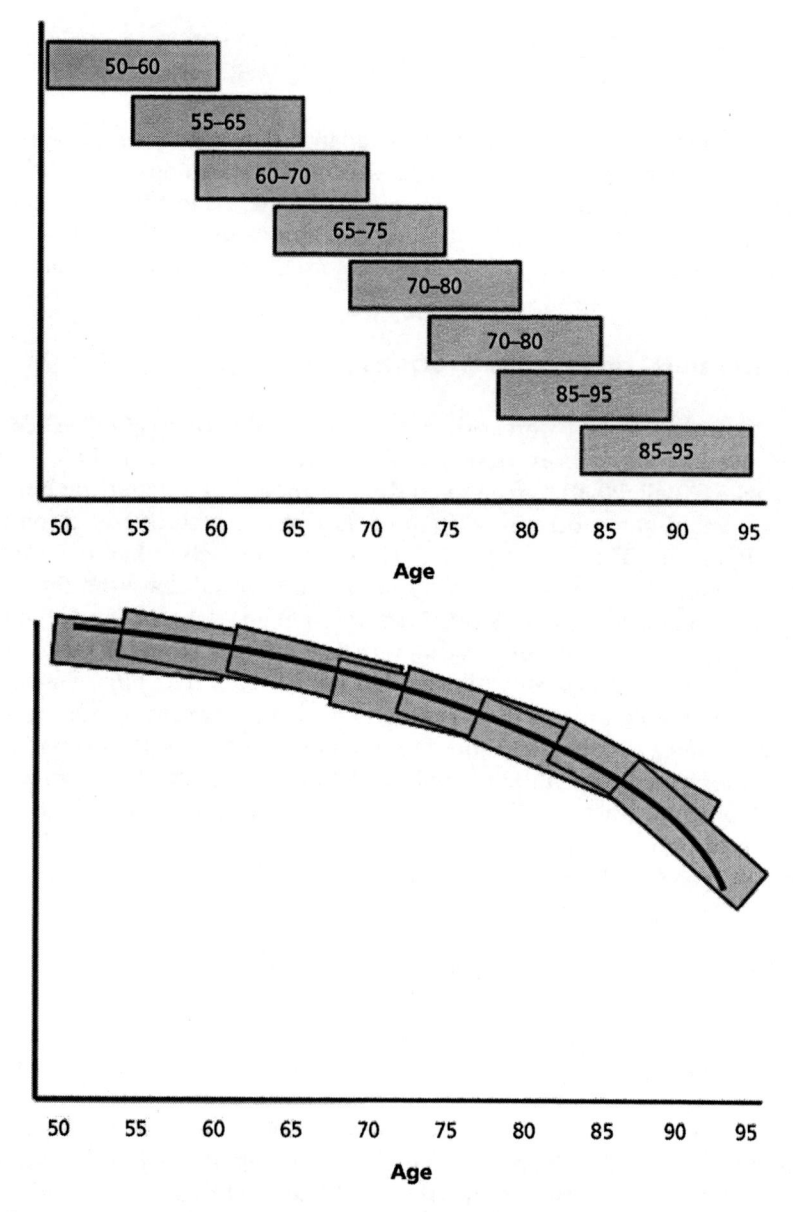

Figure 10.1 Example of an age-accelerated longitudinal design.

$SD = 3$ years) at the study beginning (baseline). This has been the most common approach by far within the cognitive aging literature. In constructing a model where age is time, individual differences would be organized around the mean outcome at a particular age (e.g., the mean of 84 years), and change would be specified as a function of the distance from that age. The use of age as time implies a theoretical model whereby cognition declines as a function of *time since birth*, such that aligning individuals based on their current age should be informative for describing individual differences in both the level and change in cognition over time (in which "time" would be age here).

Although age is measured longitudinally, if persons differ in age at baseline (i.e., they range from 79 to 100 years here), then age is also measured cross-sectionally. Therefore, it is useful to index the relative amount of cross-sectional versus longitudinal information available in the age predictor variable. We can do this by estimating an ICC for age (using equation 10.2) as derived from specifying time-varying age as an outcome in an empty model (using equation 10.1). In the example data, the ICC for age was .47, indicating that 47% of the variance in age was cross-sectional (i.e., due to initial age differences), whereas 53% was longitudinal (i.e., due to observed age changes during the study). Thus, although our theoretical model is based on the idea of "aging," only about half of the variance in age will be directly informative about within-person age changes. The rest of the age variance will be informative about preexisting differences between persons of different ages instead.

Death as Time

An alternative approach that has become increasingly popular within cognitive aging is to index change as a function of years to death instead of age, or *time to death*, given that participants ranged from −16 to 0 years to death ($M = -6$ years, $SD = 4$ years) at baseline. In constructing a model in which death is time, individual differences would be organized around the mean outcome at a particular distance from death (e.g., the mean of −6 years), and change would be specified as a function of the distance from that point. The use of death as time implies a theoretical model whereby cognition declines as a function of *impending death* (i.e., terminal decline), such that aligning individuals based on their current distance from death should be informative for describing individual differences in level and change in cognition over time, rather than based on their current age. In other words, it matters how many years one has left, not how many years one has already had. The ICC for time to death was .24, indicating that 24% of the information in death as time is between persons who enter the study at different durations to death (i.e., cross-sectional variance), whereas 76% is within-persons (i.e., longitudinal variance) as they grow closer to the end of their lives during the study.

Dementia as Time

A third option for "time" is based on a common important event: Given that everyone in the sample has been or will be diagnosed with dementia, we could also index change using proximity to the dementia diagnosis, or *time to dementia*. Participants ranged from −12 to 18 years from diagnosis ($M = 0$ years, $SD = 5$ years) at baseline, indicating that some participants entered the study already having been diagnosed with dementia, whereas others received a diagnosis at some point during or after the study. The use of dementia as time implies a theoretical model whereby cognition declines as a function of *dementia disease progression*, such that aligning individuals based on their current time with the disease (without regard to age or years to death) should be informative for describing individual differences in level and change in cognition over time. The ICC for time to dementia was .71, indicating that 71% of the information in dementia as time is between persons who enter the study with different amounts of disease progression (i.e., cross-sectional variance), whereas 29% is within persons relative to their own progression observed during the study (i.e., longitudinal variance). One significant limitation in using dementia as time, however, is that age of dementia onset can only be estimated, in contrast to observable events that have defined dates, such as birth or death. Thus, the variable for time to dementia diagnosis will contain measurement error, whereas the variables for time since birth or time to death (that are known rather than estimated) should not.

Each metric of time (time since birth, time to death, and time to dementia) forms an accelerated design in its own right, in that persons differ at baseline in each measure, and they also differ in how much of their information is actually cross-sectional (24–71%). Furthermore, the baseline values for these time dimensions are surprisingly uncorrelated. Age is only correlated with time to death at $r = .23$ and with time to dementia at $r = .17$, although time to death and time to dementia are correlated more highly at $r = .52$ (given that dementia can be a cause of death). Thus, these alternative metrics of time will align different persons in very different ways.

Time as Time

Finally, a less obvious choice for organizing individual differences is simply "time" itself, or *time in study*, which ranges from 0 to 8 years with an ICC of exactly 0, indicating that time in study represents solely longitudinal information. The use of time in study as time makes no theoretical statement whatsoever—individuals are simply organized around their baseline level of performance and their change from baseline. Thus, when used by itself, time in study ignores individual differences in time since birth, time to death, and time to dementia. As we will see later, however, such an uninformative metric for time may actually be useful in empirically distinguishing among those distinct temporal processes.

Visualizing Alternative Metrics of Time

A useful descriptive exercise in evaluating alternative metrics of time is to construct plots of individual trajectories with an overlaid trajectory of the model-estimated means at each measurement occasion within that time metric. Figure 10.2 shows four such plots for the MMSE outcome: time since birth (top left), time to death (top right), time to dementia (bottom left), and time in study (bottom right). Because MMSE is also used to assess the presence of dementia, the time to dementia plot is somewhat circular, but it nevertheless illustrates an idealized scenario in which the mean trajectory (as shown by the heavy black line) is a good descriptor of the patterns shown in the individual trajectories. That is, we can informally judge the appropriateness of a given metric of time by the similarity of the mean and individual trajectories—time to dementia appears to be a useful way to describe change in MMSE. An example of a poor match between the mean and individual trajectories can be seen for time since birth, which shows a much shallower rate of decline across age on average than what is shown by any individual. The same is true to a lesser extent for time to death. In contrast, the mean slope across time in study seems to match the individual trajectories fairly well, although there is noticeably greater heterogeneity in mean level relative to that shown in the accelerated time metrics (age, death, or dementia).

Figure 10.3 shows the same types of plots for the Object Recall memory outcome. Here the "best" metric of time is not nearly as evident, although the same general patterns appear: Time to dementia arguably seems to organize the individual trajectories around the mean trajectory mostly closely, followed by time to death and time in study, followed by time since birth.

Modeling Alternative Metrics of Time

Age as Time

Those mean and individual trajectories can then be modeled via fixed and random effects, in which fixed effects represent sample average effects and random effects represent deviations from each of those sample average effects for a given individual. Given that age is a commonly used metric of time, we can begin by constructing a model for change including fixed and random effects of age. Furthermore, we can approximate the apparent

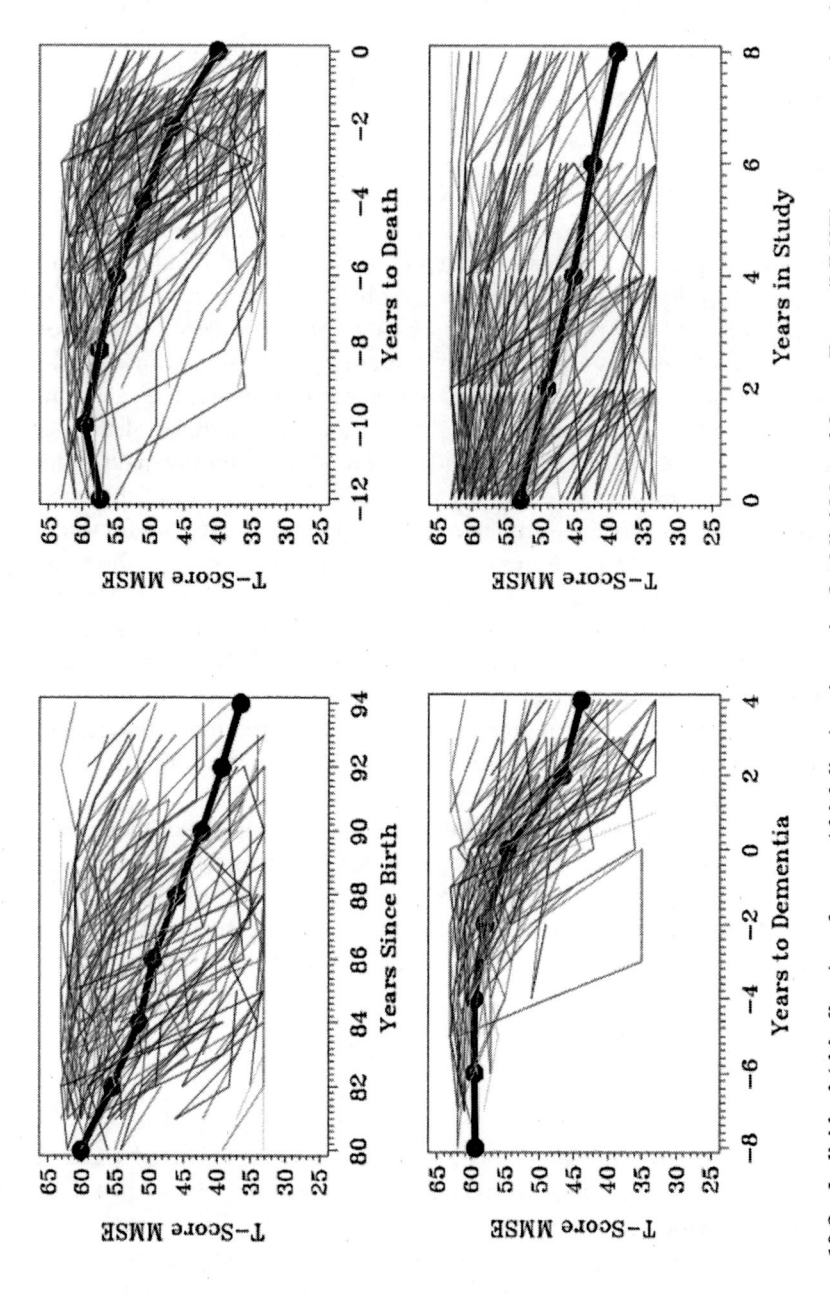

Figure 10.2 Individual (thin lines) and mean (thick line) trajectories for Mini-Mental Status Exam (MMSE) across years since birth (age; top left), years to death (top right), years to dementia diagnosis (bottom left), and years in study (bottom right).

Considering Alternative Metrics of Time ▪ 267

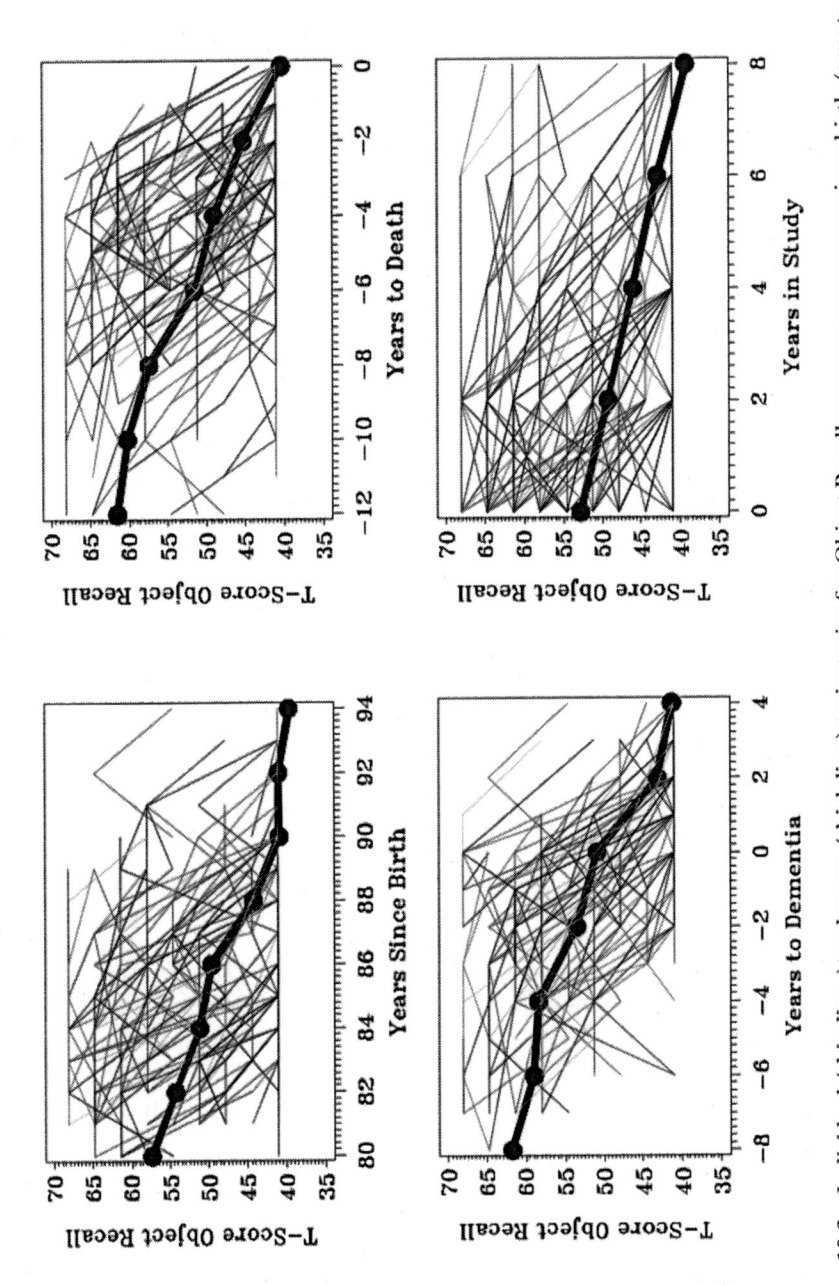

Figure 10.3 Individual (thin lines) and mean (thick line) trajectories for Object Recall memory across years since birth (age; top left), years to death (top right), years to dementia diagnosis (bottom left), and years in study (bottom right).

nonlinearity in the pattern of change across age with a quadratic effect of age, as shown in equation 10.3:

Level 1: $\quad y_{ti} = \beta_{0i} + \beta_{1i}(Age_{ti} - 84) + \beta_{2i}(Age_{ti} - 84)^2 + e_{ti}$ \quad (10.3)

Level 2: $\quad \beta_{0i} = \gamma_{00} + U_{0i}$

$\qquad\qquad \beta_{1i} = \gamma_{10} + U_{1i}$

$\qquad\qquad \beta_{2i} = \gamma_{20} + U_{2i}$

in which y_{ti} is again the outcome at time t for individual i. The level-1 model constructs an outcome at each occasion using an individual intercept, linear age slope, and quadratic age slope, as represented by the placeholders β_{0i}, β_{1i}, and β_{2i}, as well as a time- and individual-specific residual e_{ti}. The subtraction of 84 from age moves the reference point for the model from that of a newborn (if using original age) to an 84-year-old (if using age centered at 84 instead). The level-2 model then constructs each person's growth terms: as a function of the fixed (average) effect for the sample (γ_{00}, γ_{10}, and γ_{20}) and the individual random effect (U_{0i}, U_{1i}, and U_{2i}). Each term varies across persons in this example model (but in practice the necessity of each fixed or random effect should be tested). The fixed intercept (γ_{00}) is the expected outcome at age 84, and thus the intercept variance ($\tau^2_{U_0}$) describes individual differences in the outcome level at age 84. Given the quadratic age slope, the fixed linear age slope (γ_{10}) is the instantaneous linear rate of change per year of age as evaluated at age 84, and thus the linear age slope variance ($\tau^2_{U_1}$) describes individual differences in the linear age slopes also as evaluated at age 84. The fixed quadratic age slope (γ_{20}) is half the rate of acceleration or deceleration; twice the quadratic slope is how the linear age slope changes per year of age. The quadratic age slope variance ($\tau^2_{U_2}$) describes individual differences in the quadratic age slopes (which are constant across age). The U_{0i}, U_{1i}, and U_{2i} level-2 random effects are assumed to have a multivariate normal distribution across persons, whereas the e_{ti} level-1 residuals are assumed to have constant variance across persons and occasions, with no covariance across occasions within persons or between persons.

Although not obvious, the age as time model in equation 10.3 makes an important assumption of *convergence*; that is, it assumes that persons of differing initial ages all converge onto the same trajectory (i.e., as shown in Figure 10.1). More conceptually, this assumption of age convergence means that the only reason that younger and older people differ is their age, or that the cross-sectional (BP) effects of age are equivalent to the longitudinal (WP) effects of age (i.e., an assumption of ergodicity). More succinctly, convergence means that it only matters *what* age you are; it does not matter *when* you were that age. Convergence is not likely to hold to the extent that the initial age range is large or to the extent that cohort effects, selection effects, or mortality effects are likely to be present. In these example data, 47% of the variation in age is cross-sectional, and thus it is an open question whether the cross-sectional and longitudinal effects of age are equivalent (i.e., whether the effects of age show convergence).

As discussed by Sliwinski, Hoffman, and Hofer (2010), age convergence can be tested empirically by using a variant of the grand-mean-centering approach that is used to decompose effects across levels in other multilevel contexts (i.e., distinguishing individual from group effects; distinguishing time-specific from individual effects), as shown in equation 10.4:

$$\text{Level 1:} \quad y_{ti} = \beta_{0i} + \beta_{1i}(\text{Age}_{ti} - 84) + \beta_{2i}(\text{Age}_{ti} - 84)^2 + e_{ti} \quad (10.4)$$

$$\text{Level 2:} \quad \beta_{0i} = \gamma_{00} + \gamma_{01}(\text{AgeT1}_i - 84) + U_{0i}$$

$$\beta_{1i} = \gamma_{10} + \gamma_{11}(\text{AgeT1}_i - 84) + U_{1i}$$

$$\beta_{2i} = \gamma_{20} + \gamma_{21}(\text{AgeT1}_i - 84) + U_{2i}$$

in which the age at baseline (AgeT1_i) has been added as a time-invariant predictor to each level-2 equation. Although the decomposition of effects across levels typically requires computation of the mean at the higher level (i.e., mean age across time rather than age at baseline), in this case the mean age is likely to be biased by missing data—persons who dropped out of the study earlier would have a lower mean age, even if they were born in the same year. Thus, age at baseline is used as a more direct representation of age cohort (although birth year should be used in studies spanning multiple years at the first occasion). If significant effects of age cohort are found on the intercept (γ_{01}) or the linear or quadratic age slopes (γ_{11} or γ_{21}), this implies *age nonconvergence*, or that age cohort has an incremental effect (i.e., a contextual effect), even after controlling for current age. In other words, it would matter *when* you were age 84. Estimated parameters from the age as time models with age cohort are given in the second columns of Tables 10.1 and 10.2 for MMSE and Object Recall, respectively, and the corresponding model-predicted trajectories are depicted in the top panels of Figure 10.4. The quadratic age slope variance was nonsignificant and was thus not retained.

The parameters from the age as time model for MMSE can be understood as follows. Because of their interactions with age cohort, the fixed intercept, linear age slope, and quadratic age slope are interpreted conditionally on age cohort; that is, they apply specifically to someone who begins the study at age 84. Thus, for that individual, the expected MMSE (in

TABLE 10.1 Model Parameters across Alternative Metrics of Time for Mini-Mental Status Exam (MMSE)

Model parameters	Time since birth Est	SE	Time to death Est	SE	Time to dementia Est	SE
Fixed effects:						
Intercept (γ_{00})	52.76**	0.89	55.99**	0.87	52.83**	0.52
Linear slope (γ_{10})	−1.70**	0.24	−1.02**	0.31	−2.16**	0.16
Quadratic slope (γ_{20})	−0.05	0.03	−0.19**	0.04	−0.09*	0.03
Cubic slope (γ_{30})					0.01**	0.00
Cohort on intercept (γ_{01})	1.09**	0.37	0.62*	0.30	0.03	0.13
Cohort on linear slope (γ_{11})	0.08	0.08	0.05	0.08	0.07	0.04
Cohort on quadratic slope (γ_{21})	−0.01*	0.01	−0.02**	0.01	0.00	0.00
Cohort on cubic slope (γ_{31})					−0.00**	0.00
Variance components:						
Residual variance (σ_e^2)	15.38**	1.53	13.61**	1.33	20.16**	1.55
Intercept variance ($\tau_{U_0}^2$)	69.18**	9.00	63.90**	10.11	12.70**	2.44
Linear slope variance ($\tau_{U_1}^2$)	1.09**	0.29	0.97**	0.24		
Intercept slope covariance ($\tau_{U_{01}}$)	1.04	1.15	−2.56*	1.28		
Deviance (−2LL)	3513		3428		3267	
AIC	3533		3448		3287	
BIC	3564		3480		3319	

Note: * $p < .05$, ** $p < .001$. LL, log likelihood; AIC, Akaike information criteria; BIC, Bayesian information criteria. *Cohort* represents the value of each time variable at baseline.

T-score units) at age 84 is 52.76 (the fixed intercept γ_{00}), the instantaneous linear rate of decline as evaluated at age 84 is 1.70 per year (γ_{10}), and that rate of linear decline becomes (nonsignificantly) more negative by 0.10 per year (twice the quadratic slope γ_{20}, whose effect was fixed only). However, significant effects of age cohort (age at baseline) were found, such that for every year older one begins the study than age 84, the intercept at age 84 is expected to be 1.09 higher (γ_{01}), the linear rate of decline at age 84 is expected to be 0.08 less negative (nonsignificant γ_{11}), and the quadratic rate of decline is expected to be 0.01 more negative (γ_{21}). Thus, for MMSE, even after controlling for current age, persons who begin the study older have an age trajectory that begins higher than expected, but with more accelerated decline. For Object Recall, a somewhat different pattern of results was found: The expected value at age 84 was 51.60 for someone who began the study at age 84 (γ_{00}), and persons who begin the study at age 85 instead of age 84 were expected to score 0.53 higher (γ_{01}) at age 84. The form of change in Object Recall was a decelerating negative function, such that the

TABLE 10.2 Model Parameters across Alternative Metrics of Time for Object Recall Memory

Model parameters	Time since birth Est	SE	Time to death Est	SE	Time to dementia Est	SE
Fixed effects:						
Intercept (γ_{00})	51.60**	0.82	54.23**	0.87	49.90**	0.68
Linear slope (γ_{10})	−1.76**	0.19	−1.79**	0.15	−1.82**	0.22
Quadratic slope (γ_{20})	0.06*	0.03			−0.11*	0.05
Cubic slope (γ_{30})					0.02**	0.01
Cohort on intercept (γ_{01})	0.53*	0.26			0.04	0.18
Cohort on linear slope (γ_{11})					0.14**	0.05
Cohort on quadratic slope (γ_{21})					−0.02**	0.01
Cohort on cubic slope (γ_{31})					−0.00**	0.00
Variance components:						
Residual variance (σ_e^2)	28.27**	3.00	29.78**	3.27	31.12**	2.59
Intercept variance ($\tau_{U_0}^2$)	62.98**	9.55	63.28**	12.65	15.05**	3.08
Linear slope variance ($\tau_{U_1}^2$)	0.72**	0.31	0.67*	0.35		
Intercept slope covariance ($\tau_{U_{01}}$)	−4.02**	1.33	−5.69**	1.88		
Deviance (−2LL)	2851		2803		2719	
AIC	2867		2815		2737	
BIC	2892		2834		2765	

Note: * $p < .05$, ** $p < .001$. LL, log likelihood; AIC, Akaike information criteria; BIC, Bayesian information criteria. *Cohort* represents the value of each time variable at baseline.

linear rate of decline at age 84 of 1.76 per year (γ_{10}) became less negative by 0.12 (twice the quadratic γ_{20}) per year. For Object Recall, however, the rates of linear and quadratic decline across age did not differ by age cohort (i.e., no γ_{11} or γ_{21} were needed).

The positive effect of age cohort on the intercept shown by both outcomes could potentially reflect a selection effect, given that the participants who are still alive and capable of agreeing to participate at older ages are not a random subsample of all participants who could have begun the study earlier—they are likely to have comparatively greater cognitive and physical function (but may be more likely to experience greater subsequent decline, at least in MMSE). It is important to note, however, that the cohort effect on the model intercept (at age 84) is necessarily an extrapolation for the older age cohorts, who did not contribute data at age 84. The cohort effect on the intercept reflects the difference predicted by the model *that should have been observed had the data been complete.* Although such an extrapolation may seem somewhat strange, that is exactly what is implied by any acceler-

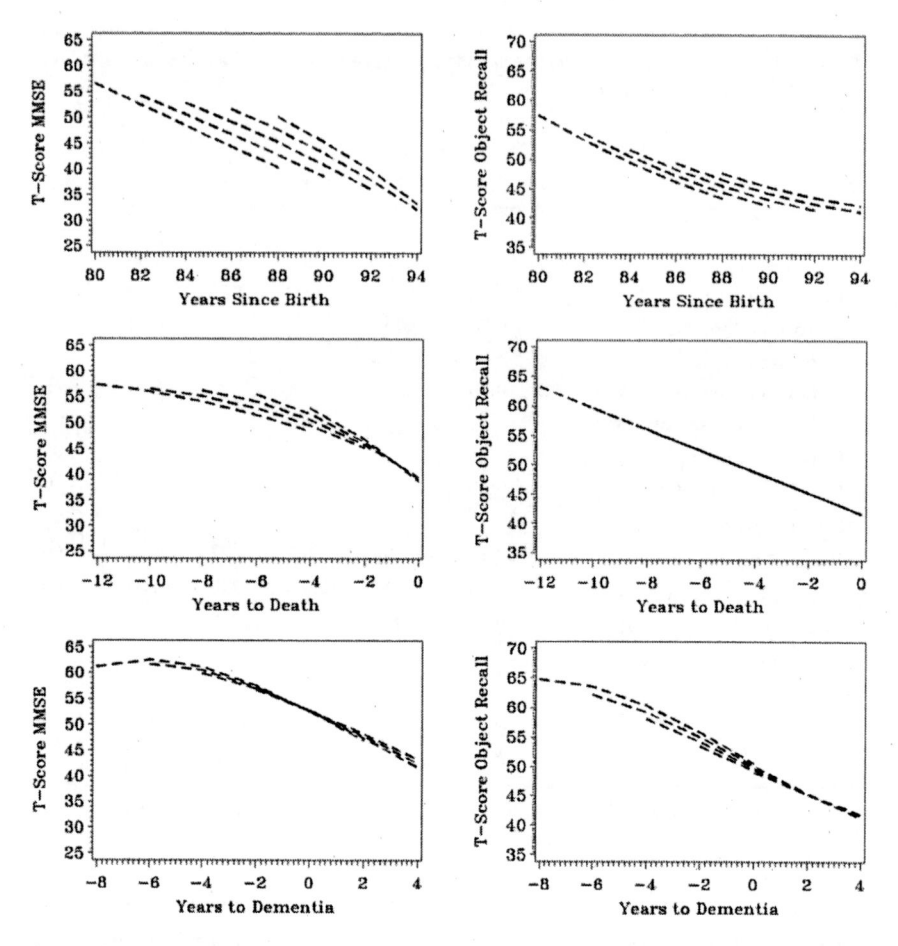

Figure 10.4 Predicted trajectories for Mini-Mental Status Exam (MMSE; left) and Object Recall memory (right) using age as time (top), death as time (middle), and dementia diagnosis as time (bottom).

ated time model—it tries to predict the overall trajectory, even though the resulting trajectory describes no actual observed individual.

Death as Time

Although time since birth is commonly used, an increasingly popular choice is to index change relative to the end of life, rather than relative to the beginning. But because time to death varies across participants at baseline (i.e., its ICC indicated that 24% of its variance was between persons), the same concerns about testing convergence apply to time to death as applied to age. Thus, we can modify the model in equation 10.4 to include time to death as the level-1 time variable (centered at 6 years prior to death) and time to death at baseline as the level-2 cohort variable. Estimated parameters from the death as time models accounting for death cohort are given in the third columns of Tables 10.1 and 10.2 for MMSE and Object Recall, respectively, and the corresponding model-predicted trajectories are depicted in the middle panels of Figure 10.4. The quadratic slope variance was again not included for either outcome.

The parameters from the death as time model for MMSE followed a very similar pattern as the age as time model. The trajectory toward death for someone who begins the study at 6 years to death (the new reference point) includes an intercept of 55.99, an instantaneous linear rate of decline at that point of 1.02 per year closer to death, and that linear rate of decline becomes more negative by 0.38 per year closer to death (i.e., an accelerating negative function). There were again effects of cohort, such that for every year closer to death one enters the study, the intercept at 6 years prior to death is greater by 0.62, the linear rate of change at 6 years prior to death is less negative by 0.05 (nonsignificant), and the quadratic rate of change is more negative by 0.02. Thus, for MMSE, persons who begin the study closer to death start out higher but have more accelerated decline (even after controlling for current years to death). For Object Recall, however, a significant linear rate of decline of 1.79 per year was predicted across all death cohorts—there was no incremental effect of beginning the study closer to death. Thus, for Object Recall, convergence of the between- and within-person effects of time to death did indeed hold (as shown by the perfectly overlapping lines in the middle right panel of Figure 10.4).

Dementia as Time

Finally, a third potential metric of time (although measured with error) is time to dementia, whereby participants are aligned using their age at diagnosis. Because 71% of its variance was between persons, the same concerns about testing convergence also apply to the effects of time to dementia. Furthermore, the model in equation 10.4 was extended to include a cubic trend as indicated in initial examinations (i.e., it included a β_{3i} placeholder at level 1, defined by just a fixed effect γ_{30} at level 2). Thus, the model included linear, quadratic, and cubic effects of time to dementia as the level-1 time variable (centered at the point of diagnosis), and effects of time to dementia at baseline as the level-2 cohort variable. Estimated parameters from the time to dementia models accounting for dementia cohort are given in the fourth columns of Tables 10.1 and 10.2 for MMSE and Object Recall, respectively, and the corresponding model-predicted trajectories are depicted in the bottom panels of Figure 10.4. None of the slope variances were significant, and so only residual and random intercept variances were retained.

The parameters from the time to dementia model for MMSE indicated an accelerating negative trajectory that eventually began to decelerate (i.e., negative linear and quadratic effects paired with a positive cubic effect), which could reflect range restriction for those scoring very low (i.e., who scored near the floor of MMSE). A significant effect of time to dementia at baseline (dementia cohort) was found only on the cubic trend, such that a lesser amount of reversal of the accelerating negative trend was found for those who began the study further along in the disease progression. For Object Recall, a very similar pattern was observed: an overall accelerating negative trend that abated further into the trajectory, although persons who began the study further along in their dementia progression showed a less negative rate of decline that accelerated more but abated less. As shown in the bottom panels of Figure 10.4, however, these dementia cohort effects do not substantially alter the overall dementia trajectories (i.e., unlike the age cohort effects that do substantially alter the age trajectories in the top panels of Figure 10.4).

Choosing amongst Alternative Metrics of Time

Model Fit

Thus far we have examined three competing variables by which change over time can be indexed: time since birth (age), time to death, and time to dementia. Each of these time metrics implies a different theoretical model and a different means by which different persons can be aligned (or not) onto a single trajectory. The next logical question is, how might one select among these alternative metrics of time? One way to compare alternative models is by using information criteria, such as the Akaike information criteria (AIC) and Bayesian information criteria (BIC) (as estimated under maximum likelihood, given that the models to be compared differ in both their fixed and random effects). Both the AIC and the BIC evaluate the fit of a model relative to the number of parameters estimated, but the BIC also includes a correction based on sample size that rewards greater parsimony. In comparing the AIC and BIC values across models for MMSE (Table 10.1) and Object Recall (Table 10.2), the most preferred model uses dementia as time, followed by death as time, and followed by age as time. This closely matches our earlier intuitions from comparing the mean and individual trajectories across alternative metrics of time (Figures 10.2 and 10.3); in those plots, the mean trajectory through dementia as time seemed to more closely match the individual trajectories.

Variance Components

Another criterion we can utilize to choose between models could be the amount of estimated variance in each model. Up to this point we have fo-

Considering Alternative Metrics of Time ▪ 275

cused on the fixed effects from the different time models, but the extent to which the model is a good descriptor of the individual data can also be evaluated by examining the variance left over both between persons and within persons. To facilitate comparison of variance components across models, the models reported in Tables 10.1 and 10.2 were reestimated with only residual and random intercept variances (given that a random slope implies the random intercept variance will change over time, and thus each intercept variance would only apply to the reference point on its time metric). As shown in the top of Figure 10.5, the residual variances

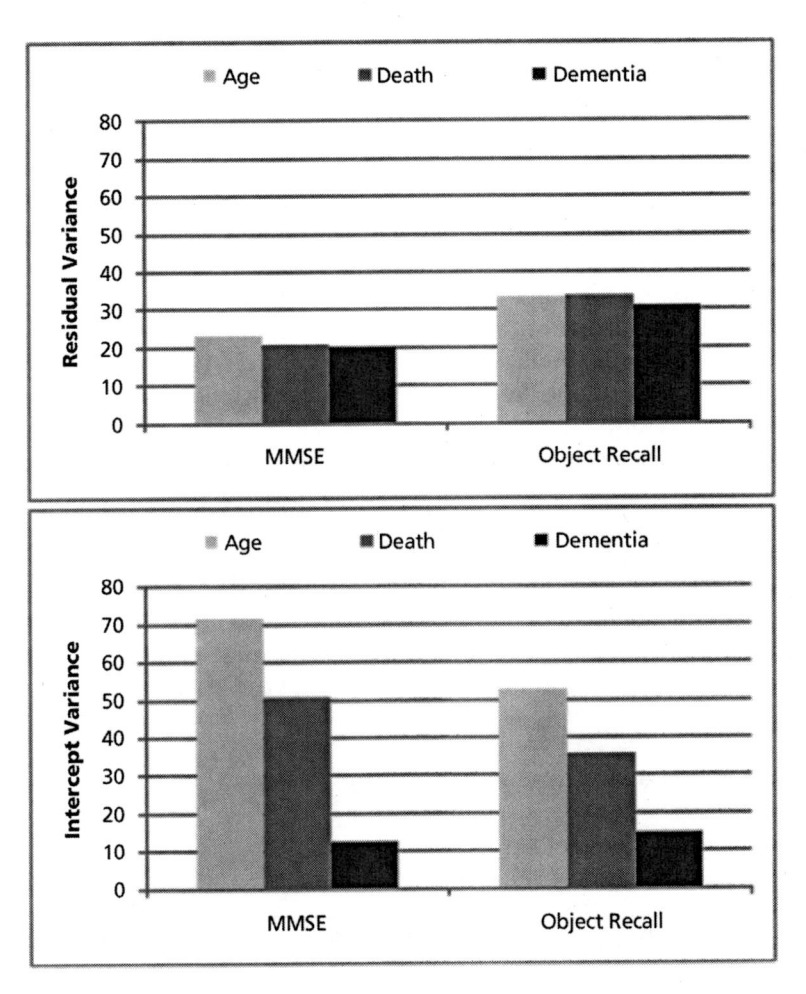

Figure 10.5 Estimated residual variance (top) and random intercept variance (bottom) for MMSE (Mini-Mental Status Exam) and Object Recall memory using age as time, death as time, and dementia diagnosis as time.

differ little between models. This is to be expected given that residual variance represents remaining within-person variation around the predicted trajectory, and within persons, these alternative time metrics are equivalent. Thus greater residual variance could be created by systematic misfit of the form of the trajectory, but these models were selected so as to maximize the fit to the data (i.e., by including higher-order polynomial functions where needed), and thus residual variance should be minimized.

In contrast, as shown in the bottom of Figure 10.5, the random intercept variances did differ markedly between models (even after controlling for cohort) due to differences in how the models aligned different persons onto the same trajectory. Thus, the intercept variance represents remaining individual differences among persons at the same point in "time" (time since birth, time to death, or time to dementia). The intercept variance is greatest for the age model, followed by the death model, followed by the dementia model, for which differences between persons are relatively minimal. Such elimination of individual differences could potentially indicate a well-fitting time metric—for instance, if dementia progression is the relevant causal process, then between-person variability should be minimized once accounting for dementia as time. The substantial age cohort effects can be taken as further evidence that age simply doesn't fit—if it did, age of entry into the study should not matter after controlling for current age (as was more the case in the time to death or time to dementia models in which cohort effects were minimal).

It is also noteworthy that no significant linear or higher-order slope variance was observed in the time to dementia models, indicating that the fixed effects were sufficient to explain the individual variation in change, too. This implies that the individual differences in change that were observed when using time since birth or time to death could have partially resulted from the misalignment of individuals with respect to time. If so, subsequent exploration of those individual differences in change would be misguided at best and misleading at worst.

What about Just Time as "Time"?

Fixed Effects of Time

Thus far we have considered the fit of three alternative metrics of time, and decided that time to dementia appears to have the best relative fit. But what about the fourth possible time metric, simply "time" itself? As discussed earlier, using time in study as time makes no theoretical statement whatsoever about what is responsible for observed change—change is simply specified relative to the baseline observation. Within persons, time is just time. In addition, because time in study contains only longitudinal

Considering Alternative Metrics of Time ▪ 277

information, concerns of testing or assuming convergence do not apply. Thus, using time in study is analogous to group-mean-centering (or person-mean-centering) in multilevel modeling, but here the level-1 effect for time is specified relative to each person's first occasion (rather than to the person's mean time).

To illustrate, consider two equivalent models of linear change across age, in which the first model is specified in terms of time and the second model is specified in terms of age, as shown in equation 10.5:

$$\text{Time Level 1: } y_{ti} = \beta_{0i} + \beta_{1i}(\text{Age}_{ti} - \text{AgeT1}_i) + e_{ti} \qquad (10.5)$$
$$\text{Time Level 2: } \beta_{0i} = \gamma_{00} + \gamma_{01}(\text{AgeT1}_i) + U_{0i}$$
$$\beta_{1i} = \gamma_{10}$$
$$\text{Age Level 1: } y_{ti} = \beta_{0i} + \beta_{1i}(\text{Age}_{ti}) + e_{ti}$$
$$\text{Age Level 2: } \beta_{0i} = \gamma_{00} + \gamma_{01}(\text{AgeT1}_i) + U_{0i}$$
$$\beta_{1i} = \gamma_{10}$$

in which the level-1 variable for current age has been replaced by current age relative to age at baseline, or simply, "time" in the time-based level-1 model. Age cohort has a main effect on the intercept only in both the time-based and age-based models. The equivalence of these two models can be shown by substituting for the β level-1 placeholders and rearranging common terms into a single-level equation, as shown in equation 10.6:

$$\text{Time-Based: } y_{ti} = \gamma_{00} + \gamma_{10}(\text{Age}_{ti} - \text{AgeT1}_i) + \gamma_{01}(\text{AgeT1}_i) + U_{0i} + e_{ti} \qquad (10.6)$$
$$\text{Time as Age: } y_{ti} = \gamma_{00} + \gamma_{10}(\text{Age}_{ti}) + (\gamma_{01} - \gamma_{10})(\text{AgeT1}_i) + U_{0i} + e_{ti}$$
$$\text{Age-Based: } y_{ti} = \gamma_{00} + \gamma_{10}(\text{Age}_{ti}) + \gamma_{01}^*(\text{AgeT1}_i) + U_{0i} + e_{ti}$$

in which the fixed intercept (γ_{00}), the fixed linear within-person effect of age (γ_{10}), the random intercept (U_{0i}), and the level-1 residual (e_{ti}) are the same across models. The effect of age cohort differs predictably across models, in that the incremental between-person effect of age cohort estimated in the age-based model of γ_{01}^* (i.e., after controlling for current age) will be produced in the time-based model by subtracting the within-person effect of age from the between-person effect of age cohort ($\gamma_{01} - \gamma_{10}$). This is because the between-person effect of age cohort in the time-based model does not control for current age (i.e., it is the total between-person effect rather than the incremental or contextual between-person effect, as in the age-based model).

Equation 10.6 describes a well-known result in the multilevel modeling literature (Snijders & Bosker, 1999): If the level-1 effect is fixed, the time-based model can be made equivalent to the age-based model, in that it will generate the same predictions and model fit (but with rearranged parameters at level 2). The same is true for any other accelerated time metric, such as time to death or time to dementia. For instance, to include time to death instead, time at level 1 would be the current time to death minus the distance from death at baseline, and distance from death at baseline would be the level-2 cohort variable. The same could be done to include time to dementia instead. Furthermore, although the level-1 age variable was not centered in equation 10.6, centering on any other constant will not change the model fit (it will only change its scale).

Although the equality in equation 10.6 is well known, what is less well known is that the fixed-effects model can also be extended to include more complex patterns of change, and yet a time-based version and an accelerated-time version (such as age) can still be made equivalent. Equation 10.7 illustrates this point by adding an interaction of age cohort with the age slope:

Time-Based: $y_{ti} = \gamma_{00} + \gamma_{10}(Age_{ti} - AgeT1_i) + \gamma_{01}(AgeT1_i) +$ (10.7)

$$\gamma_{02}(AgeT1_i)^2 + \gamma_{11}(Age_{ti} - AgeT1_i)(AgeT1_i) + U_{0i} + e_{ti}$$

Time as Age: $y_{ti} = \gamma_{00} + \gamma_{10}(Age_{ti}) + (\gamma_{01} - \gamma_{10})(AgeT1_i) +$

$$(\gamma_{02} - \gamma_{11})(AgeT1_i)^2 + \gamma_{11}(Age_{ti})(AgeT1_i) + U_{0i} + e_{ti}$$

Age-Based: $y_{ti} = \gamma_{00} + \gamma_{10}(Age_{ti}) + \gamma_{01}^*(AgeT1_i) +$

$$\gamma_{02}^*(AgeT1_i)^2 + \gamma_{11}(Age_{ti})(AgeT1_i) + U_{0i} + e_{ti}$$

in which a quadratic effect of age cohort is also added in order to maintain equivalency. In equation 10.7 the fixed intercept (γ_{00}), linear within-person effect of age (γ_{10}), age cohort by age interaction (γ_{11}), random intercept (U_{0i}), and level-1 residual (e_{ti}) are the same across models. The linear and quadratic age cohort effects differ across models in the same predictable way as before, in that the age-based model provides direct estimates of the incremental effects of age cohort (after controlling for current age), whereas the time-based model provides direct estimates of the total effects of age cohort instead (not controlling for current age). Finally, these models with a quadratic effect of age at level 1 will also be equivalent, as shown in equation 10.8:

Time-Based: $y_{ti} = \gamma_{00} + \gamma_{10}(Age_{ti} - AgeT1_i) + \gamma_{20}(Age_{ti} - AgeT1_i)^2 +$ (10.8)
$$\gamma_{01}(AgeT1_i) + \gamma_{02}(AgeT1_i)^2 +$$
$$\gamma_{11}(Age_{ti} - AgeT1_i)(AgeT1_i) +$$
$$U_{0i} + e_{ti}$$

Time as Age: $y_{ti} = \gamma_{00} + \gamma_{10}(Age_{ti}) + \gamma_{20}(Age_{ti})^2 + (\gamma_{01} - \gamma_{10})(AgeT1_i) +$
$$(\gamma_{02} + \gamma_{20} - \gamma_{11})(AgeT1_i)^2 + (\gamma_{11} - 2\gamma_{20})(Age_{ti})(AgeT1_i) +$$
$$U_{0i} + e_{ti}$$

Age-Based: $y_{ti} = \gamma_{00} + \gamma_{10}(Age_{ti}) + \gamma_{20}(Age_{ti})^2 + \gamma_{01}^*(AgeT1_i) +$
$$\gamma_{02}^*(AgeT1_i)^2 + \gamma_{11}(Age_{ti})(AgeT1_i) +$$
$$U_{0i} + e_{ti}$$

in which the fixed intercept (γ_{00}), linear within-person effect of age (γ_{10}), quadratic within-person effect of age (γ_{20}), random intercept (U_{0i}), and level-1 residual (e_{ti}) are the same across models. The age by age cohort interaction and the linear and quadratic age cohort effects differ across models in the same predictable way as before (i.e., incremental vs. total effects).

Random Effects of Time

The point of showing both the time-based and accelerated-time versions of the same model is this: So long as the level-1 effects are fixed, using time in study (i.e., rather than using direct age in an accelerated-time version) can nevertheless result in equivalent (just slightly rearranged) models. But what if the level-1 effects are random? In this case, we need only examine a simple model to see that the time-based and accelerated-time models cannot be made equivalent, as demonstrated using age as accelerated time in equation 10.9:

Time-Based: $y_{ti} = \gamma_{00} + \gamma_{10}(Age_{ti} - AgeT1_i) + \gamma_{01}(AgeT1_i) +$ (10.9)
$$U_{0i} + U_{1i}(Age_{ti} - AgeT1_i) + e_{ti}$$

Time as Age: $y_{ti} = \gamma_{00} + \gamma_{10}(Age_{ti}) + (\gamma_{01} - \gamma_{10})(AgeT1_i) +$
$$U_{0i} + U_{1i}(Age_{ti}) - U_{1i}(AgeT1_i) + e_{ti}$$

Age-Based: $y_{ti} = \gamma_{00} + \gamma_{10}(Age_{ti}) + \gamma_{01}^*(AgeT1_i) +$
$$U_{0i} + U_{1i}(Age_{ti}) + e_{ti}$$

in which a random linear slope for level-1 time/age has been added to allow individuals to differ in their linear rates of change. As shown, in the time-based model, the random slope does not include any baseline variance in time/age, whereas in the age-based model, the random slope does include baseline variance in time/age. Thus, if the level-1 effect of time/age is random, the time-based and accelerated-time models cannot be made equivalent.

So, given the need for a random slope for change over time, which model should be used—a time-based model or an accelerated-time model (e.g., age, time to death, time to dementia)? Previously we used information criteria (ML AIC and BIC) to select amongst the accelerated models (age, death, dementia), and we could do the same to select between the time-based and accelerated-time versions of each index. In this case, though, the AIC and BIC values of the time-based models were largely comparable to their accelerated-time corollaries, which seems to suggest that either version within a given metric (time or accelerated time) would be adequate (although the models for time to dementia fit relatively better than those using age or death).

In discussing this issue for multilevel models more generally, Raudenbush and Bryk (2002, pp. 143–149) present their recommendation to group-mean-center level-1 effects with random slopes, which is analogous to recommending the time-based model variants here. To place their rationale in this context, they note that when substantial variation is observed between persons in the accelerated time metric at baseline, the random intercept variance will likely be estimated with differential precision in the time-based and accelerated-time variants of the same model because of its different interpretation in each. In the time-based model variant, the intercept variance represents individual differences at baseline (or when time = 0), whereas in the accelerated-time model variant, the intercept variance represents individual differences when the accelerated-time metric is 0 (e.g., age 84 or 6 years prior to death). Thus, the intercept in the accelerated-time model variant will require greater extrapolation for those cases in which 0 is not actually observed, resulting in lower reliability and greater shrinkage of the intercept toward the mean. That intercept shrinkage can cause the individual slopes to become homogenized, with the result that the slope variance for the level-1 random effect will be smaller than it should be in the accelerated-time model variants, but accurately estimated in the time-based model variants.

This conjecture was tested in the example data by comparing the slope variance estimates from equation 10.8, in which the time-based versions and accelerated-time versions of the age and death models were specified equivalently in terms of fixed effects, and differed only in their random slopes. The dementia models were not included given that no slope variance

Considering Alternative Metrics of Time ▪ 281

was found. As shown in Figure 10.6, the random slope variance was indeed 33–77% larger in the time-based model variants than in the corresponding accelerated-time variants for both the age and death models, suggesting that the downward bias described by Raudenbush and Bryk (2002) was found in these example data as well. Unless the true model parameters are

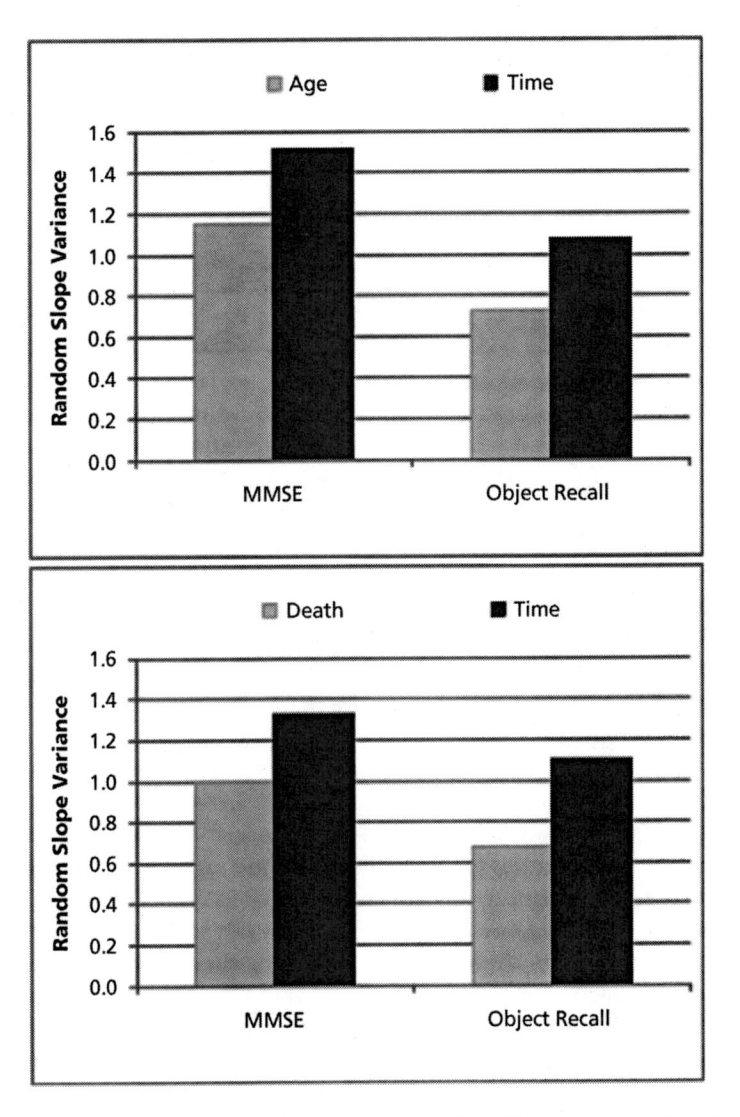

Figure 10.6 Estimated slope variance for MMSE (Mini-Mental Status Exam) and Object Recall memory across the time-based and accelerated-time models using age as time and death as time.

known, however, we cannot be certain if the slope variance in the accelerated-time models was in fact underestimated, or if the greater slope variance reported in the time-based models was actually overestimated instead.

However, these two alternative explanations have also been examined by the author via simulation (Hoffman & Templin, 2008). These simulation results (available upon request) indicated that when data were simulated using a time-based model but analyzed using an accelerated-time model instead, the slope variance was indeed underestimated by up to 50% across conditions, with larger bias found for the conditions with fewer occasions of measurement and with greater variance in the accelerated-time variable at baseline. Given that downward bias in the slope variance should generally limit the power to detect significant predictors of change, this suggests that the time-based versions of the accelerated-time models should be preferred.

Alternative Metrics of Time as Competing Theories

Let us summarize what we have learned so far about using time as "time": if used by itself, time in study is an uninformative time metric, in that change is specified relative to the baseline value (and not relative to a given distance from birth, death, or diagnosis). To make time in study informative for representing differential processes or cause of change, equations 10.5–10.9 paired time in study (at level 1) with age at baseline (age cohort at level 2) in order to reproduce the parameters from the age as time models. Time to death at baseline or time to dementia at baseline could have similarly been included instead at level 2 in order to reproduce those alternative time models. Furthermore, although the time-based and accelerated-time model variants can be made equivalent in their fixed effects, they cannot be made equivalent in their random effects, and it is in accurately quantifying the random slope variance that the time-based model variants seem to have an edge.

But perhaps the most compelling argument for using time as "time" comes from the potential to allow different time metrics (representing different causes of change) to directly compete (or interact) with one another. For instance, why do some people begin the study with lower levels of cognition? Is it their age, distance from death, or their amount of dementia progression? Each time metric's baseline value could be included at level 2 as a competing main effect in order to predict the individual intercepts. Similarly, why do some people decline more rapidly than others? Each time metric's baseline value could also be included as a competing interaction with time in study to also predict the individual slopes. Thus, by using just time as "time" we can obtain a clear and direct estimate of the unique contribution of each alternative temporal process, and we can do so without

Considering Alternative Metrics of Time ▪ 283

any making any assumptions about (or conducting tests for) convergence of its between- and within-person effects.

To illustrate, a final time-as-time model was estimated, as shown in equation 10.10:

Level 1: $y_{ti} = \beta_{0i} + \beta_{1i}(\text{Time}_{ti}) + e_{ti}$ (10.10)

Level 2: $\beta_{0i} = \gamma_{00} + \gamma_{01}(\text{AgeT1}_i) + \gamma_{02}(\text{DeathT1}_i) + \gamma_{03}(\text{DemT1}_i) + U_{0i}$

$\beta_{1i} = \gamma_{10} + \gamma_{11}(\text{AgeT1}_i) + \gamma_{12}(\text{DeathT1}_i) + \gamma_{13}(\text{DemT1}_i) + U_{1i}$

in which time in study was included at level 1 and in which effects of each alternative time metric (age, death, and dementia) were also included for the intercept and linear time slope (the quadratic time slopes were not significant and were thus not included). Results are given in Table 10.3. As shown in the second column for MMSE, only dementia progression at baseline was significantly related to a lower initial score, and only being closer to death at baseline was significantly related to a greater rate of decline. As shown in the third column for Object Recall, age, time to death, and time

TABLE 10.3 Model Parameters Using Multiple Metrics of Time

Model parameters	Mini-Mental Status Exam Est	SE	Object Recall Est	SE
Fixed effects:				
Intercept (γ_{00})	53.07**	0.50	51.81**	0.73
Linear time slope (γ_{10})	−2.17**	0.14	−1.80**	0.20
Age cohort on intercept (γ_{01})	−0.26	0.15	−0.62**	0.22
Age cohort on slope (γ_{11})	−0.03	0.05	0.13*	0.06
Death cohort on intercept (γ_{02})	−0.06	0.16	−0.56*	0.24
Death cohort on slope (γ_{12})	−0.21**	0.05	−0.06	0.06
Dementia cohort on intercept (γ_{03})	−1.48**	0.11	−1.18**	0.17
Dementia cohort on slope (γ_{13})	0.03	0.03	0.00	0.05
Variance components:				
Residual variance (σ_e^2)	14.50**	1.37	25.96**	2.67
Intercept variance ($\tau_{U_0}^2$)	22.90**	3.89	31.04**	6.42
Linear slope variance ($\tau_{U_1}^2$)	1.18**	0.28	0.87**	0.34
Intercept slope covariance ($\tau_{U_{01}}$)	−2.84**	0.91	−3.53**	1.24
Deviance (−2LL)	3280		2728	
AIC	3304		2752	
BIC	3342		2790	

Note: * $p < .05$, ** $p < .001$. LL, log likelihood; AIC, Akaike information criteria; BIC, Bayesian information criteria. *Cohort* represents the value of each time variable at baseline.

to dementia at baseline were each uniquely related to lower initial memory scores, with the largest effect (in difference per year) found for dementia. Although age significantly predicted rate of decline, older persons were actually predicted to decline less.

CONCLUSIONS

The focus of this chapter was to identify and describe the decisions surrounding the use of multiple potential ways of clocking time in longitudinal studies; that is, alternative metrics of time. Although the decision of what "time" should be is likely to be made on theoretical grounds, in many instances multiple processes may potentially be responsible for observed change, and thus multiple time metrics may need to be considered as a result. Thus, in addition to theoretically motivated choices for time, empirical indices such as differential model fit (ML AIC and BIC) and estimates of between-person heterogeneity may also be useful in comparing amongst multiple plausible metrics of time. In particular, one needs to be aware that greater heterogeneity between persons can be partially due to a misalignment of different individuals with respect to time and, if so, exploring predictors of this heterogeneity may not be informative.

Complicating matters, however, is that persons may differ in "time" at the beginning of a study (i.e., if time is accelerated so that the range of time covered is greater than that observed for any one individual). In this case, one needs to attend to the possibility that the cross-sectional and longitudinal effects of accelerated time may differ, and thus to test for their convergence accordingly. Although models were presented in this chapter to do so (e.g., equation 10.4), these models test for nonconvergence of a particular form (e.g., only a linear effect of age cohort on each growth term), and thus do not preclude the necessity of more complex models to fully disentangle the between- and within-person effects of time (and their possible interactions).

These issues led us to consider a simpler but potentially more useful metric: "time" itself. Although at face value it is the most uninformative choice, specifying time as a function of study duration (i.e., time from baseline) seems to have several advantages. First, because the pattern of change to be approximated by the fixed effects in a time-based model is based solely on within-person variance (and the number of occasions per person), the overall functional form of change can likely be described more parsimoniously (i.e., a linear model may be sufficient given only three or four occasions per person). But when used in combination with person-level predictors representing initial status on other informative metrics of time (e.g., age, time to death, time to dementia), even highly complex trajectories can be represented by a time-based model, given that time-based and accelerated-time versions of the same model can be made equivalent in terms of their fixed effects. In addition, because the random slope variance can be downwardly biased in accelerated-time models, using time-based model variants instead may better recover the true amount of individual differences in change. Furthermore, using time as "time" also permits the inclusion of participants who have not experienced a target event upon which a time metric would otherwise be constructed. For instance, persons without a dementia diagnosis could not be included in a time to dementia model, although they could be included in a time in study model (in which dementia presence and timing could still be included via level-2 predictors).

Finally, perhaps the most compelling support for the use of time as "time" is the fact that it can never be wrong! The use of time in study as time makes no assumptions about why individuals differ a priori, which can be a good thing in absence of strong theory (or when that theory is incorrect). In addition, because time is based solely on longitudinal information, one need not worry about convergence. For instance, in the example data, the between- and within-person effects of age did not converge (i.e., there were effects of age cohort in addition to current age), and the use of age as time produced a pattern of fixed effects that ultimately described the individual data very poorly. This is because using age as time aligned different individuals along a time metric with questionable relevance. In contrast, by using time in study we can instead frame the fit of alternative time metrics as a series of testable hypotheses and easily compare the relative contributions of each. Although the other time metrics could also be added as level-2 predictors in the accelerated time models (e.g., one could estimate an age as time model with time to death as a level-2 predictor), the results would ultimately be less straightforward to interpret, given that the level-2 effects of the accelerated time metric are incremental (i.e., age cohort effects after controlling for current age) whereas the level-2 effects of the other metrics would be total (i.e., total death cohort effects, not after controlling for current years to death), and that age nonconvergence could still be a problem.

In closing, the issues surrounding what time should be and how time should be specified in statistical models for change can be quite complicated. Nevertheless, such deliberations are an important precursor to drawing useful conclusions from longitudinal data, and I hope this chapter will be helpful for those contemplating what time (it) is in their own work.

ACKNOWLEDGMENTS

I would like to thank Scott Hofer, Andrea Piccinin, and Martin Sliwinski for their many helpful discussions and insights on this topic; Jonathan Templin for his helpful feedback on earlier drafts; and Boo Johansson for the use of the OCTO-Twin data in the example analyses.

REFERENCES

Baltes, P.B., Cornelius, S. W., & Nesselroade, J. R. (1979). Cohort effects in developmental psychology. In J. R. Nesselroade & P. B. Baltes (Eds.), *Longitudinal research in the study of behavior and development* (pp. 61–87). New York: Academic Press.

Baltes, P. B., & Nesselroade, J. R. (1979). History and rationale of longitudinal research. In J. R. Nesselroade & P. B. Baltes (Eds.), *Longitudinal research in the study of behavior and development* (pp. 1–39). New York: Academic Press.

Bell, R. Q. (1953). Convergence: An accelerated longitudinal approach. *Child Development, 24*, 145–152.

Folstein, M. F, Folstein, S. E., & McHugh, P. R. (1975). "Mini-Mental State": A practical method for grading the cognitive status of patients for the clinician. *Journal of Psychiatric Research, 17*, 189–198.

Hedeker, D., & Gibbons, R. D. (2006). *Longitudinal data analysis.* New York: Wiley.

Hofer, S. M., & Sliwinski, M. J. (2006). Design and analysis of longitudinal studies of aging. In J. E. Birren & K. W. Schaie (Eds.), *Handbook of the psychology of aging* (6th ed., pp. 15–37). San Diego, CA: Academic Press.

Hoffman, L., & Stawski, R. (2009). Persons as contexts: Evaluating between-person and within-person effects in longitudinal analysis. *Research in Human Development, 6*, 97–100.

Hoffman, L., & Templin, J. L. (2008, April). *The impact of alternative specifications of time on examining individual differences in change.* Poster presented at the Cognitive Aging Conference, Atlanta, GA.

Johansson, B. (1988). *The MIR-Memory in-Reality Test.* Stockholm, Sweden: Author.

Johansson, B., Hofer, S. M., Allaire, J. C., Maldonado-Molina, M., Piccinin, A. M., Berg, S., et al. (2004). Change in memory and cognitive functioning in the oldest-old: The effects of proximity to death in genetically related individuals over a six-year period. *Psychology and Aging, 19,*145–156.

Johansson, B., Whitfield, K., Pedersen, N. L., Hofer, S. M., Ahern, F., & McClearn, G. E. (1999). Origins of individual differences in episodic memory in the oldest-old: A population-based study of identical and same-sex fraternal twins aged 80 and older. Journal of Gerontology: *Psychological Sciences, 54B*, P173-P179.

McArdle, J. J., & Bell, R. Q. (2000). An introduction to latent growth curve models for developmental data analysis. In T. D. Little, K. U. Schnabel, & J. Baumert (Eds.), *Modeling longitudinal and multilevel data* (pp. 69–107). Mahwah, NJ: Erlbaum.

Raudenbush, S. W., & Bryk, A. S. (2002). *Hierarchical linear models: Applications and data analysis methods* (2nd ed.). Thousand Oaks, CA: Sage.

Schaie, K. W. (1965). A general model for the study of developmental problems. *Psychological Bulletin, 64*, 92–107.

Schaie, K. W. (2008). Historical patterns and processes of cognitive aging. In S. M. Hofer & D. F. Alwin (Eds.), *Handbook of cognitive aging: Interdisciplinary perspectives* (pp. 368–383). Thousand Oaks, CA: Sage.

Sliwinski, M. J., Hoffman, L., & Hofer, S. M. (2010). Evaluating convergence of within-person change and between-person age differences in age-heterogeneous longitudinal studies. *Research in Human Development, 7*, 45–60.

Snijders, T. A. B., & Bosker, R. (1999). *Multilevel analysis.* Thousand Oaks, CA: Sage.

CHAPTER 11

VALID MEASUREMENT WITHOUT FACTORIAL INVARIANCE

A Longitudinal Example

Michael C. Edwards
The Ohio State University

Robert J. Wirth
Vector Psychometric Group, LLC

INTRODUCTION

Measurement

At its most basic level, measurement is the process of using observable qualities of a construct to assign a number reflecting those observable qualities. Although it is essential that the assigning of numbers be based on some observable feature(s), the construct itself may or may not be directly observable. Take height, for example. By using a ruler we are able to numerically state how tall someone is in a metric that we have chosen. We can observe height, but there is useful precision in being able to label it with a specific number. Consider temperature as another example. To determine if a child has a fever, one could use a thermometer. In a mercury thermometer, the thing we are interested in (temperature) causes a change in the thing we can see (the mercury in the thermometer). We cannot directly see a child's temperature—our understanding about temperature is possible through the quantification of observable phenomena. By defining a scale that is anchored to other observable behaviors (e.g., freezing and boiling of water), we are able to communicate about temperature in a consistent and standard way. However, we must also consider pressure, which affects the way in which mercury changes in response to temperature. If we are able to measure pressure, we can account for the effect it has on our measurement of temperature. Conversely, if we do not know the pressure in a current situation, but know the pressure from our original measurements, by assessing something that is the same temperature in both conditions, we can deduce the difference in pressure between the two conditions.

In the social and health sciences the quantities we are interested in studying are seldom height and temperature, but rather constructs such as math ability, cognitive functioning, depression, or delinquency. Although these constructs differ in important ways from those of height and temperature, there are also conceptual similarities. We desire a way to assign a number, based on something observable, that reflects an individual's standing on a construct. Or, as more eloquently stated by Lord and Novick (1968):

> Usually a well-developed theory contains one or more formal models which give concrete structure to the general concepts of the theory. These models may be viewed as explications of portions of the general theory. Such models, in turn, are connected systematically with directly observable phenomena. The function of such models is to permit the logical deduction of general and specific relationships that have not been empirically demonstrated but that may be demonstrable. (p. 15)

Creating mathematical and statistical models that achieve this goal has been a primary interest of quantitative psychologists for the past (roughly) 110 years. One of the most widely known contributions of psychometricians is classical test theory (CTT). In its most basic form, CTT can be represented as

$$x_i = \tau_i + e_i, \tag{11.1}$$

where, for the ith person, x_i is the observed score, τ_i is the true score, and e_i is the error. It is common to make three additional assumptions such that

$$E(x_i) = \tau_i, \tag{11.2}$$

$$E(e_i) = 0, \quad (11.3)$$

$$\sigma_{\tau e} = 0, \quad (11.4)$$

where $E(\ )$ is the expected value and $\sigma_{\tau e}$ is the covariation between the true score and the error. In words, equations 11.2–11.4 state that the average observed score is the true score, the average error is zero, and the true score and the error are not correlated. The true score can be understood from (at least) two different perspectives. Technically speaking, it is an expected value; it is the score we expect a person to obtain if they took the test[1] infinitely many times and we averaged over those repeated assessments. Second, we can think about it conceptually as the person's actual level of the construct we are measuring. Put another way, it is the score we would expect to observe if we could measure the construct without error.

The CTT model outlined above has been very useful, but it has some critical limitations. Equation 11.1 is the most common way in which true score theory (analogous to CTT) is described—unfortunately, it is wrong. A more accurate representation of equation 11.1 would be

$$x_{ik} = \tau_{ik} + e_{ik}, \quad (11.5)$$

where all terms are as previously described, with a new k index that indicates test. Thus, x_{ik} is the observed score for person i on test k. This seems like a very minor omission until the consequences are fully considered. The true score then is *not* the actual level of the trait we're measuring. It is the actual level of the trait we're measuring for person i on scale k. If we used a different test (or even a subset of items from that test) every person could have a different true score. This does not match with our conceptual expectations of measurement—an individual's true level of depression should not change as a function of the scale being used to assess it. Without some consistency in scaling and meaning, modeling such scores longitudinally would be extremely difficult.

Usefulness of Latent Variables

A latent variable (according to one of many possible definitions) is an unobservable construct assumed to have some distribution in the population (Bollen, 2002). Based on this definition, CTT can be thought of as a latent variable model (LVM), as the true score described above fits into this definition. If true scores are viewed as latent variables it must be admitted that they are not particularly useful ones. The specificity of the true score (applies to only a single scale by person interaction) means that even conceptually there is no construct outside/beyond the instrument used to assess it. If we are willing to move into more explicitly latent variable-based measurement models we can overcome this disadvantage while simultaneously accruing other useful benefits.

We introduce factor analysis and item response theory (IRT) briefly in this section. Numerous manuscript- and book-length treatments of both exist and are of extremely high quality. Among our favorites are Browne (2001), Fabrigar, Wegener, MacCallum, and Strahan (1999), and MacCallum (2009) for exploratory factor analysis (EFA); Bollen (1989) and MacCallum (2009) for confirmatory factor analysis (CFA); and Edwards (2009), Thissen and Orlando (2001), and Thissen and Steinberg (2009) for IRT.

Stated very simply, factor analysis is a series of regressions where the predictor is latent. Factor loadings are analogous to regression coefficients (i.e., slopes) and indicate how large a change is expected in a particular measured variable given a one-unit increase in the latent construct. Just like regression, if the outcome is categorical (e.g., a yes/no response to an item on a scale), a nonlinear model must be used. Logistic regression is to linear regression as IRT is to factor analysis—IRT is a nonlinear factor analysis model (Wirth & Edwards, 2007). For example, one of the more widely used IRT models, the two-parameter logistic model (2PLM), can be written as

$$P(x_{ij}=1|\theta_i) = \frac{1}{1+\exp[-a_j(\theta_i - b_j)]}, \quad (11.6)$$

where x_{ij} is the observed response from person i to item j, θ_i is the latent score for person i, a_j is the slope for item j, and b_j is the severity parameter for item j. This bears a strong similarity to logistic regression models, with the exception of the presence of the latent variable (θ). Equation 11.6 states that the probability of someone endorsing an item (the 2PLM is for dichotomous responses) is a (nonlinear) function of that person's level of the construct (θ_i) and properties of the item (a_j and b_j). It is typically assumed that the latent construct follows a standard normal distribution. Higher slopes correspond to items that are more strongly influenced by the latent trait. The severity parameters indicate the point along the latent continuum where an individual has a 50% chance of endorsing a particular item. Thus, an item with a b-value of –1.5 has a 50% chance of being endorsed by someone who is 1.5 standard deviations below the mean.

An alternative way to present the 2PLM is

$$P(x_{ij}=1|\theta_i) = \frac{1}{1+\exp[d_j - a_j\theta_i]}, \quad (11.7)$$

where all parameters are as previously defined with the exception of d_j, which is an intercept parameter equal to the product of a_j and b_j. The only difference between equation 11.7 and equation 11.6 is that the a_j term is distributed out and the resulting $a_j b_j$ term is relabeled d_j. Although this is not a common way to write the unidimensional 2PLM, it has advantages when exploring multidimensional versions of this model (as we shall do in a subsequent section).

The graded response model (GRM; Samejima, 1969) is an extension of the 2PLM, which can accommodate more than two ordered categories. The GRM defines the probability of choosing a particular response category as

$$P(x_{ij} = c \mid \theta_i) = \frac{1}{1+\exp[-a_j(\theta_i - b_{jc})]} - \frac{1}{1+\exp[-a_j(\theta_i - b_{jc+1})]}, \quad (11.8)$$

where c is the observed response category chosen and all other terms are as previously defined. The severity parameters now have an additional subscript as there are $C-1$ of these, where C is the total number of response options. This is a cursory description of the GRM; for a more complete description, see Thissen, Nelson, Rosa, and McLeod (2001).

The 2PLM and GRM are unidimensional models, as they posit the existence of only one latent trait. More complicated multidimensional models exist (Cai, 2010a; Edwards, 2010), which can accommodate situations where the constructs in question are more dimensionally complex. Estimation for some of these multidimensional models has been difficult, but recent advances in estimation and computation, along with the increasing availability of software, should make these models more accessible.

As our modeling capabilities increase, we will be better able to choose models that more faithfully reflect our conceptualizations of constructs we are interested in studying. In some cases, a construct cannot be boiled down (fruitfully) into a single number. Multidimensional models recognize that any given item may be measuring more than one thing. In situations such as this, item responses can be influenced by more than one latent construct. This results in individual items having more than one slope—there is a separate slope for each construct to which an item is related. Multidimensional models are different from their unidimensional analogs in other respects as well, but for the purposes of this chapter these more complicated issues can be ignored. The interested reader is referred to Edwards (2010) and Cai (2010b) for more thorough treatments of these models.

A good starting place to introduce multidimensional item response theory (MIRT) is a simple two-dimensional extension of the 2PLM, which, expanding on equation 11.7, would look like

$$P(x_{ij} = 1 \mid \theta_i) = \frac{1}{1+\exp[d_j - a_{1j}\theta_{1i} - a_{2j}\theta_{2i}]}, \quad (11.9)$$

where all terms are as previously defined with the addition of a vector of latent scores for each individual (θ_i) and a new subscript on slopes and latent scores to track which of two latent dimensions each one corresponds to. Verbally, this model states that the probability of someone endorsing an item is a (nonlinear) function of that person's level on two constructs (θ_{1i}, θ_{2i}) and properties of the item (a_{1j}, a_{2j}, and d_j). Consider an item that is influenced by both anxiety and depression. In that instance the probability that someone endorses this particular item is a function of their individual levels of anxiety and depression and how the constructs of anxiety and depression are related to this particular item.

In other instances the two factors influencing an individual's probability of endorsing a question are not of equal value. One factor may be of primary influence while another is considered a "nuisance" factor. One example of this would be depression items that consider somatic symptoms. If the goal is to assess depression, overall differences in general health may cause individuals to endorse somatic items for reasons other than their level of depression. If general health is not modeled, then endorsement of this item will be interpreted as evidence of increased depression. In such a case a MIRT model may be used to account for the influence of general health and provide a more "pure" depression score.

The model we describe here, a multidimensional 2PLM, is a very simple example. Multidimensional analogs exist for almost all IRT models (of which there are many) and these can expand to accommodate any number of factors. As the number of factors increases, the difficulty of parameter estimation increases. Recent advances in estimation have allowed us much greater flexibility in our measurement models and we now have the capacity to use models with many latent variables. This has led to an expansion of the kinds of situations our measurement models are able to accurately represent. This is an important point, as described in greater detail in the next section.

STATISTICAL VALIDITY

The concepts of reliability and validity are central to measurement. As stated by Thissen and Wainer (2001), "we can define *validity* as measuring the right thing, and *reliability* as measuring the thing right" (p. 11). In any framework, CTT or otherwise, the reliability of scores relates to the proportion of observed variability that is "true" variability. In CTT this relates to true score variance as opposed to error variance. The observed variance is a combination of these two entities, and the higher the proportion of observed variance that is attributable to true score variance, the higher the reliability. Coefficient α (Cronbach, 1951) is the most commonly used statistic to estimate this quantity within the CTT framework. Different measures are used to assess score reliability in IRT or factor-analytic frameworks, but the basic ideas are the same.

Validity issues are somewhat tougher to deal with. As defined by Messick (1993), "Validity is an integrated evaluative judgment of the degree to which empirical evidence and theoretical rationales support the *adequacy* and *appropriateness* of *inferences* and *actions* based on test scores or other modes of assessment" (p. 13). There is a rich literature on validity and there exists a fairly well-established taxonomy of types of validity evidence (e.g., content, convergent, discriminant). We would like to propose making a distinction between substantive and statistical types of validity. The substantive domain captures much of what already exists in terms of validity—it focuses on how scores relate to the outside world. Substantive validity focuses on the collection of evidence that we are measuring what we claim to be measuring and includes common types of validity such as content and construct validity. Statistical validity is the extent to which the measurement model we are using provides an accurate representation of the construct(s) we wish to measure.

Using the concepts of CTT and IRT, we can illustrate one way in which, in our view, IRT has the potential to provide more statistically valid scores/models. In CTT, individual estimates are based on unit weighted combinations of item responses—endorsing an item has the same impact on the total score regardless of the item's content. In speaking with researchers, this is not usually in line with how they conceptualize the constructs they are intending to study. In the case of depression, it seems desirable to have a measurement model that is capable of differentially weighting endorsements of "I felt blue" and "I tried to commit suicide." Although ad-hoc weights can be added in the CTT framework, they are external to the model. If the construct a researcher is trying to study is conceptualized such that different symptoms (we use this term generically here) imply different levels of severity, a model that does not accommodate such features (such as a CTT model) does not offer a statistically valid representation of the construct.

In the remainder of this chapter we describe other situations where issues of statistical validity highlight strengths of LVMs. We begin with a discussion of studying latent constructs longitudinally before moving into a brief discussion of measurement invariance. Although there is a substantial literature on invariance in the structural equation modeling (SEM) framework, many of the core conclusions in this literature stand in stark contrast to literature (and common practice) in the IRT framework. In this chapter we demonstrate that the level of invariance needed to make valid inferences is far less than what has been previously suggested. Through simulated examples we demonstrate that, with modern statistical techniques, it is not even necessary that the same number of constructs exists over occasions of measurement. We close with some concluding thoughts about the fruitful uses of these models in practice.

STUDYING LATENT CONSTRUCTS LONGITUDINALLY

Researchers who are interested in studying a construct over time face unique challenges from a measurement perspective (Bauer & Hussong, 2009; Curran, 2009; Curran & Hussong, 2009). If the time frame is long enough, or in a developmentally active period, the construct itself can evolve within the assessment window. There are several ways this can happen. First, the items that appropriately assess a construct could change as the context the individual inhabits shifts. For example, it is perfectly reasonable to ask a school-age child about school-based behaviors, but not so for a 45-year-old who has been out of school for over a quarter century. In this case, the construct may not have changed, but the relevant indicators of the construct may have. This can lead to a second difficulty: changing dimensionality. Adding a block of items that are school-specific to a set of non-school-specific items may create an additional "school" factor due to the shared context of the school items. This is not to say that these items do not *also* measure the construct of interest, but that they can in fact be measuring two constructs. In most cases, the school factor is not of primary interest. If it is not modeled properly, however, variance attributable to this factor will influence estimates and inferences about the primary construct. A model that does not account for the multiple sources of variation in the item responses would be less statistically valid.

In other cases, a construct may change over time whereby new dimensions "grow out" of the existing ones. In such cases, the original primary factor is more or less intact. We currently have potentially statistically valid measurement models to handle "growing" (or "shrinking") dimensions when the primary factor remains intact. Of course, it also seems entirely possible that at some ages a construct is, for example, one dimension and at another age it is two. This kind of change poses interesting challenges both from a measurement perspective and a conceptual one. In instances where a unitary construct bifurcates at some point in time, it is not immediately clear how to best obtain a statistically valid model. In the following sections we elaborate on issues of changing relationships between indicators and constructs (measurement noninvariance) and changing dimensionality.

Measurement Invariance

In factor analysis, the stability of relations between indicators and factors (and among factors) across groups is known as *measurement invariance*. If these relations are not stable, the cumbersome term *measurement noninvariance* has been frequently used. The same concept in the IRT framework is referred to as *differential item functioning* (DIF) and we rely primarily on this nomenclature throughout much of the remainder of the chapter. The term "groups" used above is intentionally vague. In nonlongitudinal settings, groups can be defined as gender, ethnicity, age, pre- and postexperiment, and so forth. In longitudinal settings it is common for groups to correspond to time.[2] A DIF analysis in this context examines whether the way in which items relate to the construct is stable over time. Detection of DIF implies that the item's relation to the construct has changed in some way. In the IRT framework (e.g., 2PLM, GRM) we look for DIF in the a and b parameters. DIF in the slopes indicates that the strength of the relation between the latent construct and an item has changed. DIF in the severity parameters indicates that an item has become a more or less severe indicator of the latent construct.

Failing to account for DIF can bias our estimates of an individual's status on the construct of interest. For example, if a subset of items are more severe for women than for men (i.e., higher b-values), we would see lower scores among women than men. Men and women may, in fact, have *the exact same distribution of the construct*, yet their observed distributions could be markedly different. Detection of DIF is its own area of research and there are many methods in existence. If DIF is present, and can be detected, it is actually quite easy to deal with. If an item behaves differently across time (or by group, such as gender), the item can be allowed to have differing parameters at each time of assessment. As long as a core set of invariant items exist (usually called an anchor), it is possible to keep comparable metrics even when other items exhibit DIF.

The mechanism through which DIF can be accommodated is called *linking* in the IRT literature. Although linking is usually thought about in educational situations where there are nonoverlapping item sets (except for an anchor), it applies equally well to noneducational situations. To an IRT model, there is no difference between an item with DIF and two different items—all the model "knows" about an item is its parameters. As far as IRT models are concerned, different parameters mean different items. By having a set of items that remain invariant over time, it is possible to use those items to place any remaining items on the same scale (i.e., in the same metric). This ensures that a score of one at time 1 means the same thing as a score of one at time 2. Linking has been standard practice in education for decades. It forms the backbone of nearly every high-stakes educational test in the United States. Despite the vast literature on DIF, there has been little discussion of the fact that, at its core, it is just an application of linking. The substantive implications are quite different, but methodologically, the models are identical. The natural way in which linking occurs in IRT—indeed, given the proper data structure, it is automatic—is arguably its most important and compelling feature. As we shall see in the next section, linking can deal with situations even more complex than DIF.

Differential Dimensionality

As previously mentioned, it seems plausible that in some, perhaps many, longitudinal situations the dimensionality of a construct could shift over time. One possible cause for such a change is due to context-specific items. In this case, the construct itself has not changed dimensionality, but the indicators used to measure that construct now measure something else as well. Items based on manifestations of delinquency in school will be indicators of delinquency, but they may additionally represent something about the school environment. The same ideas could be applied to multiple raters. Although parents and clinicians are (ostensibly) reporting about the same construct, each reporter is responsible for predictable variance in the responses. A longitudinal study that has parents, clinicians, multiple teachers, and even target reporting used at different phases would encounter a dynamic and dimensionally complex situation. In keeping with the terminology of DIF, we have labeled this phenomenon *differential dimensionality*.

From a modeling perspective, DIF and differential dimensionality are quite distinct. From a statistical validity standpoint they both pose serious threats to a model's ability to provide scores that faithfully represent our conceptualization of a construct. In our own experience, the most common form of differential dimensionality is induced by shifting contexts where behavior is observed: Children can move from a time period when they are primarily in the home to a time period where they are in school, young adults can move from school (or college) into a work environment, and older adults can move from a work environment to retirement. For many constructs, there are context-specific questions that exist to capture salient behaviors. Edwards and Wirth (2009) described in detail, and demonstrated using simulated data, that it is possible to recover longitudinal trends while using different items at different occasions of measurement. Here, we extend these ideas to situations where changing items alters the latent dimensionality. As was true with changing item sets in the unidimensional case, linking will once again allow us to maintain a comparable metric over occasions of measurement in the multidimensional case.

EXAMPLES OF DIFFERENTIAL DIMENSIONALITY USING SIMULATED DATA

The examples in this chapter focus on estimating the measurement model for a hypothetical depression scale[3] over three assessment periods (times 1, 2, and 3). The items used on this hypothetical scale are, in part, a function of the respondent's age (pediatric, adult, and geriatric populations). As can be seen in Figure 11.1, 10 of the items (items 1–10) are used regardless of age.

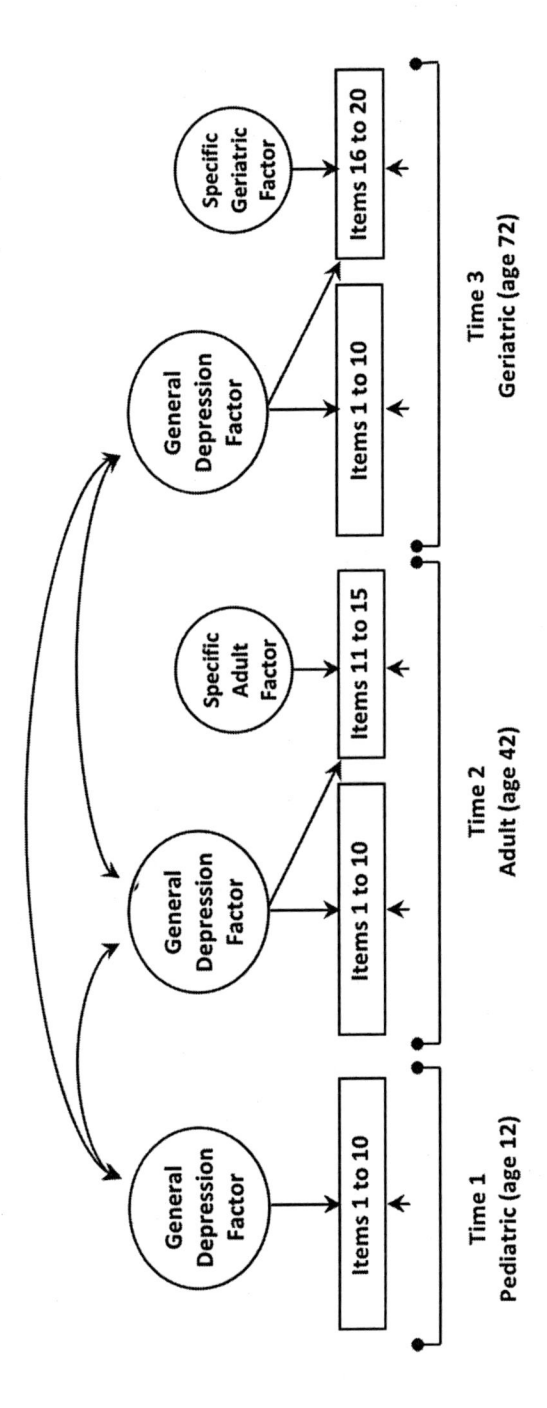

Valid Measurement Without Factorial Invariance ■ 299

Figure 11.1 A graphical representation of a hypothetical longitudinal model of depression where the items and dimensionality of the measurement model changes from time 1 (age 12) to time 2 (age 42) and then again at time 3 (age 72). Circles denote primary and specific factors (constructs). Rectangles represent sets of items. Single-headed arrows originating from a circle and ending at a rectangle denote directional influence (sets of item slopes where there is a unique slope for every item listed in the rectangle). Single-headed arrows originating from space and ending at a rectangle denotes a set of error variances (one for each item listed in the rectangle). Dual-headed arrows between circles denote a nonzero covariance between those two factors.

Five additional items are used when assessing adults. These five items (items 11–15) help to assess depression that may arise from common adult life stressors (e.g., work, sick parents). Because these five items share something in common (life stressors common in adulthood) beyond general depression, there is a dependency among these new items that can be accounted for by the addition of a specific "adult" factor. When individuals are older and move into the geriatric population, the original 10 items are still used, the five adult-specific items are no longer relevant, but now five new items (items 16–20) are included in the assessment. Just as with the five adult-specific items, these five geriatric-specific items share a commonality besides depression. For this reason, the five geriatric items also require a specific factor to account for the additional item dependencies. As can be seen in Figure 11.1, if individuals are assessed at three ages (say, 12, 42, and 72 years of age), the item sets making up the scale and the dimensionality of the scale may change over time. The time-1 assessment (age 12, pediatrics) includes just 10 items. The time-2 assessment (age 42, adult) includes 15 items, 10 of which were seen at age 12 and five of which are adult-specific items. The time-3 assessment (age 72, geriatrics) includes 15 items, 10 of which were seen at ages 12 and 42 and five of which are geriatric specific. The measurement model thus changes from a one-dimensional model at time 1 to a two-dimensional model at time 2. The model remains two-dimensional at time 3, but the meaning of the second specific factor changes from time 2 to time 3.

Data Generation

The model used to generate the data for the following example was a direct extension of the model outlined above and shown graphically in Figure 11.1. Item parameters (see Table 11.1) were generated from distributions representative of the items found in the psychological literature (Hill, 2004). While the items were all assumed to be invariant over time (i.e., did not show age DIF), each of the items was generated to have a unique relation to the construct of depression. That is, as is commonly found in practice, the slopes and severity parameters varied across items. The data were generated via a multidimensional version of the GRM and were created to correspond to items with five response alternatives. Although there are several ways the multidimensional GRM can be written, the following is consistent with the unidimensional representation given in equation 11.8 above:

$$P(x_{ij} = c \mid \theta_i) = \frac{1}{1+\exp[d_{jc} - \sum_{k=1}^{K} a_{kj}\theta_{ki}]} - \frac{1}{1+\exp[d_{jc+1} - \sum_{k=1}^{K} a_{kj}\theta_{ki}]}, \quad (11.10)$$

Valid Measurement Without Factorial Invariance • 301

TABLE 11.1 Generating Item Parameter Values by Time of Assessment

Item		Time 1							Time 2								Time 3					
		a_1	a_2	a_3	b_1	b_2	b_3	b_4	a_1	a_2	a_3	b_1	b_2	b_3	b_4	a_1	a_2	a_3	b_1	b_2	b_3	b_4
Common	1	2.2			-1.7	-1.0	0.1	0.9	2.2			-1.7	-1.0	0.1	0.9	2.2			-1.7	-1.0	0.1	0.9
	2	1.9			-1.3	-0.3	0.7	1.9	1.9			-1.3	-0.3	0.7	1.9	1.9			-1.3	-0.3	0.7	1.9
	3	1.3			-1.5	-0.8	0.1	1.3	1.3			-1.5	-0.8	0.1	1.3	1.3			-1.5	-0.8	0.1	1.3
	4	2.0			-1.8	-0.9	0.1	1.3	2.0			-1.8	-0.9	0.1	1.3	2.0			-1.8	-0.9	0.1	1.3
	5	2.1			-1.6	-1.0	-0.1	0.7	2.1			-1.6	-1.0	-0.1	0.7	2.1			-1.6	-1.0	-0.1	0.7
	6	1.7			-0.3	0.8	1.7	2.7	1.7			-0.3	0.8	1.7	2.7	1.7			-0.3	0.8	1.7	2.7
	7	2.0			-1.3	-0.6	0.5	1.4	2.0			-1.3	-0.6	0.5	1.4	2.0			-1.3	-0.6	0.5	1.4
	8	1.8			-1.1	-0.0	0.9	1.6	1.8			-1.1	0.0	0.9	1.6	1.8			-1.1	0.0	0.9	1.6
	9	1.4			-0.9	-0.1	1.0	2.3	1.4			-0.9	0.1	1.0	2.3	1.4			-0.9	0.1	1.0	2.3
	10	1.3			-1.4	-0.2	0.9	2.2	1.3			-1.4	-0.2	0.9	2.2	1.3			-1.4	-0.2	0.9	2.2
Adult	11								1.8	0.7		-0.8	0.1	1.5	2.6							
	12								2.2	0.9		-0.5	0.2	1.4	2.5							
	13								1.9	0.8		-1.5	-0.9	0.0	0.8							
	14								1.9	0.9		-2.1	-1.4	-0.5	0.7							
	15								1.7	0.7		-1.8	-0.5	0.3	1.5							
Geriatric	16															2.3		0.6	-1.8	-0.9	-0.2	0.8
	17															1.9		0.8	-2.5	-1.7	-0.9	0.3
	18															1.9		0.8	-1.0	0.1	1.2	2.3
	19															1.6		0.9	-2.1	-1.3	0.0	0.8
	20															2.2		0.9	-2.0	-1.0	-0.1	0.6

where all parameters are as previously defined and the k subscript denotes dimensions up to K dimensions.

The mean of the general factor was generated to increase linearly over time such that the mean of the general factor at times 1, 2, and 3 was 0, 0.3, and 0.6, respectively. The variance of the latent factor was also generated to increase over time such that the variance of the general factor at times 1, 2, and 3 was 1.0, 1.2, and 1.4, respectively (see Table 11.2 for the covariance structure among the general factors). The specific factors were generated to have mean and variances of zero and unity, respectively, and to be orthogonal to all other factors in the model.

A sample containing 3,000 respondents was simulated using the R software (R Development Core Team, 2009). A subsample of 300 respondents was selected from the original 3,000 simulated respondents to demonstrate the ability to regain population mean and variance structures with small samples. Parameter estimates based on each sample ($N = 3,000$ and $N = 300$) were obtained for the model, as outlined in Figure 11.1. More specifically, items 1–10 were assumed to be invariant over time and thus had their parameters constrained to equality (within item). Items 11–15 (time 2) and 16–20 (time 3) had parameters that were freely estimated. The latent mean and variance at time 1 were constrained to zero and unity, respectively. All other general factor mean and covariance parameters were freely estimated. All specific factor means and variances were constrained to zero and unity, respectively, which is required to set the scale for these latent variables. The specific factors were also constrained to be orthogonal to all other factors. Model parameter values were estimated using flexMIRT (Cai, 2012).

TABLE 11.2 Generating Values for the General Factor Mean (μ) and Covariance (φ) Structure

Time		1 $\hat{\varphi}_{t1}$	2 $\hat{\varphi}_{t2}$	3 $\hat{\varphi}_{t3}$
1	φ_{1t}	1.00	0.40	0.20
2	φ_{2t}	0.44	1.20	0.30
3	φ_{3t}	0.24	0.39	1.40
	μ_t	0.00	0.30	0.60

Note: Variances are on the diagonal, covariance below the diagonal, and correlations (bolded) above the diagonal.

Results

The examples here were designed to highlight how valid scores can be obtained in the presence of differential dimensionality. Using a sample size of 3,000, the model did a good job of regaining the generating values. As can be seen in Table 11.3, the root mean square error (RMSE) for the item characteristics were all at or below 0.07. In the case of the RMSE, smaller numbers are better, with zero suggesting that all item parameters were regained perfectly. A value of 0.07 suggests that the item parameter estimates obtained with this sample varied little, on average, from the generating (or population) values. Maybe more importantly for the discussion here, the model was able to regain the latent mean and covariance structure. As can be seen in Table 11.4, the results suggest that individuals increased in their depression approximately 0.3 units between each assessment. The results also suggested that the variability in depression increased over time with variance estimates at time 1, 2, and 3 equal to 1.0, 1.2, and 1.4, respectively.

Reducing the sample size to 300 resulted in very similar findings. As can be seen in Table 11.3, while the RMSEs for the $N = 300$ example were larger than those obtained with a sample size of 3,000, the values were still relatively small (< .20, with one exception). As with the larger sample, the estimates of the latent mean and variance structure closely resembled the generating values. Thus, even with a sample of 300, a researcher would conclude that individuals, on average, increased in their depression approximately 0.2 units from time 1 to time 2 and 0.3 units from time 2 to time 3. One would also conclude from these results that the variability in depression varied over each assessment from 1.0 to 1.4 to 1.3 for times 1, 2, and 3, respectively.

These examples highlight the ability of LVMs to provide statistically valid representations of the constructs when the dimensionality of the construct (or at least the measure) changes over time. Because we are able to have

TABLE 11.3 Root Mean Square Error (RMSE) of the Item Parameters in the $N = 3{,}000$ and $N = 300$ Invariant Item Parameter Examples

Factor		$N = 3{,}000$	$N = 300$
General depression	a_1	0.05	0.20
Specific adult	a_2	0.07	0.40
Specific geriatric	a_3	0.06	0.18
	b_1	0.04	0.13
	b_2	0.05	0.12
	b_3	0.04	0.10
	b_4	0.05	0.12

TABLE 11.4 General Factor Mean (μ) and Covariance (φ) Parameter Estimates and Standard Errors (se) for the $N = 3{,}000$ and $N = 300$ Invariant Item Example

			$N = 3{,}000$							$N = 300$			
		1		2		3			1		2		3	
Time	$\hat{\varphi}_{t1}$	(se)	$\hat{\varphi}_{t2}$	(se)	$\hat{\varphi}_{t3}$	(se)		$\hat{\varphi}_{t1}$	(se)	$\hat{\varphi}_{t2}$	(se)	$\hat{\varphi}_{t3}$	(se)
1 $\hat{\varphi}_{1t}$	1.00*	—	0.41	—	0.17	—		1.00*	—	0.37	—	0.20	—
2 $\hat{\varphi}_{2t}$	0.44	(0.02)	1.15	(0.05)	0.30	—		0.44	(0.09)	1.45	(0.23)	0.32	—
3 $\hat{\varphi}_{3t}$	0.20	(0.02)	0.38	(0.03)	1.39	(0.06)		0.23	(0.10)	0.44	(0.13)	1.34	(0.22)
$\hat{\mu}_t$	0.00*	—	0.32	0.02	0.61	(0.03)		0.00*	—	0.24	0.11	0.54	(0.11)

Note: Variance estimates are on the diagonal, covariance below the diagonal, and correlations (bolded) above the diagonal. * Denotes fixed parameter values.

statistically valid models, we are also able to regain proper mean and covariance structures over time in the presence of this changing dimensionality. While we hope that these examples demonstrated the potential utility of LVMs in parameterizing statistically valid models, the examples did assume that all items were invariant over time. This assumption is not always feasible in practice. The next set of examples addresses this added complexity.

Differential Dimensionality with DIF

The model used for these examples is likely much closer to what researchers may encounter is practice: item characteristics changing over time in addition to the dimensionality of the scale changing. We again use our hypothetical depression scale that changes in dimensionality over time and incorporates different items (and specific factors) into the assessment depending on the age of the respondent. However, in the previous example items seen at multiple time points (or across multiple ages) maintained stable measurement properties over those ages. That is, the items' parameters were invariant over time. In this example we remove this constraint and allow (some of) the items' parameters to change over time.

Method

For this example the same structure was used as in the previous example (see Figure 11.1). However, six of the 10 items that are seen across all ages have item characteristics that change as a function of age (i.e., six of the items exhibit age DIF). The new parameter values for the non-invariant items (items 1, 2, 3, 8, 9, and 10) can be found in Table 11.5. As seen in this table, items 1–3 have DIF from time 1 to time 2, but are invariant from time 2 to time 3. Items 8–10 are invariant from time 1 to time 2, but have DIF from time 2 to time 3. All other item and latent parameter values remain unchanged. One sample ($N = 3{,}000$) was again generated. This sample and a second subset ($N = 300$) of the simulated responses were fit to this model using flexMIRT.

Results

In the presence of both differential dimensionality and DIF, accurate parameter estimates could be regained with a sample size of 3,000. As can be seen in Table 11.6, the RMSE values suggest that, with $N = 3{,}000$, the item parameters deviate only slightly, on average, from the generating values. These RMSE values are in agreement with previous simulations conducted

TABLE 11.5 Generating Item Parameter Values by Time of Assessment for the Noninvariant Item Examples

Item	Time 1				Time 2					Time 3				
	a_1	b_1	b_2	b_3	b_4	a_1	b_1	b_2	b_3	b_4	a_1	b_1	b_2	b_3	b_4
1	2.2	−1.7	−1.0	0.1	0.9	1.7	−2.2	−1.5	−0.4	0.4	1.7	−2.2	−1.5	−0.4	0.4
2	1.9	−1.3	−0.3	0.7	1.9	1.5	−1.8	−0.8	0.2	1.4	1.5	−1.8	−0.8	0.2	1.4
3	1.3	−1.5	−0.8	0.1	1.3	1.0	−2.0	−1.3	−0.4	0.8	1.0	−2.0	−1.3	−0.4	0.8
8	1.8	−1.1	0.0	0.9	1.6	1.8	−1.1	0.0	0.9	1.6	2.1	−0.6	0.5	1.4	2.1
9	1.4	−0.9	0.1	1.0	2.3	1.4	−0.9	0.1	1.0	2.3	1.7	−0.4	0.6	1.5	2.8
10	1.3	−1.4	−0.2	0.9	2.2	1.3	−1.4	−0.2	0.9	2.2	1.6	−0.9	0.3	1.4	2.7

Note: All other generating values remain unchanged from Tables 11.1 and 11.2.

TABLE 11.6 Root Mean Square Error (RMSE) of the Item Parameters in the N = 3,000 and N = 300 Noninvariant Item Parameter Examples

Factor		N = 3,000	N = 300
General depression	a_1	0.05	0.20
Specific adult	a_2	0.11	0.21
Specific geriatric	a_3	0.12	0.30
	b_1	0.05	0.27
	b_2	0.05	0.09
	b_3	0.03	0.10
	b_4	0.03	0.13

to examine recovery of GRM parameters as a function of sample size (Reise & Yu, 1990). The ability to accurately regain the generating values was not restricted to the item characteristics. The results of these analyses suggest that a researcher would correctly conclude that individuals increased in their level of depression, on average, from 0.0 at time 1 to 0.3 at time 2 and then to 0.6 at time 3. Examining the results in Table 11.7, a researcher would also conclude that the variability in depression also increased over time (1.0, 1.2, and 1.4 for times 1, 2, and 3, respectively).

Valid conclusions can still be reached in the presence of differential dimensionality and DIF (assuming the model is statistically valid) even with rather small samples (see RMSE values in Table 11.6). Indeed, using a sample size of 300 instead of 3,000, a researcher's conclusions would change very little (see Table 11.7).

It is important to point out that the models in these examples are properly specified. The likelihood of specifying a model correctly increases as the complexity of the model decreases. In cases such as the hypothetical examples here, much care would have to be taken to ensure that both dimensionality and item constrains are properly accounted for. Obtaining a statistically valid model would include, among other things, that all important factors are included (e.g., no additional areas of local dependence in the model), the correct item model is chosen (2PLM vs. three-parameter logistic model), and that the cross-item or cross-time constraints are reasonable. We do not wish to minimize the importance and work that must go into developing the proper model. Instead, we wish to focus on the "big picture": If you can develop a statistically valid model, even when the model is highly complex, one can obtain accurate estimates of an individual's or group of individuals' standing on a construct.

TABLE 11.7 General Factor Mean (μ) and Covariance (φ) Parameter Estimates and Standard Errors (se) for the $N = 3{,}000$ and $N = 300$ Noninvariant Item Example

		$N = 3{,}000$						$N = 300$				
	1		2		3		1		2		3	
Time	$\hat{\varphi}_{t1}$	(se)	$\hat{\varphi}_{t2}$	(se)	$\hat{\varphi}_{t3}$	(se)	$\hat{\varphi}_{t1}$	(se)	$\hat{\varphi}_{t2}$	(se)	$\hat{\varphi}_{t3}$	(se)
1 $\hat{\varphi}_{1t}$	1.00*	—	**0.42**	—	**0.24**	—	1.00*	—	**0.34**	—	**0.25**	—
2 $\hat{\varphi}_{2t}$	0.46	(0.02)	1.19	(0.05)	**0.31**	—	0.36	(0.09)	1.14	(0.23)	**0.28**	—
3 $\hat{\varphi}_{3t}$	0.29	(0.02)	0.40	(0.03)	1.44	(0.07)	0.30	(0.11)	0.36	(0.13)	1.46	(0.29)
$\hat{\mu}_t$	0.00*	—	0.32	(0.02)	0.58	(0.03)	0.00*	—	0.32	(0.12)	0.57	(0.13)

Note: Variance estimates are on the diagonal, covariance below the diagonal, and correlations (bolded) above the diagonal. * Denotes fixed parameter values.

CONCLUSION

In this chapter we have provided a brief introduction to IRT and compared it (and other modern LVMs) to CTT. We described the idea of statistical validity and noted how modern LVMs have the potential to provide better statistical validity than CTT-based measurement models. Simulated data were used to demonstrate that by using IRT, it is possible to recover changes in latent means and variances over time in the presence of differential dimensionality. The simulations show that these methods are effective with large ($N = 3{,}000$) and smaller ($N = 300$) sample sizes and even when differential dimensionality and DIF coexist.

Some topics have been excluded from this chapter so that we could focus on the issues just mentioned. There is a close analytic relation between factor analysis and IRT such that IRT can really be viewed as a nonlinear factor-analytic model. As was pointed out by Wirth and Edwards (2007), IRT- and SEM-based factor-analytic models with categorical indicators can be collectively thought of as item factor models. Given this, all of the analyses done in this chapter could be done within the SEM framework (and using any number of SEM software packages). We use a relatively new software package and estimator to obtain what are thought of traditionally as IRT-based parameter estimates (i.e., parameters in the GRM) due to the added tools available with traditional IRT-based model parameterizations (see Wirth & Edwards, 2007, for a discussion of the tools found with IRT- and SEM-based item factor models). We expect that for simpler models, like the kind that were used here, differences between the statistical frameworks/software/estimation would be minimal. This may not be the case in more complex situations. The examples presented here were not designed to address this issue.

The simulated examples focus on a situation where the changing dimensionality is in a sense an artifact of context-specific items. We do not explore the more complicated situation where a single factor bifurcates into two different factors at some point along a developmental trajectory. While this is a fascinating idea, it requires more attention than we could devote to it in this chapter and we thus chose to do no more than mention its existence.

We hope the concept of statistical validity is useful and can help researchers think more deeply about the relations between their conceptualizations of a construct and the capabilities of the measurement models they use. The simulated examples are not all-encompassing—indeed we only simulate one set of data for each example. We can draw some macro-level conclusions about the success of parameter recovery, but we cannot offer more nuanced analyses that would be possible with a full simulation study. However, the point was not to conduct a massive simulation study, but rather to illustrate via simulation a class of problems that researchers may often face but until recently could not easily be addressed with the models, estimation, or software that were available to them. Both authors of this chapter are quantitative methodologists and we do not know whether other researchers may find a use for these models. Our hope is that by demonstrating the existence of these techniques, researchers will be able to apply the general concepts to their particular situations.

NOTES

1. We use the terms *test, scale, instrument,* and *assessment* interchangeably throughout this chapter.
2. We use the terms *time, assessment,* and *age* interchangeably throughout this chapter.
3. It is important to note that the authors are not experts in depression and we do not wish to suggest that the hypothetical structure proposed here in any way reflects the "true" structure of depression. We simply chose the topic of depression as an example due to its familiarity. We leave the theoretical makeup of depression to the experts.

REFERENCES

Bauer, D. J., & Hussong, A. M. (2009). Psychometric approaches for developing commensurate measures across independent studies: Traditional and new models. *Psychological Methods, 2,* 101–125.

Bollen, K. A. (1989). *Structural equation with latent variables.* New York: Wiley.

Bollen, K. A. (2002). Latent variables in psychology and the social sciences. *Annual Review of Psychology, 53,* 605–634.

Browne, M. W. (2001). An overview of analytic rotation in exploratory factor analysis. *Multivariate Behavioral Research, 36,* 111–150.

Cai, L. (2010a). Metropolis-Hastings Robbins-Monro algorithm for confirmatory item factor analysis. *Journal of Educational and Behavioral Statistics, 35,* 307–335.

Cai, L. (2010b). A two-tier full-information item factor analysis model with applications. *Psychometrika, 75,* 581–612.

Cai, L. (2012). flexMIRT™ version 1.86: A numerical engine for multilevel item factor analysis and test scoring. [Computer software]. Seattle: WA: Vector Psychometric Group, LLC.

Cronbach, L. J. (1951). Coefficient alpha and the internal structure of tests. *Psychometrika, 16,* 297–334.

Curran, P. J. (2009). The seemingly quixotic pursuit of a cumulative psychological science: Introduction to the special issue. *Psychological Methods, 2,* 77–80.

Curran, P. J., & Hussong, A. M. (2009). Integrative data analysis: The simultaneous analysis of multiple data sets. *Psychological Methods, 2,* 81–100.

Edwards, M. C. (2009). An introduction to item response theory using the Need for Cognition Scale. *Social and Personality Psychology Compass, 3,* 507–529.

Edwards, M. C. (2010). A Markov chain Monte Carlo approach to confirmatory item factor analysis. *Psychometrika, 75,* 474–497.

Edwards, M. C., & Wirth, R. J. (2009). Measurement and the study of change. *Research in Human Development, 6,* 74–96.

Fabrigar, L. R., Wegener, D. T., MacCallum, R. C., & Strahan, E. J. (1999). Evaluating the use of exploratory facotr analysis in psychological research. *Psychological Methods, 4,* 272–299.

Hill, C. D. (2004). Precision of parameter estimates for the graded item response model. Unpublished master's thesis, University of North Carolina at Chapel Hill.

Lord, F. M., & Novick, M. R. (1968). *Statistical theories of mental test scores.* Reading, MA: Addison-Wesley.

MacCallum, R. C. (2009). Factor analysis. In R. Millsap & A. Maydeu-Olivares (Eds.), *The Sage handbook of quantitative methods in psychology* (pp. 123–147). London: Sage.

Messick, S. (1993). Validity. In R. L. Linn (Ed.), *Educational measurement* (pp. 13–103). Phoenix, AZ: Oryx Press.

R Development Core Team. (2009). R: A language and environment for statistical computing. R foundation for statistical computing. Vienna, Austria: Author.

Reise, S. P., & Yu, J. (1990). Parameter recovery in the graded response model using Multilog. *Journal of Educational Measurement, 27,* 133–144.

Samejima, F. (1969). Estimation of latent ability using a response pattern of graded scores. *Psychometrika Monograph,* 17.

Thissen, D., Nelson, L., Rosa, K., & McLeod, L. D. (2001). Item response theory for items scored in more than two categories. In D. Thissen & H. Wainer (Eds.), *Test scoring* (pp. 141–186). Mahwah, NJ: Erlbaum.

Thissen, D., & Orlando, M. (2001). Item response theory for items scored in two categories. In D. Thissen & H. Wainer (Eds.), *Test scoring* (pp. 73–140). Mahwah, NJ: Erlbaum.

Thissen, D., & Steinberg, L. (2009). Item response theory. In R. Millsap & A. Maydeu-Olivares (Eds.), *The Sage handbook of quantitative methods in psychology* (pp. 148–177). London: Sage.

Thissen, D., & Wainer, H. (2001). An overview of test scoring. In D. Thissen & H. Wainer (Eds.), *Test scoring* (pp. 1–19). Mahwah, NJ: Erlbaum.

Wirth, R. J., & Edwards, M. C. (2007). Item factor analysis: Current approaches and future directions. *Psychological Methods, 12,* 58–79.

CHAPTER 12

THE DISCRIMINATION-CENSORING PARADOX IN ITEM RESPONSE GROWTH MODELS

Jennifer Koran
Southern Illinois University

INTRODUCTION

One of the greatest remaining practical challenges in growth modeling is the interface of growth modeling methodology with measurement methodology. While some researchers focus on the development of reliable and flexible modeling methodologies for growth, other researchers focus on fundamental issues of how growth is measured. As an example of the latter, researchers have often approached growth measurement challenges from the perspective of vertical scaling, applying test-equating methodology to create a linked scale across increasingly difficult forms of an assessment. Both growth modeling and measurement methodologies must be addressed for growth to be effectively modeled in practice. However, these components are often addressed separately. Developments in both areas and in growth analysis as a whole may be hampered because the interface between these two areas has been largely ignored.

Advances in Longitudinal Methods in the Social and Behavioral Sciences, pages 313–332
Copyright © 2012 by Information Age Publishing
All rights of reproduction in any form reserved.

Consider current practice in modeling growth in individual students' academic abilities over time. This process typically uses several statistical models or transformations to move from data representing a student's scored responses on individual test items to inferences about changes in the student's underlying ability. First, a measurement model, often from the family of item response models, is used to move from a student's responses to many individual items to a single test score that provides an estimate of the student's proficiency at the time he or she answered the items. Then a vertical scaling transformation may be needed to put scores from increasingly difficult tests on a developmental, or vertical, scale. Finally, a trajectory for the individual scaled estimates of proficiency may be estimated in a growth model, such as one from the latent growth curve model or linear mixed-effect model frameworks (Bollen & Curran, 2006; Duncan, Duncan, & Strycker, 2006; Fitzmaurice, Laird, & Ware, 2011; Hancock & Lawrence, 2006; Singer & Willett, 2003).

Each of these steps has received a great deal of focused research attention isolated from the other steps. For example, much measurement research focuses on the estimation and fit of item response models. Researchers concerned with vertical scaling are working to address substantive concerns regarding the vertical alignment of content in a way that makes a vertical scale meaningful. Likewise, growth modeling researchers study issues such as the effect of misspecification of the growth trajectory.

More recently, some researchers (e.g., Hung, 2010; Koran, 2009; Segawa, 2005; Zheng & Wilson, 2009) have turned to an approach that attempts to integrate the measurement, or item response, model with the growth model. While a universal lexicon for this integrated approach has not yet been well established to date, in this chapter I refer to it as an *item response growth model*.

Because the item response growth model approach is still emerging in the literature as of this writing, this chapter begins with an overview of the item response growth model approach. The item response growth model will then be used to examine a phenomenon that occurs when unique item discrimination parameters are estimated as part of such a model. This phenomenon is termed the *discrimination-censoring paradox*. In the final section of the chapter, potential resolutions of the paradox are explored and recommendations are provided.

INTEGRATED ITEM RESPONSE MODELS FOR GROWTH

To address the diverse needs of the readership of this volume, this section begins with a very brief general explanation of item response models as a measurement methodology. An overview of the historical context of item response growth models follows. This section culminates in a description of

The Discrimination-Censoring Paradox in Item Response Growth Models ▪ 315

how a two-parameter logistic item response model is extended to an item response growth model.

Overview of Item Response Models

Item response theory, while originally devised in the 1950s, has gained in popularity since microcomputers became available in the 1970s to carry out the calculations associated with fitting item response models to data. In this case the data are the scores on each test or questionnaire item from each individual examinee or survey participant in the sample. Most of the item response models in use today are variations on logistic regression in which a model is specified to predict whether a given examinee will obtain a correct or incorrect answer to a given item (or above or below a given score in the case that the item is not scored dichotomously). This prediction depends, of course, on characteristics of the person (examinee or survey participant), such as his or her ability or latent propensity, as well as on characteristics of the particular item, such as how difficult the item is or how well it is able to discriminate high-ability (propensity) persons from low-ability (propensity) persons. The person characteristics and item characteristics cannot be directly observed. They are considered latent, and parameters representing these characteristics are included in the model.

One of the simplest item response models is the one-parameter logistic item response (Rasch) model (see also Hambleton, Swaminathan, & Rogers, 1991),

$$P(y_{pi} = 1 \mid \theta_p) = \frac{\exp(\theta_p - b_i)}{1 + \exp(\theta_p - b_i)} \qquad (12.1)$$

where y_{pi} is the observed binary response of 0 or 1 from person $p = 1, 2, \ldots, N$ on indicator (item) $i = 1, 2, \ldots, I_p$. In this model there is one person parameter θ_p and one item parameter b_i. Here θ_p represents the level of ability or latent propensity of person p (examinee). There may be multiple-person parameters if multiple abilities or propensities are being assessed in the same test or survey instrument, as in multidimensional item response models. The item parameter b_i is the indicator (item) location parameter, which represents the location of the item on the same latent continuum as the person's (examinee's) ability level.

The model may also be extended to include additional item parameters. A common example is the two-parameter logistic model,

$$P(y_{pi} = 1 \mid \theta_p) = \frac{\exp(a_i(\theta_p - b_i))}{1 + \exp(a_i(\theta_p - b_i))} \qquad (12.2)$$

where a_i is the indicator (item) discrimination parameter for item i. This parameter represents how well the particular indicator can discriminate persons located above from those located below the indicator on the latent scale.

History

The most recent approach to modeling growth directly from item responses is certainly not the first attempt to do so. Over the past four decades several models have been proposed for modeling item response data from repeated measurements over time from the perspective of the item response theory framework.

Fischer's (1976) linear logistic latent trait model with relaxed assumptions is perhaps the first item response model to accommodate repeated-measures data. Fischer's model incorporated one or more treatment effects, which could include the effect of time to create a growth model. However, it has been noted that since the treatment effects are assumed to be the same for all individuals measured at the same time intervals, this model is not appropriate for measuring individual differences in change over time (Embretson, 1991).

The use of multidimensional item response models has also been proposed with repeated-measures data. Andersen (1985), Wang, Wilson, and Adams (1998), and te Marvelde, Glas, Van Landeghem, and Van Damme (2006) presented multidimensional item response models that included different but correlated latent dimensions at each time point. At each new time point the level on the latent construct is registered under a new dimension, rather than as an amount of change since a prior time point. Change scores must be computed outside of the model and are vulnerable to some of the same limitations as traditional difference scores. Thus, these models have also been noted to be inadequate for measuring individual differences in change over time (Roberts & Ma, 2006).

Building upon the multidimensional approach, the latent change model approach acknowledged that longitudinal data are not just repeated measurements but *ordered* repeated measurements over time. Embretson's (1991) multidimensional Rasch model for learning and change presented perhaps the first longitudinal item response model consistent with major advances in modeling differences in individual latent trajectories over time in other frameworks (i.e., latent growth curve modeling and generalized linear mixed modeling). As with the Fischer (1976), Andersen (1985), and Wang et al. (1998) models, Embretson's model was developed within the Rasch family of item response models. This model parameterized the latent construct by registering some level at the initial time point and including a change score, or modifiability, at each subsequent time point. This parameterization computed change scores within the model, and thus avoided an inverse relation between the reliability of the change score and the correlation between the two measures.

Roberts and Ma (2006) likewise followed Embretson's approach to extend the generalized partial credit model for multiple measurements over time. Unlike the te Marvelde et al. (2006) model, which was also a multivariate extension of the generalized partial credit model, this model was parameterized in terms of change scores.

$$P(y_{pit} = c \mid \theta^*_{p1},\ldots,\theta^*_{pT}) = \frac{\exp\left(\sum_{k=0}^{c} a_{i(t)} \left[\sum_{q=1}^{t} \theta^*_{pq} - b_{i(t)k}\right]\right)}{\sum_{w=0}^{M_i} \exp\left(\sum_{k=0}^{w} a_{i(t)} \left[\sum_{q=1}^{t} \theta^*_{pq} - b_{i(t)k}\right]\right)}, \quad (12.3)$$

where y_{pit} is the observed polytomous response in category $c = 0, 1, \ldots, M_i$ from person $p = 1, 2, \ldots, N$ on indicator (item) $i = 1, 2, \ldots, I_{pt}$ at time point $t = 1, 2, \ldots, T$; a_i is the indicator (item) discrimination parameter for item i at time point t, $\theta^*_{pt} = \theta_{pt} - \theta_{p(t-1)}$ represents the change in person p's level of skill or ability between two subsequent time points t and $t-1$, and $b_{i(t)k}$ is the kth step location parameter for item i at time t, representing the point on the latent continuum at which each response category becomes more probable than the one preceding it.

When contrasted against the most recent growth modeling developments in other frameworks, however, the item response models presented by Embretson (1991) and Roberts and Ma (2006) have two notable limitations. First, these models are restricted to circumstances in which all examinees are measured at the same time points. They cannot be used in situations in which examinees are tested at different points in time, as in some formative or embedded assessment programs. Second, they do not impose a functional form on the growth. Thus, they do not allow for model-based testing of a particular functional form for growth, as might be desired for studies in education and human development. Both models employ a piecewise-defined trajectory, in which each measured time point defines its own piece in the model. As the number of time points increases, the number of dimensions, and thus the computational intensity of the model, also necessarily increase. It is ironic that item response theory authors, such as Embretson and Roberts and Ma, have extolled the virtues of using item response theory to measure change, and yet so little systematic development has taken place for growth models in this framework.

Explanatory Item Response Model Framework

Through the decades item response theory has generally maintained its own niche as a measurement modeling framework, including the use of its own conventional notation and terminology (some of which was discussed earlier). In 2004, DeBoeck and Wilson edited a book that reframed Rasch and two-parameter logistic item response models as special cases of the general class of nonlinear mixed-effects models, which have broad applicability beyond measurement modeling. For example, within the nonlinear mixed model framework the two-parameter logistic model presented earlier would be denoted as:

$$\text{logit}(y_{pi}) = \eta_{pi} = \sum_{i=1}^{I} a_i \theta_p X_{pi} + \sum_{i=1}^{I} \beta_i X_{pi} \qquad (12.4)$$

where y_{pi} is the observed binary response of 0 or 1 from person $p = 1, 2, \ldots, N$ on indicator $i = 1, 2, \ldots, I_p$, a_i is the item discrimination parameter for indicator (item) i, θ_p represents the person's level of skill or ability, X_{pi} is an indicator variable that takes the value 1 if person p was administered item i at time t and 0 otherwise, and $\beta_i = a_i b_i$, where b_i is the indicator (item) location parameter. The notation η_{pi} represents the expected value of a latent continuous variable underlying the observed response y_{pi}. This expected value is predicted by the systematic component of the model, which is a function of the item indicator variables X_{pi} as well as the latent item and person parameters. Because the observed item response data have only two discrete categories (1 or 0; e.g., right or wrong), it is necessary to transform the data onto a continuous scale. This is achieved using the logit transformation. This transformation divides the probability of observing a 1 by the probability of observing a 0 and then takes the natural logarithm of the result. Item parameters, such as item difficulty and item discrimination, often are allowed to take on different values for each item and are considered fixed effects. Person parameters, such as θ_p, are considered random effects.

A symbolic representation of this model is shown in Figure 12.1. In this representation random variables are represented by circles drawn with broken lines. Fixed variables are represented by circles drawn with solid lines. The curved connecting line between y_{pi} and π_{pi} represents the Bernoulli distribution for a single trial in which the item response y_{pi} may result in a value of 0 or 1. The π_{pi} term represents the probability that the observed response y_{pi} is 1. The straight connecting line represents the logit transformation of π_{pi} to the linear predictor η_{pi}. The arrows represent additive portions composing the linear predictor. Two such additive components are

The Discrimination-Censoring Paradox in Item Response Growth Models ▪ 319

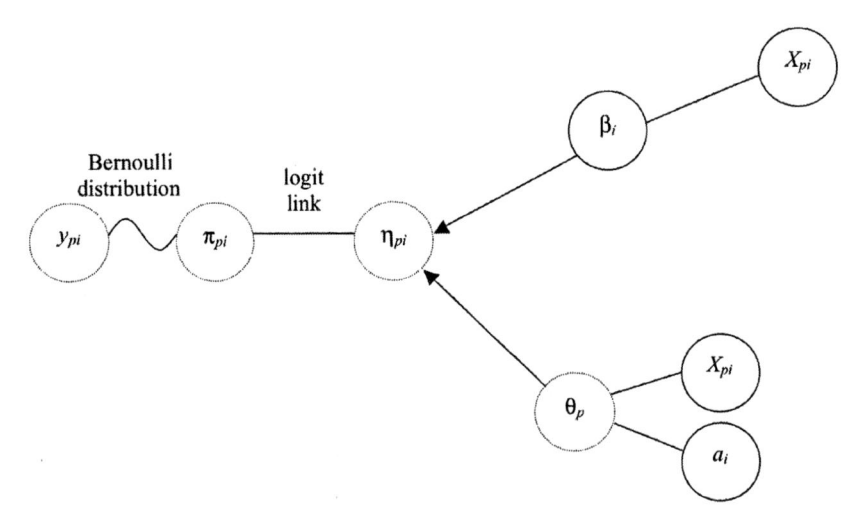

Figure 12.1 Symbolic model for the two-parameter logistic item response model. The convention used in this diagram closely follows that used in De Boeck and Wilson (2004).

depicted: one containing the item location within the parameter β_i and the other isolating the item discrimination parameter a_i.

The representation of item response models in the nonlinear mixed-effects model framework made it easier to see how covariates could be incorporated into item response models to explain item parameters, person parameters, or both. Thus, DeBoeck and Wilson (2004) referred to these models as *explanatory item response models*. By positing relations among latent person parameters and manifest indicators of time, item response growth models are one manifestation of explanatory item response models, although DeBoeck and Wilson did not explicitly include growth models in their book. Framed in this way, item response growth models have the same advantages as the more popular growth models in the linear and nonlinear mixed-effects model frameworks. That is, they allow examinees to be measured at different time points and allow an a priori hypothesized model for the growth trajectory to be fitted to the data.

The integrated item response growth model presented in this chapter extends beyond previous item response models for longitudinal data by specifying a functional form for the growth of individual examinees. In addition, this model includes item discrimination parameters, thus extending the item response growth model beyond a similar model in the Rasch family that has been investigated by Zheng and Wilson (2009).

Description of a Two-Parameter Logistic Item Response (Latent) Growth Model

This section presents an integrated item response growth model that is an extension of the two-parameter logistic item response model (described previously). In addition to the two types of item parameters discussed in the general overview of item response theory, there are two person parameters in this item response growth model. Within the nonlinear mixed model framework, a version of the model expressing growth as a linear trajectory is denoted as:

$$\text{logit}(y_{pit}) = \eta_{pit} = \sum_{i=1}^{I} a_i \theta_p X_{pit} + t \sum_{i=1}^{I} a_i \delta_p X_{pit} - \sum_{i=1}^{I} \beta_i X_{pit} \quad (12.5)$$

where y_{pit} is the observed binary response of 0 or 1 from person $p = 1, 2, \ldots, N$ on indicator $i = 1, 2, \ldots, I_{pt}$ at a duration of time t since the first measurement, a_i is the item discrimination parameter for item i, θ_p represents the examinee's level of skill or ability at the initial time of assessment, X_{pit} is an item indicator that takes the value 1 if person p was administered item i at time t and 0 otherwise, δ_p models the change in examinee ability as an increment per unit of time, and $\beta_i = a_i b_i$, where b_i is the item location parameter. The notation η_{pit} represents the expected value of a latent continuous variable underlying the observed response y_{pit}. This expected value is predicted by the systematic component of the model, which is a function of the item indicator variables X_{pit} as well as the latent item and person parameters. In the item response growth model presented here, θ_p represents the examinee's level of skill or ability at the initial time of assessment. An additional person parameter, represented by δ_p, models the change in this ability as an increment (or decrement) over time. The person parameters θ_p and δ_p are both random variables in the model. That is, their values vary across individuals so that not all individuals need start with the same level of ability θ_p nor increase at the same rate δ_p.

A symbolic representation of this model is shown in Figure 12.2. The symbolic conventions are as described in Figure 12.1. The additive components composing the linear predictor shown include one component containing the item location within the parameter β and other components containing the structural parameters for the growth trajectory, depicted here for the linear trajectory as including the parameters θ_p and δ_p.

The person parameters θ_p and δ_p are normally distributed random variables with mean vector $[0\ \mu_\delta]'$ and variance/covariance matrix

$$T = \begin{bmatrix} 1 & \\ \tau_{10} & \tau_{11} \end{bmatrix}.$$

The Discrimination-Censoring Paradox in Item Response Growth Models ▪ 321

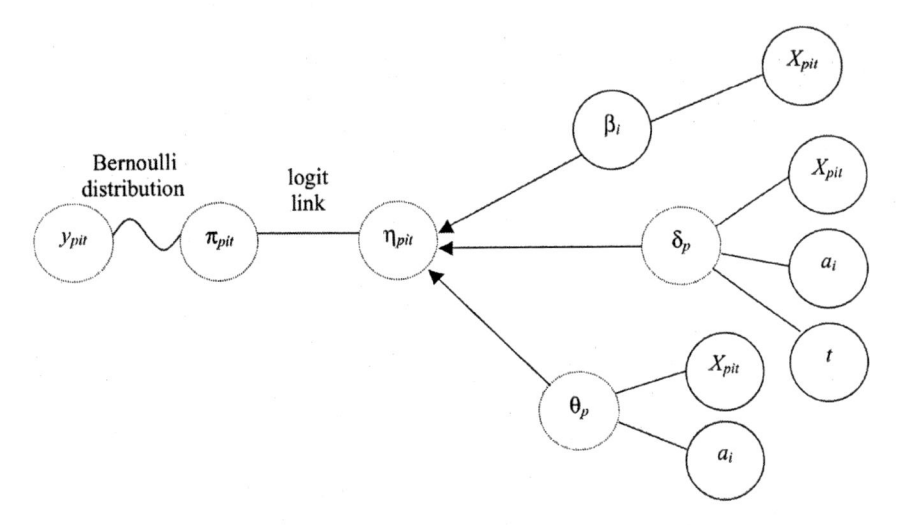

Figure 12.2 Symbolic model for the two-parameter logistic item response growth model. The convention used in this diagram closely follows that used in De Boeck and Wilson (2004).

The mean and variance of θ are fixed to 0 and 1, respectively, to identify the model. This is the traditional item response theory approach to removing the indeterminacy in the latent scale. In addition, the variance of the residuals is assumed to be normally distributed with mean 0 and variance 1.

It should be noted that the linear trajectory version of the model has been presented here and is sufficient for our purpose, but other forms for the growth trajectory could be used in this item response growth model as well. Indeed, the proposed model of linear growth may be too simplistic in some applications. Growth in areas such as elementary reading may be characterized by a change in the rate of growth over time at some critical transition point(s). This can be modeled using a piecewise linear growth trajectory. Other more gradual changes in the rate may be modeled by instead extending the model to include a quadratic term. For example, a quadratic form of the model could be represented as

$$\text{logit}(y_{pit}) = \eta_{pit} = \sum_{i=1}^{I} a_i \theta_p X_{pit} + t \sum_{i=1}^{I} a_i \delta_{1p} X_{pit} + t^2 \sum_{i=1}^{I} a_i \delta_{2p} X_{pit} - \sum_{i=1}^{I} \beta_i X_{pit} \quad (12.6)$$

where the notation has been modified slightly to allow δ_{1p} to represent linear growth (growth rate) as in the linear model, and an additional term has been added to include an additional random effect δ_{2p}, which represents the change in acceleration of the growth rate over time.

DISCRIMINATION-CENSORING PARADOX

The paradox at the heart of this chapter arises where a problem that is well known in latent growth modeling meets a challenge that is well known in item response theory. In latent growth modeling there is great concern with the effects of censoring in the data used to estimate individual growth trajectories. Censoring occurs when some upper or lower bound on the measurement of a characteristic results in a recorded value that fails to distinguish the level of an individual with a true level of the characteristic that is outside of the measured range.

Of particular concern in growth modeling are floor or ceiling effects, where individuals may fall below the lowest measured level or above the highest measured level of the instrument being used. Figure 12.3 depicts an individual growth trajectory that has been impacted by a ceiling effect. The measurement instrument is able to accurately discern the individual's latent propensity for the first four time points. This is shown in the four solid dots on the left side of Figure 12.3. In this particular case the individual's latent ability or propensity continues to grow at the same rate over the course of the next three time points. This is shown by the open circles on the right side of Figure 12.3. However, this person has reached the ceiling on the measurement instrument. For example, the individual may have mastered the most difficult item administered. Thus, the observed level of latent ability or propensity, represented by the solid dots on the right

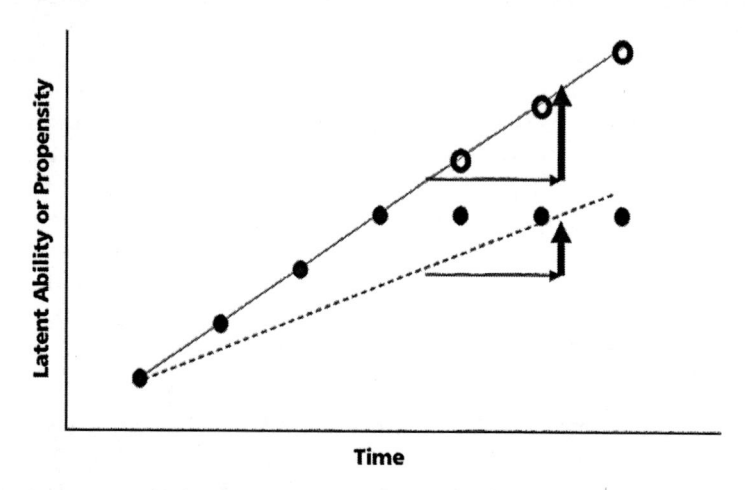

Figure 12.3 Ceiling effect on measurement of individual growth trajectory. Solid points represent observed measurements. Open points represent the measurement values without the presence of a ceiling effect. The solid line represents the true linear growth. The dashed line represents the estimated linear growth based on the observed measurements.

side of Figure 12.3, shows a leveling-off where the ceiling has been reached. The true linear trajectory is marked by a solid line in the figure. However, the best fit line to the observed points, shown by the dashed line in the figure, shows an underestimated slope representing the rate of growth. This example demonstrates that, while the individuals are located outside the range of the instrument, differences in their levels of the characteristic are not discernible, even though they may in fact be growing. While there are ways to model censoring for manifest variables, the problem is less easily resolved when growth is being observed in a latent characteristic. Wang, Zhang, McArdle, and Salthouse (2009) found that ceiling effects in latent growth models often resulted in underestimation of the magnitude of growth and incorrect model selection.

Likewise, the challenge of estimating item discrimination parameters is well known in the item response theory literature. Numerous simulation studies show that item discrimination parameter estimates are less stable than item location parameter estimates (Sireci, 1991; Yen, 1987; Yoes, 1995). This generally means that larger sample sizes are required to achieve reasonably stable estimation of the item discrimination parameters, but it also means that appropriate information is needed to effectively estimate these parameters. That is, just as in logistic regression, it is necessary to have a sufficient number of responses of 1 from persons located above the item on the scale and 0s from persons below the item on the scale in order to estimate the item discrimination parameter (positive discrimination case; the opposite would be true in the case of negative discrimination). This is because the item discrimination parameter essentially functions as the beta weight or slope would in a typical logistic regression model.

To avoid the effect of censoring in an item response growth model, it is necessary to have a sufficient number of items with adequate discrimination located both above and below the person's location *at each time point*. If all the items located above (below) the person's latent ability or propensity have very low discrimination, those items are not able to clearly demonstrate the person's location, since persons with very different latent propensities will have very similar probabilities of answering the item correctly. Essentially, information at the extreme ends of the latent ability distribution is sparse for the given time point.

The information needs for estimating item discrimination and person locations, respectively, come into conflict when both sets of parameters are to be estimated simultaneously from the same data. This conflict as it is observed in item response (latent) growth models may be called the *discrimination-censoring paradox*. To understand why this conflict is necessarily a paradox, it may be useful to picture the distribution of person ability or propensity and the item locations on the same latent continuum, as in Figure 12.4. This represents the latent propensity distribution (represented

Distribution of latent propensity

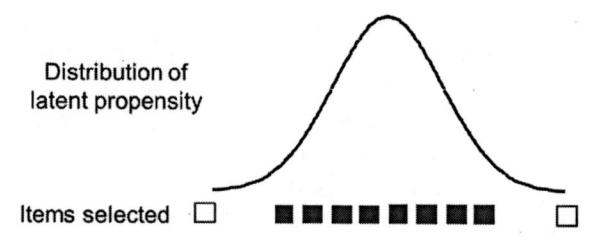

Items selected ☐ ■■■■■■■■ ☐

Figure 12.4 Depiction of persons and items located on the same latent continuum. The squares represent the locations of items along the latent continuum. The density curve represents the distribution of latent propensity or ability in the group of persons (examinees).

by the normal curve) and the choice of items on the instrument used to measure it (represented by squares located along the latent continuum), both at a single point in time within the larger longitudinal study.

To avoid the effects of censoring to obtain accurate growth parameter estimates, there will need to be some items with very low locations administered and some items with very high locations administered to at least some persons at some point during the study. Items with these extreme locations for the given time point in Figure 12.4 are represented by unshaded squares. However, to obtain stable estimates of the discrimination parameters for such items, there is a need to have some individuals respond in a way that is consistent with a location above the item's location as well as some individuals respond in a way that is consistent with a location below the item's location. When the extreme end of the latent continuum at any given time point is observed as in Figure 12.4, it should be noted that some person or item in the dataset at hand must occupy the lowest (highest) position on the latent continuum. Thus, it is not possible to have persons located both above and below the lowest (highest) item while at the same time having items located both above and below the lowest (highest) individual person on the latent continuum. One or the other can be true, but not both. This issue can be avoided in cross-sectional design situations where censoring is less problematic. In these cases there is no trajectory to be estimated both within and across persons.

Previous research has shown that the item selection design affects the quality of parameter recovery in a two-parameter logistic version of an item response growth model (Koran, 2009). Koran (2009) chose a broad spread of the generating item locations in an attempt to avoid the well-known effect of censored item response data in contributing to the underestimation of the growth rate and the covariance between the growth rate and initial status. Due to a lack of full information about the true growth, in censoring there is a shrinking or contracting of the underlying vertical scale. However, a stretching or inflation of the underlying vertical scale was instead observed in Koran's study. Thus, an effect opposite to the effect of censoring was observed.

The Discrimination-Censoring Paradox in Item Response Growth Models ▪ 325

What does vertical scale inflation look like? Koran (2009) found both an overestimation of the (mean) growth rate and an overestimation of the covariance between the growth rate and initial status. Items with low generated locations on the latent continuum ("easy" items) had estimated locations that were lower on the latent continuum (i.e., appeared easier). Items with high generated locations ("hard" items) had estimated locations that were higher on the latent continuum (i.e., appeared harder). Figure 12.5

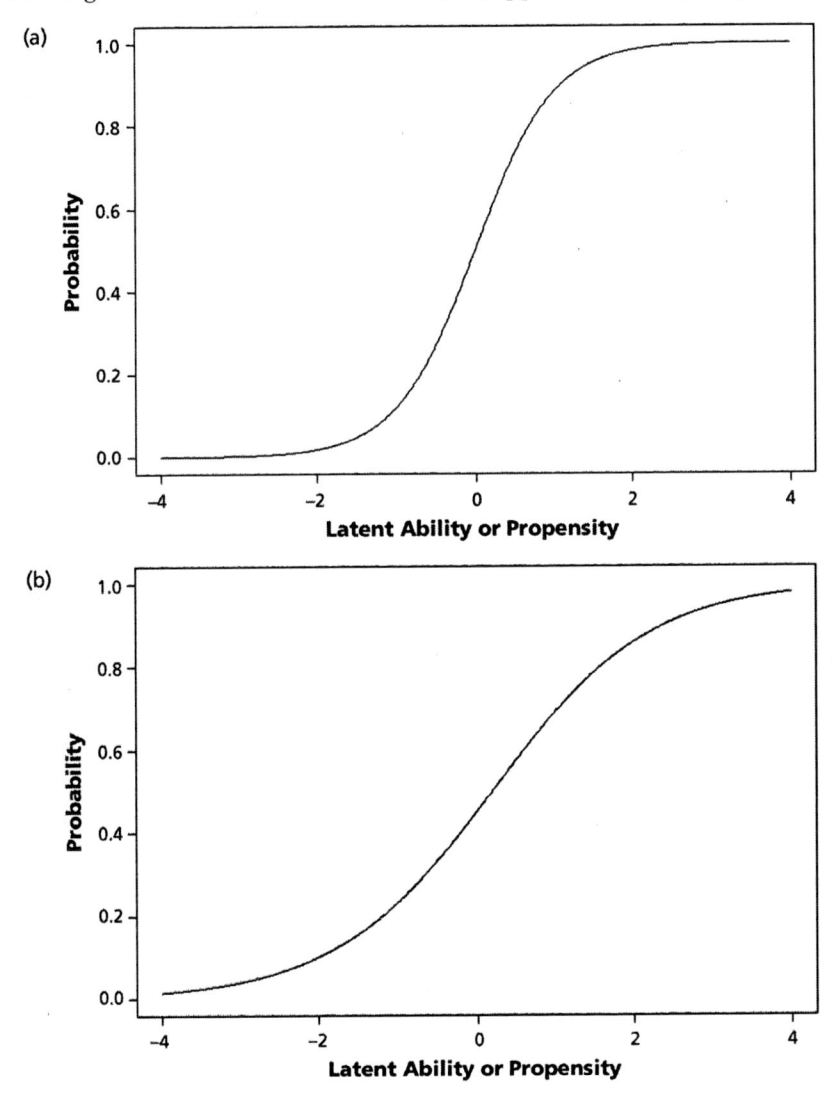

Figure 12.5 Logistic curves for a single item (a) without scale inflation and (b) with scale inflation.

demonstrates what happens to the item discrimination (slope) parameter when the latent continuum is stretched. Figure 12.5 depicts a logistic curve (item characteristic curve, or ICC) for an individual item. The item discrimination is the steepness of this curve. Panel A shows the logistic curve on the intended latent scale; Panel B shows the same curve when the latent scale has been stretched. Notice that the curve is less steep in Panel B. Indeed, Koran noticed a consistent underestimation of the item discrimination (slope) parameter in her recovery study.

STEPS TOWARD RESOLVING THE DISCRIMINATION-CENSORING PARADOX

There are two major types of approaches for addressing the discrimination-censoring paradox: the research design approach and the data analysis/statistical modeling approach. The following two subsections describe ways in which these approaches might address the discrimination-censoring paradox.

Longitudinal Research Design

Koran (2009) showed that the item selection design affects the magnitude of the bias that is observed as a result of the discrimination-censoring paradox. While the effects of the paradox remain, they may be minimized by attempting to match the item locations to the distribution of latent ability at each time point. In practice longitudinal designs can accomplish this to a limited extent. Adaptive testing in which persons are administered items with locations close to the approximate location of the individual may help to reduce some of the problems with sparse item information by producing a better balance of 0s to 1s on extremely easy or difficult items.

The inclusion of a strategic "bridge sample" is a technique that has been used in national longitudinal datasets in education where measurement occasions may be as far as 2 or 3 years apart (e.g., Najarian, Pollack, & Sorongon, 2009). Additional groups of examinees are measured on only one occasion and their item responses are included in the calibration of item parameters. That is, in places where sparse item information is anticipated, members of a bridge sample could be included at a single time point. These individuals do not contribute to the estimation of growth since they are assessed at a single time point. This may be especially helpful in estimating item discrimination parameters for items located at the beginning and end of the longitudinal latent scale. Thus, a strategic approach may be to include bridge samples of lower and higher average ability (propensity) than the growth sample at the beginning and end points of data collection, respectively, assuming a positive direction of growth. So long as censoring is avoided in the growth sample, then the parameter estimates from an integrated item response growth model may accurately reflect the true parameters. The need for bridge samples in the middle of longitudinal data collection can be limited if the spacing of measurements relative to the magnitude of growth is taken into consideration. More research is needed to verify the benefits and identify limitations of using bridge samples with integrated item response growth models.

The desire to get more out of statistical modeling in the form of information about the growth trajectories of individuals brings about the challenge to take accurate measurements at every time point for each individual. To take more away from a statistical model, effort must be directed to achieve the necessary quality of measurement. The discrimination-censoring paradox shows that the quality of the measurement is affected by how carefully the items administered are matched to individual ability (propensity) and how well examinee abilities (propensities) are matched to the item. The effective design of growth studies requires more time and effort invested in preliminary studies and may benefit from more flexibility in data collection designs across individuals and during the course of the study.

Data Analysis and Growth Modeling

Effective research design is essential but often not exercised optimally due to limitations in practice. However, there are some potential approaches for dealing with the discrimination-censoring paradox through data analysis and modeling techniques.

In previous research with the integrated item response growth model (Koran, 2009), it appears that the effect of the discrimination-censoring paradox is that the vertical scale produced differs from the generating scale by some constant. Thus, another approach that may be considered is to adjust the scale by a constant. However, without knowing the generating values of the parameters, it would be difficult to directly calculate the value of the constant in practice. It may be possible to place a constraint, such as the average of the item discrimination parameters must be equal to 1, to achieve the rescaling without requiring the direct calculation of the scaling constant.

Another potential statistical solution for the discrimination-censoring paradox is to separate the item parameter estimation from the item response growth model. That is, item parameters would be estimated as a first step, and the subsequent item response growth model would treat the item parameters as known values. This approach keeps the measurement model and the growth model united. However, the integrated item response growth model does not actually operate any differently given that the item parameters were treated as fixed effects in the model. Measurement error and the uncertainty associated with the lack of fit of the measurement model are still incorporated into the growth model. Thus, the implications of measurement error for the growth model results should not be any different whether the values of the item parameters are estimated at the same time the growth model parameters are estimated or whether the item parameter estimation occurs in a separate step. In fact, when the estimation algorithm takes advantage of the conditional independence assumption in the course of estimating the item and growth parameters in the model (see Koran, 2009, for further explanation), it is effectively separating item and growth parameter estimation. The current item parameter estimates are treated as fixed, known values during the steps when growth parameter estimates are updated to new values.

However, this avenue for resolving the paradox itself produces a new challenge. The population of latent propensity including all time points is not normally distributed and possibly not independent without conditioning the examinees. The latter issue may not be a concern since individual examinees are changing (growing) between the measurements at different time points. In effect, when the individual is assessed the next time, he or she is a "new person." This is why a common persons design is not sufficient to link a vertical scale; the linking of the vertical scale must also rest on some common items across time points. The former issue, however, needs to be addressed. In the process of parameter estimation, some form for the latent distribution must be assumed. Item parameter estimation in item response theory typically assumes normally distributed latent ability. If item responses from all time points are used in a single concurrent calibration, then the density of this mixture distribution across time points may have a shape that is far from the typical normal shape assumed by most item response calibration software.

The more rapid the general rate of growth relative to the static population variance in the latent propensity at any given time point, the less the mixture of these distributions will resemble a normal curve. The top of Figure 12.6 (part a), depicts an example illustration with four time points. In this figure a normally distributed latent propensity has been assumed for the population of examinees at each time point with the variances of these distributions held constant over time points. In this example there is steady mean growth, resulting in the four normal curves being equally spaced. The bottom of Figure 12.6 (part b) shows that the mixture of these distributions is substantially more platykurtic (has substantially greater kurtosis) than a normal distribution. For situations when the variance of the latent

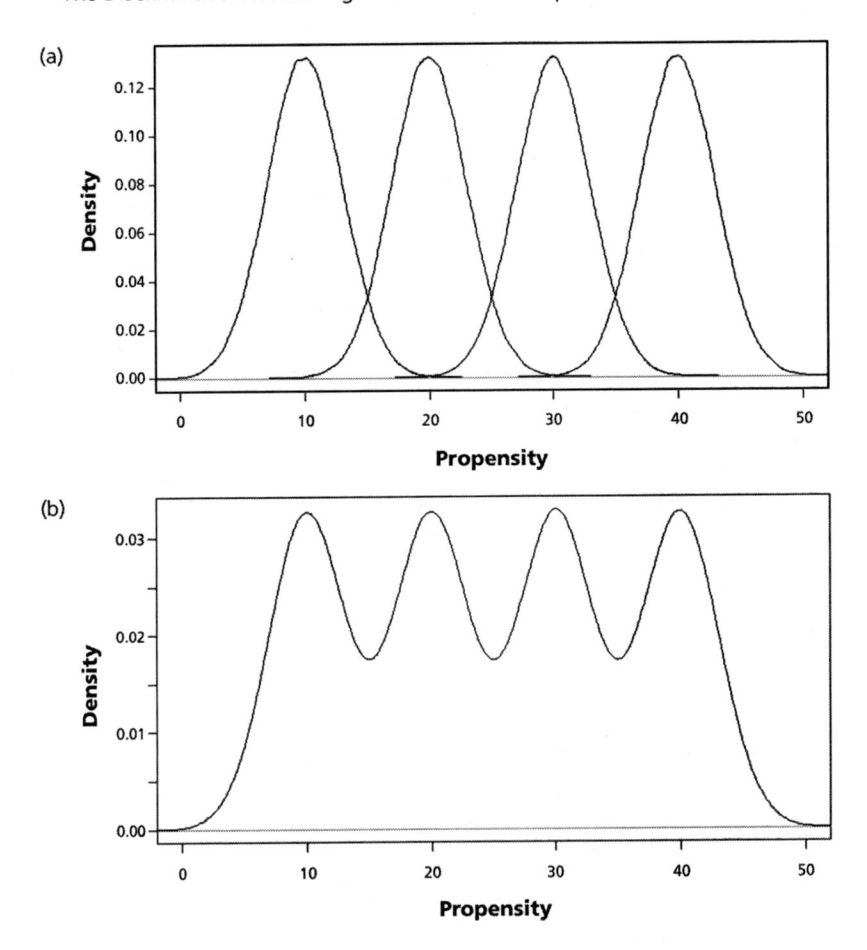

Figure 12.6 Distribution of latent propensity at (a) four time points and (b) mixture distribution of latent propensity at four time points.

propensity steadily increases or decreases across time points, there is also great potential for the mixture distribution to be heavily skewed as well.

Research on methods for estimating item response model parameters in the context of nonnormal latent ability or propensity distributions has been ongoing. In cross-sectional contexts a popular approach has been the empirical histogram method (Mislevy, 1984). A more recently proposed option has been to apply curve fitting methods. In cross-sectional contexts both Ramsay curves (Woods, 2006; Woods & Thissen, 2006) and Davidian curves (Woods & Lin, 2009) have been investigated. These methods involve fitting multiple models (sometimes as many as 25) to the data and choosing the most desirable curve to model the latent distribution.

CONCLUSION

This chapter has focused on illuminating the discrimination-censoring paradox. Why take time to describe a paradox that does not yet have a satisfactory resolution? First, the discrimination-censoring paradox and item response (latent) growth models in general offer a different and unique perspective on the construction of vertical scales. This may ultimately lead to the generation of solutions that help to resolve long-standing issues with vertical scaling and methodological artifacts in growth modeling. Second, the integrated item response model brings this paradox to light, and allows researchers to address it conscientiously rather than using a default approach.

Integrated item response growth models address the entire growth modeling process that currently involves several transformations to move from student responses to individual test items to implications about growth in a student body. Thus, it ties together several distinct areas of active research in the psychometric literature that deal with issues in each transformation in isolation from the others. The integrated approach provides a leverage point for consideration of the quality of the interaction among multiple components in the process. The effects of the discrimination-censoring paradox suggest a particular relationship between the characteristics of measurement at the item level and the resulting quantification of growth, as mediated by the latent vertical scale. Thus, continued research of the item response growth model concept will have implications for ongoing research in item response modeling, vertical scaling, and growth modeling in general.

ACKNOWLEDGMENTS

The explanations of highly abstract concepts in this chapter were clarified in response to helpful feedback from Valerie Boyer and Bobbi Knapp. The author is grateful for their support.

REFERENCES

Andersen, E. B. (1985). Estimating latent correlations between repeated testings. *Psychometrika, 50,* 3–16.

Bollen, K. A., & Curran, P. J. (2006). *Latent curve models: A structural equation perspective.* Hoboken, NJ: Wiley-Interscience.

DeBoeck, P., & Wilson, M. (2004). *Explanatory item response models: A generalized linear and nonlinear approach.* New York: Springer.

Duncan, T. E., Duncan, S. C., & Strycker, L. A. (2006). *An introduction to latent variable growth curve modeling: Concepts, issues, and applications* (2nd ed.). Mahwah, NJ: Erlbaum.

Embretson, S. E. (1991). A multidimensional latent trait model for measuring learning and change. *Psychometrika, 56,* 495–515.
Fischer, G. H. (1976). Some probabilistic models for measuring change. In D. N. M. de Gruijter & L. J. van der Kamp (Eds.), *Advances in psychological and educational measurement* (pp. 97–110). New York: Wiley.
Fitzmaurice, G. M., Laird, N. M., & Ware, J. H. (2011). *Applied longitudinal analysis* (2nd ed.). New York: Wiley.
Hambleton, R. K., Swaminathan, H., & Rogers, H. J. (1991). *Fundamentals of item response theory.* Newbury Park, CA: Sage.
Hancock, G. R., & Lawrence, F. R. (2006). Using latent growth models to evaluate longitudinal change. In G. R. Hancock & R. O. Mueller (Eds.), *Structural equation modeling: A second course* (pp. 171–196). Greenwood, CT: Information Age Publishing.
Hung, L. (2010). The multigroup multilevel categorical latent growth curve models. *Multivariate Behavioral Research, 45,* 359–392.
Koran, J. (2009). *An integrated item response model for evaluating individual students' growth in educational achievement.* Unpublished doctoral dissertation, University of Maryland, College Park.
Mislevy, R. (1984). Estimating latent distributions. *Psychometrika, 49,* 359–381.
Najarian, M., Pollack, J. M., & Sorongon, A.G. (2009). *Early Childhood Longitudinal Study, Kindergarten Class of 1998–99 (ECLS-K), Psychometric Report for the Eighth Grade* (NCES 2009–002). Washington, DC: National Center for Education Statistics, Institute of Education Sciences, U.S. Department of Education.
Roberts, J. S., & Ma, Q. (2006). IRT models for the assessment of change across repeated measurements. In R. W. Lissitz (Ed.), *Longitudinal and value added modeling of student performance* (pp. 100–127). Maple Grove, MN: JAM Press.
SAS Institute. (1999). *SAS/STAT user's guide version 8.* Cary, NC: Author.
Segawa, E. (2005). A growth model for multilevel ordinal data. *Journal of Educational and Behavioral Statistics, 30,* 369–396.
Singer, J. D., & Willett, J. B. (2003). *Applied longitudinal data analysis: Modeling change and event occurrence.* New York: Oxford University Press.
Sireci, S. G. (1991). *"Sample-independent" item parameters? An investigation of the stability of IRT item parameters estimated from small data sets.* Paper presented the annual meeting of the Northeastern Educational Research Association, Ellenville, NY.
te Marvelde, J. M., Glas, C. A. W., Van Landeghem, G., & Van Damme, J. (2006). Application of multidimensional item response theory models to longitudinal data. *Educational and Psychological Measurement, 66,* 5–34.
Wang, L., Zhang, Z., McArdle, J. J., & Salthouse, T. A. (2009). Investigating ceiling effects in longitudinal data analysis. *Multivariate Behavioral Research, 43,* 476–496.
Wang, W., Wilson, M., & Adams, R. J. (1998). Measuring individual differences in change with Rasch models. *Journal of Outcome Measurement, 2,* 240–265.
Woods, C. M. (2006). Ramsay-curve item response theory to detect and correct for non-normal latent variables. *Psychological Methods, 11,* 253–270.
Woods, C. M., & Lin, N. (2009). Item response theory with estimation of the latent density using Davidian curves. *Applied Psychological Measurement, 33,* 102–117.

Woods, C. M., & Thissen, D. (2006). Item response theory with estimation of the latent population distribution using spline-based densities. *Psychometrika, 71,* 281–301.

Yen, W. M. (1987). A comparison of the efficiency and accuracy of BILOG and LOGIST. *Psychometrika, 52,* 275–291.

Yoes, M. (1995). *An updated comparison of micro-computer based item parameter estimation procedures used with the 3-parameter IRT model.* Saint Paul, MN: Assessment Systems Corporation.

Zheng, X., & Wilson, M.R. (2009). *An IRT-based linear growth model for longitudinal data.* Paper presented at the annual meeting of the American Educational Research Association, San Diego, CA.

ABOUT THE CONTRIBUTORS

Shelley A. Blozis, PhD, is Associate Professor of Psychology, Center Statistician, and Executive Committee Member of the Asian American Center on Disparities Research, and a member of the Nursing Science and Health-Care Leadership Graduate Group at the University of California, Davis. Her research interests concern mixed-effects models for longitudinal data and sensitivity analysis of mixed models when data are missing. Dr. Blozis's research has appeared in *Psychological Methods, the Journal of Educational and Behavioral Statistics, Structural Equation Modeling, Child Development*, and *Psychology and Aging*. She is currently Associate Editor of the American Psychological Association's *Dictionary of Statistics and Research Methods in Psychology*. She has served on the editorial board of *Psychological Methods* since 2003 and has taught courses and professional workshops in mixed-effects models.

Casey L. Codd is currently a PhD student at The Ohio State University. Her research interests include psychometric methods, latent variable models, and analysis of longitudinal data, with particular emphasis on nonlinear relationships.

David E. Conroy, PhD, is Professor of Kinesiology and Human Development and Family Studies at The Pennsylvania State University. His research interests concern motivation with particular emphasis on achievement motivation and motivation for physical activity. Dr. Conroy's work has appeared in journals such as *Annals of Behavioral Medicine, Developmental Psychology*, the *Journal of Personality*, and the *Journal of Sport and Exercise Psychology*. He is on the editorial boards for several journals, including *Assessment, Interna-*

tional Review of Sport & Exercise Psychology, Journal of Applied Sport Psychology, Journal of Sport and Exercise Psychology, Psychology of Sport and Exercise, and *Sport, Exercise and Performance Psychology.* Dr. Conroy's research has been funded by the National Institutes of Health.

Robert Cudeck is a member of the Psychology Department at The Ohio State University. His research interests are concerned with applications of latent variable models to behavioral data.

Patrick J. Curran, PhD, is Professor in the L.L. Thurstone Psychometric Laboratory in the Department of Psychology at the University of North Carolina at Chapel Hill. His quantitative area of research is focused on the development, evaluation, and application of statistical models for the study of individual stability and change over time. His substantive area of research is focused on the study of risk and protective factors in the development of child and adolescent substance use. Dr. Curran has published over 70 scientific papers and chapters and has coauthored a textbook with Ken Bollen on latent curve analysis. He has served as Associate Editor for *Psychological Methods* and has been on the editorial boards of seven scientific journals as well as a member of multiple grant review panels for the National Institutes of Health and the National Science Foundation.

Michael C. Edwards, PhD, is Associate Professor in the quantitative area of the Psychology Department at The Ohio State University. His research interests focus on modern psychometrics with an emphasis on item response theory (IRT), factor analysis, and computerized adaptive testing.

Emilio Ferrer, PhD, is Professor in the Department of Psychology at the University of California, Davis. His research interests include methods to analyze change and intraindividual variability, in particular latent change models and dynamical systems. Dr. Ferrer's current research in this area involves techniques to model dyadic interactions and the neural changes underlying the development of fluid reasoning. This research is currently funded by the National Science Foundation and the National Institutes of Health. He is coeditor of the recent volume *Statistical Methods for Modeling Human Dynamics.*

Gregory R. Hancock, PhD, is Professor and Chair of the Measurement, Statistics and Evaluation program in the Department of Human Development and Quantitative Methodology at the University of Maryland, College Park, and Director of the Center for Integrated Latent Variable Research. His research interests include structural equation modeling (SEM) and latent growth models, and the use of latent variables in (quasi)experimental design. Dr. Hancock's research has appeared in such journals as *Psychometri-*

ka, *Multivariate Behavioral Research, Structural Equation Modeling: A Multidisciplinary Journal, the British Journal of Mathematical and Statistical Psychology,* the *Journal of Educational and Behavioral Statistics,* and *Educational and Psychological Measurement.* He also coedited the volumes *Structural Equation Modeling: A Second Course* (2006), *Advances in Latent Variable Mixture Models* (2008), and *The Reviewer's Guide to Quantitative Methods in the Social Sciences* (2010). He is past chair (three terms) of the SEM special interest group of the American Educational Research Association (AERA), serves on the editorial board of a number of journals, is Associate Editor of *Structural Equation Modeling: A Multidisciplinary Journal,* has taught dozens of methodological workshops in the United States and abroad, and is a Fellow of AERA and the recipient of the Jacob Cohen Award for Distinguished Contributions to Teaching and Mentoring by Division 5 of the American Psychological Association.

Jeffrey R. Harring, PhD, is Associate Professor in Measurement, Statistics and Evaluation at the University of Maryland, College Park. He teaches quantitative methods courses encompassing topics on experimental design and multiple regression analysis. He also teaches advanced graduate seminars on longitudinal data analysis, simulation design, computational statistics, and finite mixture models. Dr. Harring's research focuses on nonlinear models for repeated measures data, nonlinear structural equation models, and mixtures of both linear and nonlinear growth models. He has published methodological papers in prominent journals such as *Multivariate Behavioral Research, Psychological Assessment,* the *Journal of Educational and Behavioral Statistics,* and *Structural Equation Modeling,* and coauthored an invited submission in the *Annual Review of Psychology.* Recently, Dr. Harring coauthored *Comparing Groups: Randomization and Bootstrap Methods Using R* (2011).

Donald Hedeker, PhD, is Professor of Biostatistics in the Division of Epidemiology and Biostatistics in the School of Public Health at the University of Illinois at Chicago. His main expertise is in the development and use of advanced statistical methods for clustered and longitudinal data, with particular emphasis on mixed-effects models. He is the primary author of several freeware computer programs for mixed-effects analysis and published, with coauthor Robert D. Gibbons, the text *Longitudinal Data Analysis* (2006). In 2000, Dr. Hedeker was named a Fellow of the American Statistical Association. He is an Associate Editor for *Statistics in Medicine* and *Journal of Statistical Software,* and a past Associate Editor for the *Journal of Educational and Behavioral Statistics.*

Lesa Hoffman, PhD, is Associate Professor in the Department of Psychology at the University of Nebraska-Lincoln where she teaches graduate courses in quantitative methods. At the core of her research is the integration of advanced quantitative methods (e.g., multilevel, structural equation, and item response modeling) to the examination of psychological and developmental processes, particularly within the study of cognitive aging. Dr. Hoffman's research has appeared in such journals as *Behavior Research Methods, Multivariate Behavioral Research, Research in Human Development,* and *Psychology and Aging.* She was elected as a member of the Society for Multivariate Experimental Psychology in 2009, received the Cattell Early Career Research Award in 2011, and has taught numerous domestic and international methodological workshops in recent years.

Andrea L. Howard, PhD, is Research Assistant Professor in Quantitative Psychology at the University of North Carolina at Chapel Hill. Her research interests focus on methods for assessing multivariate change over time, particularly in relation to child and adolescent internalizing and externalizing behaviors and substance use.

Amanda Hyde is a PhD student in the Kinesiology Department at The Pennsylvania State University. Her research interests include controlled and automatic forms of physical activity motivation and methods for quantifying long- and short-term change. Her research has been published in journals such as the *Journal of Sport and Exercise Psychology* and *Psychology of Sport and Exercise.*

Booil Jo, PhD, is Associate Professor of Biostatistics in the Department of Psychiatry and Behavioral Sciences at Stanford University. Her research interests include latent variable modeling, causal inference, design/analyses of clinical trials, and longitudinal/missing data analysis. Dr. Jo's research has appeared in such journals as *Psychological Methods, Journal of Educational and Behavioral Statistics, Statistics in Medicine, Statistics and Its Interface,* and *Biostatistics.* For the past decade, her research has been focused on developing and identifying models that can provide practical guidelines for causal inference in randomized trials especially in prevention intervention contexts. Specific topics include causal inference taking into account various complications such as treatment noncompliance, nested data, mediation, missing data, and longitudinal data.

Jennifer Koran, PhD, is Assistant Professor in the Educational Measurement and Statistics Program at Southern Illinois University Carbondale. Her interests are in measurement and statistics applied to the behavioral and social sciences. Her current research focuses on methodological issues with latent growth models and categorical measures. Dr. Koran's research has been funded by the Educational Testing Service. She has presented papers annually at meetings of the American Educational Research Association and the National Council on Measurement in Education and published in *Structural Equation Modeling: A Multidisciplinary Journal.* She serves on the editorial board for *Frontiers in Quantitative Psychology and Measurement* and reviews for the *Journal of Educational Measurement* and the *Journal of Educational Psychology.*

Stephanie Lane is a doctoral student in the L.L. Thurstone Psychometric Lab in the Department of Psychology at the University of North Carolina at Chapel Hill. Her research interests include the development and application of novel techniques for examining individual variability in stability and change over time with an emphasis on the estimation of interactions among latent growth factors.

Taehun Lee, PhD, is a postdoctoral researcher in the advanced quantitative methodology program in the School of Education at the University of California at Los Angeles. His research interests concern methodological/statistical issues surrounding estimation, evaluation, and selection of latent variable models, which include factor analysis models, structural equation models, multilevel models and item response theory models. Dr. Lee's current research in this area involves addressing uncertainties involved in parameter estimation, model-data fit evaluation, and missing data imputation. He is also interested in applications of statistical models for the study of individual differences and change over time.

Robert MacCallum, PhD, is Professor of Psychology at the University of North Carolina at Chapel Hill. His research interests focus on methods for analysis and modeling of correlational and longitudinal data, including factor analysis, structural equation modeling, and latent curve models. Within these areas he has worked on various issues including model estimation and evaluation, power analysis for testing models, and the nature and management of sources of error in modeling. Dr. MacCallum's current interests involve the study of uncertainty inherent in results of statistical models. He is former director of the L. L. Thurstone Psychometric Laboratory at UNC, and former president of the Society for Multivariate Experimental Psychology. In 2011 he received the Samuel J. Messick Award for distinguished scientific contributions from Division 5 of the American Psychological Association.

Robin Mermelstein, PhD, is Director of the Institute for Health Research and Policy, Professor in the Department of Psychology, and Clinical Professor of Community Health Sciences at the University of Illinois at Chicago (UIC). She is also the Director of the Novel Translational and Collaborative Studies Core of UIC's Center for Clinical and Translational Sciences. Dr. Mermelstein has been active in cancer prevention and tobacco-related research for over 20 years, with continuous National Institutes of Health funding as a Principal Investigator since 1986. Over the past 15 years, she has devoted much of her research efforts to the issue of adolescent and young adult smoking using ecological momentary assessment approaches and understanding the dynamic relationships between subjective and objective contexts and smoking.

Lauren Molloy is a doctoral candidate in the Human Development and Family Studies Program at The Pennsylvania State University. She is interested in the integration of social network analysis and methods sensitive to intraindividual variability to advance understanding of basic social developmental processes and the evaluation of preventive interventions. Currently, with funding from Penn State's Network Science Initiative, she is the Principal Investigator on an innovative social network study in which she is developing and testing a new research paradigm to examine time-varying intragroup dynamics in group-based intervention settings and their relation to intervention outcomes.

Aaron Pincus, PhD, is Professor of Psychology at The Pennsylvania State University where he teaches personality assessment and psychotherapy for the doctoral program in clinical psychology. His research includes the development of new assessment measures and methods based on the interpersonal circumplex model, as well as the integration of personality, psychopathology, and psychotherapy using interpersonal assessment. He also developed the recently published Pathological Narcissism Inventory. Dr. Pincus is a Fellow of the Society for Personality Assessment and received the 2007 American Psychological Association Division 12/American Psychological Foundation Theodore Millon Award for contributions to personality psychology. He has served as an Associate Editor for *Psychological Assessment* and is currently an Associate Editor for *Assessment.*

Kristopher J. Preacher, PhD, is Assistant Professor in the Quantitative Methods Program at Vanderbilt University. His research concerns the use and combination of structural equation modeling and multilevel modeling to model correlational and longitudinal data. Other interests include developing techniques to test mediation and moderation hypotheses, bridging the gap between substantive theory and statistical practice, and studying model evaluation and model selection in the application of multivariate methods to social science questions. He serves on the editorial boards of *Psychological Methods, Journal of Counseling Psychology, Communication Methods and Measures,* and *Multivariate Behavioral Research.*

Nilam Ram, PhD, is Assistant Professor of Human Development and Family Studies at The Pennsylvania State University. He developed interest in intraindividual concepts and methods while working in the financial markets and through study of quantitative psychology. His research interests center on how short-term changes (e.g., processes such as learning, information processing, emotion regulation, etc.) develop over the course of the life span and how intraindividual change and variability study designs (e.g., measurement bursts) might contribute to our knowledge base. Current projects include examinations of age differences in short-term dynamics at the interface of cognition, affect, and temperament; cyclic and other systematic patterns in the day-to-day progression of emotions; and change in cognition and well-being over the life span, particularly in old age. Together with colleagues Dr. Ram is working to develop a variety of methods for coupling together processes that proceed on different time scales, as well as multiperson extensions of intraindividual analytic techniques that maintain a focus on the individual while still tackling issues of aggregation and generalizability.

Joel Steele, PhD, is Assistant Professor in the Department of Psychology at Portland State University. His research involves longitudinal data analysis using linear, nonlinear, and dynamic systems-based models. Methodologically, his interests revolve around the translation of substantive theories into testable mathematical models that can be applied to empirical data. His work has spanned various substantive fields including autism, academic achievement, romantic relationships, and infant-mother mental health.

Robert J. Wirth, PhD, is Managing Partner for Vector Psychometric Group, LLC. His research focuses on modern psychometrics with an emphasis on measurement invariance in longitudinal models within the factor analysis, structural equation, and item response theory frameworks. Dr. Wirth has published numerous book chapters and journal articles appearing in outlets such as *Psychological Methods, Medical Care, Psychological Assessment, Journal of Abnormal Psychology, Health Psychology,* and *Child Development.* He regularly serves as a reviewer for a variety of quantitative and substantive journals.

CPSIA information can be obtained at www.ICGtesting.com
Printed in the USA
LVOW10s1729040214

372315LV00001B/5/P